# Fast Track Web Programming

## A Programmer's Guide to
## Mastering Web Technologies

# Fast Track Web Programming

## A Programmer's Guide to Mastering Web Technologies

## Dave Cintron

**Wiley Computer Publishing**

**John Wiley & Sons, Inc.**

NEW YORK · CHICHESTER · WEINHEIM · BRISBANE · SINGAPORE · TORONTO

Publisher: Robert Ipsen
Editor: Cary Sullivan
Electronic Products, Associate Editor: Mike Sosa
Managing Editor: Brian Snapp
Text Design & Composition: Benchmark Productions, Inc.

Designations used by companies to distinguish their products are often claimed as trademarks. In all instances where John Wiley & Sons, Inc., is aware of a claim, the product names appear in initial capital or ALL CAPITAL LETTERS. Readers, however, should contact the appropriate companies for more complete information regarding trademarks and registration.

This publication is designed to provide accurate and authoritative information in regard to the subject matter covered. It is sold with the understanding that the publisher is not engaged in professional services. If professional advice or other expert assistance is required, the services of a competent professional person should be sought.

*Library of Congress Cataloging-in-Publication Data:*

Cintron, David, 1956–
   Fast track Web programming : a programmer's guide to mastering Web technologies / David Cintron.
      p. cm.
   ISBN 0-471-32426-4 (pbk. : alk. paper)
   1. Internet programming.   2. Web sites--Design.   I. Title.
   QA76.625.C56   1999
   005.2'76--dc21                                                      98-50462
                                                                            CIP

Printed in the United States of America.
10 9 8 7 6 5 4 3 2 1

# Contents

# Acknowledgments

Grateful thanks to Damon Wood of SD/Web98 for permission to cover the show.

I'd also like to thank Netscape's Suzanne Anthony and Susan Walton, who got me in the door to interview some of the major players of the Web game, and to Tom Paquin and Eric Byunn for their time.

Walter Brugger and Mike Tilse at Earthlink, for courteously providing access to their facilities.

The Microsoft crew, including Adam Denning, Garth Bruce, and Peter Plamondon, for taking time from their hectic schedules to bring me into the fold.

Jeremy Allaire of Allaire Corporation.

Maureen Loftus of Cybercash.

Eliza Osborne and Erik Smith of Sun Microsystems.

Eric Tachibana of Extropia.

Finally, to Kevin Epstein of RealNetworks, whom I actually had to interview twice due to a major malfunction.

Thanks also to the following Internet entities for their permission to include stuff in the book: Brian Chmielewski, the major contributing author and editor of *Web Promote Weekly* (www.webpromote.com) and Jane Benson of ISOC (www.isoc.com).

My high school friend James Roskind who was kind enough to review the section on security and give me a little guidance in this cryptic area.

And the biggest thanks of all to my editors Cary Sullivan and Christina Berry!

# Introduction

Earthlink Equipment Room—Pasadena, CA.

Check out the picture. This is the real thing. Actually it's only about half of the real thing! There's just as much stuff to the right of the picture, including their *OC-48* 622 *MBPS* fiber-optic uplink to *UUNET*.

Racks and racks of data communications equipment. This is what you're dealing with when you dial into Earthlink Network. Most Internet Service Providers (ISPs) probably do not have this sophisticated of a setup. If you look closely you can see the earthquake tension wires running at a slight angle that bolt every rack of equipment to the foundation. The whole shebang sits on a raised floor. Around the outside of the room are high-capacity uninterruptible power supplies (UPS) and water-cooled air conditioning units. Out back they have a gas generator that will run the whole place all by itself. Los Angeles could be hit with a 9.9 and Earthlink Network would still be up and running. Now that's an ISP that's never going down!

# Welcome

Welcome to *Fast Track Web Programming: A Programmer's Guide to Mastering Web Technologies.* Get ready, because in this book we will dive into the world of Web programming the way it really is out there in the real world! I first got interested in writing this book when I walked into the computer science section of several major bookstore chains and found that despite the numerous racks of books on computer technology, there was no single source that would give me a decent overview of everything I was looking at.

There was a rack over here for HTML programming, a rack over there for Java programming, another one for C and C++ programming; books on the Internet, books on Windows. Not only that, but all of the books were 300, 400, some of them 800 or more pages.

All I wanted to know was, where should I begin? What's the big picture???

Well, finally, we have it all in one place. It's right here. I've done all the work for you.

It has been my goal to take the technologies that comprise the World Wide Web and put them into a framework that gives a perspective not just on what they are and how to learn them, but on *what they are used for* and *why they should be learned*, and *what relevance they have* to someone who needs to make a decision about his or her future in the world of Internet programming.

It's not beyond most of us to learn how to program simple Web pages in a week, but a really serious programmer is looking at choosing a language or set of languages that take at least weeks to study, months to master, and years to get to the guru chair.

The decision of what path we take is often defined by fate; fate being the job we ended up with depending upon the necessity of some moment in our lives. But the person making the mid-life career change, or the rare individual who actually plans out his or her life decade by decade (always amazes me how they do that), deserves to be able to make an informed decision. Ideally they will find someone who can show them the path so they can thankfully find their way.

Well, maybe someday you can thank me!

# Who Should Read This Book

This book is for those who want to learn how to do Web programming professionally. You may be one of these people:

- A legacy programmer from the DOS world. You want to get into Windows and Internet programming because with the year 2000 coming and everyone being forced to upgrade, you're going to need a new job pretty soon! Even though you haven't gotten up the courage to take the dive, you've opened this book, so now's the time!

■ An armchair jockey who's been shooting out Web pages from the hip. Maybe you don't really grasp the big picture, or the jargon's been putting you to sleep. You know a lot of Internet programmers who get by with borrowing applets and scripts from bulletin boards and Web sites, but they don't really know how to write them. This book will give you a real start so you can originate, not just imitate.

■ A new programmer who wants to get serious and professional and enter the real world of Windows and Internet programming. This will take you there.

## Overview of the Book

In this book, I have done my best to give you everything you need to know to become an Internet "player." Once you get through this, you should be able to show up at any conference and understand what everyone is talking about, and by the end you should be right up there on the leading edge, ready to talk tech and look smart.

To this end, here's the inside story on what all these Internet technologies are *really* used for! Money makes the world go around and, well, the World Wide Web is powered by the money people pay to use it. You'll know what's going on so that more of that money can eventually end up in your hands, the hands of an Internet programmer.

On the Internet, money translates into e-commerce (electronic commerce), and we cover that, too! This is the fastest growing area of the Internet, as far as programming is concerned. I will show you how this works and how you can be a part of it.

As a special bonus, there are interviews with top people at the heart of the Internet world, people who can tell you just what goes on in those equipment rooms, programmer shops, and corporate meetings!

Finally, there are links to the products that are used to create the programs that use the technologies to run the Internet as described in this book. They are here for you to use, to learn, and to build your future career.

And I have your attention, don't I?

## Overview of the Technology

The word *language* is quickly becoming difficult to fit into the scope of what are fast becoming things called *technologies*. Java is a language, but it is really more than that. It is a technology not just for communicating something, as the word *language* implies, but a technology for accomplishing something, as technology does. The same concept applies to the other languages as they evolve into technologies.

The concept of a language evolving into a technology starts with a programming language new on the market and moves through a phase in which implementations of this language expand to the point where the base becomes so broad that it arrives as a dynamic force. This shows up as things like thousands and thousands of Java applications out there on the Web, accessible all over the world, running 24 hours a day, doing things for their authors and for us. This is a force, set in motion by what can only be called a *technology*.

These technologies bring our culture to a new level that involves not only the exchange of information, but the delivery of services and products to us in unprecedented volume. In this book we will show you how to use these technologies in the real world.

Our literary mountain is capped with the new technologies of e-commerce. Electronic commerce is driving the expansion of the Internet *and* our future.

## How This Book Is Organized

In the first two chapters we start off with an overview of the Internet. Not just another boring lecture on its history and who invented this and that, but an in-depth, easy-to-understand clarification on what the Internet is today. We're talking about the nuts and bolts of the Internet and how it works. That's how it REALLY works from the Network Operations Center Manager of Earthlink, manager of probably the largest concentration of Internet hardware any ISP has ever had in one place.

The third chapter gets into programming, starting out with the basics of the types of programming we find on the Internet. Then we move on to a chapter for each language we need to know.

In the next six chapters we learn the basics of each language that is used to construct the Internet, of what kind of stuff the Internet is built. We learn why these pieces were designed they way they were, and why there are so many languages needed to accomplish the business of the Internet.

Each language, or family of languages, has its own chapter. We discuss not just how these languages are programmed, but how they are implemented on the Internet. By *implemented* we mean under the different systems that make up the Internet, the actual machines and operating systems. This is important because as we have seen at least in the news and hopefully in our experience, one software company does not necessarily want to do something the way another software company does. This leads to different implementations of what is supposed to be the same programming language. To overcome the confusion this causes, you need to know how these languages are implemented—and we tell you that.

The languages discussed include:

- HTML
- Dynamic HTML
- JavaScript
- Visual Basic
- PERL
- The basics of Java

The last thing addressed in the language section of the book is databases. These are the technologies that hold the data that makes searchable bodies of information searchable, whether it is simply information or a collection of products for sale. This brings us to our final section.

The last chapter talks about where Internet programming is headed.

One of the big trends in Internet programming is toward programming browsers to take advantage of new Internet capabilities such as faster speeds, the availability of audio and video, and whatever else people like you will be dreaming up in the not-too-distant future.

Another big trend is, of course, e-commerce. Sales over the World Wide Web are increasing exponentially (meaning they are increasing at an increasing rate). I was an eager attendee of Spring Internet World at the Los Angeles Coliseum this year, and the overwhelming theme of this trade show was E-COMMERCE! It seemed everyone had something to sell that had to do with selling something over the Internet.

Finally, with the merging of communications technologies such as High Definition Television, Digital Television, and ultra-high-speed cable and fiber-optic modem lines, who knows what the future will hold?

## Define Your Terms!

There are a lot of terms used in this book. We do our best to define as many as seems necessary, but if you don't understand a term, look it up. You can't understand what you're reading if you don't understand all the words. This may seem too simple but believe me, there are plenty of people out there who have been told they don't need to do this, that they can figure it out by reading the context. This just ain't true. Help us bring the American education system back on track. Look up those words! Don't be lazy! Don't embarrass yourself! The alternative is to give a blank stare when your friend (or boss) brings you a programming question. Believe me, any programming guru can spit out definitions so fast and long that it leaves you in awe and you start using the word *guru* to describe those people because it seems they have psychic power.

Actually, Microsoft has just recently published a really good computer dictionary. As my friend Roger would say, better buy it. Better buy it. Better buy it. Better buy it.

## What a Beginner Should Know

I assume that you're Web savvy, you're online, and you know how to get around. Maybe you've written a Web page, maybe not, but in any case you've seen plenty of them and you've probably looked at the source code. And finally, you've got to be computer savvy.

What I don't assume is that you've worked with Unix or that you know a whole lot about DOS. There's no big need to learn either one for what you will be doing here. It's possible to write Web pages and get around without having to work with the OS, but it helps to know your way around both Windows and Unix file systems.

There is a nasty rumor out there that DOS is dead. This is not at all true. Accessing the command line prompt enables you to use utilities to figure out what's going on that you just can't do in Windows. I have a friend who works in tech support for a major ISP, and knowing DOS has helped get him promoted! DOS is easy. So if you don't know DOS, you should learn it and get access to the public domain DOS utilities that help you to look around at the DOS level. Some tools I have used constantly for years are "list," "whereis," and "mf" (maxfind). These can be found at Internet sites that offer freeware utilities, such as the Ziff-Davis Web site, www.zdnet.com.

You don't need to study any Unix to understand this book, but once you've gotten in deep enough you should consider doing this to help you move onward and upward. Unix is the OS that runs most of the Web server hardware out there, so it follows that most Web hosting accounts are on Unix machines. If you haven't worked on a Unix machine I suggest you find a friend or someone who can get you onto one, or if you're really ambitious you can even get a hold of Linux and install it as a second OS on your own system. There are versions out there that are free, or for just about $50 you can buy one that will install pretty easily.

Get yourself a simple book on how to use Unix and vi (that's vee eye, not vie), the Unix text editor. And I mean *simple* because Unix is anything but simple, so it's best if you make it as easy on yourself as possible. Unix is everywhere on the Internet, so the sooner you familiarize yourself with it, the better. You don't have to be a Unix guru; in fact, it's enough if you just learn how to read directory listings and use basic commands. This will at least come in handy when you get into using *ftp*, *telnet*, and *rlogin* to Unix *hosts*.

## Tools You Will Need

The bare minimum you need to start with is an Internet browser and Internet access. Then, if you're serious about writing Web pages, which I assume you are, you need to get yourself some space on a server somewhere. These days all providers, as far as I know, provide at least a couple of megabytes of space with any paid Internet access account—if they want to be competitive. Don't be discouraged if you only have a little bit of Web space; you can fit quite a lot in just a couple of megabytes. Just because disk space is measured by the gigabyte on new PCs these days doesn't change the fact that the size of Web pages and graphics is still measured by the kilobyte.

Moving along, there is a companion Web site to this book that provides links to every other tool that we mention. There are a lot of tools you can get for free as freeware or trial downloads. You should download them and check them out, and if you find them useful, make good use of them.

To program HTML you should have a Web page editor, although it's not completely necessary. There really are no good tools out there with which to program in Dynamic HTML and JavaScript unless you want to fork over several hundred dollars for one of the newer visual development tools, and these won't necessarily help you learn anyway, since it's better if you write the code yourself.

Visual Basic, PERL, and Java require development tools, and these are all downloadable for free via the links given at the companion site:

*www.wiley.com/compbooks/cintron*

Okay, now that you're fully briefed, let's get started!

# What Has the Internet Become?

Our tour of Internet programming begins with an introduction to the Internet itself. Even if you are a seasoned surfer, you still may not have taken the time to find out very much about where the Internet came from or how it's really put together. In this chapter I'll be showing you some pretty cool statistics on the 'Net and defining some core terminology that you may not have even known that you needed to know! And if you are somewhat new to the Internet, this chapter offers an introduction that may just give you an insider's edge over some of your more experienced 'Net surfing friends.

In short, I believe just about anyone can benefit from the information presented here. We'll also be taking a look at how computer networks work in general because that's what the Internet is all about. And finally, we'll have our first heart-to-heart talk with an experienced Internet professional working in a high-profile company.

## The Internet Defined

The Internet went public in 1993 with the introduction of browsers. Back then you could count the number of public ISPs (Internet Service Providers) on one hand.

Since then, the Internet has grown into a network of thousands of ISPs, cascading out from the main backbone providers to national ISP networks on super-high-speed fiber OC-48 optic links (see Table 1.1 later in this chapter) to statewide ISP networks on high-speed OC-12 leased lines, to citywide ISP networks on medium-speed T3 leased lines, to local yokels starting an ISP business in their hometown with a simple T1 link.

# DEFINITION: INTERNET

**A worldwide network of computers and *data communications* equipment, open for membership to *anyone* who has the know-how and wants to be a part of the network, and open for access to *everyone*. Originally put together as a communications network by American university research facilities combined with U.S. government Department of Defense funding, the Internet is now a worldwide enterprise that belongs to the public.**

The Internet is now linked to networks in Europe, Asia, South America, Australia, and Africa. In fact, the Internet has even advanced to the point that you can access live cameras in Antarctica, and get a weather report from Mars (that's right, the planet).

We've moved from one Internet language, HTML, to a half-dozen major languages like Java and JavaScript, plus hundreds of development tools.

The Internet is now available to nearly every household in the world equipped with a telephone line. It has enabled us to communicate with anyone else on the Internet—no matter what his or her physical location—in seconds and at virtually no cost. It has enabled us to find information that would otherwise be time-consuming, difficult, or impossible to locate, in seconds and at virtually no cost. It has enabled us to shop, buy, and have merchandise delivered without leaving home.

# INTERESTING SITES!

**www.jennicam.org**
**With Internet cameras in her apartment snapping a new shot every 2 minutes, Jenni is the original Truman. Her online life has even gotten her an appearance on the David Letterman show. You too can keep your eye on Jenni 24 hours a day.**

**www.links.net**
**Justin keeps his diary on the Internet, complete with pictures, and he's even been the star of a documentary film on Internet culture. "Home Page," a film by Doug Block, premiered at Web98 last June.**

**www.dove.net.au/~punky/Worldmap.html**
**This map gives you access to hundreds of cameras around the world uploading live images to the Internet on a regular basis.**

**nova.stanford.edu/projects/mgs/late.html**
**This page is not currently live, but will post weather reports from Mars as soon as the Mars Global Surveyor starts transmitting data back to the JPL in Pasadena, California.**

## How Much Has the Internet Grown?

In 1988 when the Internet was first plugged in to a T1 backbone (see Figure 1.1), there were a total of about 50,000 hosts online mostly consisting of colleges and universities, government and military agencies, and all in the United States. In 1993, when the World Wide Web came online, the number of hosts had just passed the 1 million mark.

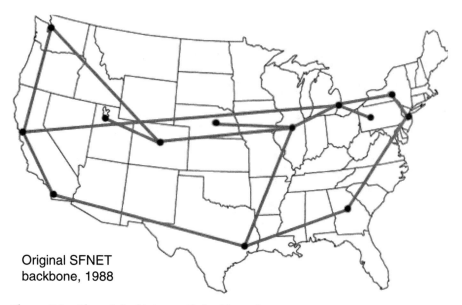

Original SFNET
backbone, 1988

**Figure 1.1**   The original Internet T1 backbone in 1988.

Growth since then has effectively been exponential, doubling every year. In fact, even if you go all the way back to 1980, growth every year is still about double.

Remember the old math problem: Would you rather get $10 a day for a month, or start with a penny on the first day and double it every day? Well, if every year you got a penny for every host online, this year you'd be collecting about $360,000. Estimates are not exact, but it looks like there are more than 36 million hosts online today scattered throughout every country in the world (see Figure 1.2), and in fact some places that are not countries, such as Antarctica, Earth orbit, and the planet Mars.

## Who Pays for the Internet?

I've heard people say the Internet is free, but that's not really true. Although it costs you virtually nothing to call in to your ISP and from there send messages and access computers all over the world, there is still plenty of money changing hands (see Figure 1.3).

First, the explosion of telephone lines is causing area code splits all over the country. The phone company is keeping very busy adding phone lines and billing us for them. Further, the need for communications equipment and long distance lines is sending stock values soaring for companies that supply it, such as MCI and Sprint. Over the next 10 years the capacity for data communications is going to have to increase by 100 times to meet the demand for streaming audio and video over the Internet.

The ISP industry has grown so fast that some ISPs are even getting listed on the stock market themselves. You pay the phone company for a line to call *your* ISP, and your ISP pays the phone company big bucks for a high-speed uplink to *its* ISP, which is probably another phone company.

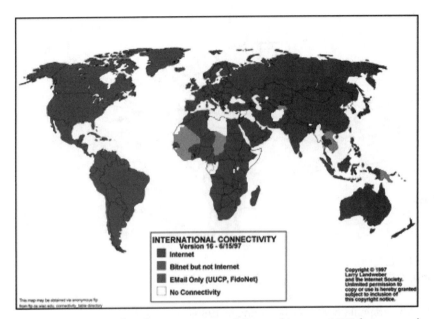

**Figure 1.2**    International Internet connectivity as of January 1998 from www.isoc.org.

There are hundreds of software companies that make the products that allow us to use and program the Internet. Starting with the big three, Netscape, Sun, and Microsoft, visit any computer-related trade show and it will be obvious that there's plenty of work out there for Internet programmers and Web designers.

Consumers alone are spending hundreds of millions of dollars. As an Internet programmer you can even get some of this to come your way.

## What's the Internet Made of?

The Internet was originally run by the National Science Foundation, hence NSFNET, but the original backbone has been shut down and now it's based on a set of Network Access Points, or NAPs, which any private backbone operator can hook into.

These NAPs are located around the country and now compose the highest level of the Internet. There are actually no official connections between NAPs, only those provided by the private networks. In fact, it is a courtesy that they link to each other to route traffic between them because there's no law or higher organizing body that says they have to do this. Figure 1.4 shows that there are enough backbone providers connecting the NAPs together that we can assume that multiple redundant high-speed connections are available between NAP points.

At the highest level we find the fastest "Optical carrier" backbone-level connections running at hundreds of megabits per second. There are enough speed standards to make a short list, as illustrated in Table 1.1.

The NAP network is really a symbolic network representing interconnectivity. Typically, an actual NAP-connected backbone provider (see Figure 1.5) is a telephone

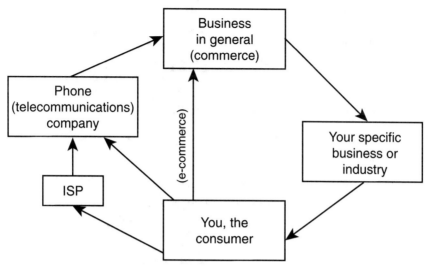

**Figure 1.3** Flow of money in to and back from the Internet.

company, since they're the ones who lay the cable, set up the microwave towers, pay for the satellites, and so on. Or it could be a major corporation who spends a great deal of money leasing the fastest and best of these lines. So moving down the hierarchy to the next level we find these big money communications corporations.

Below the level of NAP backbone provider we have the Regional Network Operators (see Figure 1.6). The line between these two can be very sloppy, because a big regional operator can lease the same high-speed lines used by the NAP backbone

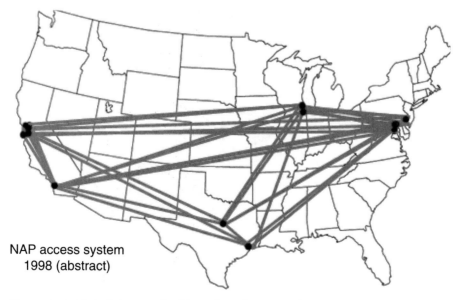

NAP access system 1998 (abstract)

**Figure 1.4** Today's Internet backbone based on NAP sites.

**Table 1.1** Telecommunications Standards

| STANDARD | SPEED | DESIGNATION |
|---|---|---|
| Transmission Level 1 | 1.544Mbps | T-1 |
| Transmission Level 3 | 45Mbps | T-3 |
| Optical Carrier Level 1 | 51.48Mbps | OC-1 |
| Optical Carrier Level 3 | 155.52Mbps | OC-3 |
| Optical Carrier Level 12 | 622.08Mbps | OC-12 |
| Optical Carrier Level 24 | 1244.16Mbps | OC-24 |
| Optical Carrier Level 48 | 2488.32Mbps | OC-48 |
| Optical Carrier Level 192 | 9.95Gbps | OC-192 |
| Optical Carrier Level 768 | 39.8Gbps | OC-768 |

providers, and they often rent small equipment rooms across the country in which they store the hardware used to provide local connectivity through one of those high-speed connections. The main difference is that these regional operators usually provide service to less densely populated areas or areas with fewer users.

At the lowest level we have the local ISP (see Figure 1.7). These companies usually have just one location. But not to be thwarted by locality, from their one location they can still lease lines to other locations where they can actually lease dial-up access and so appear to have a larger base from which to sign up new customers. The slowest connections an ISP

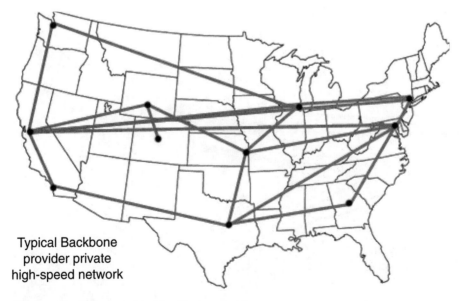

Typical Backbone
provider private
high-speed network

**Figure 1.5** NAP-connected backbone provider.

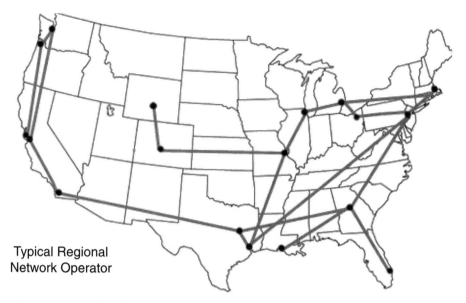

Typical Regional
Network Operator

**Figure 1.6** Regional Network Operator connectivity.

can offer range from the T-1 leased line at 1.544Mbps down through the 128kbps ISDN (Integrated Services Digital Network) or 56kbps leased line. This last one used to be a big deal but these days it's the same as a modem line, although in this case the modem would always be connected. The truth is, anything above 56kbps has to be a digital line.

The evolution of modem speeds has been slowly but steadily increasing, as illustrated in Table 1.2.

**Table 1.2** Modem Speed Evolution

| SPEED | DATE | SOURCE |
| --- | --- | --- |
| 300 baud | 1960s | Back then only the phone company could make modems! |
| 1200 baud | 1970s | This represents the phone company's idea of progress? |
| 2400 baud | 1980s | As soon as the phone company was deregulated, things picked up. |
| 9600 baud | 1990s | Much more progress here with a little private research! |
| 14400 baud | 1995 | This was the first Internet-enabling modem speed! |
| 28800 baud | 1996 | Modem surfing any slower than this can be painful! |
| 56K baud | 1997 | Barely a standard at this point, 56K access now competes with ISDN! |
| ADSL | 1998 | > T1 speed, this is the phone company's answer to cable modems. |
| Cable | 1998 | > T1 speed, fast download but slow upload, which is okay. |

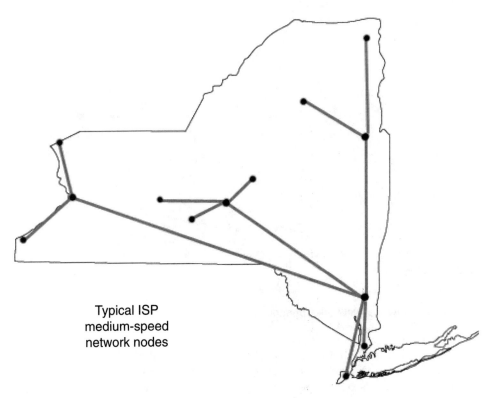

Typical ISP
medium-speed
network nodes

**Figure 1.7**  Typical ISP connectivity.

We've come a long way from the time when the phone company had a monopoly on modems. Up until it was deregulated you couldn't even buy your own telephone; you had to rent it from the phone company! Needless to say, the variety of models available was about as exciting as the current selection of plywood at the local hardware store.

That's all behind us now. The advancing march of cable modems and the phone company's ADSL service threatens to put the ISPs in the position of having to provide humongous bandwidth or possibly surrender that portion of the market to the big corporate ISPs who can afford it.

The cable modem and ADSL (Asymmetric Digital Subscriber Line) line will either make the future more Internet oriented or more expensive. Currently, an optical line giving several hundred megabits per second is special, but when we get to providing movies, HDTV, and other video services over the Internet, it won't be so special anymore. What used to service all of Pittsburgh will be just about enough for the houses in your neighborhood.

Oh, I left one level out. There's the corporate, small business, or individual Internet presence that has just one server at one location. Of course they all have only one connection to their ISP, although their ISP can be at any level! Even if you're just running a server out of your house you can choose a local ISP, a Regional Network Operator as an ISP, or even one of the NAP-connected access providers such as Sprint, MCI, or IBM.

This is where the line gets really sloppy. Just because you're at the bottom of the hierarchy doesn't mean you have to connect to the next level up. You can connect to any level that will provide connectivity to you.

## What Is an Intranet?

The Internet is a network that lies between networks and unites them. An *intranet* is an Internet-type computer network within itself. This is kind of a contradiction in terms. We have had computer networks for over 30 years and never called them intranets. Now that we have the Internet, we have to distinguish between the known model of private computer networks and an Internet-style private computer network. Hence the term *intranet*.

## DEFINITION: INTRA- AND INTER-

**Intra- is a prefix meaning within or inside. Inter- is a prefix meaning between. For example, interactive means between the computer and user and intergalactic means between galaxies, while intragalactic means within the same galaxy.**

In an intranet, we create Web pages that provide company information and training, send e-mail to each other, even submit vacation requests and other communications through forms on Web pages. This type of network usually allows users to access the Internet, but is blocked off from unauthorized access by a *firewall*.

A firewall is a server set up so that all traffic into and out of the network has to go through it, and it is set up to either permit or deny traffic according to where it's coming from, where it's going, and what it is. Traffic can be restricted according to which user is initiating it either inside or outside the network so that only authorized users can send and receive data to the network. Traffic can also be restricted by the computer it is coming from or going to so that only specific computers or servers can connect to the network. Traffic can also be restricted by the kind of service that is being used, such as file transfers, mail, and so forth.

## What Is a Computer Network?

To many, this may be obvious: It's a bunch of computers connected together. That's true, but there are several options here. First, they must all use the same type of connection. To connect the computers together we put a communications card in each one. This card has a connector like a modem but works at a much higher speed. We can connect all the connectors together in a few different ways. They may have a central server with centralized data stored on a disk drive, or they may simply be connected to a hub that just routes data between them.

Computer networks can be made of just two computers or they can be big, made of several smaller networks. Of course the Internet is the biggest, but we'll work up to that.

The Local Area Network (LAN) is usually confined to a floor or building and has one or two servers, the idea being that it's very local. A typical LAN configuration is shown in Figure 1.8.

Local Area Network

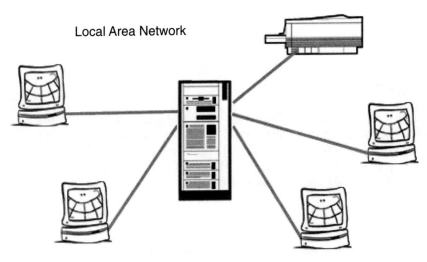

**Figure 1.8** Typical LAN configuration.

The Wide Area Network (WAN) is composed of two or more LANs, as shown in Figure 1.9. There's a little more to it in that each network within itself may not be connected together by the same kind of equipment. The Macs on the left and the PCs on the right may need a negotiator to translate the communications from one network to the other.

A WAN could be distributed throughout a large building, several buildings, or even between cities or countries. The link between them should be invisible to the user. A new trend is for corporations to pay an ISP to connect them together, which is much less expensive than leasing long-distance high-speed lines, especially when an international connection is involved. This is called a Virtual Private Network (VPN).

to another LAN

to the Internet

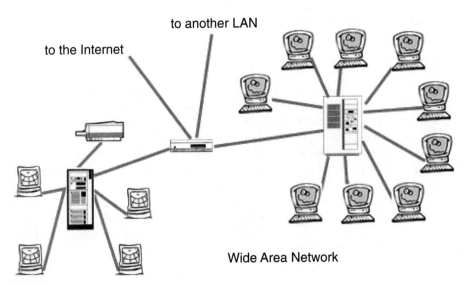

Wide Area Network

**Figure 1.9** Typical WAN configuration.

## What Kinds of LANs Are There?

There are basically three ways to configure a LAN, as shown in Figures 1.10, 1.11, and 1.12. These are called *hub, bus,* and *ring*. These are different network *topologies* and all use different types of equipment.

## DEFINITION: TOPOLOGY

**Topology refers to the way in which a network is laid out. It makes more sense if you go back to the root of topology, topos, which means place, plus -logy, which means theory or science. It is a science of places, or more specifically, how places relate to each other, which is just what is needed to build a network.**

The connection between a computer and the equipment routing the data is always Ethernet. Ethernet is a standard for communications and not a type of connector. Ethernet connectors can be coaxial cable, fiber optic, or twisted pair wire. In all cases, they attach at the back of the computer and look like either a telephone plug type of connector or a BNC connector (also known as a British Naval Connector to those who do their homework), which is a coaxial cable connector that locks together.

The original Ethernet standard was 10Mbps. We now have Fast Ethernet, which is 100Mbps. If you are in a university, the government, a large corporation, or an ISP, you may have an Ethernet connection to the Internet, hooked straight in at maximum warp. Up and coming is Gigabit Ethernet, which is 1000Mbps.

In a bus-type Ethernet network (Figure 1.10), data is put on the bus by one computer and all the other Ethernet cards can read it. The one to which it is addressed processes it and the others ignore it.

Hub networks (Figure 1.11) are pretty easy to configure; all you have to do is plug the computers in to the hub. If one gets disconnected there are no consequences to the rest of the network. Data goes directly from source to destination. This topology is also called a *star*.

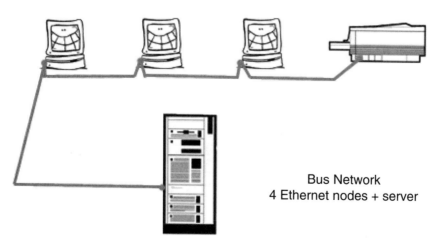

Bus Network
4 Ethernet nodes + server

**Figure 1.10** Bus-configured LAN.

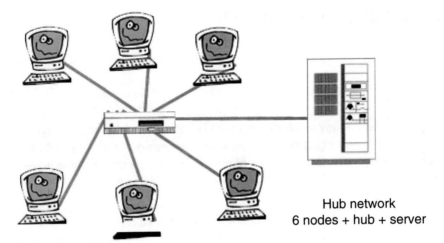

**Figure 1.11**    Hub-configured LAN.

The ring network (Figure 1.12) is similar to the hub, but the hub is built in to the server, and within the server is the ring structure. The ports are internally connected in a ring that passes the data around in a circle. Each computer in turn reads the data sent. If the data is meant for them it is processed; if not, it is passed along. This type of network is also called a *token ring* with the pieces of data passed along called *tokens*. Because of the wide availability of Ethernet equipment and hubs and the ease of configuring them (you can pretty much buy them off the shelf these days), the ring network is not seen very much, especially in the business world.

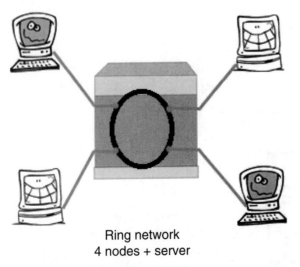

**Figure 1.12**    Ring-configured LAN.

## How Do Networks Communicate with Each Other?

You can get pretty creative with network topologies, connecting hubs to buses and so on. This is all done through a kind of equipment referred to as *routers*. These fall into a few not quite separate classes of equipment called *gateways, routers,* and *bridges.*

A gateway is the entrance point to a LAN from the outside. It may have to do some translations in the type of communications used both for data coming in and for data going out, and may perform a security function.

A router does just that, routes communications to the destination. Routers may also be gateways if they are the entrance point to the LAN. Routers are essential to Internet communications.

A bridge technically just connects two similar LANs using the same type of communications, but now we have *brouters*, which are bridge-routers that might as well be called *gateways*. The most common use of the simple bridge is to connect LANs together to form a WAN.

It's not difficult to take the preceding LAN illustrations and paste them together to form an ever-growing picture of how the Internet is constructed, as I have attempted to do for you in Figure 1.13.

As you will recall, the backbone of the Internet is the Network Access Points. All roads lead back to the NAPs, which are the highest level of interconnection. Without the NAPs, the Internet would be a conglomerate of disagreeable networks where traffic could become lost or forgotten.

History often repeats itself, and in this case the Internet is following the same pattern that the telephone did soon after its commercial start. In New York at the turn of the

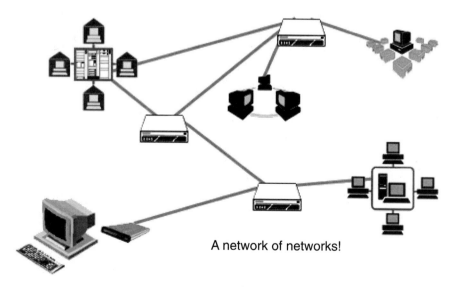

A network of networks!

**Figure 1.13**    LANs, routers, modems, workstations, and servers.

twentieth century there were phone lines hanging off of poles all over the city and several different, incompatible telephone companies from which to choose. Just because you had a telephone didn't mean you could call someone else with a telephone!

So telephone exchanges were set up, which persist to this day—the original electronic Network Access Points. And it seems that someday soon these will be replaced by or transformed into Internet communications exchanges.

## INTERESTING SITES!

*www.isoc.org*
**The Internet Society is the main Internet administrative organization (ISOC is discussed in more detail in Chapter 2, "How Does the Internet Work?").**

*www.isoc.org/zakon/Internet/*
**Hobbes' Internet World is a site of its own within the ISOC site and is just brimming with 'Net facts!**

## What Is Client/Server?

Client/server is to computers what customer-waiter is to food. If you are on a computer network, your workstation is the client, and the network file server is the server.

The special thing that makes *client/server* a term worth remembering is that it describes the concept in software in which you have a program running on the end-user workstation called a *client*, which communicates with a program running on the server, again called a *server*, as shown in Figure 1.14. These two programs are made to work with each other. For example, you can have a client/server database in which the client and server work together to maximize the speed and accuracy of data access and updates.

*Server* is becoming a term used for too many things. A server can be a computer that holds files in a central location, delivering up information when requested. A server can be a program running on a server computer. A server can be a program that interfaces with a client program. A server can be a waiter.

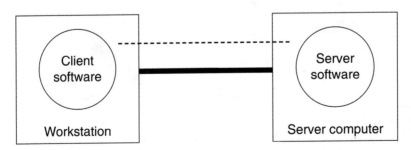

The Client/Server concept

**Figure 1.14**   Client/server.

# The Internet as a Virtual World

If you stop to think about what the Internet really is, there are two separate but equally important parts to it. First, the connection of wires and circuits which without electricity is nothing more than a lot of dead metal. And second, what? An incredible symphony of electrical charge and impulse. A universe of electronic information that weighs nothing and can't be observed. A world that exists parallel to and tries to mirror and enhance our own. A virtual world.

## What Is Location Independence?

In spite of all the geography and topology associated with the networks that make up the Internet, you do not need to know a single thing about any of it because the Internet is location independent. The location of the servers, routers, or data you're looking for, transmitting, or viewing has nothing to do with your ability to look for it, transmit it, or view it. This is all handled by the network, and is invisible to you.

This leaves us with the question of how to find things in such a network. If there are no spatial references, how can anything be located? The William Gibson novel *Neuromancer* (Ace Books, 1984) put forward the concept that we could go into a virtual reality space created by a computer that would translate the no-dimensional world of computer data into the three-dimensional world of living beings. This concept has been picked up on and used in many books, movies, and even television shows.

The term *virtual* can throw you for a bit of a loop because it's used in place of *almost*, which isn't quite correct in this case. The better definition is "apparent" rather than "real." It looks real, but what you see isn't what it appears to be—it's just an image without solid form.

Unfortunately, today there is no such virtual reality to navigate the Internet. I liken an Internet search to being in the Library of Congress (one of the largest containers of information in the world) in the dark with no map after an earthquake that has thrown all the books, papers, files, and everything and anything else on the floor and tossed them around a bit.

## How Can I Find Things on the Internet?

In 1994, when the Web was new and there was no way to find things on it, two guys at Stanford University started a hobby of cataloging their favorite Web pages into their computer. Then they wrote a program to go out and catalog any and all pages. Then they found that thousands of people were accessing their catalog every day. Then someone came along and invested some money, and Yahoo! became big business.

It became such a big business that now search engines are a business of their own. There are hundreds of search engines out there, but the top 10 were rated by the *WebPromote* newsletter in April 1998, as shown in Table 1.3. Yahoo! far outpaces the number-2 spot by double the access.

**Table 1.3**   Search Engine Statistics

| RANK/SEARCH ENGINE | REACH (%) | UNIQUE VISITORS (MILLIONS) |
|---|---|---|
| 1.   Yahoo! | 41.5 | 15.2 |
| 2.   Excite | 20.7 | 7.6 |
| 3.   InfoSeek | 17.3 | 6.3 |
| 4.   Lycos | 12.7 | 4.7 |
| 5.   AltaVista | 9.2 | 3.4 |
| 6.   WebCrawler | 7.6 | 2.8 |
| 7.   HotBot | 5.4 | 2.0 |
| 8.   Search.com | 3.5 | 1.3 |
| 9.   LookSmart | 2.8 | 1.0 |
| 10.  DejaNews | 1.9 | 0.7 |

From looking at the Yahoo! homepage (see Figure 1.15) you can see how commercial the Web has become. Banner ads offer credit cards, prizes, travel bargains, and merchandise. Technically, Yahoo! is not a "search engine" but a *directory* since its contents are actually cataloged by people. Nevertheless Yahoo! does have a partner, Inktomi, who supplies the search engine component of Yahoo! that responds when you need to look beyond the Yahoo! cataloged sites.

The Internet directory/search engine is a vastly important utility for the public, which means advertisers have a captive audience.

## How Much Information Is on the Internet?

The incredible quantity of Web pages online forces us to use search engines to find what we want, and their astounding capacity to store data is reflected in conducting a trivial search. All of the search engines will reject a search query for the word or letter "a" as did AltaVista, but it did give a statistic on the result:

```
No matches were found.
Ignored: a: 789026114
```

There are reported to be over 140 million Web pages right now and AltaVista has cataloged not only those pages but the text they contain, finding nearly 800 million occurrences of the word "a." Even more astounding is that it took only a split second for it to reject all of them!

The reply from an advertising inquiry to Yahoo! boasts that they are the #1 Web site in the world with 1 million people per day accessing over 65 million Web pages per day!

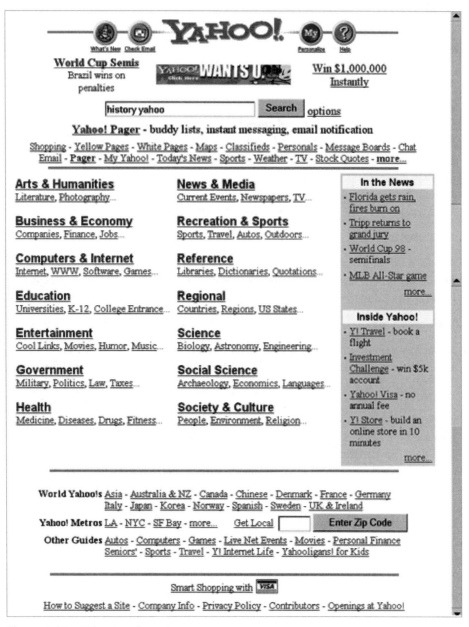

**Figure 1.15**    Yahoo! main page.

Simply searching the Internet to find out about the Internet can be fascinating. There are hundreds of search engines with information on any topic imaginable. Some search engines have diversified into specialty areas. Search engine features are continually changing and features will continue to become more widespread. These include multiple language capability, personalization (where you make choices about the information that is displayed when you visit the page), news, tools, and more.

# INTERESTING SITES!

*www.yahoo.com*

Yahoo! offers travel services, stock quotes, and online store creation and hosting as well as localized search engines for large cities.

| Try: | For: |
|---|---|
| *search.yahoo.com* | **Advanced search options** |
| *people.yahoo.com* | **Finding a friend** |
| *travel.yahoo.com* | **Travel arrangements** |
| *quote.yahoo.com* | **Stock quotes** |
| *store.yahoo.com* | **Online store tools** |
| *local.yahoo.com* | **Local searches by city (ny.,sf.,etc.)** |

*www.altavista.com*

AltaVista offers search capability in several languages, and the engine can actually be purchased and used in your own corporate Web site. Try asking it a question; it's pretty good with this.

*www.excite.com*

Excite has a feature on every search result with which you can search for "more pages like this one," which can often (but not always) help find your search target.

*www.infoseek.com*

InfoSeek offers a downloadable button that installs directly into a Web browser, giving InfoSeek search access without having to detour to the InfoSeek site. InfoSeek also has multiple-language search pages.

*www.lycos.com*

Lycos offers a search filtering program that will block out objectionable material. Lycos also has a "more like this" feature on search results.

*www.Webcrawler.com*

WebCrawler offers a toolbox that gives particularly helpful information on specific topics. WebCrawler is now owned by Excite.

*www.hotbot.com*

HotBot is a more avant-garde site owned by *Wired* magazine. HotBot offers free online use of its search engine for your own Web site. Search just your site or the whole Web.

*www.dejanews.com*

DejaNews gives GUI-style access to Internet newsgroups, making it quick and easy to use this feature of the Internet.

# How Do Search Engines Catalog Information?

Web pages get indexed when programs running on search engine servers read Web pages and sort through their textual content to find out what they are all about. In addition to the text that is displayed to the viewer, Web page authors can also put information into pages that explicitly state to the search engines what the Web page is about.

Each search engine has a different way of cataloging pages, so searches will end up with different results on different search engines. This can be advantageous: If you can't find something you're looking for with one of them, just try another. Eventually you'll end up with a favorite or two. Yahoo! was set up to categorize sites, not individual pages, and the site categorization is done by real people looking at the sites.

There are two problems to be solved when it comes to cataloging the Internet. The first is that there are so many pages. The second is that they keep changing! Just because something was cataloged today doesn't mean it will still be there tomorrow. And even if it is still there, it may not be the same page as it was yesterday!

At first, the search engines claimed they had their robots or crawlers roving the Internet and finding pages to add to the index. I have not found this to be true. The job of continually rechecking pages already indexed is enough to keep any number of robot rovers busy day and night. When a page turns up missing it's called a *broken link*, and there are plenty of these hanging around.

To get a site or page indexed, you have to go to the search engine and submit your request in a page written specifically for the purpose of accepting the entry of pages to be cataloged. Some engines claim their robots will go out and search an entire site if you enter only the single site address, but I have not found this to be true either. In contacting tech support about this, I was told to just go ahead and enter the address of every single page I wanted indexed. This can be time-consuming, but it's really the best way. When it comes to having my sites indexed, I trust no one. I submit my own requests and follow up on the results.

A few days, or a couple of weeks later your site will appear when searched for. There are tips and tricks to ensure it comes up where you want it to and to ensure speedy indexing.

There are also those who hide added inapplicable information in their Web pages in an attempt to get search engines to display their site no matter what you're looking for. This is called *spamming*.

## DEFINITION: SPAM

**Spam is a word that describes unwanted Internet content. There are two main categories of spam: unsolicited e-mail sent out in large quantities to people who didn't ask for it, and irrelevant search engine criteria that causes mis-indexing of the Web page.**

Both search engine companies and Internet service providers are campaigning against spam because it clogs the information superhighway. Spam e-mail distributors sending out millions of messages all at once can bring a halt to traffic in the affected pathways. Spam in search engines gives unwanted results that make the search engine companies work harder to give us what we asked for, and make the rest of us work harder to find what we're looking for.

## What Are Newsgroups?

Newsgroups come from a pre-Internet bulletin board service called *Usenet*. Originally set up at Duke University, newsgroups were meant to keep academics informed of progress in their field. Having become absorbed into the Internet, newsgroups now cover anything from hard news to very informal discussion forums.

There are literally thousands of newsgroups for every subject, from the sublime to the ridiculous. Newsgroups have names like rec.arts.startrek, a discussion group under the top-level recreation, second-level arts, Star Trek branch. Anyone can find a newsgroup and read and post messages. The easiest way I have found is through DejaNews, mentioned earlier as dejanews.com.

Table 1.4 lists the more popular of the at least 50 top-level newsgroups.

## What Other Services Are There on the Internet?

There are plenty of services to be found on the Internet, one of which is Internet radio. You can listen to the radio on the Internet from stations all over the world. All you have

**Table 1.4**    Top-Level Newsgroup Categories

| NAME | FUNCTION |
| --- | --- |
| bionet | The biological sciences. |
| biz | Business and commerce. |
| comp | Computers: technically oriented. |
| k12 | Education. |
| news | Just plain news. |
| rec | Recreation: hobbies, sports, and interests. |
| sci | High science. |
| soc | Society and cultural issues. |
| bit | This is actually an e-mail newsgroup where you are e-mailed every posting, and is another service the Internet inherited. This one was started in 1986 and called *BITNET*. |

to do to listen to Internet radio is to download the RealAudio player from www.real.com and search for a radio station. Internet radio is made possible by streaming audio technology. Audio information is sent just like any other information, decoded and played through speakers (see Figure 1.16).

Another new service is called *push technology*. Typical browsing has users pulling information off the Internet; *push* means the Internet sends you the data without your having to ask for it (of course you do ask for it, but just once, and it keeps coming). One of the major players in this league is the PointCast Network, which delivers news information to your screen. Download the PointCast program from pointcast.com, and as long as you are connected, up-to-the-minute news, weather, and sports information will dance across your screen (see Figure 1.17).

## INTERESTING SITES!

**www.pointcast.com**
**PointCast network provides continual news, weather, sports, stocks, or whatever your preference!**

**www.bbc.co.uk/radio5/**
**Listen to a different viewpoint with BBC radio.**

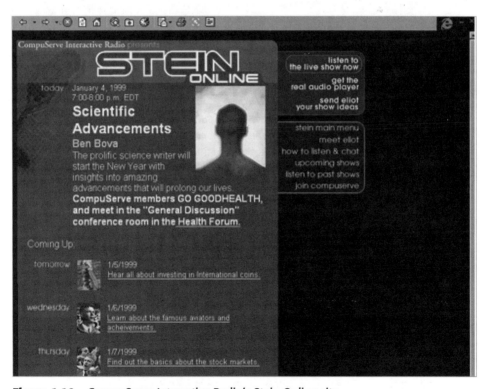

**Figure 1.16**   CompuServe Interactive Radio's Stein Online site.

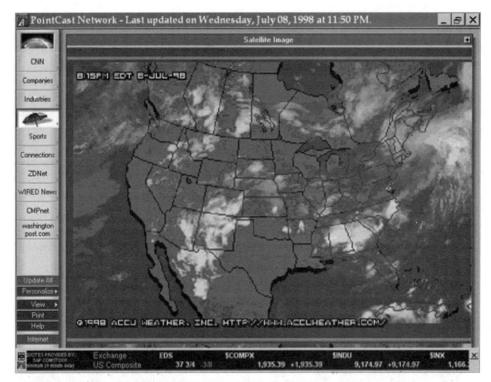

**Figure 1.17**    PointCast push display.

## INTERVIEW

*Mike Tilse, Network Operations Center Manager, Earthlink Network, Inc.*

Earthlink is one of the biggest ISPs on the planet. In fact, it's now a publicly traded company, which means it's listed in the stock market.

Earthlink is an enormous place. Located in Pasadena, California, Earthlink occupies two large buildings and has over 1500 employees. Mike Tilse is in charge of taking care of hardware and software that provides all Earthlink Internet services.

Mike runs the Earthlink Network Operations Center (NOC). NOC installations can be awesome places, and more and more of them are springing up around the world to monitor and handle network status 24 hours a day, 7 days a week. With business riding on server uptime *[depending on servers staying in operation]*, no expense is spared on network integrity.

*What's your job here at Earthlink?*
I have about 20 people in my department and I have several areas under me which are nonintuitive from my title. I do have the Network Operations Center under me, which is the monitoring group. That's the area in the data center that's monitored 24 x 7.

That group physically is a communication-in-and-out function for information development. For things of a technical nature, like if things are broken or coordination needs to be established or an upgrade or an outage or those kinds of things. If there's a problem or people need to be told that there are problems that need to be fixed, that stuff all goes in and out through the NOC.

I also have another area, Advanced Technical Services, or ATS. They handle things like customers who have dedicated connections to Earthlink. Setting up what are called *frame relay lines* or ISDN, that kind of stuff. I have a guy who handles that area for me, sort of like my submanager, and he does a lot of the programming and kinds of things that are necessary for various tools. He sorts out high-level technical problems and does evaluations on equipment, all sorts of different types of things. He's basically on his own personal career path to being a programmer.

I have another area called Manager Technical Services, which is actually where I started out. They handle customer account problems at a high level. People call in to tech support and if tech support can't handle them, a request is made to hand specific problems to MTS. MTS handles those things, they fix corrupted mailboxes. It's sort of a mini system administrator kind of function in that they have the same group access as the system administrators have. They have kind of a limited subset of duties that have to do with dealing with the specifics of customer accounts. They don't handle the vast majority of system administration—they're not system administrators—but to do what they do, they have to have the same level of access.

And then we have a sort of other group in MTS called *hostmaster*, which is comprised of people who handle the domain name requests, updating zone files, making sure that the data's correct, moving domains from another company to our company, interacting with the InterNIC, all that stuff.

*What do you do mostly?*
I hire good people who I don't have to manage, and then I manage them very lightly. I give them direction where they need direction, and I point out that things are not correct. I do performance reviews, I set direction and tone for the different areas.

*Do you have to leave some latitude for people working in these technologies since everything's very new and we're all learning?*
You have various different strategies as a manager. I could say any business has. You can micromanage people and treat them like machines and tell them every little step that they have to do, on which basis you could probably never manage more than one or two people effectively. It swamps all your time, so that's not really practical. If you want something to get done you have to have people who can manage themselves. I always hire people who are smart, inquisitive, curious, who pick up things fast; not necessarily the most technically skilled people, but the people who will be the most technically skilled, the people who want to be the most technically skilled, people who are fast talkers. This is one of the divisions that we make, informally, in IT, between us and the rest of the company and the rest of the world. Are they fast talkers or are they slow talkers. Can they get their concepts across? Are they easily confused? Those are personnel aspects that really make a difference when you try to get someone a job and can rely on them to do it.

*Did you come up through the network hierarchy?*
When I started, I started very early in Earthlink's history and I was the MTS. I must have lucked out. The Manager of Technical Services, that's who I was. I was the only guy. I

learned the job in about two weeks from the guy who was leaving the position. Thereafter for almost a year I worked 70 hours, more than 70-hour weeks. Finally I got another guy working for me and helping out, then I got some more people and more people and they made me the NOC manager and now I have more people than anybody else in the department.

*What technologies did you have to learn to do your job?*
Unix skills, vi editing skills, how the domain name system worked, what you're supposed to do and what you shouldn't do. There are very easy ways to crash your domain name system if you do something it doesn't like. The whole thing can go down; it's getting more robust as time goes on, but there's still just certain things you can't do. Being reliable, being willing to be here to do a very specific job that requires accuracy to do it accurately all the time.

*You're maintaining this huge network, is this all pretty much administering it through the setup files and knowing how the system works?*
That's fundamental, because you have to figure it's all based on communication of one kind or another. If you know the fundamentals of communication you know what portions of those communications can go wrong. If you're trained with that then you know you're dealing with dumb machines that only understand things in a certain way. You have to be able to "think" in the certain way that the machines do.

You have to understand what the protocols are and how they work—the level that I was working at when I was involved more technically. I didn't have to know every little bit and byte, that wasn't what I was handling. But I did have to know the specifics of how the mail files worked. I had to know the specifics of what machine did what, where it got its files from, and what it did with those files so that I knew I was changing the right file to get the effect that I wanted.

I learned a lot of that on the job. A lot of people just showed me things, a lot of people pointed at things to read, all that stuff. I'm not a programming person, particularly. I in my job, and most of the things that my people do, am basically involved in configuration and maintenance of programs that other people do. The standard programs like sendmail, or the domain name system, or these different aspects of Unix, account privileges and those kinds of things. So there's not a lot of program creation going on but what happens is, because you're using these standard programs, you can do things to simplify them. You can use scripting, you can use PERL.

PERL is probably a major, *major* skill that anybody who wants to work in the Internet area should have. PERL is being used to program all kinds of integration and interfacing both in Unix and in Web servers, doing things like logging stuff, parsing logs, pulling things out of log files, doing little useful utility kind of things that aren't standard programs that people have already done and that have what you want. If you know PERL, you can hack together little utilities that make your life easier as an administrator or as a programmer.

If you're building applications that you actually want to do something that nothing else does the way you want it to do then, yeah, you need to know C++, Java, that kind of stuff. Things are sort of moving toward Java being very useful for a number of things. If you know C, then you're going to be able to debug things. You're going to be able to look at the source.

If you're talking about, we're going to put in a new [Internet] service, because the system administrator has to do that. When we come up with a new service that people want that we want to implement on our servers, we're going to have to know how to compile programs for different platforms. You're going to have to know how to configure it, install it, apply grease in all the correct places. You have to know about how to do the administration with it, shell scripts and stuff to help set it up. You may need to look at the source code and you may need to write programming modules, C modules, or something like that to do some specific thing that this larger standard program doesn't quite do for you. You may need to apply some glue.

We have a Unix programming department, and they do applications that need to be done. Where programming comes in is, you're going to have things like database programs. You're going to buy a generic database like Oracle, which we have, but to interface it to your system you have to have a database administrator. Take our mail system, for instance. If we wanted to investigate users before we allowed them to send mail to our mail system, instead of accepting any mail coming in whatsoever, we would have to do that as a database. So then somebody would have to write the pieces that sendmail is going to use to interface to the Oracle database to get that information, and that's not a standard piece. So you have programmers to write those applications, those things to fit these standardized services that work very well, to interface between and convert information that you want on the other end. That's a whole area where you need C++ and database programmers.

***Do you think Java will ever replace C++?***
It may to a large degree, but I think there's still going to be a lot of things that are Web based that are going to be quick where you want cross-platform compatibility that are going to work very well in Java, and Java's going to be an important piece of all that. But you're going to still have some background proprietary behind the firewall systems and specialized systems where you're going to want that thing precompiled and it's just got to be fast. If you can shave 5 milliseconds off an application and you're doing 20 million transactions a week, now that's a lot of time!

***Do you see any trend in the way things are going as far as Web programming is concerned, based on your experience over the last four years?***
I think we're going through something that any new enterprise goes through in its sort of immature state. You basically have a set of standards and you have a set of capabilities. Then a lot of people explored how you can do those things with those capabilities, and that was like the early days of the Internet, early days of bulletin boards, early days of the ARPA, and all of that. So what came out of that was the best, the most efficient, robust, and simple way for people to understand, way to do that, which was TCP/IP. And that became the standard for the Internet. So once you had this sort of winning protocol, this winning way of doing things, then a lot people jumped on it and made it the foundation for other things. That became a building block. So then you have all these people came up with all these different ways to do all these other neat things with TCP/IP as a building block. So the Web came out as being another building block on that protocol. And of course FTP and other things were also very solid building blocks as protocols, but the Web, the HTTP protocol, is really solid. So now you have another explosion of all the things people can do. Things like delivering video, delivering voice. We're now going through a sorting-out period, where a lot of people are going to go, what is the best

protocol to do all these other little neat things. And those then, if they're broad enough, if they're general enough and robust enough, will become building blocks for other explosions.

*Evolutionary, survival of the fittest?*
Exactly. And sometimes the most elegant, wonderful kind of thing just doesn't win because it's just too complex for people to understand—it's too clever. The thing that wins is the thing that works every time you use it; it's reliable and it's simple and it may not do everything it could possibly do, it may not allow for all possibilities, but if it's a solid enough building block and reliable enough, more people build on it and it continues to work.

These things we're talking about are standards. They become standards because they're useful. They don't become standards because of their marketing.

If jeans are made in such as way that the principles of making jeans becomes the standard principles of the jeans-making industries, like Levi's, same thing.

*We'd have an explosion of jeans?*
Exactly. One thing that's going to happen is that cryptography is going to settle out to some degree on some standard. The other thing is that this kind of thing favors open standards. Nonproprietary standards. Standards where the source code is available. Standards where people can understand it and actually be secure in their understanding of it and that it does only what it says it does and not something else. That's what all this government attempt to enforce cryptographic protocols where you have key recovery and all this crap, those are never going ahead.

*Do you have to deal with cryptography?*
Sure, we're getting into that because we're doing virtual private networks where you have to have cryptography.

*What's a virtual private network?*
It's a way, through Internet connectivity, to communicate from their computer to any other computer on the Internet. Instead of installing a separate wire that carries only their internal traffic, what they do is between the two locations that they want to communicate securely, they put in encryption routers, one on each end, and one encrypts and the other decrypts, or they both actually do both. So any time you're sending data that you want to be encrypted or that you want to be secure, it encrypts that data before it sticks it in the packets and puts it on the network. And then at your end when you're receiving that data, it decrypts it and delivers it to your computer. It's a virtual private network because it doesn't exist in fact, it's not a separate secure line that only your traffic goes over. It's a public network and anybody can see those packets, but because they're encrypted it's private.

This is a big thing. A lot of people are doing this because it's very expensive to set up private wires, and it's not that expensive to get connected to the Internet. If you can put a reliable encryption/decryption solution that creates a virtual network on the Internet between your businesses you can use the Internet for your own private network and be secure that nobody's getting your data. There are people who are setting them up. They may just be buying network services from us, we don't necessarily have anything to do with VPN. We just route the traffic like any other traffic.

It's basically sending things in clear text, which is an open standard for data communication like ASCII. It's in numbers and you can easily convert it into readable data. If someone were to put a computer on that network that could read the traffic going by, it could convert basically anything that isn't encrypted into human-readable text and people could read it and discover all the secrets, anything that was going by on that network, even passwords, they're just text. And if somebody were actually looking at those packets of data they could figure out what the passwords are. There's even programs called, like, snoop, and there's others that you can run on a typical Unix box to capture the packets and send them to you.

People want us to [provide cryptography services] and it's one of the product mixes that any Internet service provider is probably going to have to get into. Certainly our salespeople are saying this is part of our business. We handle business customers, we sell private Internet connections to businesses for business purposes, as well as dial-up networks, and we sell high-speed links to people.

### So that's a trend?
There's going to be more and more of that. And one of the other trends is the fact that there's this huge problem with spam and there's a huge problem with crackers.

### What's a cracker?
Someone who breaks into a computer system. *Hacker* is generally considered to be an affectionate name. Someone who's a hacker means that he or she is skilled, knowledgeable. Crackers are people who just want to destroy things.

### What do you see for the future of the Internet?
The future of security is not going to be so much in security but in accountability. Everyone will have a digital signature and everything that's done will have a record, an audit trail with that signature.

The technologies that will survive are those that will not break down when you handle 30,000 or 50,000 users at once. It's fine in a university environment to handle 100 or so users but not in the ISP business.

The people that will get the jobs are those who understand and can work with the technologies that they're using, like today if you understand and can configure Internet routing, you can pretty much name your price.

You can visit Earthlink at www.earthlink.net.

## Summary

In this chapter I've shown you the Internet from the outside in. In the next chapter, we're going to look at the Internet from the inside out!

CHAPTER

2

# How Does the Internet Work?

Chapter 1, "What Has the Internet Become?" described how the Internet works hardware-wise. In this chapter, we'll see how the Internet works software-wise. If you've ever wondered how your Web browser does its job, how the Web addresses you select are located and retrieved, or how a Web page makes it around the world in the blink of an eye, then wonder no more.

By the end of this chapter you'll be able to speak with confidence about the high-tech world of Internet communications, or even better, understand what these network guys are talking about with all their acronyms.

You'll be able to find out just how many milliseconds it takes to get a response from any Web site, and you'll know exactly what's going back and forth between your computer and the Web when you're online. And finally, if there's anything more you want to find out, you'll know how to get in touch directly with the people who manage the Web itself!

## The Internet as a Network of Networks

The Internet has been made possible by the use of standard data communications protocols. Every computer in the world that is on the Internet understands this specific set of protocols. In fact, there's a whole administrative system for proposing, accepting, revising, and updating these communications standards. We'll be going into these protocols and how they work in this chapter.

## DEFINITION: PROTOCOL

**Protocol is a code of conduct to follow to ensure that people don't misunderstand each other. The same holds true for computers. A communications protocol is a standardized method for transmitting data between computers in a way that it can be sent, received, and processed without error. In short, what makes the Internet work is that the machines all understand each other, no matter what version of Unix, Windows, DOS, or any other operating system they're using. They all speak the same digital language.**

# What Is the World Wide Web?

The World Wide Web (WWW) is a *subset* of the Internet. When we look up a Web site using the *www* prefix, as in:

```
http://www.cintronics.com
```

the *www* is meant to give you a Web page in hypertext format. At least that is how it was originally designed by Tim Berners-Lee who invented the World Wide Web as a global hypertext project back in 1990! Although today some Web addresses do not start with *www*, if they're hypertext, they're part of the World Wide Web.

The WWW is all the hypertext in the world linked together as one large entity.

## DEFINITION: HYPERTEXT

**Hypertext is a method of linking text together. The key to hypertext is the links that can go from any part of one page to any part of the same or another page. That's all there is to it. Hypertext Markup Language (HTML) is a language for hypertext layout. The purpose of the original Web browser, Mosaic, was to display formatted hypertext.**

**Of course, there is more to hypertext than jumping from point to point. The theory is that hypertext can create a unified knowledge base that unites all of the information in the universe into an interlinked whole. If we were to cross-reference every relevant piece of information with every other, not only would our Web documents become colorful, they would represent a complete and formidable knowledge engine. When we extend this idea into further forms of data storage, such as audio and video, we come up with a larger concept called *hypermedia*, all kept in a world called *hyperspace*!**

HTTP is the primary protocol that all Web browsers are programmed to use. This means that the Web uses HTTP as opposed to FTP (File Transfer Protocol) and other protocols in use on the Internet.

# DEFINITION: HTTP

**HTTP is HyperText Transfer Protocol. This is the protocol used to send hypertext information back and forth on the Internet. We'll be taking a look at this later.**

This would not be a physical subset, meaning that some computers use HTTP and some use FTP (actually, all servers should be equipped to use both of these protocols and more), but when a browser requests a Web page from a server, it is asking for it in HTTP language. If it's not sent in HTTP, the page won't be displayed on your screen as hypertext. Don't get confused by the www in the URL; it's HTTP that makes the Web!

## What Is a Domain?

Originally, a domain was one of the main hosts or subnetworks of the Internet, and a domain name was a way to access that specific host or network. These days a domain can be anything from a single Web page sharing space on a single computer with thousands of other domains, to a Web site of any size, to an entire network. The thing that makes the domain is addressibility, which leads us to define the *domain name*.

A domain name is the central part of the Internet address, like *cintronics.com*. Whatever precedes it, like www or search or plastic.explosives, is a local name (called a *subdomain*) assigned by the server network manager. The Internet is only concerned with the last part of the name, the domain name, which it associates with a specific server.

Domain names are split into two parts: the first (or top) level and second level. The second-level domain is the name you choose. The first-level domain is the extension (there are currently seven), plus over 100 country codes. The seven extensions are listed in Table 2.1. The first-level domain is assigned according to what kind of domain

**Table 2.1**   Top-Level Domains

| DOMAIN | MEANING |
| --- | --- |
| .arpa | ARPANET |
| .com | Commercial (most domains are commercial) |
| .edu | Educational institutions |
| .gov | Government domains |
| .mil | Military domains |
| .net | ISP domains |
| .org | Mostly nonprofit, public service organizations |
| .us | United States |
| .uk | United Kingdom |
| .jp | Japan |
| .sg | Singapore |

it represents. The domain name system is flexible and can vary slightly from country to country. You can check the up-to-the-minute status of all of the top-level domains that are in use or under serious consideration at www.iana.org/domain-names.html.

### Who Assigns Domain Names?

An ever-growing body of Internet administration organizations maintains lists of domain names. The domain names are picked by those who want to use them, and then an administrative fee is paid to register the name with one of these organizations. You can't expect somebody to keep track of millions of domain names for free!

Currently, if you live in the Western hemisphere you'll probably pay $35/year to Network Solutions, the registration arm of InterNIC (Internet Network Information Center), to own the domain name of your choice (as long as it's not already taken). The fee is usually $70 up front for the first two years and then $35 per year thereafter.

You can register a domain name over the Internet and have it assigned immediately. Just log into www.internic.net and register your name. They'll send you a bill, and if you don't pay it you just lose the name.

## What Is a URL?

The Uniform Resource Locator (URL) is used to find an exact target within a domain, and it can be broken down into five parts. A full URL would read http://www .prolotherapy.com/prolohelp.html.

The first part is the protocol designator such as http:// or ftp://. This designates which communications resource on the destination server will be used to service the request, whether it's hypertext, file transfer, or another. The default value your browser will assign is the http:// prefix, making it the part we most usually omit. This part of the URL is also called the *scheme* or *access method*.

The second part is the subdomain name, which the browser defaults to www.

The third part is the actual domain name, which has no default value.

The fourth part is the port number. You won't see this unless you're using the type of Internet protocols made for managing, updating, and debugging networks and connections. This was the original way of designating protocol, used with the original form of domain name addresses, which was entirely numeric. Most protocols do not have designators like http and ftp. In fact, http normally uses port 80, which would be written after a colon as :80, although a server may be configured with a different port number. A word of warning: This will not work when you type it into a URL unless you know exactly when to use it.

The fifth part of the URL is also optional and gives the *path* of a specific file to access. Again, there is a default where the Web server will deliver up any file named *index* with a valid HTML extension, such as index.htm, index.html, or index.shtml. Shtml stands for server HTML, which means the page contains something for the server to process, like a hit counter.

### How Does the Internet Find a URL?

Once you get a domain name, you will also need a domain-level account on the Web server on which you place your site. Once you have a domain-level account, then you need to get the IP address of the server where your megabytes are allocated from the ISP network administrator.

## DEFINITION: IP ADDRESS

**IP means *Internet Protocol*. Every domain on the Internet is assigned a unique number. This number is 12 digits long (four sets of 3 digits each) and is called the *IP address*. When you type in a domain name this is translated into the 12-digit number. For example, when you type in cintronics.com, your ISP connects you to 208.234.16.25.**

Once you have the IP address, you tell the InterNIC what this is. Once they program this into the Internet, voilá! It really does seem like magic the first time you see it happen.

There's a bit more to this process, which we'll explore in depth in the next section. The InterNIC, or the organization that maintains the domain name list in your geographical area, conspires with an organization maintaining the IP address list to publish a directory of what name goes with what number. This is called an *Internet phone book*. This list is continually updated on an international basis, and there are special servers whose function is solely to respond to domain name lookups. You can imagine how many of these occur each second during high-traffic periods!

### From Browser to Provider to Router to Server

Figure 2.1 is a simple diagram of the data path followed in Internet communications between a browser and server. Like the old song, *Dry Bones* . . .

> The browser's connected to the provider . . .
> The provider's connected to the router . . .
> The router's connected to the server . . .
> Oh, hear the word of the protocol . . .

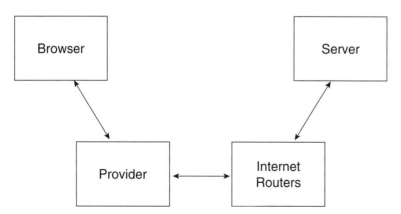

**Figure 2.1** Basic Internet communication path.

All kidding aside, each of these steps involve several detailed processes, each of which will be described in depth later in this chapter.

## The Browser's Role

The first step in Internet communications is when the browser calls a program to make a dial-up connection to your local ISP access number. On Windows computers using dial-up connections, this program is called *Winsock*. The browser accesses the modem and instructs it to dial the number specified in the Dial-Up Networking settings. The modem dials and establishes a physical connection (an electronic signal that goes from your modem to their modem) to the ISP modem.

Once the physical connection is established, the communications program establishes a software connection based on specific communications protocols.

## The Provider's Role

In the second step of the communication process, a server on the provider's end runs a program that constantly checks for incoming calls. These programs are called *daemons*. When a call is received, the server establishes the connection. Because of the huge amount of traffic a provider has to handle, the server you connect to may only have the job of maintaining the communications link. This server may then route each task you ask it to perform to specialized servers that handle specific tasks, such as e-mail or a Web page request. Most likely you have asked for a Web page by name, like www.phunmen.com.

The provider translates this physical name into an Internet protocol type name. Perhaps you've seen these; for example, 208.234.16.25 is the same as www.cintronics.com. Once we have the numerical Internet address we can start routing.

## The Router's Role

The Internet has a lot of routers on it. These routers use the numeric address to route traffic from source to destination and back. In fact, messages do not always get routed all together. They are broken up into pieces and these pieces do not necessarily all follow the same path to get to their destination, but they do get there. At times you may wait until the browser says it cannot establish a connection with the server. In this case, it could be that the server is down or simply that the reply is taking too long because of a traffic jam.

## The Server's Role

The final step is the destination server. This is set up much like the server at your ISP. It runs programs that wait to receive, or listen for, an incoming request. When this occurs the destination server sets up a connection, delivers the requested information, and terminates the connection with the ISP server. This all happens very fast.

# DEFINITION: SERVER

**A server is a computer with two features: (1) It's hardwired into the Internet, and (2) It has a great deal of specialized server software. The technology of Internet servers is fairly complex and is growing rapidly, so if you want to understand it, you've got to do a lot of studying and make sure you understand one thing before you go on to another.**

We've already taken a quick look at the different options for hardwiring into the Internet, from a 56kbps leased line all the way to an OC-48 fiber optic connection. Let's take a brief look at server software.

First you need the basic server software. If you want to set up your own software this is a win-win situation because what is reputed to be the best and most common Web server available is also free! The Apache server is available to download with all the source code at no cost. Apache is also the original Web server, which was *patched* up by the original group who added features to it. Hence it was named, *A Patchy server*. What's new is that you no longer have to compile it yourself; you can download an executable form. What's not new is that you have to install and configure it yourself, but there's a lot of helpful people out there to assist you.

On the Web server that is responding to incoming requests for Internet services run a series of daemons that provide services for all the various protocol services that a server must be ready to respond to. Exactly what daemons are running and what they do is governed by a series of files that must be configured by the server administrator. Under a Graphical User Interface, or GUI (that means some form of Windows-based server such as Windows NT), this job is made easier for the beginner by the user-friendly interface. On other servers this job is mostly done with a text editor, although improved administrator tools are starting to come on the market.

You now have the beginnings of a running Web server. You also have a series of options for what plug-in services you are going to support! These include features such as streaming audio and video, database services available from database software companies, security and e-commerce options, and so forth. These options and more go into making up a Web server. Companies such as Sun, Netscape, IBM, Microsoft, Lotus, and Novell are all offering new and improved Web server software.

# Internet Architecture

Now that you have some kind of an idea how information is bandied about on the Internet by server software, we're going to take a look at the underlying design that makes this work.

# DEFINITION: ARCHITECTURE

**This word is no different in computers than it is in building construction. It means the way something is built; in this case, the way the network called the Internet is built so that it will stay standing. In the case of the Internet, the architecture is a**

specification that defines exactly how electronic communication will occur between computers on the Internet, since the Internet is all about communication.

## Layered Architecture

Figure 2.2 illustrates a hierarchy of Internet communication. The top and bottom layers are what we can see physically, but it's the gears that turn between browser and modem that make all of this mesh together.

The modem obviously does the work of physically transmitting electronic signals, and cares not what they contain but only that they are sent and received without error.

The Internet protocol, or IP layer, does the work of routing communications, and again cares not what they contain but only that they go to the right place.

The Transport Control protocol layer does the work of sending and receiving communications, and still does not care what they contain, only that they are sent and received. The difference between this and the modem is that the modem handles physical signals, and TCP handles messages handed to it by the application program.

The application program interfaces with TCP to send and receive complete communications.

The Internet is designed to carry communication in layers. Each layer has a specific task. This is supposed to simplify things, and when you understand how it works, you can see that it does. This method keeps an application program from having to figure out how to perform the task of another layer. No matter what layer it is on, all it has to do is its specific function.

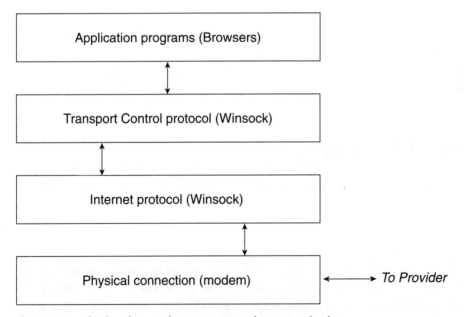

**Figure 2.2**    The four layers of Internet network communication.

This is easy if you think of it in terms of driving a car. When you drive, you shouldn't have to worry about how the car works. You turn it on and point it where you want to go. Likewise, the car doesn't have to figure out how to drive, it only has to keep the engine running. And finally, the road doesn't have to worry about keeping the car running or how to drive it, it just has to provide the route.

Between each layer there are programs that provide the communications between each layer. Like the steering wheel and tires that provide an interface between the driver, car, and road, these programs pass the data back and forth between the different levels of Internet architecture.

## NOTE
The end purpose of Internet architecture is to enable programs on one machine, in each layer, to only have to communicate with programs in other machines in the same layer. Let's take a closer look at this.

### How Does Layered Architecture Work?

Let's say, for example, that your application program sends a request for a database search on a search engine. This is an application-to-application request. This request is passed onto the Winsock program, which handles both the Transport and Internet layers. These two layers combined is a technology called *TCP/IP*.

## DEFINITION: TCP/IP
TCP/IP is the protocol that makes the Internet work. This stands for a combination of Transport Control Protocol/Internet Protocol. TCP is a protocol that does what it says. It controls transport, the communication of data. IP is the numerical method of Internet addressing mentioned earlier. Every computer on the Internet has a unique IP address and all data is routed using the IP protocol; and every computer network that is hooked into the Internet must have a method of handling TCP/IP messages even if they do not use TCP/IP for their private network protocol, but IPX/SPX (Internet Packet eXchange/Sequenced Packet eXchange, a NetWare protocol used by Novell) or NetBEUI (NetBIOS Enhanced User Interface, a protocol used by Windows networks).

The TCP layer takes responsibility for ensuring the communication is completed. It keeps a list (called a *queue*) of messages in progress. Every message that is sent should have an acknowledgment sent back, and every message that is received (except for an acknowledgment) is in turn sent an acknowledgment. TCP performs specific tasks if acknowledgments are not received, messages come in later than expected, or if messages have missing or corrupted data. For example, messages are given a certain amount of time to make the trip, or they are considered late and discarded, even if they *do* come back. Of course, they are not tossed without a message being sent to the offending server that their late messages have been given the boot. The point is that the TCP layer in the Winsock program on your computer communicates only with the TCP layer on the host computer to which you are connected.

As you can see in Figure 2.3, the TCP layer converts messages that are handed to it by the application layer into TCP format by adding the TCP control information to the front of the message, now called a TCP header, and then hands the whole message over to the IP layer. The IP layer takes responsibility for ensuring that the communications are correctly routed. The first thing the IP layer does with every message is to convert its www style address into a numerical IP address. It tacks the IP address to the front of the TCP format message, which now makes it an IP format message. Again, the IP protocol on your machine was designed to talk only to the IP layer out there on the Internet, so it takes the message it has converted to IP format and fires this out to the physical connection layer.

The physical connection layer performs the transmission of the data. You could say this layer converts the IP messages to an electronic format. This layer is all electronic and relies on programming that resides on or in the physical network card, such as an Ethernet interface, or phone line interface card, meaning modem. These little wonders have protocols of their own—we never see them, but we do in fact hear them every time we fire up a modem dialer. This is the song of the physical layers communicating.

Keep in mind that TCP/IP does not come into action until the physical connection has been established. Then, one at a time, the layer architecture is built up to the top. First IP, then TCP, then the application layer can begin operation across the network.

At each level, the protocol handling a data block either adds its protocol-specific information to or removes it from that data. When sending a message, each protocol layer will add the information required by the same protocol layer at the receiving end, then pass the message on the layer below, which treats the entire message block as a single unit. When receiving a message, the protocol layer will process and remove that information before passing the remaining data to the layer above. If there is an error, an error message is returned back to the transmitting layer in the same fashion.

## Communications Protocols

I suppose all protocols are actually communications protocols, since they're meant to make smooth communication occur, whether between two countries or two computers. As far as the Internet goes you have to have both ends of the connection speaking the same language, and not talking out of turn. It gets a bit more complicated than that when you apply protocols to layered architecture.

To put it more simply, each layer speaks its own language but not the language of other layers, so adds its own protocol information to the message, kind of like the post office. You put a message in an envelope (HTTP), which gets addressed by you (TCP), which gets picked up and bar-coded by the post office (IP) and put on a truck and/or airplane (modem), routed to your mailbox (IP), given to the right person at the address (TCP), and opened and read (HTTP). After all, this stuff was designed by people just like us.

## How Does the Browser Communicate with the Provider?

To connect to the Internet the first step is to make the connection between browser and provider. This is accomplished in four steps. First, the modem makes a physical connection to the ISP. Then the ISP's security authorization must be granted through a login, and once that gate is opened you have to be assigned an IP address in order for

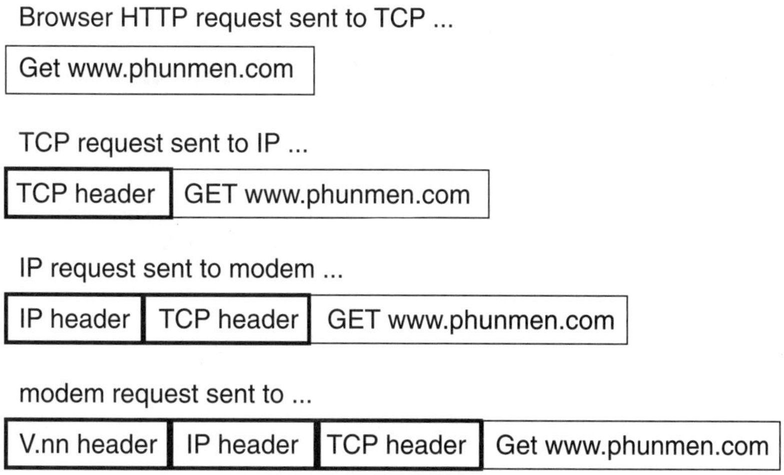

Browser HTTP request sent to TCP ...

| Get www.phunmen.com |
|---|

TCP request sent to IP ...

| TCP header | GET www.phunmen.com |
|---|---|

IP request sent to modem ...

| IP header | TCP header | GET www.phunmen.com |
|---|---|---|

modem request sent to ...

| V.nn header | IP header | TCP header | Get www.phunmen.com |
|---|---|---|---|

**Figure 2.3**   Layered protocol data handling.

any server to be able to route HTTP messages back to you. And finally, you have to start the party going by sending one yourself!

### The Modem Connection

A dial-up connection first requires the computer to use the modem to dial the provider. This is normally accomplished by the browser itself but there's no rule saying you couldn't use any program that will tell the modem to dial out. In Windows 9x, the Dial-Up Networking utility may call the Dial-Up Scripting tool to do this. It can even be done manually. All the browser really cares about is having a clear channel through the communications port so it can establish a TCP/IP connection.

All modems use the Hayes command set. This is a series of modem commands invented for the Hayes modem, which was created after the deregulation of the telephone companies. The browser's communication with the modem begins by initializing the modem and ends with a message indicating success or failure. Such a cycle of communication is shown in Table 2.2. Modem responses are in *italics*.

The Hayes command set is good to know. If you're having real problems with a modem, you can go into a shareware program (or another modem direct-connect program like Telix) and see if the modem is responding and what happens when it receives commands. If nothing else, you can use it to do a direct connect for file transfers and remote logins from Unix machines either as a user or as a Web host with an account on the machine.

A modem should come with a manual that lists which options are valid. Every modem is slightly different, which is why you have to pick your modem from a list every time you set up a program. The selection determines what options the modem initialization string will set. Table 2.3 lists several Hayes modem commands.

**INFORMATIVE SITE!**
*www.delta.com/delta/products*
**Telix shareware**

**Table 2.2**    Hayes Modem Commands and Responses

| DATA | MEANING |
|------|---------|
| AT | Attention. (Is the modem there?) |
| OK | Acknowledged (Modem is here.) |
| ATZ | Attention, initialize modem. Z means clear all settings. (This is usually a much longer string depending on modem options available.) |
| OK | Acknowledged |
| ATDT 181898899791 | Attention, dial this number using tone dialing (DT). The modem will put the line off hook, dial, and if a carrier signal is detected, connect. |
| CONNECT 33600 or LINE BUSY | Connected at 33600bps. Busy signal. |
| NO DIALTONE | Couldn't even dial out! |
| NO CARRIER | No answer, at least not by a modem. |

**Table 2.3**    Useful Hayes Modem Commands

| COMMAND | MEANING |
|---------|---------|
| A/ | Repeat last command (easy way to redial). |
| ATS0=1 | Set auto answer on. (S0=0 would be off). |
| ATA | Answer the phone right now (pick up the line and give a carrier signal). |
| ATDP9,5551212 | Dial on a pulse phone (comma makes it pause for a second). |
| ATE1 | Echo my commands back (otherwise you won't see them). |
| ATH | Hang up the phone right now. |
| ATL3 | Set maximum speaker volume (options are 0 for off, 1, 2, and 3). |
| ATQ1 | Do NOT display result codes (quiet mode). |
| ATV1 | Display result codes in text (0 for numbers!). |
| +++ | Return to command mode. Used while online! (must be typed slowly). |

### The Login

Once the modem has established a physical data link, the next step is to log in. This is just like logging in to any computer that requires a login, and it may be automated or manual. Either you or your computer have a text conversation with the host server to validate your authority to use the service. The login used to have to be done manually but is now automated by tools such as dial-up networking.

### The IP Connection

After logging in successfully, you are assigned an IP address. Remember, these are Internet addresses and this means that you are now temporarily a full-fledged Internet computer. You have to be if you're going to send a request from an ISP in Los Angeles to a server in London and expect a response. Your IP address is assigned out of a pool that your service provider has available. This happens behind the scenes, so you won't know what that address is going to be.

## DEFINITION: BITS AND BYTES

**It helps to understand computer hardware to better understand computer software. A *bit* is the original memory unit, consisting of a single on or off switch, representing the number 1 or 0, and physically represented as an electrical charge at a specific location on a chip. A byte is 4 bits, which in binary arithmetic gives you a number between 0 and 15. Two bytes can be combined to represent a number between 0 and 255 (or 16 * 16 less 1), and 4 bytes will represent a number up to 65,535, etc.**

An IP address is 32-bits long, broken down into four sections of 8 bits, or four numbers between 0 and 256. IP addresses are assigned to networks in batches—the size of the batch depends on the size of the network. Your ISP has a chunk of IP addresses available to assign to the computers within its own network of servers it is hosting and dial-up users.

Your ISP has been assigned a block of these numbers through the InterNIC; for example, an ISP may have been assigned IP addresses 208.234.16.0 through 208.234.16.256. ISPs are free to assign the last part of the IP address to their computers as they please.

## INFORMATIVE SITES!

*www.internic.net*
**The InterNIC**

*www.iana.org*
**The Internet Assigned Numbers Authority**

*www.arin.net*
**The American Registry for Internet Numbers**

*www.nic.mil or nic.ddn.mil*
**DoD Network Information Center**

*www.nic.gov*
**U.S. Government NIC**                                         *Continues*

# INFORMATIVE SITES! *(CONTINUED)*

*www.ripe.net*
**Reseaux IP Europeens**

*www.apnic.net*
**Asia-Pacific NIC**

---

## THE INTERNIC, IP ADDRESSES, AND THE DOMAIN NAME SYSTEM

The domain name system was created to supplement the dotted decimal IP address notation into a more user-friendly Internet addressing scheme, where users no longer would have to keep track of IP addresses.

In order to match domain names up to their IP addresses, an increasing number of administrative bodies are being created. First, we had the InterNIC, which stands for Internetwork Information Center. The InterNIC's job was to keep track of what domain names were assigned, to whom they belonged, when they expired, and to what IP addresses they were assigned.

This job has now been split up into several parts: the InterNIC for the Western hemisphere and some other parts of the world, RIPE for Europe, and APNIC for the Asia/Pacific region. The job of keeping track of IP addresses has been moved over to ARIN, the American Registry for Internet Numbers. We also have IANA, the Internet Assigned Numbers Authority, to coordinate what is being done with domain names and IP addresses in the United States. There are even more organizations that cover .gov and .mil domains, Canada, Mexico, etc.

The end result is that these painstakingly maintained tables of IP addresses and domain names are exported to Internet routers the world over on a regular basis. This is an automated process that can take days to reach the most remote of third-world networks.

---

## The HTTP Connection

Now you've got a modem connection and an IP address. Assuming you're Web browsing, the next step is to get a Web page. The HTTP protocol is text-based (since it occurs at the highest network layer) and fairly easy to understand. The browser sends out a GET or POST request to the server with additional information to identify how to answer the request, as shown in the following code:

```
GET / HTTP/1.1
Accept: image/gif, image/x-xbitmap, image/jpeg, image/pjpeg, */*
Accept-Language: en-us
Accept-Encoding: gzip, deflate
User-Agent: Mozilla/4.0 (compatible; MSIE 4.01;Windows 98)
Host: www.prolotherapy.com
Connection: Keep-Alive
Extension: Security/Remote-Passphrase
```

Table 2.4 translates the meaning of each of the tags in this HTTP header. It's called a *header* because it's at the beginning of the HTTP content.

**Table 2.4**  HTTP Header Tags

| TAG | MEANING |
| --- | --- |
| GET: | Identifies the request as HTTP version 1.1. |
| Accept: | Identifies what image formats are accepted: gif, bitmap, jpeg, or anything else! |
| Accept-Language: | Specifies the language as U.S. English . . . there are translators out there. |
| Accept-Encoding: | Says that zip data compression is OK. |
| User-Agent: | Identifies the user agent, or browser and OS. |
| Host: | Requests the homepage for www.prolotherapy.com. |
| Connection: | Specifies to keep the connection open, or alive. |
| Extension: | Something about security . . . |

The Connection line tells the server not to close the connection right away because in this case we're not going to close the connection once we receive this one page. Now this request must be routed.

## How Does the Provider Communicate with the Routers?

It's not enough to connect to a provider, get TCP/IP fired up, and send out a request for a Web page. Now that HTTP message has to find its way to the right server. Everything rides on an assumption that the domain name you just requested really exists. The question is where, and that's where the domain name servers come in.

### The Domain Name Server

The first step on the provider's end is to convert the domain name for the Web page requested into an IP address. Because this task is the sine qua non (Latin for without which not) of the Internet, there is an entire network of domain name servers set up to accomplish this task.

The originating server calls a program called a *name resolver*. This program accesses a table on the server with the address of the local name server. This is either on the same computer or at another IP address on the local network. Either way, the name server is accessed by its IP address. If on the local machine, the IP address is always the same, 127.0.0.1.

The name server will either have the IP address of the requested DNS (Domain Name Server) already on file or it will have to query a remote name server for the answer. The only reasons it would have the address already on file is either that it is part of the local network or it is in the cached list of recently requested addresses.

The domain name system is set up in a hierarchical fashion, as illustrated in Figure 2.4. This handles the problem of finding addresses without every DNS server having to keep a list of every DNS address, which would be impossible. If the local name

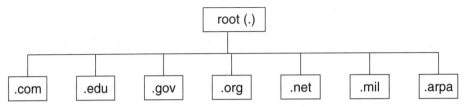

**Figure 2.4**    The domain name hierarchy.

server does not have the IP address requested, it accesses a file on the server with a list of one or more remote name servers. The DNS system is set up so that name resolution can be separated out by top-level domain. You can designate one server to look up addresses for the .com domain, another for .edu, and so on.

There are a lot of fun little tests you can do with ping. One thing it will do is show you the first nine hops, or nodes traversed, on the packet's journey. If you do this, you'll see that the packets do not always follow the same path to the same server.

In a large private network there may be an internal hierarchy of name servers, but an ISP is most likely to go straight to the top, to the root name server, designated by a lone . (a period, or in Web terms, "dot nothing").

The root name server will relay the address resolution request to the appropriate server of the requested domain. This request, having gone all the way up the hierarchy, now goes all the way down until it reaches a name server that has the exact address of the requested domain. This scheme follows the network numbering scheme mentioned earlier, which is also called *dotted decimal notation*. IP addresses are handed out according

---

### IP ADDRESSES, LOOPBACK, AND PING

The IP address 127.0.0.1 is called the *loopback* address and is also used for testing. You can send IP messages from yourself to yourself to see if your server is working internally because the messages never leave the network.

*Ping* is an Internet service used to see if a server is responding. Pinging the loopback takes zero time because the data packets don't actually have to go anywhere.

C:\WINDOWS> ping 127.0.0.1

Pinging 127.0.0.1 with 32 bytes of data:Reply from 127.0.0.1: bytes=32 time<10ms TTL=128Reply from 127.0.0.1: bytes=32 time<10ms TTL=128

Reply from 127.0.0.1: bytes=32 time<10ms TTL=128Reply from 127.0.0.1: bytes=32 time<10ms TTL=128

Ping statistics for 127.0.0.1:Packets: Sent = 4, Received = 4, Lost = 0 (0% loss),

Approximate round-trip times in milli-seconds:

Minimum = 0ms, Maximum = 0ms, Average = 0ms

Now let's ping a remote server.

C:\WINDOWS> ping 208.234.16.25

Pinging 208.234.16.25 with 32 bytes of data:Reply from 208.234.16.25: bytes=32 time=393ms TTL=51Reply from 208.234.16.25: bytes=32 time=361ms TTL=51Reply from

**Table 2.5**   IP Network Classes

| CLASS | NETWORK ADDRESS | LOCAL HOST ADDRESSES | # NETS POSSIBLE | # NET NODES |
|-------|-----------------|----------------------|-----------------|-------------|
| A | 1. to 126. | 0.0.1 to 255.255.254 | 126 | 16777214 |
| B | 128.0 to 191.254 | 0.1 to 255.254 | 16256 | 65534 |
| C | 224.0.0 to 255.255.255 | 0 to 254 | 2072640 | 254 |

to the size of the network that needs them. A network will be assigned either the first part of the IP address only, or the first and second, or the first, second, and third. The actual number handed out is called the *network* (or *subnet) mask*, because the network addresses will have that part as a fixed value with the rest of the address variable.

The IP address assignment scheme is listed in Table 2.5. Some addresses are reserved, so not all are available.

The name resolution request will eventually end up at the name server for the specific network the final destination is a part of. This name server will hand back the full four-part IP address of the destination domain.

So, in summary, the domain name request starts with the application, moves up the name server hierarchy as far as it needs to go to resolve the top-level domain, then back down the hierarchy toward the destination until the exact network connection is identified. The IP address of this node will be transmitted back through the name server network until it comes back to you with the answer—all faster than a speeding bullet. But not too fast to be shown in Figure 2.5.

208.234.16.25: bytes=32 time=369ms TTL=51 Reply from 208.234.16.25: bytes=32 time=358ms TTL=51

Ping statistics for 208.234.16.25:   Packets: Sent = 4, Received = 4, Lost = 0 (0% loss), Approximate round trip times in milli-seconds: Minimum = 358ms, Maximum = 393ms, Average = 370ms

Pinging cintronics.com took about one-third of a second for each data packet.

The TTL figure on the right means *time to live*. As you can see on the loopback ping, this started out at 128. Every network node it passes through then subtracts 1 from this count. If the count gets to 0, the data packet is tossed.

The term *time to live* came from the original concept that this would represent the time in seconds to allow the packet to continue transmission. In the fiber optic world of the Internet, this data packet could circle the world several times before expiring, so the rule was added that each node would subtract one second regardless of the actual transmission time. The purpose of this is to keep packets from loading up the network when they either don't have anywhere to go because of a traffic problem or a nonexistent destination.

In this case, since the entire round trip from my ping in Los Angeles to the server in North Carolina and back took only a third of a second, and the packets returned with a TTL of 51, it turns out that each of these data packets was processed by 77 routing nodes during their brief 370-millisecond voyage!

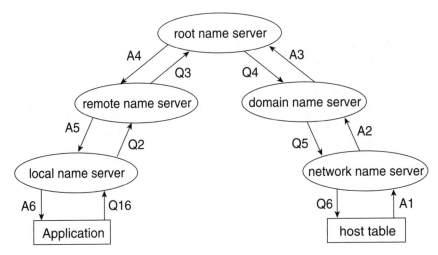

**Figure 2.5**   Domain name hierarchy in action.

Table 2.6 lists the locations of the root name servers on the Internet. As the Internet started out as an American enterprise, servers A through H are all in the United States, and most are part of or close to a U.S. military base. As we progress it seems more international servers will appear.

**Table 2.6**   Root Servers Around the World

| ROOT SERVER NAME | IP ADDRESS | PHYSICAL LOCATION |
|---|---|---|
| A.ROOT-SERVERS.NET | 198.41.0.4 | Herndon, VA |
| B.ROOT-SERVERS.NET | 128.9.0.107 | Marina del Rey, CA |
| C.ROOT-SERVERS.NET | 192.33.4.12 | Herndon, VA |
| D.ROOT-SERVERS.NET | 128.8.10.90 | College Park, MD |
| E.ROOT-SERVERS.NET | 92.203.230.10 | Moffett Field, CA |
| F.ROOT-SERVERS.NET | 192.5.5.241 | Woodside, CA |
| G.ROOT-SERVERS.NET | 192.112.36.4 | Vienna, VA |
| H.ROOT-SERVERS.NET | 128.63.2.53 | Aberdeen Proving Grounds, MD |
| I.ROOT-SERVERS.NET | 192.36.148.17 | Stockholm, Sweden |
| J.ROOT-SERVERS.NET | 198.41.0.10 | Baltimore, MD |
| K.ROOT-SERVERS.NET | 193.0.14.129 | Amsterdam, Netherlands |
| L.ROOT-SERVERS.NET | 198.32.64.12 | Marina del Rey, CA |
| M.ROOT-SERVERS.NET | 202.12.27.33 | Somewhere in Japan |

## IPV4, IPV6, AND IPNG

The current version of IP in use is version 4. If you add up the number of possible networks using this scheme, the total is just over 2 million, with the total number of IP addresses at just over 16 million. A few years ago this seemed like plenty, but now we actually are in danger of running out of numbers.

Enter IP version 6, also called *IP next generation* or *IPng*. The IPv4 address is four parts of 8 bits each, making 32 bits. The IPv6 address is 128 bits long. The number of computers that would be supported by IPv6 translates to:
340,282,366,920,938,463,463,374,607,431,768,211,456.

We're not sure exactly when IPv6 might become a reality. There are a few more things to work out, and the entire Internet would have to be reprogrammed to handle the new routing numbers.

Also in the works is expansion of top-level domains. A group of seven new top-level domains were almost added to the Web recently, but this was put off for a while. These top-level domains were .arts, .rec, .per, .store, .info, .firm, and .web. It's certain that this scheme will be expanded in the near future once the powers that be can agree on an expansion plan. It's even been proposed to have a .sex to pigeonhole this category of controversial material into an identifiable domain of its own.

IANA has made a public statement on this subject:

"IANA continues to receive applications for, and inquiries about, new generic TLDs. Given the ongoing discussions about the creation of a new Internet organization that are taking place throughout the Internet community, as recommended in the U.S. Government's white paper on "Management of Internet Names and Addresses," no new generic TLDs will be established at this time. The process and criteria for adding domains will almost certainly fall within the responsibility of the new organization. Please be patient as IANA and the Internet evolve in this transitional period, and the Internet community works toward consensus in establishing this new organization.

We encourage you to participate publicly concerning this issue and other issues involved with Internet governance through "our comments" mailbox. All mail received at this mailbox about these issues is posted on this Web site under "Public Comments.""

Once the destination IP address has been returned in response to the name resolution request, the provider can start sending requests across to the destination server.

## How Does the Router Communicate with the Server?

Provider to Routers and Routers to Servers are all the same communications protocols. However, I will introduce one final concept in this section, which applies to exactly what form data takes as it is moved across the Internet.

The Internet is a packet-switched network. All data is packaged in TCP and IP headers and sent through routers which have their own hardware communications protocols.

This is kind of like sending out a bunch of carrier pigeons, each with an equal chunk of the message, and putting it back together after they land. Hopefully they would all take an efficient route and show up on the other side; otherwise, your message would be lost.

# DEFINITION: PACKET SWITCHING

**A packet is a block of data packaged for transmission. Data packets are smaller pieces of a larger block of data that is broken down and sent in the individual packets, then received and reassembled. On the Internet, data is sent without regard to exactly how it will arrive at its destination since this is the job of the routers, not the servers. Switching is changing. In packet switching, individual packets of data may go one way or another, their route switched according to what is most efficient at that time.**

## *An Example Communications Cycle*

Let's take a look at an actual Internet communications cycle captured from the modem port. We'll start with the modem login, the go through the raw HTTP protocol requests for the www.prolotherapy.com homepage, and finally go over the HTTP acknowledgments and final delivery of content.

Outgoing commands (issued by our computer) are in ***bold italic.*** Incoming data is in plain text.

First comes our modem access, with PC/modem communications . . .

```
AT
AT
OK
AT&F E0V1&C1&D2S95=45 S0=0 AT&FE0V1&C1 &D2S95=45S0=0
AT&F E0V1&C1&D2S95=45 S0=0 AT&FE0V1&C1 &D2S95=45S0=0
OK
ATS7=60S30=0 L0M1\N3%C3&K3B0N 1X4
OK
ATDT;
OK
ATDT9889791
CARRIER 28800
PROTOCOL: LAP-M
COMPRESSION: V.42BIS
CONNECT 28800
Host Name:
CPS
User ID:
(my user id)
Password:
(my password)
PPP: Connected to 0041 PQG1
```

The first command to the modem is AT, and the modem echoes our commands until the E0 command is given embedded in the first initialization string. Once the dial-up command is given as *ATDT9889791,* the hardware protocol takes over until the physical connection is made, and we don't see the results until we get a successful V.42 physical connection reported as *CONNECT 28800,* etc.

Now we are again in the between-protocols zone (like we were when the modem was attempting to establish a physical connection) and we have to log in to the host. Once that is accomplished, a PPP (Point to Point Protocol) link is established, and we can move into the HTTP zone.

Our browser requests the page as described in the previous section.

```
GET / HTTP/1.1
Accept: image/gif, image/x-xbitmap, image/jpeg, image/pjpeg, */*
Accept-Language: en-us
Accept-Encoding: gzip, deflate
User-Agent: Mozilla/4.0 (compatible; MSIE 4.01;Windows 98)
Host: www.prolotherapy.com
Connection: Keep-Alive
Extension: Security/Remote-Passphrase
```

The server returns an HTTP acknowledgment of our HTTP request, telling us the date and time, server type, echoing our connection request, and that an HTML content type is to follow.

```
HTTP/1.1 200 OK
Date: Sun, 19 Jul 1998 02:07:34 GMT
Server: Apache/1.2.5
Keep-Alive: timeout=15, max=100
Connection: Keep-Alive
Transfer-Encoding: chunked
Content-Type: text/html
```

And now the actual Web page . . .

```
HTTP/1.0 200 OK

Server: Netscape-Communications/1.12

Last-modified: Friday, 23-Jun-98 14:54:39 GMT

Content-length: 1466

Content-type: text/plain

<!DOCTYPE HTML PUBLIC "-//SoftQuad//DTD HoTMetaL PRO
4.0::19970916::extensions to HTML 4.0//EN" "hmpro4.dtd">
<HTML>
<HEAD><TITLE>Prolotherapy.com home page</TITLE>
<META NAME="keywords"
CONTENT="prolotherapy, arthritis, back pain, sports injury, non-surgical
treatment, chronic pain">
<META NAME="description"
CONTENT="a comprehensive information database on Prolotherapy, a non-
surgical and permanent treatment for chronic pain">
</HEAD>
```

```
<BODY BACKGROUND="images/Musclesb.GIF">
<TABLE WIDTH="100%"><TR>
<TD WIDTH="112" HEIGHT="214"></TD><TD WIDTH="485" HEIGHT="214">
<TABLE WIDTH="100%"><TR><TD HEIGHT="71"></TD><TD HEIGHT="71"></TD>
</TR>
<TR><TD HEIGHT="100"></TD><TD HEIGHT="100">
<A HREF="prolobooks.htm"><IMG SRC=""></A><A HREF="prolobooks.htm">
<IMG SRC="images/books.GIF" ALT="order books" WIDTH="141" HEIGHT="159"
ALIGN="RIGHT" BORDER="0"></A></TD>
</TR></TABLE></TD>
</TR>
<TR><TD WIDTH="112" ROWSPAN="3"><A HREF="prolotherapy.htm">
<IMG SRC="images/map.gif" ALT="sitemap" WIDTH="108" HEIGHT="288"
BORDER="0"></A></TD>
<TD WIDTH="485">
<P><FONT SIZE="+2" COLOR="#008000" FACE="Euromode,Arial,Helvetica">
<A HREF="prolodefine.htm"><I>What is prolotherapy?</I></A></FONT></P>
<P><FONT SIZE="+2" COLOR="#FF0080" FACE="Euromode,Arial,Helvetica">
<A HREF="prolohelp.htm"><I>Can prolotherapy help me?</I></A></FONT></P>
<P><FONT SIZE="+2" COLOR="#8000FF" FACE="Euromode,Arial,Helvetica"><I>
<A HREF="proloshaw.htm">Where can I get prolotherapy?</A></I></FONT></P>
<P><FONT SIZE="+2" COLOR="#8000FF" FACE="Euromode,Arial,Helvetica"><I>
<A HREF="proloinfo.htm">More information on prolotherapy</A></I></FONT>
</P></TD></TR>
<TR><TD WIDTH="485"><BR>
<HR COLOR="#008000" SIZE="12"><BR>
</TD></TR>
<TR><TD WIDTH="485"><FONT SIZE="+1">
<FONT FACE="Nasalization,Arial,Helvetica">
<I>Web site designed by
<A HREF="http://www.cintronics.com">Cintronics</A></I></FONT><BR>
</FONT><BR>
<IMG SRC="/cgi-bin/Count.cgi?sh=F|df=prolotherapy.dat"> </TD>
</TR>
</TABLE>
</BODY>
</HTML>
```

Hold on, we're not finished yet. We need pictures! These are sent separately, and in fact are all requested up front and sent in the order in which they were requested. The following is one example of an image request:

```
GET /images/Musclesb.GIF HTTP/1.1
Accept: */*
Referer: http://www.prolotherapy.com/
Accept-Language: en-us
Accept-Encoding: gzip, deflate
If-Modified-Since: Wed, 18 Mar 1998 06:43:01 GMT
If-None-Match: "255d5-6bcb-350f6cf5"
User-Agent: Mozilla/4.0 (compatible; MSIE4.01; Windows 98)
Host: www.prolotherapy.com
```

```
Connection: Keep-Alive
Extension: Security/Remote-Passphrase
```

We are requesting Musclesb.gif, a background image of a human body. The server will first acknowledge the request.

There seems to be a bit of image cache handling going on here with the If-Modified-Since: line. *Caching* is the process of saving information in a place from which it can be more quickly retrieved, and is used as a way to speed things up. The dictionary defines a *cache* as a hiding place and this is applicable to computer scenarios. If the image has not been modified, it doesn't need to be sent again and can be read from the local system based on a label for the cached file. These labels are called *Entity tags* and there are two examples here: the string of numbers and letters in the In-None-Match: line in the preceding code, and the ETag: line in the code following this paragraph. This acknowledgment says that this specific image was not modified, echoing back the If-None-Match label as an ETag to identify which one.

```
HTTP/1.1 304 Not Modified
Date: Sun,19 Jul 1998 02:07:36 GMT
Server: Apache/1.2.5
Connection: Keep-Alive
Keep-Alive: timeout=15,max=99
ETag: "255d5-6bcb-350f6cf5"
```

Finally, if the server needs to send the picture, it will be sent in a separate communication.

```
HTTP/1.1 200 OK
Date: Sun, 19 Jul 1998 02:07:37 GMT
Server: Apache/1.2.5
Keep-Alive: timeout=15,max=99
Connection: Keep-Alive
Transfer-Encoding: chunked
Content-Type: image/gif
(binary image file follows)
```

That is a example of a full HTTP communications cycle.

**NOTE**
These communication cycles were captured using ModemWatch98, part of the ComSpy program, which is part of the SpySuite package available from Prudens, Inc. at www.spywindows.com, or through this book's companion Web site at www.wiley.com/compbooks/cintron.

The final page for this communication cycle is shown in Figure 2.6.

### The Internet as a Managed Network

I often liken the Internet to the Wild West. There are a few rules, no sheriff, and people do as they please. But this analogy only applies to content. In the United States we have

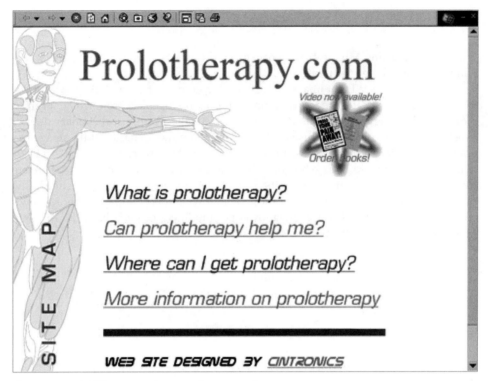

**Figure 2.6**    HTTP content, browser interpreted.

extreme freedom of speech, and some people choose to take this as far as it will go (which is pretty far).

Where standards are concerned, there are a lot of people out there trying to keep order. To this end, there are two categories of organizations at work: those composed mostly of technical professionals, and those made up of corporate members. At the highest levels, we have the Internet Society (ISOC) consisting mostly of individual members, and the W3C (World Wide Web Consortium) consisting entirely of corporate membership. ISOC is also at the top level of a hierarchy of Internet organizations that help them to achieve their purposes.

In looking through these organizations, it seems they all have the same goals. They do, although they are accomplishing them in different ways and seem careful to create a mutually beneficial relationship. A graphic timeline of these groups is shown in Figure 2.7.

## *ISOC*

The Internet Society was formed in 1992 and its mission statement is "To assure the beneficial, open evolution of the global Internet and its related Internetworking technologies through leadership in standards, issues, and education."

The Internet Society is a professional membership society with more than 100 organizational and 6000 individual members in over 100 countries. It provides leadership

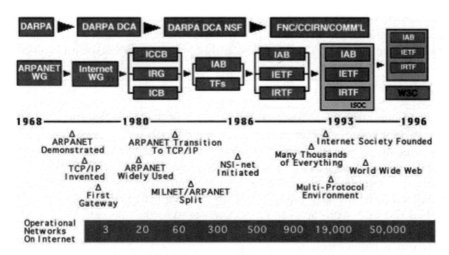

**Figure 2.7**   Acronym timeline! (courtesy of ISOC)

in addressing issues that confront the future of the Internet, and is the organizational home for the groups responsible for Internet infrastructure standards, including the Internet Engineering Task Force (IETF) and the Internet Architecture Board (IAB).

ISOC's principal purpose is to maintain and extend the development and availability of the Internet and its associated technologies and applications, both as an end in itself and as a means of enabling organizations, professions, and individuals worldwide to more effectively collaborate, cooperate, and innovate in their respective fields and interests.

The specific goals and purposes of ISOC include:

- Development, maintenance, evolution, and dissemination of standards for the Internet and its Internetworking technologies and applications

- Growth and evolution of the Internet architecture

- Maintenance and evolution of effective administrative processes necessary for operation of the global Internet and Internets

- Education and research related to the Internet and Internetworking

- Harmonization of actions and activities at international levels to facilitate the development and availability of the Internet

- Collection and dissemination of information related to the Internet and Internetworking, including histories and archives

- Assisting technologically developing countries, areas, and peoples in implementing and evolving their Internet infrastructure and use

- Liaison with other organizations, governments, and the general public for coordination, collaboration, and education in effecting the above purposes

In short, the Internet Society is a professional society that is concerned with the growth and evolution of the worldwide Internet, with the way in which the Internet is and can be used, and with the social, political, and technical issues that arise as a result.

## The IAB

The Internet Architecture Board has been around since 1983 in another form called the Internet Activities Board, another group that was originally a U.S. government-run body. The original IAB was started by ARPA (the Advanced Research Projects Agency) in 1979 under the acronym ICCB (Internet Configuration Control Board). In 1990, IAB began making its minutes public and as of 1992, it became a part of the Internet Society. The IAB publishes the technical standards for the Internet and provides oversight of the architecture for the protocols and procedures used by the Internet.

The Internet Architecture Board (IAB) is a technical advisory group of the Internet Society. Its responsibilities include:

- **Architectural Oversight:** The IAB provides oversight of the architecture for the protocols and procedures used by the Internet.

- **Standards Process Oversight and Appeal:** The IAB provides oversight of the process used to create Internet Standards. The IAB serves as an appeals board for complaints of improper execution of the standards process.

- **RFC Series and IANA:** The IAB is responsible for editorial management and publication of the Request for Comments (RFC) document series, and for administration of the various Internet assigned numbers.

- **External Liaison:** The IAB acts as representative of the interests of the Internet Society in liaison relationships with other organizations concerned with standards and other technical and organizational issues relevant to the worldwide Internet.

- **Advice to ISOC:** The IAB acts as a source of advice and guidance to the Board of Trustees and Officers of the Internet Society concerning technical, architectural, procedural, and (where appropriate) policy matters pertaining to the Internet and its enabling technologies.

- **IESG Selection:** The IAB appoints a new IETF chair and all other IESG candidates from a list provided by the IETF nominating committee.

## The IETF

The Internet Engineering Task Force has been around since 1986 and was originally formed by vendors who sold to the U.S. government, since the government owned the Internet back then. The IETF has since become a part of ISOC.

The IETF is a loosely self-organized group of people who make technical and other contributions to the engineering and evolution of the Internet and its technologies. It is the principal body engaged in the development of new Internet standard specifications.

Its mission includes:

- Identifying, and proposing solutions to, pressing operational and technical problems in the Internet
- Specifying the development or usage of protocols and the near-term architecture to solve such technical problems for the Internet
- Making recommendations to the Internet Engineering Steering Group (IESG) regarding the standardization of protocols and protocol usage in the Internet
- Facilitating technology transfer from the Internet Research Task Force (IRTF) to the wider Internet community
- Providing a forum for the exchange of information within the Internet community among vendors, users, researchers, agency contractors, and network managers

The IETF meeting is not a conference, although there are technical presentations. The IETF is not a traditional standards organization, although many specifications are produced that become standards. The IETF is made up of volunteers who meet three times a year to fulfill the IETF mission.

There is no membership in the IETF; anyone may register for and attend any meeting.

## IESG

The Internet Engineering Steering Group is part of the IETF and is responsible for technical management of IETF activities and the Internet standards process. As part of ISOC, it administers the process according to the rules and procedures that have been ratified by ISOC Trustees. The IESG is directly responsible for the actions associated with entry into and movement along the Internet "standards track," including final approval of specifications as Internet Standards.

One of the primary tasks the IESG is working on is issues relating to IPv6.

## IRTF

The Internet Research Task Force is also part of ISOC. Its purpose is a more farsighted version of the IESG, "to promote research of importance to the evolution of the future Internet by creating focused, long-term, and small Research Groups working on topics related to Internet protocols, applications, architecture, and technology."

These groups work on topics related to Internet protocols, applications, architecture, and technology. Research Groups are expected to have the stable long-term membership needed to promote the development of research collaboration and teamwork in exploring research issues. Participation is by individual contributors, rather than by representatives of organizations.

## IANA

The Internet Assigned Numbers Authority is the newest of the Internet management organizations, and is responsible for assigning a number, or "unique identifier," to everything involving a standard or protocol that needs one. The IANA doesn't assign IP addresses, but it does coordinate how IP addresses are assigned.

The new independent IANA organization will have responsibilities in three interrelated areas: Internet Protocol addresses, domain names, and protocol parameters. This will include the root server system and the work carried out currently by the existing IANA. The new IANA goal is "to preserve the central coordinating functions of the global Internet for the public good."

## W3C

W3C is the nickname of the World Wide Web Consortium. The W3C is run by Tim Berners-Lee, creator of the World Wide Web, or W$^3$ as it is sometimes called. Tim invented the Web when he was working at CERN, a European particle physics laboratory in 1989. CERN is French (again) for European Nuclear Research Center. The W3C has partner groups in Europe through INRIA (another French acronym) and in Japan through Keio University. The MIT Laboratory for Computer Science in the United States is also involved. The W3C was started with funds from DARPA and the European Commission.

The W3C purpose is "to develop common protocols to enhance the interoperability and lead the evolution of the World Wide Web," which means that the W3C creates specifications, reviews and publishes them so that the Web can expand with open, agreed-upon standards. Not just an ivory tower organization that churns out mandates for its subjects, the W3C is a member organization with over 250 corporations. Membership is not cheap, and perusing the list of members makes it evident that any self-respecting Internet company has joined. More specific goals of the W3C are stated as "Superior Web Technology" and "Universal Web Accessibility," both through the process of open development and member organizations; and "Responsible Web Application," which goes back to content.

Loosely, the W3C works in this way: Members are organized into activity groups approved by the W3C that look at areas of the Internet in which they have an interest. When they come up with something, they write up a submission that goes to the Director for approval. If he approves this, it becomes a *working draft*. The group works this up into a specification that is called a *proposed recommendation*. If the Director again approves this, it is voted on by the group and, if approved, becomes an *approved recommendation*. This can then be submitted to IESG under ISOC to become an *Internet standard*. The approved recommendation is something that people can now work with, which achieves the W3C goal.

The W3C's latest news is the approval of SMIL (Synchronized Media Integration Language, described in Chapter 12!) as an official recommendation. Over the last year, the W3C has also released approved recommendations such as HTML 4.0, XML 1.0, and CSS2.

## INFORMATIVE SITES!

*www.isoc.org*
**ISOC**

*www.isi.edu/iab*
**IAB**

*www.ietf.org*
**IETF**

*www.ietf.org/iesg*
**IESG**

*www.irtf.org*
**IRTF**

*www.w3c.org*
**W3C**

## What Is an Internet Standard?

The preceding references to RFCs and standards are more than just talk. There is a very specific route through which standards evolve to become official.

### DEFINITION: RFC

**RFC means *Request for Comment* and RFCs are very important; they contain all of the protocols in use throughout the Internet. If you become responsible for managing a network or writing code that performs communication cycles in a specific protocol, the RFC for that protocol will be your primary reference.**

**RFCs started out as being simple e-mail proposals requesting input from peers working on Internet protocols back in 1969. Now they are sophisticated documents that lay out an exact proposal from top to bottom. Some RFCs are informational, giving information such as what is an RFC, a list of RFCs, and introductory information on protocols and the Internet. You can find them all in the ISOC Internet Repository at www.isoc.org.**

The IETF recommends and approves working groups that are run by the IESG under the IETF. These groups can consist of anyone interested in the subject matter. A working group will form a core IESG design team to tackle the task of putting together a specification. This process takes 9–18 months, and during this phase the specification is called an *Internet draft*. When this draft is completed, meets with the consensus of the working group, and gets on the standards track, it is given the status of *RFC*.

Once an RFC has been published, it can now get on the standards track as a *proposed standard*. To move to the next level, at least two separate implementations of this specification must have been working together for at least six months. Then the spec can be upgraded to a *draft standard*. To achieve the pinnacle emblem of full *Internet standard*, the spec must show significant experience, interest, and stability.

Organizations such as the W3C submit RFCs to the IETF, which are published as informational documents. What happens after that is up to the IETF, whose members could very well be members of the W3C.

A list of all assigned Internet standards to date can be found in Appendix A, "Internet Standards Index."

RFC 2324 is an easy-to-read example of a protocol specification. Not to be taken too seriously, Hypertext Coffee Pot Protocol has been released in fun and is included as Appendix B, "RFC 2324: Hypertext Coffee Pot Control Protocol." This document tells us that we can address coffee pots attached to the Internet using an HTTP-like protocol in this way:

```
BREW coffee://pot.cintronics.com/kitchen?Half-and-half HTCPCP/1.0
accept-additions: milk-type/*

user-agent: Mozilla/3.01Gold (WinNT; I)"

connection: Keep-Awake
```

## INTERVIEW

### Tom Paquin, the Mozilla group

If you spend some time rummaging around in the Netscape site, aptly named www.netscape.com, you may eventually find yourself in a series of pages about something called *Mozilla*. Actually, the Mozilla group has its own Web site aptly named www.mozilla.org. With the Mozilla group, Netscape has put its source for the Navigator browser into an open source release. This means that they are looking for developers to take hold of the browser code, component by component, and enhance it in a way that will contribute to the development of Internet browsing by the will of the people.

Tom is manager of the Mozilla group, which is located in the development area of Netscape.

In this interview, you're going to hear what's going on in the world of browser development and how you can be a part of it. So over to Tom, who seems to prefer the term *hacking* to *programming*.

### Tom, what is Mozilla?

Mozilla was the code name for our 1.0 product. Before we shipped the product and we were hacking it up on our Web browser, you always need a code name for your product and the code name was Mozilla.

### But what does Mozilla really mean?

I guess *Mosaic killer*. There's what we call a user agent in a Web browser. When a Web browser contacts a server, one of the things it transmits is what is called a *user agent*. It's the header that identifies what kind of client is talking to the server so it can make decisions based on that. So in our user agent we put the name Mozilla and it stuck. He was our mascot and then one of the sales guys put him on T-shirts and next thing you know he's all over our Web site and so on and so on.

### Is the Mozilla project Outside Netscape?

It's an open source release of Mozilla we hope to be Mozilla 5.0 or whatever, the next major release of the Navigator. We were already working on it when we decided to go with an open source strategy. When you have an open source strategy you need to deal with the programmers on the Net. You need to be able to give them a place to ask their questions, voice their opinions, provide their changes and repairs, give forums for discussion so they can tie into what you're doing as opposed to holding back. In order to cultivate their assistance you need this marketplace of ideas where people go to do all this stuff so we created mozilla.org to do that. Netscape took their sources, cleaned them up, made them legal, gave them to Mozilla and said "be the steward."

Everyone who works for Mozilla works for me, and I work for a guy who works for Netscape. We're all a part of Netscape. Our mission and our charter are very clearly delineated. Our job is to take care of Net developers who tell Netscape to get lost when they're going to do something that is inconsistent with what will engage our developers. I work for Netscape but it's my job to make sure that development is consistent.

And to Netscape, for all intents and purposes, that is good. They will reap the rewards if they get people out there engaged and contributing. Then Netscape can take advantage of all this contribution and put it into the products and ship them. The logic behind this is there are a lot more smart people out there than there are in here. If we could get just 1 percent of them working on our source then wow, wouldn't that be fine.

So Netscape gives all their source to Mozilla and builds a machine inside Netscape where they can build their products based on Mozilla sources. Then they can turn their machinery around and pull the source back into Netscape, do their work and then make sure Mozilla sources reflect the changes that have been made inside Netscape. To the extent that there's a third party out there working on the same code that someone inside Netscape is working on, coordination needs to occur. Mozilla's in charge of making sure coordination occurs.

*With all these great minds working on the browser side then, what is Netscape concentrating on?*
It turns out that when you have a company trying to build product based on open sources, be it Navigator or whatever, it takes work. Problem one is it takes work to take a product that's an open source thing and turn it into a product your customers want. Problem two is in today's world almost all the people who know how to develop on the Mozilla code base work here. So it's going to be a while because of the large complex code base before there are a lot of people out there who can practically hack Mozilla.

If it was like a Unix kernel, and there are way, way, tons of people out there who can do Unix kernels, then perhaps you wouldn't need a full-bore entire product division working on Mozilla here at Netscape. But the case is that they aren't out there, so our product division is going pretty much like it always was, the difference is we're maintaining our code in a public way. To the extent that it's legal, I mean the crypto guys aren't because of the government and the Java guys aren't because of licensing sources, we don't have the license from Sun. So we want everything that we can put out, out.

*So this means that if one person is coordinating the development of that component, you could actually say in the case of IMGLIB you could get somebody like yourself working for maybe Adobe who would want to sponsor this person and do all of their image stuff?*
Oh yeah, that's the whole deal. There's a guy named Brendan Eich who's responsible for this list. And if like the network newsgroups are all coming down and saying, "we've got this image stuff and it's broken here and not working there and we're trying to get a hold of this person here and they won't give us the time of day, won't answer our questions, won't let us check in our code," etc., Brendan's going to take care of that.

But absolutely, if we could figure out a way to create a thing here called Java and they were willing and it made sense to put Sun or a Sun employee as the one here then absolutely, truly, in a heartbeat. I don't want to hear, "danger, all Netscape people!" That's the problem and I want to fix that. I want the world engaged.

**Where do you see this going in five years?**
Well right now this stuff is a bunch of fairly incestuous code in libraries that are linked together, but the interfaces are clearly descendant of a large project instead of very separately developed modules that can be called regardless of what application you're running in.

We need to fix the technology to get to a client-based model where people can live independently of where their work is located. We're going to over time see a lot of location-independent server-based stuff. You know Web mail is a good thing but being able to log in to any old Web server and read my mail is a good thing. The more stuff you put on my client side, the less able I am, or the more expensive it is to do that, because every time I go somewhere my data has to come with me. If my data is on the server and my server's fast, I like that a lot, so I think we're going toward a lot more server-side applications, so learning how to write server-side applications like CGI, PERL, and all those things is very important.

Scalability is going to be hard because every time we turn around it's not you and your 50 buddies anymore, it's you and your 4000 cohorts. Writing scalable systems is going to be important. I think huge increases in the amount of related data are going to occur. Right now we have a severe manageability problem. You do a Web search, it's huge, 354,000 hits. OK, I'll add AND this and NOT that. Great, so now it's down to 370 hits so now I have to wade through 370 Web pages, most of which are not what I want. You're going to see a lot of innovation in this space . . . things that you and I haven't thought about.

Interfaces where people can come by and plug in new concepts. We have a thing now called a *plug-in interface*. Writing a plug-in in something, that's valuable to know how to do and I need these people, some more of them.

**Is writing a plug-in a fairly easy thing to do?**
The original goal of the plug-in was to provide a simple interface where you could take your big giant chunk of legacy code. You've got, for example, Macromedia Director, and you want director movies to run right in Navigator. What will happen is when Navigator starts up it goes through the plug-ins directory and loads the plug-ins and identifies what MIME types are handled. Then later on when it gets the MIME type, and every document you ever get on the Web has a MIME type, when it sees the MIME type it'll look to see if it has a handle for this. I've got a director movie? Here's the call I need to handle that.

**You mentioned security space earlier. What did you mean by that?**
Security is a lot more than cryptography, and it's hard because security's one of these things where I build walls and fences and put up TV cameras and guard dogs and I assert that no one can break though this door. And I get all the experts to inspect my gate and my door and my lock and everything else and I get the world's best locksmith out to try to pick my lock, and they all fail. I can run around thumping my chest and saying "see? I'm secure. You can't get through this lock." Meanwhile there's a guy tunneling right under the whole mess and I forgot, oh wow, there's dirt under there, a guy could get across. So

it's really hard, so you figure out that people can dig tunnels and you fix that and the next thing you know they go over the wall in a hot air balloon.

The hard thing about security is to figure out what kinds of things you need to defend against, and there's all these ingenious idiots out there who have thought of something you haven't thought of, and most of the attacks we've seen, some of them are just spectacularly brilliant and some of them aren't, who would have thought that you can go four or five steps sideways in this very wacky way, and some of them are just stumbled upon.

The point is that if you are going to put up something like a store or a banking system or you want to be a consultant at a company that is trying to get Internet enabled and they're concerned about their data or the defense of their machines on a private network, you need to understand where the strengths are, where the weaknesses are, what's understood, what's not understood, what kinds of things should set off alarms in your head. The information space is fairly rich, there's a lot of stuff there you need to get before you can legitimately say "OK, I think I can speak about this." But there's a huge amount of ignorance out there in this case because very few people have really had to live there in a serious way.

So that ignorance is a demand because as soon as people really want to go out and do stuff on the Internet, they're going to want to know about it or at least they're going to want to have somebody they trust to help them: "I worry about it and you're OK," or "I worry about it, here are what all of your risks are." There are very few people who understand that space.

### What do the defined security standards have to do with?

Besides encryption of data, all firewalls are security devices. You have data integrity. Say I'm the CEO of Netscape and I send a report out to the executive council, why do I have any reason to believe they received the same report that I sent? That matters. Five years ago it might have been pretty hard for Joe Schmoe to screw with data; nowadays it's not that hard anymore, and perhaps Joe Schmoe doesn't care if he gets caught. A lot of the world's defenses against wacky kinds of attack are that you can't do that untraceably. Well, the guy who shot Robert Kennedy didn't care, or maybe he cared, I don't know, but the guy's dead. So integrity of data matters, authentication of users matters, authentication of who you're talking to in an open network environment matters. Spoofing is a big deal, it's pretty easy to spoof stuff, people don't tend to do it but it could be done.

There are other simple things. There's a popular lore that anybody could break down the Internet by attacking the routers. It's pretty true, if somebody put a couple machines up on the Net that started advertising bogus routing information, the Net would come into a chaotic state pretty quickly. Now the weenies of the world who run the Internet know this so they've got defenses set up. They could bring the Internet down, clean it up, figure out what's going on, and bring it back up again. The world would not die, but it would be an interesting half hour.

### Do you think one of the reasons this field is wide open is that this is very far away?

One of the problems is, what is sovereignty on the Internet? Where does the U.S. get off saying gambling on the Internet is illegal and if they say that, what are they going to do about it? There's some server in the Bahamas that's running, an American citizen has a bank account in the Bahamas, the money never leaves the Bahamas, but they sit in

Tennessee and place bets. How are they going to control that without absolutely shutting down the Net? How are you going to say people can't get on this if they're in Japan? There are places in the world where it's very very difficult to prevent anything, and once you've got one place you can get on this, traceability's toast.

I could go to one of the financial servers and scramble all the data, simply encrypt it. If they don't have the keys, the data's gone. Now maybe they have things backed up, but these are the concerns of corporations. It's not just development directions, companies care a lot as well, it's a big space.

*Do you have any advice to future Internet programmers?*
If I were going to start in this area, I wouldn't care a lot about the insides of the Navigator. I would care a lot about plug-ins and the kinds of things I'm going to need to write to play with Mozilla in order to enable my programming content. I care a lot about programming server-side applications and stuff like that and I care a lot about what I can do in JavaScript and friends to make stuff happen on the client side. Those things are huge. The security thing is probably another book, another whole area.

And it's not just content, it's Web applications. I don't fill out paper forms anymore to request vacation. I just point and click and select what I want to take a vacation from this day to that day. Somebody had to write the CGI script behind that. All these Web stores, a few years ago you could make money as a consultant putting up a store for somebody. "Hi there, L.L. Bean, sure I'll create a Web site for you. I know you don't have a lot of programmers in your company and you don't want to become a software shop, I'll do it for you." The next step is to write a program that you can hand to somebody and say, "Here's my program. It will make a store for you," and that's what we're actually seeing now happening. There's banking, there's database applications. What happens in application space is you used to have Intuit is your money manager thing and you have Word which is your document manager thing, and Excel which is your spreadsheet thing. These things are going away. What's happening is all these applications are becoming Web based. You have one interface called your browser and the people who wrote for example, Quicken, don't have to worry about who you are anymore, they just do an HTML and JavaScript text box and this whole business about Mac or Windows doesn't matter anymore.

*So you think we're moving from an application-dependent interface to a browser-dependent global kind of application?*
Yes, and HTML isn't quite there yet but it's getting pushed. XML is going to help a lot in syntactic space. There's other things that are going to help, but for sure people are writing applications all over the place now that say "don't worry about what the guys got, go to the browser." And the server, it's great, the information's on some central company server that you want your 4000 seats to be able to deal with. A few years ago you bought 4000 copies of the xyz application which probably spoke to some server through some private communication. Screw that. Put your application on your server and assume they have browsers.

I think the real bulk of the work is going to be clients as front ends to service apps in a big way. We're seeing it now. I think if you actually counted how many people are doing what kind of work, actual humans and actual work now in Web space, you'd find out that's where the dominant activity is.

*What about browser compatibility and competition?*
I doubt it would be very hard for Microsoft to keep up with source code that's publicly viewable. What's important to the Web is that there aren't competing and different ways of doing things. A guy who's writing an application doesn't want to have to worry about what browser you have. So if the Mozilla DNA, the behavioral characteristics and what makes it work, are caught in everywhere, based on the vote of the people who are contributing code, I think Netscape wins, Netscape's happy, and Netscape's more useful. Netscape is about making the Internet useful. The pie gets bigger for all of us businesses who are trying to make money off the Internet.

Our documentation is now out there. The whole friggin' world can say "change it," or "yes this is the right way for it to be," or "we've done the analysis and the result is this is the way it ought to go." There's no closed doors where some company pops up and says "we know what's best and we'll tell you." It's in open debate and everybody gets to toe the line.

*Thank you, Tom!*

For more information on the Mozilla project, go to www.mozilla.org.
For more information on Netscape development, go to developer.netscape.com.
To see a secret message, type "about:mozilla" in the Navigator URL box.

# Summary

In this chapter you've seen the Internet from the inside out, what makes it tick, who makes it tick, and where to find them.

In the next chapter we're going to look at how the Internet is programmed.

CHAPTER

3

# Programming, Scripting, and Applets

Now that the secrets of the Internet have been revealed in Chapters 1 and 2 where you got a thorough and eye-opening breakdown of exactly how the Internet works, it's time to prepare yourself to join the ranks of those who are busy programming the Internet. The first step is to learn about how programming is done.

Reading this chapter will not only save you months of experience in the "school of hard knocks," it will give you a good grounding in the techniques of programming. If you've never programmed before and are totally unfamiliar with what programming is, I suggest you get involved in some kind of introductory activity. This talk is meant for those who have had at least a little programming experience and it gives a powerful overview of all aspects of computer programming technologies and how they relate to modern programming techniques and the Internet.

By the end of this chapter you'll have a top-to-bottom understanding of what programming is all about, including just what the phrase "object oriented" means, a subject whole books have been written about!

## Programming Languages

It used to be that programmers only needed to learn one language. You would learn your language and program everything in that one language. Your user interface, databases, everything was taken care of by the programming language without having to learn additional languages.

Those times are gone, at least for now.

You write your basic Web page in HTML. It looks good but it needs a little flair, so you find a Java *applet* that does some cool stuff. Maybe you need the user to fill out a form and you find a *CGI* script written by a generous person who put his or her *PERL* code into the *public domain*. You borrow that, but it's not enough. You want to validate the input, so you add a little *JavaScript*. And if you're really adventurous, you go for the latest and the greatest: a clever *cascading style sheet* or a few lines of *Dynamic HTML* or . . . don't let this throw you! All of these technologies and more are taught in this book.

To be an Internet programmer in today's market, you'll need to learn several languages. If you expect to do a good job, you can't keep borrowing other people's code. Even if you don't write your own, you still have to know what all the code means. There is a tremendous future in Internet-style programming and if you can do the job, it's yours for the taking.

# Programming Basics

Programming starts with the specification for a programming language. These specifications are usually much harder to read than the language itself and have to be deciphered by people who write books on programming. Computer languages are written so that coding can be done in plain text that is oriented to mathematical and textual expressions people can read, like salesTaxRate=8.75 or print('hello world').

COBOL (COmmon Business Oriented Language) is an example of a language that was meant to be easily read, and despite predictions that its end is near, it's going to be a long time before the 10 billion lines of COBOL code in government and big business computers will be replaced. The year 2000 is doing a lot to get people to upgrade their systems, but in a lot of cases the expense of out and out redoing this code is prohibitive and all that's getting done is patch, patch, patch.

In today's programming world, language diversity abounds! But the bottom line is that all languages are limited to doing the same things, they can only do what the CPU instruction set is capable of. These are basically limited to add this to that, move that over there, and compare that to this. Every computer instruction is built on this foundation. Division, multiplication, and subtraction are all based on modifications to the process of adding. Compare operations have a lot of options, greater than, less than, and so forth, but they all come down to different interpretations of the result of the simple compare operation. Boolean operations such as AND, OR, NAND, NOR are variations on add and compare.

In computer programming, mathematical proficiency is important—computers are number-crunching machines. Even if you're just processing text, text is represented numerically. And when it comes to graphics and game programming, counting pixel positions, changes, and direction should occur only slightly more slowly in your head than it does in the computer.

If you want to get way, way down into the CPU chip itself, there's a style of programming that few have heard of: *microcode*. On the CPU chip itself is an even smaller and more low-level instruction set than the machine language codes, and the machine language instructions are actually broken down into microcode as they are executed!

Microcode is based on the specific architecture of the CPU and includes instructions that move data around the ALU (Arithmetic-Logic Unit) on the chip and down specific pathways to perform CPU-specific logical functions that make up machine language instructions. Only chip designers write microcode to implement what you see as the machine language instruction set. Intel's MMX (Multi-Media eXtension) is probably the most widely known example of a CPU instruction set.

## Compilers

There are high-level languages and low-level languages, sometimes also referred to as first-, second-, third-, and fourth-generation languages. The closer the instructions in the language correspond with the CPU instruction set, the lower the level is. A high-level language instruction could translate into hundreds, or even thousands, of low-level instructions. For example, writing a high-level command such as window.open ('Hello world') would take quite a few machine language steps to accomplish!

The first generation of computer languages was machine languages written in cryptic numerical code and doing only one tiny step at a time. The second generation was assembly languages, easier to read and write but still tied to the instruction set. The third generation was the first high-level languages and are the wordy type languages that remain popular after many decades (such as COBOL and Fortran), which translate one line into many CPU instructions but are still lengthy and laborious to work in. Fourth-generation languages, also known as 4GLs, are meant to be clear, concise, and easy to use, but a step up from the third-generation by doing things like advanced database queries in a single instruction.

Once a programming language has been spec'd, the next step is to get the language to where it can be used. A compiler is written, which translates the text-based code into machine language. Machine language is based on the instruction set implemented on the CPU on which the program will run. Ultimately, a program must be translated into machine language, even if it goes through one or more other forms first. Only a machine language translation of the program will run on a computer, period.

In a program, there is data and there are instructions. When the compiler goes through a program, it separates these out. Some languages require you to declare all of your data names, variables, blocks, or sections up front before a single instruction occurs. Other programs let you declare on the fly. Either way, the compiler has to allocate enough space for all of them. (Except in C, where the program can allocate and deallocate space, but that's a feature, meaning an additional useful function.) But even in C, the compiler has to know the names and types of all data before it can start the job of compiling the instructions because the instructions will operate on the data.

A compiler cannot be written in the same language that is being implemented. There is a science to writing compilers, and because we don't want to write a compiler in another high-level language, many of them are written in assembly language. Assembly language is called a low-level language because it's down there one step from the binary machine code.

Assembly language is machine code made human readable, but it still reflects machine instructions one for one. One line of assembly language code is one machine instruction. A compiler that compiles assembler code into machine code is not called a

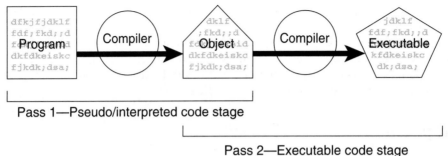

Pass 1—Pseudo/interpreted code stage

Pass 2—Executable code stage

**Figure 3.1**    The two stages of compiling.

*compiler*, it's called an *assembler*. The C language is the closest to assembly language because it was intended to translate into fast executables by reason of its likeness to machine code (but it's still called a high-level language).

There are two stages to compiling a program, called *passes*, as illustrated in Figure 3.1. Some compilers are very efficient and do both passes at once, but it still takes two passes. The first pass compiles the human-written program into what we call *pseudocode*, or *intermediate* code, or *object* code. Do not confuse object code with object-oriented programming. The term *object code* has been around a lot longer and refers to how the compiler performs its task.

The compiler's first pass translates every piece of data and instruction into tables and symbolic codes that the compiler or runtime can understand when it goes to interpret this intermediate code. Pseudocode can only be understood either by the compiler performing its second pass, which translates intermediate code into machine code, or by a runtime that has been written to both perform the second compiler pass and then execute the result. If this sounds familiar it's because Java bytecode is pseudocode and the Java Virtual Machine (Java VM), is a runtime. (See sidebar, *How Does a Compiler Work?*)

## Object Code and Subroutines

In the early days of programming, all programs were written as monolithic (literally "one stone") self-contained units needing nothing more to do their destined task. As memory capacity and therefore program size grew, program size became unwieldy and programmers got tired of writing the same code over and over. So they invented a way to write certain workhorse routines just once and call on their services from the main program they were writing.

These smaller programs would be called *subroutines* and would somehow be linked to the main program at the object code stage before being compiled to a (still monolithic) machine language program. The object-oriented term for subroutines is *methods*, but if subroutines are good enough for the computers on Star Trek, they're good enough for us. These external subroutines are also compiled to object code. You can't compile them to machine code because they are going to be linked with the main program first!

*Linking* means resolving data addresses between programs. Subroutines written and compiled in files outside the main program have unresolved data references, meaning we've referred to data we haven't declared. These are permitted because the subroutine is not declared as a main procedure, but they have to be resolved before the program can

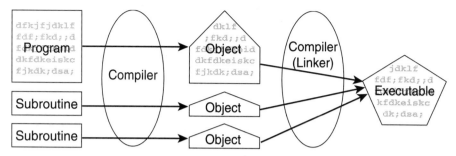

**Figure 3.2**   Compiling with external subroutines.

be executed. Object code is code that defines these data and instruction sections as objects in a way that these references can be resolved, or linked together. In some languages the second-pass compilers are also called *linkers* and are totally separate from the first-pass compilers. These take a compiled main procedure and its compiled external subroutines and make one executable. This process is shown in Figure 3.2.

## Runtime Systems

Beyond workhorse programmer-written subroutines that might display data entry boxes in a certain way, or define a standard print format, there are subroutines that do low-level system tasks such as accepting input keys through the keyboard device handler or reading and writing the disk directory structure. Nothing a computer does is automatic! Somebody has to write the code and it has to be run somewhere in the program.

So again, rather than writing this code for every program, programmers found a way to load these routines into memory in such a way that they are invisible to the programmer and don't even have to be thought about. This is called a *runtime* system because it loads at runtime, not at link time or compile time.

There are two ways of compiling programs: pass one to pseudocode only, and pass one and two to executable code. Both are executable, but only the code compiled to machine level can be qualified to be what we call a *standalone* program, which needs nothing more than its own file to run. The exact way in which programs are to be executed depends on how the language is designed.

Some languages are not designed for their executables to be run as standalones. These languages use a runtime system to provide services to the running program, as shown in Figure 3.3. This runtime may be installed on the computer as an always-present entity. There are several related terms for this depending on the operating system. On Unix we can call it a *daemon*. On DOS it's a *TSR* (Terminate and Stay Resident). On a Novell Network it can be an *NLM* (Netware Loadable Module). The bottom line is that it is loaded in memory before the program is run. It can even be loaded just before running the program and unloaded after, which we just call a plain *runtime*. A final option to make a program into a standalone executable is to compile it to actually contain the entire runtime.

The services a runtime provides are several. The simplest runtime may just handle system calls, interpreting display and print requests, and in doing so, acts as an interface between the program and the operating system. A runtime may also execute

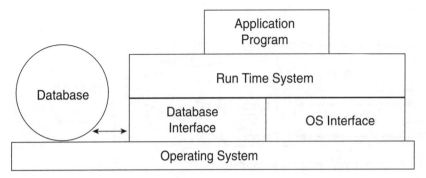

**Figure 3.3**    Runtime system function.

pseudocode because it is interpreted as it goes along. This takes more time than running a machine code compiled program, but it also makes the code more portable. Like in Java, you can compile the program once and run it on many different platforms without recompiling for each one. The platform runtime interprets the system calls and executes them in the OS, taking this knowledge task away from the programmer.

A more sophisticated runtime may include an entire database function, providing services that open and close files, store and retrieve data, perform searches, even with an entire query language. Back in the 1960s these functions were not available in any package or runtime and had to all be written by hand. In the 1970s, some database packages began to emerge and evolve through the 1980s. Back then this was the only way to maintain a sophisticated database. Advances in the science of programming have led us to better ways to do this, although these advances are still based on the same principles.

The Java VM is a runtime that is loaded by the browser when an applet is detected. This takes time, as we have all waited for the "loading java" message. The bytecode is downloaded and it is read, interpreted, and executed, one bytecode at a time. There are ways of improving the efficiency of this process, all of which are being looked at by various companies involved in Java development. One is to store the machine compiled code as it is interpreted so the next time it is run it does not have to be reinterpreted. Another is to put the interpreter into hardware!

In a nutshell, that's programming.

## Scripting

If you've read the preceding sidebar, I can tell you that scripting is 100-percent interpretive. If you haven't read it, then read it so you can understand what interpretive code means.

Scripting languages such as VBScript and JavaScript are all interpreted at runtime. They are compiled and executed on the spot by the browser. These kinds of languages have grown out of traditional programming languages from the need to have sophisticated code to control command flow at the OS prompt level. The first and

## HOW DOES A COMPILER WORK?

Here's a brief example of compiler function. Remember, a compiler is a program, too. We'll set about compiling a tiny program written in a made-up language.

```
proc main( ) {
openOutput (sysout);
timeNow = time( );
print (sysout,'Good Morning Vietnam! Its ',timeNow);
close (sysout);
}
```

As a programmer, what would you do with this? We have to have our first-pass compiler program translate it into something that our second-pass compiler program can process, and it's easiest to write a program to process varying kinds of data input into tables.

So we start by writing a first-pass compiler to read one line at a time. Based on the function keyword at the start of the line, we call a routine to translate statements based on those keywords. After translating, our table building procedure results in this.

```
START
PROC      main
DATA      main
DATA$1    LIT        26      Good Morning Vietnam! Its
DATA$2    TIM        8       00000000
CODE      main
OPN       sysout
PRT       sysout             DATA$1
PRT       sysout             DATA$2
CLS       sysout
END
```

This simple table is now set up to either be interpreted or processed into machine code. The truth is, this looks a lot like assembly language.

The DATA and CODE tags let our compiler have a little easier time following along.

The data section describes the space allocated to both variables, initializes their content, and contains easy table references (DATA$n) for the instruction section.

The instruction section has translated our keywords into 3-letter codes giving a 1,2,3,4 straightforward open, print, print, close.

Several useful features are included in our little first-pass compiler. The second-pass compiler has the option to format the time output based on its TIM type declared in the data section. Some would say the START and END tags are unnecessary, but personally I like to know that I'm dealing with a complete file and that when I've reached the end, it's really the end. Further, it could be possible to stuff several procedures (subroutines, methods, whatever) into a single file so the tag main can be used to identify which sections belong to which.

Like I said, compiler writing is a science of its own. Now you can think how much fun the people had who wrote the compiler that handles everything you throw at it!

best scripting languages were those controlling shell commands in Unix. This leaked over a bit to other operating systems and now to the Web.

Server-side scripts are now coming into play in the form of applications like Active Server Pages. Active Server Pages is a scheme from Microsoft that simply means the *server* does something *active* with the script on the *page*, rather than passively palming it off to the browser. This brings things like database access into the realm of scripting.

Scripting languages trade speed of execution for flexibility of function, meaning the interpretive part slows them down but adds features not found in compiled code. For example, data variables in scripting languages do not have to be declared and can be interpreted as any data type, converting them on the fly. This is because we compile as we go, so nothing is set in stone. It also makes some things easier and shortens the code.

Scripting also allows a great deal of interactivity with the content of Web pages. We can use scripting to change the content of a Web page as we go, or to spit out an entirely new page to the user based on user input. Compiled code is not allowed this flexibility because it has to run in a separate window to protect the browser and the user's computer from crashes and security violations. Thus, the scripting language has become the go-between of browsers and applets, taking parameters from the browser and passing them to the applet to control execution. The way the browser compartments this function is illustrated in Figure 3.4. We'll be going into this in great detail when dealing with the scripting languages themselves in later chapters.

## JavaScript

JavaScript is a language designed to be placed entirely in Web pages. As Web pages are made entirely of text, they cannot contain any kind of program that has already been compiled. JavaScript is meant to be interpreted as it is read by the browser, but is executed, like any language, in response to user actions.

Figure 3.5 is a short example of JavaScript. This script would be placed right in a Web page and causes a menu to appear when the mouse is moved over the menu title. The menu disappears when the mouse is moved off the title.

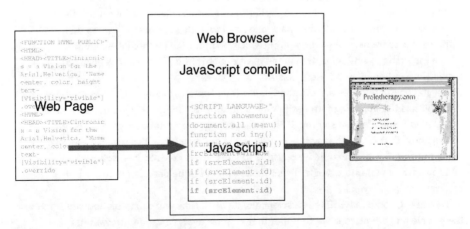

**Figure 3.4**  Browser script handling.

```
<SCRIPT LANGUAGE="javascript">
function showmenu(menu) {
  ... code to show the menu ...
}
function hidemenu(menu) {
  ... code to hide the menu ...
}
</SCRIPT>
<BODY>
    <DIV ONMOUSEOVER="showmenu('professional')"
         ONMOUSEOUT="hidemenu('professional')">
    <IMG SRC="professional.GIF">
       <DIV ID="professional" CLASS="menuhide">
       <A HREF="fasttrack.htm">author</A><BR>
       <A HREF="Webmenu.htm">Web design</A><BR>
       <A HREF="digitalvideo.htm">digital video production</A><BR>
       <A HREF="resume.htm">resume bank</A>
       </DIV>
    </DIV>
</BODY>
```

**Figure 3.5**   An example of JavaScript.

The script is enclosed in a set of HTML <SCRIPT></SCRIPT> tags and is identified to the browser with LANGUAGE="javascript". There are then two functions declared, one to show and one to hide the menu. The code, although very short, is a bit too complex to explain here, so it is not shown.

The script calls are placed in the body of the Web page taking advantage of built-in event handling provided by the browser. One simple statement causes the ONMOUSEOVER event to trigger the *showmenu* function and the ONMOUSEOUT event to trigger the *hidemenu* function.

The first <DIV> statement creates the division that the browser keeps track of so that when the mouse enters its display area, the event handlers will be activated. This division only contains two things: an image called "professional.gif" and another division.

The second <DIV> tag is used to create an arbitrary division called "professional." This division starts out with a hidden menu of four items that point to other Web pages with the <A HREF=... ></A> hypertext address reference tag set.

When the mouse event handlers come in to play, they are executed on this inner "professional" division that is contained within the outer division. The result is shown in Figure 3.6.

# Components

Components are programs that are not standalone, but are routines that can be called upon by other programs to perform a specific task. Components must be written in a specific way to qualify as callable; that is, so their methods can be called by any other program.

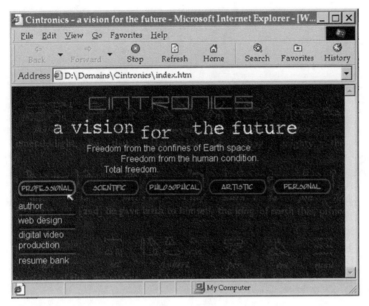

**Figure 3.6**   JavaScript in action.

For example, an applet is a component, but so is the Java VM! These are both programs that run inside of and which are at the service of other programs. The applet runs inside the Java VM, and the Java VM runs inside the browser. In fact, these are not just components; since they are also objects, they are *component objects*.

## Applets

An applet is an executable Java program that is placed in a Web page. The difference between an applet and a full-fledged Java program is only the security limitations placed on the applet by the Web browser. There is no technical reason a Java program placed in a Web page could not do things like handle your accounting, update your software, and even optimize or format your hard drive.

That's the whole problem. Browsers have been programmed so that Java programs running within them can't do any harm to our computers.

In fact, the only reading and writing an applet is permitted to do is to files on its home server. This way, an applet can be used to look up database records at a central site and display the results in its applet window. It can accept input from that window and display results back—but that's it. This allows us to program database inquiries, write interactive game programs, or anything else that expires once we leave the page. An industrious site could store individual data about users on its own server, but this could become cumbersome, outdated, and unused if users did not frequently return to the site.

Not to despair, there are people out there working on cryptographic solutions to provide the security we need. The restricted area in which applets are allowed to play is called the *sandbox*. How this is handled by the browser is shown in Figure 3.7. It is possible that with digital signature encryption (see Chapter 11, "Security and E-Commerce"), these applets can have their source verified as being a trusted site and they can be let out of the sandbox, even if just a little bit.

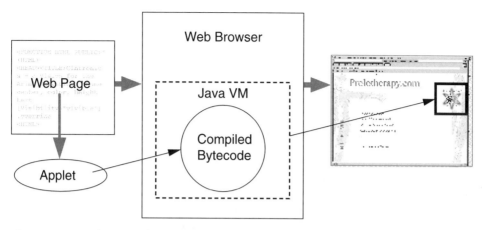

**Figure 3.7**    Applet compilation and control.

## ActiveX Controls

ActiveX is not a language or a product. ActiveX is a specification from Microsoft for components.

The primary differences between an applet and ActiveX control are these. Applets are always written in Java, whereas ActiveX controls can be written in Java, C++, Visual Basic, or anything else that will run on the user's computer. Applets are downloaded and then run under the Java VM and are discarded afterwards. ActiveX controls are downloaded and actually installed on the user's computer and afterwards they are available to the Web browser or any other application that wants to use them from there on out. Applets run in the sandbox and cannot do anything with data on the user's computer. ActiveX controls have free rein.

ActiveX controls can do this because of increased security. Every ActiveX control has a sophisticated class ID number that identifies where it came from so that if anyone ever wrote an ActiveX control with a malicious Trojan Horse inside of it, he or she could be hauled out in public and suitably tarred and feathered. This ID number installs on your computer and is used to call up the ActiveX control when it is needed in the future. As an example, the class ID number for the Surround Video control is *928626A3-6B98-11CF-90B4-00AA00A4011F*. This ID number has to be used in the Web page and anything else that calls the control.

**NOTE**
The drawback to ActiveX controls is that they are executables that have to be compiled for the user's specific OS, so pages that include them have to be written to detect the OS in use and download the correct control, not to mention that you'd have to have controls written for every OS for your page to work. A good example of an ActiveX control is the Microsoft Surround Video, which can be seen at www.microsoft.com/ie/homeuser/mmedia/netsuke.htm. You can find out more about ActiveX at www.microsoft.com/activex.

# Object-Oriented Programming

Object oriented programming is the latest successful advancement in programming style. Programming concepts have come a long way, and we're going to explore this to come to a better understanding of what object-oriented programming represents.

## Von Neumann Programming

The original concept of a computer program did not involve storing any data in the computer. Programs were punched onto paper tape with holes in it that represented the binary code, read in by what passed for a computer back in the 1940s, and the results were spit out, probably on another paper tape. Eventually, someone realized that you might store the program and data permanently in the computer so things could go faster.

Von Neumann programming is characterized by sequential processing: straight down the line, start to finish. The program listing shown in Figure 3.8 is a COBOL example of a Von Neumann-style program.

```
identification division.
      program-id. warp.

      data division.
      working-storage section.

      01 fdistance          pic 9(13)v9(5).
      01 fwarp              pic 9(13)v9(5).
      01 warpfactor         pic 99v99.
      01 traveltime         pic 9(13)v9(5).
      01 travelfmt          pic zz,zz9.99.

      procedure division.

          display "Light years" at 1020.
          display "Warp speed" at 1220.
          display "Days travel" at 1420.

          accept fdistance at 1035.
          accept fwarp at 1235.

          compute warpfactor = 2**(fwarp - 1).
          compute traveltime = (fdistance / warpfactor) * 365.25.

          move traveltime to travelfmt.
          display travelfmt at 1435.

          stop run.
```

**Figure 3.8**   Von Neumann warp drive calculator (COBOL).

This simple program allows the user to input the distance in light years and the warp factor to calculate the number of days travel time.

The program first declares all of the working variables. "pic" is for *picture* in COBOL and is used to define the data type. "01" is a top-level declaration. "v" is an implied decimal point. "z" is a format character to replace zeroes with blanks.

Older languages allow you to declare the exact size of a number, even though internally the data is stored in the same way data types are declared these days in Java and C. The program displays tags at cursor coordinates based on the 24 × 80 DOS screen size, accepts input, does the calculation, and displays the result. The calculation is based on warp factor 1 = the speed of light (or c for short), warp factor $x = c * 2^{(warp\ factor - 1)}$.

The program is simple to read (being written in COBOL) and contains no subroutine calls. Since this type of programming evolved in the paper tape program era, a pure Von Neumann program would probably not have any GOTO statements.

The point of this exercise is that this program has a very obvious separation of data space and instruction space. You can easily visualize the one-for-one representation between data and instructions and their internal representation in memory.

## Structured Programming

Structured programming is a step beyond Von Neumann programming. It involves breaking code up into chunks that can be more easily managed than a program full of GOTO statements. A large program can turn into what is termed *spaghetti code*, because when you try to visualize the program structure in your head with all its GOTO statements it looks like a pile of cooked spaghetti.

Structured programming was an answer to this. The perfect structured program would contain no GOTO statements and would be a series of internal subroutine calls to little routines each no more than about 20 lines long. This gets into a lot of deep nested calling where subroutines call subroutines that call subroutines, but you can build a much larger program that can be more easily debugged.

Figure 3.9 illustrates the warp drive program rewritten in structured form, even though it's really a bit short for that. I'm going to stretch COBOL a bit into a pseudo-language by adding statements to demonstrate the concepts that will help bridge the gap towards object-oriented programming.

The top-level procedure of the program is a single statement that calls an internal subroutine to perform a four-step procedure. This makes it very easy to see the entire program structure in a single glance. The beauty of this is that any size program can be structured with these few steps! This program is executed repeatedly until the user presses the Escape key.

I have distinguished internal subroutine calls from external subroutine calls by using the *xcall* statement for external subroutines. Internal subroutine calls do not need to include any variable references as these are available to all internal routines. External subroutine calls must have variables included so we pass them by specifying a list of variables in parentheses separated by commas. The called subroutine will be in the form of a program originally compiled separately, and will begin with a statement referring to the exact array of variables passed. If there is any difference in the number of variables or data type, the program will unfortunately crash, unable to perform its task.

```
identification division.
      program-id. warp.

      data division.
      working-storage section.

      01 fdistance          pic 9(13)v9(5).
      01 fwarp              pic 9(13)v9(5).
      01 warpfactor         pic 99v99.
      01 traveltime         pic 9(13)v9(5).
      01 travelfmt          pic zz,zz9.99.
      01 function-key       pic xx.
      01 escape-key         pic xx value "1B".

      procedure division.

            perform startwarp until function-key = escape-key.
            stop run.

      startwarp.

            call display-screen.
            call get-input.
            call compute-time.
            call show-result.
            return.

      display-screen.

            xcall display ("Light years",10,20).
            xcall display ("Warp speed",12,20).
            xcall display ("Days travel",14,20).
            return.

      get-input.

            xcall input (fdistance,10,35,function-key).
            xcall input (fwarp,12,35,function-key).
            return.

      compute-time.

            compute warpfactor = 2**(fwarp - 1).
            compute traveltime = (fdistance / warpfactor) * 365.25.
            return.

      show-result.

            move traveltime to travelfmt.
            xcall display (travelfmt,14,35).
            return.
```

**Figure 3.9** Structured warp drive calculator.

```
proc display (string,row,col);

    data;
        string          ,a80;
        row             ,d2;
        col             ,d2;

    proc;
        display string at row,col;
        return;
```

**Figure 3.10**   External subroutine.

Figure 3.10 illustrates a simplified example of the display external subroutine written in a pseudo-language.

In this style of subroutine call, all variables passed in either direction are included in the array. The called subroutine can change the values of the variables passed, and the changes will be reflected when the subroutine returns to the calling program. This is reflected in the *xcall input* statement where the value of a function key pressed is sent back. The hexadecimal value 1B stands for the Escape key and tells the program to terminate.

Experienced programmers looking at this scheme will appreciate the utility of structured programming, but they also realize that object-oriented programming takes this a step further, saving a great deal of time and code space and adding more functionality. For example, the programs we have seen include no GUI interfaces and minimal display and input handling.

## What Is Object-Oriented Programming?

Object-oriented programming is represented in many books as a way of thinking of code blocks as actual physical objects like a tree, but I am not going to take that approach. We're going to start from the ground up, no pun intended.

Object-oriented programming is different from traditional programming in many ways. Object-oriented programs can still be structured. There is still nothing wrong with the concept of structured programming. Structured programming is used as an example here because it was considered a very significant advancement in programming technology in the late 1970s and early 1980s.

One of the reasons early programs were Von Neumann oriented was memory limitations. It used to be that you had to squeeze as much code into so little space that programmers would pride themselves on such genius as writing a full-featured input routine that would compile to 3K. When a 64K memory board costs $1,000 and the OS has to run in half that space, you're really working to get anything done at all. As prices decreased and memory capacity increased, programmers became a little freer with their styles and program sizes. As available memory has expanded, so has programming technology. Now back to objects.

## Object Features

First, an object is still a program but instead of just looking at the program from the inside out, we can look at the program from the outside in. Looking at a block of code in this way is like having all programs function as an external subroutine but again, the external subroutine interface has been greatly improved. You may have heard about *Bean* programming. This is what Beans are all about: using preprogrammed routines as subroutines to a larger program. The special thing about Beans is that they are generic and can apply to a lot of situations.

One of the slavishly tedious things in traditional programming is using external subroutines. These save work over inline code by allowing us to reuse this code over and over with simple calls instead of having to write it anew each time, like programming a speed dial on our phone. But external subroutines are used so much that simply calling them becomes a lot of busy work. Let's compare this to the world before conference calling, and say you want to coordinate with three other people on what movie to see. You call one, ask him or her, then call the third and fourth persons and get their options. Then you would have to call each one back again and confirm. It works but it's tedious, and after a while might drive you crazy. There has to be a better way.

I once had to write a program that would print the same data to four printers at once in different formats. These were an invoice, a picking ticket (used in the warehouse to pick the items out), a shipping label, and something else, I forget what. Using my full-featured COBOL I had to take the inhouse external print subroutine and make three clones, one for each additional printer. Why? Because the print routine stored values like the line number and page number internally. Furthermore, it opened and closed the printer so that it couldn't possibly be used for more than one data stream. Then I had to call these routines PRINT1, PRINT2, PRINT3 . . . you get the idea.

Had this been an object-oriented language, I would not have had to do any of this. I could have invoked the same routine four times and it would have created four different objects, each one with the same behavior and separate data, with only four lines of code.

```
Print1 = new Print(lpt1:)
Print2 = new Print(lpt2:)
Print3 = new Print(lpt3:)
Print4 = new Print(lpt4:)
```

Second, an object is a program that contains both data and a programming term new to this section, *behavior*. Behavior means that the object has more than one internal function (read this as *subroutine*) that can be called upon. In the multimedia world of the Internet, we could look at an object as being able to control the stream of audio data with functions just like a record, tape, CD, or DVD player (pick your generation).

Figure 3.11 shows the outline of code for an object called AudioPlayer, and the GUI result of that code is shown in Figure 3.12. Now, to call that code from another object-oriented program is very simple. We declare the object as an AudioPlayer object, initialize the object, open, play, and stop/close.

Only the open routine gets a value passed to it because the rest of the routines depend on the file already having been opened. As a note, when the program is exited, the close routine should be automatically called. Closing a file releases the link between the program and the file and is good form. Otherwise, this relationship can remain on lists the

```
AudioPlayer player;
player = new AudioPlayer;
player.open (newyorknewyork);
player.play();
player.stop();
```

**Figure 3.11**   Fast-and-easy object code.

operating system maintains, and these will get longer and longer as more files do not get closed. This can also keep memory tied up that is not being used. This process is also called *housekeeping* or *garbage collection*.

This is a very simplified code skeleton and does not provide for choosing the file, etc., but with the illustration, it is meant to show the relationship between an object-oriented program, the object it calls, and what this object represents.

Third, objects are designed to be inserted in statements as if they were variables. The term *object* stretches the concept of a variable because an object can be far more sophisticated than just a data item. Yet paradoxically, objects can be treated as simple data items because of the mechanism of returned values. Although an object can be sent any number of variable/objects (let's call them *parameters*) when it is called, an object always sends back (or returns) either no values or one value, and if one, it always *returns it in place of the reference to the object itself.*

For example, here is a statement from the upcoming object-oriented version of the warpspeed program:

```
fdistance = getFloat(distance.getText());
```

This statement first calls a routine called getText that returns the contents of a text entry box; in this case, the box called *distance*. At runtime this value is put into the parentheses in place of the object. If this value were "9.5" the statement would then get interpreted as this, converting the text value to a floating-point number:

```
fdistance = getFloat("9.5");
```

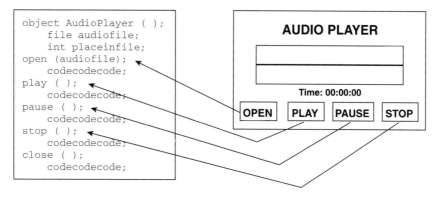

**Figure 3.12**   Object behavior in action.

This can get very complex, actually nesting several calls on a single line, which gets an incredible amount of things done in a single statement. This statements boils down to the floating-point number $.95 \times 10^1$:

```
fdistance = 0.95E+01
```

And fourth, object-oriented programming offers the opportunity to easily access huge libraries of external subroutines. I am offending an entire generation of programmers here with my terminology because I should be calling object-oriented subroutines *methods*.

In traditional programming language packages, the most the average package had to offer (as far as what are called *system subroutines*) was database I/O (input/output), mathematical functions, and some display tricks to spice things up a bit. Languages such as Java and C include much larger libraries called API (Application Program Interface) libraries. With the tremendous distribution potential of the Internet, API libraries can be published and assimilated around the globe within days. We have APIs for Internet communications, APIs for security, Microsoft APIs (ISAPI), Netscape APIs (NSAPI), and on and on.

### Tying It All Together

An object can be viewed as a bundle of data and methods. It is initiated into existence and can be so numerous times, each time creating a new *instance*. *Instance* is an important word that means an occurrence of an object. This object contains behavior that can be invoked. Objects will maintain their state, meaning their data will remain stationary unless acted upon, just like in Newton's first law of motion. In other words, when you call the object again you can depend on the object being in the same condition it was at the end of its previous call.

There are many more features to an object-oriented language, but these are not necessary to describe what object-oriented programming is. These include things such as event handling, which covers responses to system events like mouse moves and clicks, and text entry and function keys as in our example program. We'll be going into these in our chapters on Java and JavaScript.

Figure 3.13 illustrates the object-oriented warpspeed calculator written as a Java applet.

The last action here is to put this in a simple HTML page to execute. Everything in this page has to be there to create the minimal HTML document structure. The only line that we are programming is the APPLET tag, which gives the name of the compiled Java code file and the size of the box the browser is to create to run the applet. You can see the Web page as written in Figure 3.14 and as displayed in Figure 3.15.

# What Is a Markup Language?

Like a scripting language, a markup language is not a compiled language, it is an interpreted language. But unlike a scripting language, it is not an executed language. Markup is not a logical progression of instructions, but a static descriptive language. It is interpreted by the browser when it is first read in, and the results are displayed in the browser window. Once that's done, the processing is over until different markup is read in and the cycle repeats.

```
import java.awt.*;
import java.lang.Float;
import java.lang.Math;

public class Warp extends java.applet.Applet {
    TextField distance, warpspeed;
    String travel;
    float fdistance, fwarp;
    double warpfactor, traveltime;

    public void init() {
        setLayout(new GridLayout(3,2,10,10));
        distance = new TextField("0");
        warpspeed = new TextField("0");
        travel = new String("0");

        add(new Label("Light years"));
        add(distance);
        add(new Label("Warp speed"));
        add(warpspeed);
    }
    public void calcWarp() {
        fdistance = getFloat(distance.getText());
        fwarp = getFloat(warpspeed.getText());
        if (fwarp == 0 | fdistance == 0) {
            traveltime = 0;
        } else {
            warpfactor = Math.pow((double)2,(double)fwarp - 1);
            traveltime = (double)(fdistance / warpfactor) * 365.25;
        }
        travel = String.valueOf(traveltime);
    }
    public float getFloat(String floatText) {
        Float FloatNum = Float.valueOf(floatText);
        return FloatNum.floatValue();
    }
    public void paint(Graphics g) {
        g.drawString("Travel days ",1,125);
        g.drawString(travel,100,125);
    }
    public boolean action(Event evt, Object arg) {
        if (evt.target instanceof TextField) {
            calcWarp();
            repaint();
            return true;
        } else
            return false;
    }
}
```

**Figure 3.13**  Object-oriented (Java) warp drive calculator.

```
<!DOCTYPE HTML PUBLIC>
<HTML>
  <HEAD>
    <TITLE>Warp speed</TITLE>
  </HEAD>
  <BODY>
      <APPLET CODE="Warp.class" WIDTH="200" HEIGHT="150"></APPLET>
  </BODY>
</HTML>
```

**Figure 3.14** Warp drive Web page.

Markup is information added to text. Markup can tell what the text means and gives information on how the text is to be interpreted by the human reader or display program. This can mean interpreted for display purposes or interpreted for the purpose of understanding what the text means. A good example of pre-Web markup is proofreader's marks, which are used to mark up text with corrections to its spelling and format.

The following is an example of markup, a partial list of skills. To this text is added markup in the form of <B>**Bold**</B>, <I>*Italics*</I>, and New line (break) <BR>.

```
<B>Computers:</B><BR>
Consultant <I>(Business, Electronic commerce, Internet)</I><BR>
Programmer<BR>
Systems Analyst<BR>
Web Designer<BR>
<B>Science:</B><BR>
Philosophical historian<BR>
Researcher<BR>
Theoretical Physicist
<B>Writer:</B><BR>
Screenwriter<BR>
Technical writer<BR>
```

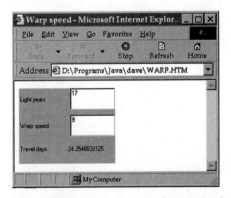

**Figure 3.15** Warp drive applet engaged.

The markup will translate the text to display like this:

```
Computers:
Consultant (Business, Electronic commerce, Internet)
Programmer
Systems Analyst Web Designer
Science:
Philosophical historian
Researcher
Theoretical Physicist
Writer:
Screenwriter
Technical writer
```

Don't be fooled by the formatting of the source document. Just because it is formatted for readability doesn't mean the interpreted output will do anything other than follow the markup commands. Without the <BR> symbols, the words would just all string·together like this:

```
Computers: Consultant (Business, Electronic commerce, Internet)
Programmer Systems Analyst Web Designer Science: Philosophical historian
Researcher Theoretical Physicist Writer: Screenwriter Technical writer
```

We'll be looking at markup languages extensively in the next chapter.

# How Is the Internet Programmed?

Now we have the task of putting this discussion together in a lucid manner to explain its relevance to the world of Internet programming. This is easy.

The Web was originally programmed with markup languages. These alone provided a tremendous amount of artistic license for designers to bring their skills to the graphical interface provided by Web browsers. But displaying static text and images has not been enough for the motion-oriented media consciousness of our society.

Next came *animated gifs*, images that moved. But this was just a distraction. The release of the Java language allowed developers the freedom to write browser plug-ins that would run applets to play audio clips, display movies, play games, and all sorts of features that are entertaining, but which at first had little to do with getting much of anything done outside of some learning and fun.

ActiveX controls were created to increase the functionality of downloaded components, since the security-limited applets did not satisfy our need for speed. ActiveX has barely scratched the surface of what is possible with the technology of using components without security limitations. ActiveX and its successors are going to go a long way.

Even with applets (and especially with ActiveX), a way was needed to control these components from the browser so they could provide better interactivity to the user. Scripting languages provided the answer. Their syntax was taken from full-fledged programming languages and their functionality was specifically designed to interface the browser with the applet or ActiveX control. This gives us even more flexibility than

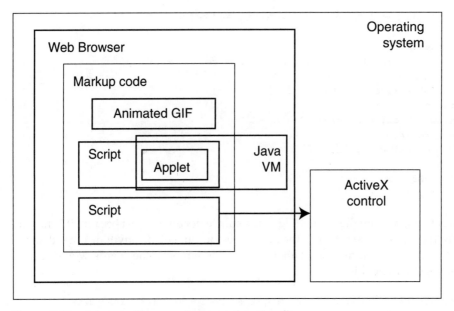

**Figure 3.16**   Integrated browser language functionality.

we could have originally imagined with the plain old markup language we started with. Even though we can display moving images and launch applets and ActiveX controls in our page, the page content is still static.

Dynamic HTML addresses these concerns and will be covered thoroughly in the next few chapters. Figure 3.16 illustrates how this multitude of languages are all orchestrated by the hard-working browser.

# How a Programmer's Mind Works

Having been a programmer myself for longer than I care to admit, I have achieved the dubious distinction wherever I go of being one of the fastest and best. I still make mistakes and it's rare that one writes a program that works exactly the way it's supposed to in the first draft, but it can happen.

The point is, I have come to an understanding of what defines the ability of a programmer. I am going to relate that to you now, and explain it.

The ability of a programmer is directly proportional to his or her ability to construct and view mental mock-ups.

What does this mean? I expect the first question is, what is a mock-up?

## DEFINITION: MOCK-UP
**A full-size model or representation chiefly for study, testing, or display.**

We have architects constructing mock-ups of buildings, war buffs building mock-ups of battles, and so forth. So now we come to a mental mock-up. What is that?

I'll give an example that will apply to the science of programming. First, I have to ask you a question: How do you get to your favorite computer store? (I have to pick something I know will be relevant to all the readers.) Now when you tell me how to get there, you will, I hope, look at a mental map of your area of the planet and give me directions based on that. That map is a mental mock-up of your part of the world as it relates to roads.

In programming we also need to achieve the ability to think in terms of steps to follow using the logic of computer capabilities. This logic is independent of what language we are using, but it does depend on an understanding of how computers work, how data is stored and retrieved, how to display and print, and so on.

When I get a programming job, I read the specs and construct a mental image of what the program is supposed to do; then I put my fingers on the keyboard and start typing. I've always had an edge on this, been quick at it; in fact, I've gotten to where I can program and talk to my oddball friends on the phone at the same time. My fellow programmers have had a little trouble understanding how I can do this, but this is how it works. I look at my well-constructed mental image of what I'm going to do. Since there is nothing I don't understand about what I'm going to do, instantly the code to accomplish this comes to mind. While I'm typing, I can talk about something else. When I run out of code, I take another look.

In the long run it doesn't really matter how long it takes to construct an image of the process you are about to encode in cybernetic steps; what matters is how correct it is. Personally, I've noticed that no matter how overdue something may be, if it's really good, people forgive your failings faster than if it were on time and wrong (that's a trade secret, by the way).

Finally, it's anybody's guess as to exactly what goes on in your head, how this mock-up is going to be constructed, and what it might look like. If you have a thorough understanding of what is needed and wanted on the customer's side of the table and of the capabilities of the programming languages you are going to be using to achieve that on your side of the table, it will be right. *Right* means it does what it's supposed to and it works. It may take some practice, but you will get better at it as you go along.

Trust me, I've been there. In fact, I'm still there.

## Summary

This may have been an intense chapter for you, but having the basics of programming down is important to understanding what it means to do the actual work of programming.

In the next chapter we're going to discuss the basics of the Web markup languages. Lest you think that these are simple, it's simply not true any more. In a few years the advances being made in creating more flexible and sophisticated methods of data storage and display, specifically for the Internet and the kind of distributed and internationalized content it represents, will mean that programming a markup language is going to be real work!

Let's get started!

CHAPTER

4

# HTML, XML, SGML

This chapter introduces the first language we will study: HTML. HTML is the platform from which the Web was launched and remains the superstructure upon which the Web is built.

All the languages mentioned in this chapter are markup languages. We'll be going over what markup is, where it came from, and where it's going. Most importantly, you'll learn HTML!

By the end of this chapter you'll not only be able to start writing Web pages, you'll be pretty much of an authority on HTML because you'll be able to tell others its history, including why it was created, what's right and wrong about it, and where it's going.

## Where Did Markup Languages Come from?

Markup languages evolved out of a desire to display text in something other than a single font and type size. For those of you who may not have been paying attention, there were no such things as CRT (read that as *Cathode Ray Tube*) terminals of any kind until 25 years ago. That may seem like a long time ago, but realize that at the time, those clunky teletype-style printed output terminals were replaced by little more than teletype-style CRT terminals.

The only significant advancement in these terminals over the following 10–15 years was the transformation of our monochrome CRT from teletype one-line-at-a-time style into a text page display style with the ability to place the cursor in a specific character position before displaying the same single-font-and-type-size text. Oh yes, and the extension of the character set to include line drawing characters.

Certainly there were experiments and expensive high-tech windows-style terminals available at some point during the 1980s but these were not in widespread use.

This brings us to the turn of the 1990s when the Macintosh and Windows operating systems changed all that. This was the very first time the general public had the ability to create electronic documents. But remember, in the beginning the Mac still had a monochrome black and white monitor. But was it fun to play with those fonts. Soon increasingly sophisticated typesetting and page layout programs became available.

There are two kinds of markup languages: the control code markup that characterizes typical word processing and page layout applications in the form of embedded property symbols that are not human readable; and HTML-style markup using plain text characters that are both human and machine readable.

As part of the experiments and expensive high-tech equipment mentioned was a technology called *SGML*. Although this is the second type of markup language that gained commercial popularity, it was actually the first to be developed.

# How Markup Languages Work

Markup languages add processing information to text and store the combination in a file that is meant to be read by a computer.

## DEFINITION: MARKUP

**Markup is extra information placed with text to describe how the text is to be interpreted. Interpretation can be accomplished by a computer program such as a Web browser for display purposes, by an information storage and retrieval system (which includes cataloging/indexing and search programs), or by a system that does both.**

Word processing programs use binary codes that are not human readable. If you open such a document with a program that does not understand the codes, all you will see is a bunch of what we call *garbage*, since people tend to denigrate (make less of) things they don't understand. Actually, this code is quite smart, but looks like nonsense to us. Hypertext markup languages use human-readable codes in plain text, even though the codes are still meant to be computer processed.

In order to get into the frame of mind to understand what markup languages are really about, you have to put aside for a minute most of what you know or have heard about HTML because HTML is all about looks, or *format*, which is the computer term for the way electronic information is presented. Formatting is not the primary reason for a markup language. The most compelling reason to add markup to a document is to give it a structure so that all of its textual components can be identified and given meaning beyond how it will appear.

For example, you can identify parts of an online store page such as PRODUCT, CATEGORY, PICTURE, PRICE, DESCRIPTION, and so forth. Let's take a page from an online store as illustrated in Figure 4.1, then we'll break it down into its elements and figure out how they should be marked up.

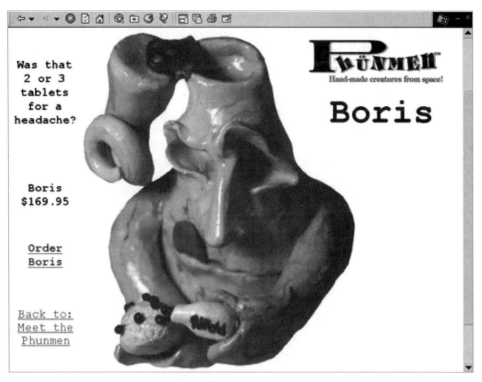

**Figure 4.1**    Boris applying aspirin to his brain.

The page shown has four elements along the left-hand margin, two along the right (one being a graphic), and a large graphic of Boris that dominates the center. We could mark this up based on element tags illustrated in Figure 4.2.

We have split each piece of information out into an element identifiable by human or machine. This format could easily be read by a search cataloging program, and used by another program to apply specific formats to each type of item. Not only that, but

```
<PRODUCT>Boris
<CATEGORY>Novelty figurine</CATEGORY>
<BANNER SRC="images/phunmen.gif"></BANNER>
<DESCRIPTION>Phunmen #4 of 43
<PICTURE SRC="images/boris.jpg"></PICTURE>
<QUOTE>Was that 2 or 3 tablets for a headache?</QUOTE>
<PRICE>$169.95</PRICE>
</DESCRIPTION>
<ORDER>Order Boris</ORDER>
<PARENT>Back to: Meet the Phunmen</PARENT>
</PRODUCT>
```

**Figure 4.2**    Boris marked up.

these items could be read from a database and built on-the-fly into this type of document, or this document could even serve as a database itself.

This type of formatting is the direction in which markup is headed, even though it may be unfamiliar to those involved in HTML style markup, which is shown in Figure 4.3.

This is just a small part of the HTML that goes into formatting this single page, and says nothing about what any of the text or images represent, only about how they are supposed to look. The page is formatted by first specifying a FONT, <B> makes the text bold, <BR> goes to a new line. <A HREF> gives the Address for a Hypertext REFerence (Web page) and IMG SRC tells the browser to display an image. All tags in this example have starting and ending pairs such as <B> </B>. There is a FONT within a FONT that tells the browser to increase the text size by 4 units (an HTML-specific quantity).

The truth is, this markup will work but won't display the page exactly the way it is shown. There are a lot more commands needed to place the elements on the page just where we want them. HTML can get very complex and hard to read, meaning hard to maintain in the future, at least without a front-end GUI interface that allows you to avoid having to read Web pages like this. But even with such an application, the quantity of Web pages in a large site, especially where a large amount of products, services, or information is offered, can make maintenance very difficult.

The point is that we have two extremes here of how markup languages can be used: one for information, the other for display. These must be merged together to give us both information and an aesthetic presentation, along with a manageable upkeep. Achieving this with markup is what this chapter is all about.

## An Example Markup Language

We could easily write a markup language of our own. When I was implementing an early text editing program called FASTXT on a DEC timesharing system back in the early 1980s, I wrote a suite of programs to allow users to store, retrieve, and print their documents without having to assign them 8.3 filenames (for example, filename.ext) or issue system commands. In order to take advantage of the new dot matrix printer features, I also wrote a program that would read their text files line by line and translate their user-typed markup into printer control codes to make text bold, italic, underlined, and such.

```
<FONT FACE="Courier New">
<B>Was that 2 or 3 tablets for a headache?</B><BR>
<B>Boris</B><BR>
<B>$169.95</B><BR>
<A HREF="betterbuyit.htm"><B>Order Boris</B></A><BR>
<A HREF="meetthephunmen.htm">Back to: Meet the Phunmen</A><BR>
<IMG SRC="images/boris.jpg">
<IMG SRC="images/phunmen.gif">
<FONT SIZE=+4><B>Boris</B></FONT>
</FONT>
```

**Figure 4.3**   Boris in HTML.

```
Interoffice [BOLD]MEMO[BEND] of the day
[BOLD]TO: [BEND]Lead programmer
[BOLD]FROM: [BEND]Markup programmer
[BOLD]DATE: [BEND]19 Apr 1986
[BOLD]RE:[BEND][ITAL]Your new markup language[IEND]
Dear Dave,
[UNDR]Can't we find an easier way to do this!!![UEND]
Sincerely,
[ITAL]Kris[IEND]
```

**Figure 4.4**   Makeshift markup memo.

Let's see how writing our own markup language would work.

The first thing to do is to pick a set of characters that will alert our program that a command has been encountered. To simplify things, these characters will not be permitted anywhere else in the text. Let's pick [ and ], because this still leaves two other choices for parentheses.

Next we pick the control codes. Let's start with [BOLD], [ITAL], and [UNDR]. We also need to know when to undo the command, so let's add [BEND], [IEND], and [UEND].

Finally, because this is a simple start, we have a few rules. First, only one command at a time. Second, commands must be started and ended on the same line, because I don't want to keep track of our users' markup mistakes.

Now let's create a document. Figure 4.4 shows how to do this.

Our program can now scan through each line, and when it hits a [, it checks the next four characters for a match to one of our codes followed by a ]. If it doesn't match, we forget about it and keep scanning to the end of the line.

If it does match, what do we do? We can't allow this code to be printed. If we remove it, we'll have blank space in the line. So we have to format a new line! Taking the first line we move the text up to the first [ into our new line, giving only:

```
Interoffice
```

Next we stick the printer control code for bold on the end of this line. Printer control codes are odd-looking, so let's say it's "^[1B" to turn on bolding. We now have:

```
"Interoffice ^[1B".
```

We then scan for the next [ ] pair with control code, finding [BEND]. We move the text from the end of the last code to the start of this code to our new line, which is "MEMO," followed by the printer command code to turn off the bolding, let's say that's "^[0B".

```
Interoffice ^[1BMEMO^[0B
```

Finally, we scan to the end of the line to finish off the text. This gives us the fully formatted line delivered to the printer:

```
Interoffice ^[1BMEMO^[0B of the day
```

With this process, the user receives a marked-up output without having to know anything about printer command codes. The result is shown in Figure 4.5.

In today's world of Windows and other GUI interfaces, PostScript laser and high-speed inkjet color printers, this kind of programming may seem caveman. But behind the scenes the people who write the PostScript encoders and printer drivers are dealing with this same thing on a level several orders of magnitude above this simple example.

Markup languages work in just this way. Our office memo would be written once then deleted or, because of all the work that went into it, modified and used again. Documents written in languages such as HTML today are not likely to be so short-lived; again, because of the work that goes into them. However, the future holds more. Corporate intranets are steering office communications towards paperless markup documents, and the only option available today is HTML. With a simplified HTML editor for office users and a working intranet, there's no reason we can't send each other more than e-mail messages. Presentations including slides, pictures, even audio and video files can be written and delivered electronically without having to put materials in binders with overhead transparencies and time-consuming duplication and distribution.

These languages go farther than just a few formatting commands. We can include a header section with information on who wrote the document and when, rather than relying on the system directory for this information, which could get lost in an e-mail or file transfer anyway. We can include indents, centering, and other alignment, tables, and (don't forget the whole reason for HTML) hypertext links.

Markup languages is a developing technology which, as you will see in the next few sections, is destined to take over the storage, retrieval, and presentation of all office documents and databases.

# SGML

Standard Generalized Markup Language (SGML) has its roots in the late 1960s when publishers first saw the need for a way to store documents in a computer. Even back

```
Interoffice MEMO of the day
TO: Lead programmer
FROM: Markup programmer
DATE: 19 Apr 1986
RE: Your new markup language
Dear Dave,
Can't we find an easier way to do this!!!
Sincerely,
```

**Figure 4.5**    Markup madness.

then, the monospaced output of a typewriter-style printer could still be enhanced by spacing, centering, overstriking, and other mechanical formatting techniques. SGML did not have an official standard specification until 1980 and was (and still is) mostly used by the government, especially the DoD and IRS, and larger corporations such as IBM.

SGML is an extremely sophisticated markup language that compares to HTML in the same way an F-15 would compare to a Cessna. SGML is such a large and complex language that we are not going to even try to give an explanation of it in this book. We will, however, discuss what SGML is all about.

SGML is actually more than a markup language, it is a language that can define other languages! That is what makes it so complex. SGML has been used to define the HTML language as the simplest of markup languages, omitting all but the most essential elements necessary to displaying text in an attractive manner.

This means that HTML is actually a *subset* of SGML. The word is that HTML is a specific *DTD* of SGML. What is a DTD? Our next subject, of course. But briefly, DTD means *Document Type Definition*. SGML was originally written to create models for different types of documents, and the DTD is the key to doing this, and HTML was designed as one of these types of documents.

HTML 0.9 was the first released HTML version. Those who have been following the progress of HTML over the last five years have seen the addition of numerous elements and attributes. The original version was meant to be pretty skimpy, and the HTML DTD has been purposely held down to a tiny shadow of its SGML parent.

SGML is actually on the Web, at least a little bit. There are SGML documents and sites out there for the aggressive Web addict. Interleaf, Inc. has an SGML browser plug-in called the Panorama viewer, available through the companion Website as an evaluation copy!

Now what we are going to do is to find out what DTDs are all about and how markup languages are being used now and will be used in the future in the marked-up world of the Internet.

## INFORMATIVE SITES!

*www.sgml.com*
**Find out more about SGML!**

*www.sq.com/resources/sgml*
**SoftQuad's SGML site!**

*www.interleaf.com/Panorama*
**Download Interleaf's Panorama Viewer!**

## DTD

A Document Type Definition is an exact specification for the structure of documents written in SGML. DTDs are written in a manner described in the SGML specification. Since SGML is such a flexible language, every SGML document must have a DTD specified for it or it can't be processed because the processing program wouldn't know what to do with the data.

From an SGML document's viewpoint, a DTD is a format that the document must adhere to. In order to be effectively processed, all of the elements contained in the document must be described within the DTD that gives the *definition* for that *type* of *document*.

Since the HTML language is described by specific SGML DTDs, it would follow that any HTML document should also declare a DTD for itself since there are separate DTDs for every version of HTML. But browsers do not care about HTML DTDs, and most pages don't even have a DTD declaration. The browsers always process the Web pages against the latest HTML version since that's what they're programmed to do.

Before this seems like too much vapor, I will explain our two examples of the Phunmen page for Boris in terms of a DTD.

If we were to create an SGML-style DTD based on the structure of our first example in Figure 4.2, the DTD would state, in the language of DTDs, that every PRODUCT element

---

## DOCUMENT TYPE DEFINITIONS AND DECLARATIONS

DTD stands for Document Type *Definition*, not *Declaration*. To make a document type declaration is to declare a document as attached to a specific DTD. Maybe they should have called the second one *DTA* to avoid this ambiguous acronym.

Here is an example of a DTD declaration made as the first line of an HTML page, declaring it as an HTML 4.0 document:

```
<!DOCTYPE HTML PUBLIC "-//W3C//DTD HTML 4.0//EN">
```

<!DOCTYPE> is the only piece of the SGML DTD spec allowed into HTML. PUBLIC means that the DTD is a published spec. Alternately, we would use SYSTEM if our spec were private. Instead of the spec that follows, you would give the URL of your DTD.

For example, the original declaration for the HTML 4.0 working DTD was:

```
<!DOCTYPE HTML SYSTEM
"http://www.w3.org/pub/WWW/MarkUp/Cougar/Cougar.dtd">
```

Continuing with our W3C public DTD, the "-" means the spec is not an official Internet standard. The truth is, none of the HTML specs have been given STD status yet! They're still RFCs. This RFC issued by the W3C is called DTD HTML 4.0 and is in English.

The purpose of having a DTD in SGML is to validate the structure of a document. This allows any program that is going to do something with this document to check it out completely before attempting to do anything with it. If the document doesn't pass the DTD test, it errors out. If our document passes muster, that is, if it conforms 100 percent to the DTD, then the parser (which reads the document and breaks it up into its defined elements before it is processed) will pass it on to the processor to be displayed, printed, or otherwise processed.

Because most Web programmers are not familiar with HTML DTDs, instead of validating HTML documents our friendly Web browsers give them carte blanche and always process the documents. Most of these pages violate some rule or another in the HTML DTD. The lack of closing tags (e.g., <P> without </P>) is by far the most frequent misdemeanor. In the future, we may not be afforded such a luxury when documents with integrated HTML, XML, and scripting have to be handled in a predictable fashion.

must have CATEGORY, BANNER, DESCRIPTION, ORDER, and PARENT elements, and then that every DESCRIPTION element must have PICTURE, QUOTE, and PRICE elements. All of these elements would in turn be defined as text, except BANNER and PICTURE, which would be .gif or .jpg files.

We haven't discussed how these elements would be displayed yet because remember, this is a simple example of SGML markup. With SGML, display is the last thing we are concerned with.

The HTML-style DTD in contrast to the SGML-style DTD is based half on structure and half on display properties. It specifies that elements in <B></B> wrappers are to be displayed in bold, and that every <A> element must have an HREF attribute. The truth is that *all* the HTML markup tags have this DTD specification behind them, telling the browser how to interpret the code you write.

---

There are HTML validators you can run your Web page through to check for DTD compliance. But watch out, you need to know which DTD to specify to make any sense of the result. For example, my HoTMetaLPRO HTML editor adds this line at the beginning of the pages it creates:

```
<!DOCTYPE HTML PUBLIC "-//SoftQuad//DTD HoTMetaL PRO
4.0::19970916::extensions to HTML 4.0//EN" "hmpro4.dtd">
```

I doubt this DTD is programmed into the W3C's HTML validator, so I would really want to use one of the W3C DTD specifications for validation instead.

To give you an example of what an XML type of DTD looks like, I will write one as just described. The DTD shown in Figure 4.6 starts with the DOCTYPE declaration as "SIMPLE [", which means that it is simply included in our document. The "]" closing tag appears at the end of the DTD.

Each element can have subelements and may or may not have attributes.

Our DTD elements start with PRODUCT, which lists its subelements in order. Then each of those elements is described, mostly boiling down to #PCDATA. The image elements have no content and so are EMPTY, but they have an SRC attribute which is the filename of the image, declared as CDATA, and which is a REQUIRED attribute.

The difference between CDATA and #PCDATA is that CDATA can contain any data whatsoever, meaning that the document parser (which is a part of the browser) will not try to interpret the text as markup. #PCDATA is restricted to text that cannot be mistaken for markup. For example, if our image file was named "<images>/phunmen!.gif", the browser would normally treat the <images> as markup. CDATA declares this text off-limits to browser interpretation.

The purpose of the DTD is to provide a model against which we can validate the document. DTDs are linked up with display properties through the use of a style sheet, and style sheets are now replacing a lot of HTML attributes. In fact, in HTML 4.0 a lot of these attributes are *deprecated*, or given has-been status, because of style sheets. A good example is the FONT tag. Instead of specifying the type FACE and font SIZE, these are placed in a style sheet.

Style sheets will be discussed in Chapter 5, "Dynamic HTML."

```
#PCDATA means "parsed character data," which is just text.
<!DOCTYPE SIMPLE [
<!ELEMENT PRODUCT (CATEGORY,BANNER,DESCRIPTION,ORDER,PARENT)>
<!ELEMENT CATEGORY (#PCDATA)>
<!ELEMENT BANNER EMPTY>
<!ATTLIST BANNER
    SRC CDATA # REQUIRED>
<!ELEMENT DESCRIPTION (#PCDATA,PICTURE,QUOTE,PRICE)>
<!ELEMENT PICTURE EMPTY>
<!ATTLIST PICTURE
    SRC CDATA # REQUIRED>
<!ELEMENT QUOTE (#PCDATA)>
<!ELEMENT PRICE (#PCDATA)>
<!ELEMENT ORDER (CDATA)>
<!ELEMENT PARENT (CDATA)>
]>
```

**Figure 4.6**   A document type definition.

# INFORMATIVE SITES!

*validator.w3.org*
**HTML validator straight from the W3C**

*watson.addy.com/*
**Dr. Watson's HTML validator**

*www.cre.canon.co.uk/~neilb/Weblint/*
**Get the lint off your Web pages!**

# XML

XML is *also* a subset of SGML.

XML (eXtensible Markup Language) is also a DTD of SGML but with XML the power of the DTD has been added back into the language! In XML we can create our own DTDs, which means we can create our own tags and specify how the content of these tags is to be displayed. Because of this, HTML is *not* included in XML, but XML has been given the power to supersede HTML. How this is done will be explained later because it involves a synergy of the power of HTML, scripting languages, style sheets, along with XML data.

Don't worry just yet, this technology is just getting on its horse. Once you understand HTML, Dynamic HTML, style sheets, and XML basics, you'll be ready to ride with the rest of the markup cowboys. How these work together is very simple and elegant.

# Writing HTML Documents

You can buy a Web page editor to write HTML documents and not ever look at the following example code. In fact, I highly recommend using a good Web page editor because writing all this code out by hand will most certainly drive even the most eager typist insane. But I do recommend looking at this code, because you want to know your options and be able to debug and stretch HTML to its limits. To do this, you have to know what HTML is made of.

That is why you're reading this book.

## Basic HTML Structure

SGML has left us the legacy of a standard markup language format, no matter what DTD our markup language is following. This means that we start by creating tags with the <TAG> format. But what is a tag really?

In HTML a tag is a command to the browser to display or otherwise process the contents of the tag set in a specific way. I also refer to the individual tags in the HTML language as *elements* of a Web page. A tag can also include *attributes*, which supply additional information about the content to be processed.

An HTML document is divided into two main sections: HEAD and BODY. Each of these sections has certain tags that can be used within it. We'll be going over these sections right away.

HTML begins with the tag <HTML>. A basic empty HTML document would contain these elements:

```
<!DOCTYPE HTML PUBLIC "your DTD goes here">
<HTML>
<HEAD></HEAD>
<BODY></BODY>
</HTML>
```

These elements are all optional! The browser will display a page just the same without any of these tags. The way I see it, the DTD may not be missed, but I think documents would look empty without these important structural tags. Besides good form, there are critical advantages to including these tags, like adding more tags that go within the HEAD tag.

### *HEAD*

The HEAD section contains basic information about the document, including its title and a description of its contents in the form of META tags. The content of the META tags was probably originally designed for human consumption but has ended up being used mainly as fuel for search engine indexing robots.

Table 4.1 lists HEAD elements including TITLE and META tags (see the example following).

**Table 4.1** HTML HEAD Elements

| HTML ELEMENT | MY COMMENTS |
|---|---|
| TITLE | This tag specifies what is displayed at the top of the Browser window. More than that, search engines will also use this tag as the title they show for your page. The world will know you by your title, so pick a good one. I dislike seeing search engine results that say "No Title." |
| META | This tag is for search engines and has two attributes: NAME and CONTENT. |
| *Attributes* | These define optional features offered by the tag. In the case of META, the tag would be meaningless without the attributes, but there are other tags soon to be seen where this is not true. Why do we call them *attributes*? The dictionary defines *attribute* as a characteristic feature, property, or quality. |
| META NAME= "keywords" "description" | Depending on what algorithms the search engines are using, the "keywords" and "description" attributes will play a part, along with the content of the BODY of your page, in how it is cataloged. |
| META CONTENT= *"keywords"* | The phrases in this attribute must be separated by commas. Please don't spam your keywords. In doing the research for this book, I did a search on SGML and good manners keeps me from telling you what came up smack in the middle of the result list, but someday it will end up in the .sex domain. |
| META CONTENT= *"description"* | Again, a good concise description of your page will go far with search engines; think of these big guys as your friends. Treat them well and they will send you more friends. |

The following code from the www.prolotherapy.com homepage is a good example of META tags. Last time I checked a search on the word *prolotherapy* in Yahoo! brought this site up in 10 out of the top 10 results. This site also rates in the top 10 in every one of the top search engines. I nailed this keyword, which also appears in the text of the page a few more times, not to mention the URL.

```
<HEAD>
<TITLE>Prolotherapy.com home page</TITLE>
<META NAME="keywords" CONTENT="prolotherapy, arthritis, back pain,
sports injury, non-surgical treatment, chronic pain">
<META NAME="description"
CONTENT="a comprehensive information database on Prolotherapy, a non-
surgical and permanent treatment for chronic pain">
</HEAD>
```

## *BODY*

The BODY tag is where we do all the work in HTML. From here on out, the HTML language will be tackled in sections. Entire books are written on HTML, so we're going to go through it in a practical and relevant manner.

Table 4.2 gives a summary of HTML BODY attributes. All of these have been *deprecated* in favor of style sheets (which we'll discuss in Chapter 5) starting with HTML 4.0, but you can still use these tags, which will probably not change for many years. Because of the velocity of technological change in the Internet programming arena (the unofficial definition of an Internet year is about three months), backward compatibility is a major issue we all have to deal with. You can imagine the amount of effort it would take to change the zillions of HTML pages on the Web over to something else, then to get the majority of users to update their browsers, and to retrain everyone to use a new alternative to HTML!

*Deprecated* is a funny word because although it and *depreciate(with an i),* have different roots, they have come to mean almost the same thing, which is "to lower the value of." If the tag is still useful, it hasn't lost any value, has it? I know that what the W3C is trying to do is to discourage its use so it can be phased out. But deprecated? I suppose it's a status thing.

### BODY META Tag

There is also a place in the BODY tag for META. The following statement will wait 30 seconds then jump to the URL given. To see how this works visit www.californiado.org.

```
<META HTTP-EQUIV="Refresh"
CONTENT="30;URL=http://www.californiado.org/aopsc.htm">
```

**Table 4.2**   HTML BODY Attributes

| BODY ATTRIBUTE | MY COMMENTS |
| --- | --- |
| BACKGROUND= "image" | This defines the background image for the page. This image will be automatically tiled to fill the screen, but if you use style sheets instead of this attribute you have more options. |
| BGCOLOR= color | This gives a color to the background, especially useful where the browser defaults to a drab gray. If used with a background image, it can keep the screen from flashing the default color before the image has loaded. Just specify the image background color. |
| TEXT=color | Specifies the BODY text color. |
| VLINK=color | Specifies what color to use for links already visited. |
| ALINK=color | Specifies what color to use for links not yet visited. |

---

**HTML COLORS**

You can use color names for the 16 colors found in 16-color selection charts, which include black, white, gray, silver, maroon, red, purple, fuschia, green, lime, olive, yellow, navy, blue, teal, and aqua.

Or, you can use the hexadecimal color triplet! Remember, hex is base 16 expressed as 01234567890ABCDEF for 0 to 16. This means 00 is zero and FF is 255 (the first F is 15x16=240 and the second F is 15).

The hex triplet gives you three pairs of HEX digits for RED, GREEN, and BLUE that looks like this: #RRGGBB. Each pair can have the values 00 for no color to FF for full saturation. These colors are additive, meaning that white is all colors in full saturation, #FFFFFF, and black is absence of color, #000000. Bright red would be #FF0000, bright green, #00FF00, and bright blue, #0000FF. You can experiment or use a color picking program to choose for you.

---

What is HTTP-EQUIV? This goes back to the real purpose of the META tag. In practice, NAME and HTTP-EQUIV are the same. If you review the HTTP examples in Chapter 2, "How Does the Internet Work?" you will see that HTTP sends along some keywords of its own as part of the protocol.

The original purpose of a META tag was to give specialized information about the document to an application accessing it so the application could make an informed decision about what to do with it. So the HTTP-EQUIV was meant to match the HTTP protocol keyword, which could be transmitted with the document. The truth is the META tag is the only tag that can go anywhere.

### BODY Elements

Table 4.3 is a list of the simplest HTML formatting tags. These all have opening and closing tags, which are required. They can be nested, which means put together one inside another; for example, <B><I> is bold italic</I></B> or <I><B>and so is </B></I>.

Table 4.4 is a list of tags that are also simple but which are almost never used. How these are actually rendered are browser-specific choices. These are the tags in HTML that attempt to specify the purpose of content, which is not really what HTML is used for. The HTML RFC suggests, but does not dictate, that these are displayed in a certain way.

Table 4.5 lists text formatting tags that have nothing to do with structure and that, again, are seldom used in favor of other tags that provide better control over how the

**Table 4.3**   HTML Simple Formatting Elements

| TAG | FUNCTION | EXAMPLE |
|-----|----------|---------|
| B | **Display text in bold.** | <B>Buy now!</B> |
| I | *Display text in italics.* | <I>This is important.</I> |
| U | <U>Display text underlined.</U> | <U>Don't forget.</U> |
| S | ~~Display text with strikethrough.~~ | <S>No longer available.</S> |
| TT | `Display text in monospace.` | <TT>x = c*t</TT> |

**Table 4.4** Rare HTML Content Formatting Elements

| TAG | FUNCTION |
|-----|----------|
| BLOCKQUOTE | Display text quoted from another source. A typical rendering might be a slight extra left and right indent, and/or italic font, and provide space above and below the quote. |
| CITE | Indicate the title of a book or other citation, typically rendered as italics. |
| CODE | Indicates an example of code, typically rendered in a monospaced font. Intended for short words or phrases of code so the PRE element is more appropriate for multiple-line listings. |
| DEL | Show text as having been deleted from the document. |
| DFN | Indicates that this is the defining instance of the enclosed term. |
| EM | Indicates an emphasized phrase, typically rendered as italics. |
| INS | Show text as having been added to the document. |
| KBD | Indicates text typed by a user, typically rendered in a monospaced font. |
| PRE | Indicates that the enclosed text is preformatted, typically rendered in a fixed-pitch font with whitespace intact and no word wrap. |
| Q | Short quotations, typically rendered with delimiting quotation marks. |
| SAMP | Indicates a sequence of literal characters, typically rendered in a monospaced font. |
| STRONG | Indicates strong emphasis, typically rendered in bold. |
| SUB, SUP | Subscript and superscript. |
| VAR | Indicates a placeholder variable, typically rendered as italic. |

text will actually display. Currently, a 1- or 2-point difference in a type style means something to Web designers. I label this *text formatting* as opposed to *content formatting* because it says nothing about what the text means.

## NOTE

**Unless you're formatting in one of the monospaced tags as listed previously, multiple spaces are always discarded, meaning that "my banana" will look the same as "my banana" will look the same as "my banana." Much Web design work goes into controlling whitespace.**

Because of lack of radar accuracy, the H1 through H6 elements tend not to be used by militant Web designers. On the other hand, BR, HR, and P are used a lot—P especially. The ALIGN attribute will align the text to the left, center, or right, or will cause it to grasp both sides of the page and pull itself apart until the line is filled.

The BR tag CLEAR attribute prevents text from displaying next to another element, particularly an image. For example, CLEAR="left" would skip past an element already

**Table 4.5**  HTML Text Formatting Elements

| TAG | FUNCTION | ATTRIBUTES |
|---|---|---|
| BR | Specifies a line break. | CLEAR="none,left,right,all" |
| H1 | Bold, very large font, centered. One or two blank lines above and below. | ALIGN="left,center,right,justify" |
| H2 | Bold, large font, flush left. One or two blank lines above and below. | ALIGN="left,center,right,justify" |
| H3 | Italic, large font, slightly indented from the left margin. One or two blank lines above and below. | ALIGN="left,center,right,justify" |
| H4 | Bold, normal font, indented more than H3. One blank line above and below. | ALIGN="left,center,right,justify" |
| H5 | Italic, normal font, indented as H4. One blank line above. | ALIGN="left,center,right,justify" |
| H6 | Bold, indented same as normal text, more than H5. One blank line above. | ALIGN="left,center,right,justify" |
| HR | A divider between sections of text; typically a full width horizontal rule. | ALIGN="left,center,right,justify" SIZE= (see below) WIDTH= (see below) NOSHADE= (see below) |
| P | Indicates a new paragraph. This will cause a line break before with extra vertical space before. Whether or not there is space after the paragraph depends on how it ends, with a closing tag or a different type of text block. | ALIGN="left,center,right,justify" |

in place on the left before ending the break and displaying the next block of text. The default is of course CLEAR="none". CLEAR="all" is the same as the illegal but illustrative command CLEAR="left+right".

Often we see a cool graphic used instead of an HR because HRs are just gray or black lines, but we can do a lot with the once useful HR tag. Width can be set as a percentage of screen size; for example, WIDTH="70%". Then we can adjust the thickness; for example, SIZE="10" will create a 10-point rule. ALIGN will similarly align the rule. You can almost make art with this kind of flexibility.

Now that we have the basics of HTML display formatting down, let's put some of them to use.

Figure 4.7 is a prehistoric Web page written in early 1996 just before HTML 3.0 was released. It uses only a few elements we haven't gone over yet, but makes heavy use of header elements and horizontal rules. (It was written by hand!) It also uses the CENTER element, long ago *deprecated,* which centers everything with wild abandon.

```
<HTML>
<HEAD>
 <TITLE>Cintronics: MicroNuclear Physics On-Line</TITLE>
</HEAD>

<BODY>
 <CENTER><FONT FACE="Eurostile","Glacier">
 <BR>
  <H1>MICRONUCLEAR PHYSICS</H1>
 <HR>
  <H2>A NEW PRESENTATION OF QUANTUM WAVE MECHANICS TOWARDS IMPROVED
      EVALUATION OF NUCLEAR PROCESSES</H2>
 <HR>
  <H3>by David A. Cintron</H3>
 <HR SIZE=10>
  <H4>Copyright &COPY 1990, 1996 by David A. Cintron.
      All rights reserved.</H4>
 </CENTER></FONT>

<HR SIZE=12>
<A NAME="aimofmnp"></A>
<CENTER><FONT FACE="Eurostile","Glacier">
THE AIM OF M.N.P. (MICRONUCLEAR PHYSICS)</FONT></CENTER>
<HR>
The aim of Micronuclear Physics is the achievement of low cost, high
volume energy production through the application of an extremely
highly efficient technology on a microscopic level.
<P>
The words atomic and nuclear have gained bad reputations because of
the
destructive nature of the atomic bomb and the failure of the nuclear
reactor to deliver safe, clean energy. The goal of M.N.P. is to
replace a bad technology based on misconception and misunderstanding,
with a good technology based on truth.
<P>
The two failed products of the atomic age, the Bomb and the Reactor,
are based on large scale out of control reactions of heavy, unstable
radioactive elements.
<P>
M.N.P. deals with individual particles and precise energy flows.
... (more text goes here) ...
<A HREF="mnptoc.htm">MNP table of contents</A>
<P>
</HTML>
<P>
```

**Figure 4.7**  A technical treatise elocuted in elementary HTML.

This Web page is formatted to make the HTML easy to read for the writer. Remember that whitespace is removed when the document is displayed, so as long as we know what our markup is doing, we can put text all over the place, skip lines, and not worry about it.

If you look closely, you'll see the &COPY tag, which displays the © symbol. We'll discuss these special characters later in the chapter. Most of the text was omitted for pain relief. You can read the entire text of this document at www.cintronics.com, in the *scientific* section.

Figure 4.8 illustrates what the MicroNuclear Physics Web page looks like with headers, rules, and paragraphs.

## Hypertext Linking

One of the features of the MNP set of pages is a way for people to get around by clicking on links.

There are two types of hypertext linking in HTML, which are listed in Table 4.6. The first is the anchor tag <A HREF= ""> (I think they should have called it an *address* tag), which refers to a local or remote URL. The HREF on this page refers to a page in the same directory by giving only the local filename, mnptoc.htm.

The other is the <A NAME= ""> tag, which creates a new anchor (or address) in the current document. In the example document, the element <A NAME="aimofmnp"></A> is called an *empty element* because it has an attribute but no content between the tags, although content is allowed. This element creates an anchor called #aimofmnp for other documents to link to.

Linking works in concert with the <A HREF= ""> element. We can have another page jump directly to this spot in this document by using the following code line. The # sign indicates that we are addressing a specific anchor within the HTML page. Note the # sign directly follows the filename.

```
<A HREF="mnp1.htm#aimofmnp">The Aim of MNP</A>
```

Or, if the referring page is not in the *cintronics* domain, we would include the full URL.

```
<A HREF="www.cintronics.com/mnp1.htm#aimofmnp">The Aim of MNP</A>
```

The browser should place our Web page so that the anchor (which cannot actually be seen) is at the top. This allows us to avoid having to skip down past everything above while manually searching for our target, by putting us smack dab in the from which place we want to start.

**Table 4.6**  Anchor Attributes

| ANCHOR ATTRIBUTE | PURPOSE | EXAMPLE |
|---|---|---|
| A NAME="*anchor*" | Anchor to link to | <A NAME="mypicture"> This is me</A> |
| A HREF="*URL*" | Link to another anchor | <A HREF="www.you.com #mypicture">Check me out!</A> |

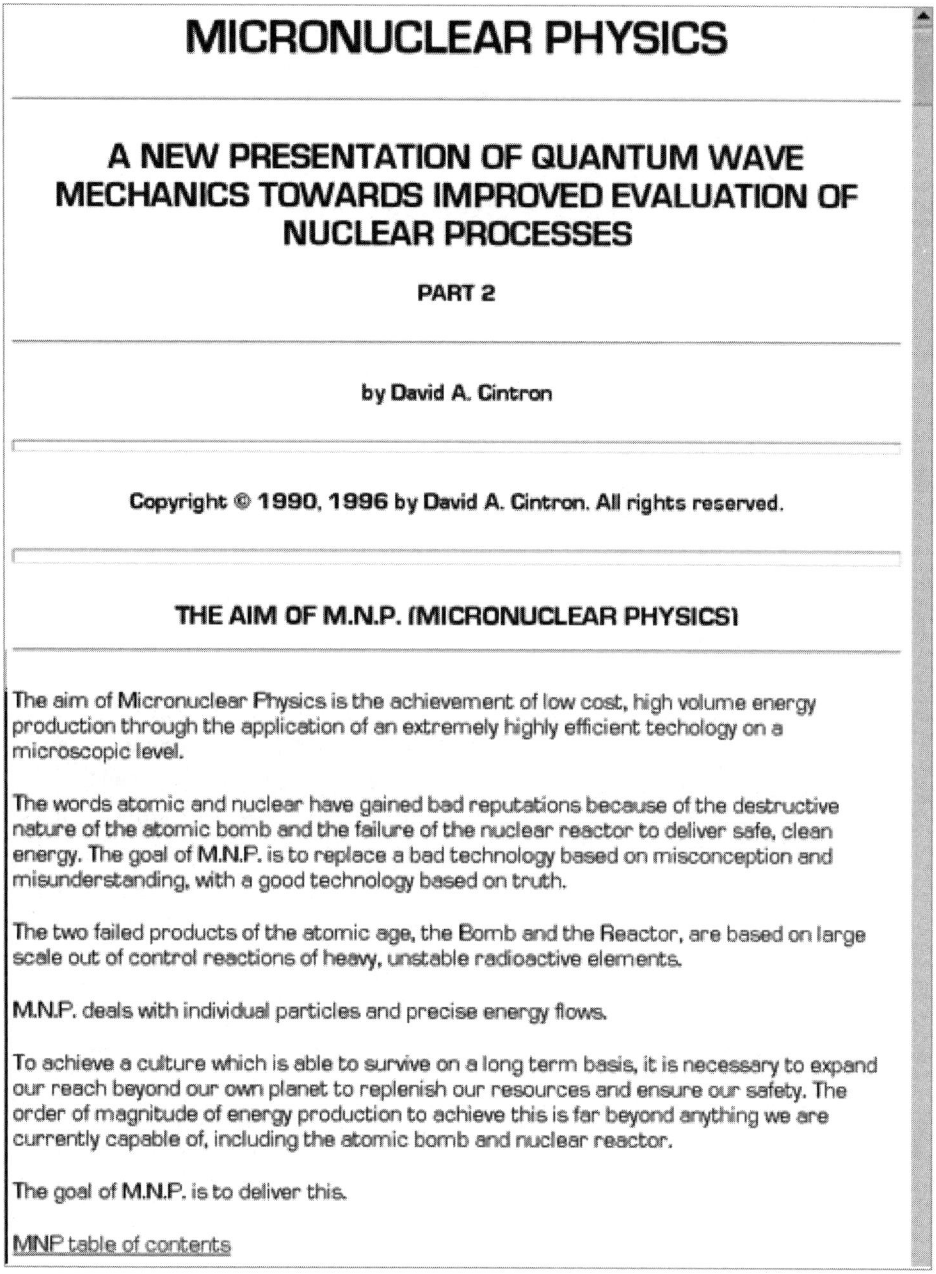

# MICRONUCLEAR PHYSICS

## A NEW PRESENTATION OF QUANTUM WAVE MECHANICS TOWARDS IMPROVED EVALUATION OF NUCLEAR PROCESSES

### PART 2

by David A. Cintron

Copyright © 1990, 1996 by David A. Cintron. All rights reserved.

### THE AIM OF M.N.P. (MICRONUCLEAR PHYSICS)

The aim of Micronuclear Physics is the achievement of low cost, high volume energy production through the application of an extremely highly efficient techology on a microscopic level.

The words atomic and nuclear have gained bad reputations because of the destructive nature of the atomic bomb and the failure of the nuclear reactor to deliver safe, clean energy. The goal of M.N.P. is to replace a bad technology based on misconception and misunderstanding, with a good technology based on truth.

The two failed products of the atomic age, the Bomb and the Reactor, are based on large scale out of control reactions of heavy, unstable radioactive elements.

M.N.P. deals with individual particles and precise energy flows.

To achieve a culture which is able to survive on a long term basis, it is necessary to expand our reach beyond our own planet to replenish our resources and ensure our safety. The order of magnitude of energy production to achieve this is far beyond anything we are currently capable of, including the atomic bomb and nuclear reactor.

The goal of M.N.P. is to deliver this.

MNP table of contents

**Figure 4.8** MNP addresses the world.

All HREF links by default are displayed with underlining, but remember that you can also change their color using BODY attributes. NAME anchors are not displayed with any special style and so are not indicated to the user at all. If no NAME anchor is given in a URL, the browser takes you to the top of the page addressed. By the way, you can use an image like this <A HREF=…>*image tag*</A> so it will also activate a link.

**NOTE**
The term *URI* is beginning to replace URL. URI means Universal Resource Identifier and a URL is a subset of the URI specification. Remember, if you hear URI you can take it to mean URL.

## Special Characters in HTML

The term *escaping characters* comes from the old cursor-positioned CRT (Cathode Ray Tube) terminal where you could send an escape-sequence to tell the CRT to do things that the user would not see, like placing the cursor or clearing the screen. Otherwise, there would have been a lot of fireworks visible to the user. This was logically called an *escape sequence* because it began with the escape character.

However, HTML escaping does not use the escape character, it starts with "&" and it is used to display markup characters or characters that aren't on the keyboard. Some of these are shown in Table 4.7. Another reason these keys aren't on the keyboard and can't go directly into HTML documents is that they are 8-bit characters. With 7 bits we can use up to 128 characters, and there are 128 more characters available when you increase to 8 bits. Some data communications equipment only transmits 7-bit characters, so these characters can be left out.

**NOTE**
I mostly use the copyright symbol, although in some medical documents I need the degree symbol for body temperature. When you need them, you need them, and here they are, the four markup symbols (&, <, > and ") and a sample of some other special characters from above 128.

**Don't forget to put the semicolon after!**

You can also use the direct decimal code for these characters. The corresponding names and decimal codes for these symbols are listed in Appendix C, "Escaped Characters."

## Lists in HTML

You can create lists in HTML that will automatically be formatted with features such as numbers, bullets, and indenting. This is a feature that leaves you little control over display specifics, but can do a lot of work for you if you're not concerned with list display.

**Table 4.7**  Special Characters

| SYMBOL | SIGN | SYMBOL | SIGN | SYMBOL | SIGN |
| --- | --- | --- | --- | --- | --- |
| &amp; | & | &pound; | £ | &aring; | å |
| &gt; | > | &copy; | © | &Aelig; | Æ |
| &lt; | < | &reg; | ® | &aelig; | æ |
| &quot; | " | &deg; | ° | &divide; | ÷ |

There are three types of lists: ordered, unordered, and definition. Each list is enclosed in a set of tags stating what kind of list it is, and can have list items, as illustrated in Table 4.8.

Ordered lists and unordered lists are the same except for the tag set. <OL> means ordered list, which will be displayed with numbers sequentially assigned. <UL> is for an unordered list, which will have bullets instead. <DL> is for definition lists, which has two item types, DT for definition term and DD for definition description. In this case, each DT list item can have DD list items.

Lists would be formatted in one of the following three ways:

| ORDERED LIST | UNORDERED LIST | DEFINITION LIST |
|---|---|---|
| <OL> Talk show hosts | <UL> Scream show hosts | <DL> Types of shows |
| <LI> Leno | <LI> Geraldo | <DT> Talk show |
| <LI> Letterman | <LI> Jerry Springer | <DD> Comedy, celebrities |
| <LI> Oprah | <LI> Sally Jessie | <DT> Scream show |
| <LI> Conan O'Brien | <LI> Jenny Jones | <DD> Actors, weirdos |
| </OL> | </UL> | </DL> |

Figure 4.9 illustrates a list used to display part of the MNP table of contents, which is shown in Figure 4.10.

## Tables in HTML

Tables in HTML are important because you can control layout, especially if you have an HTML editor that lets you drag and drop, click, and move elements around. The only feature that outdoes tables is *dynamic positioning,* a feature in Dynamic HTML, which will be discussed in Chapter 5.

To create a table, we start with the tag TABLE. The TABLE tag takes a WIDTH attribute, which can be set as a percentage of screen width (making the table size according to the user's screen settings), or as an actual number of pixels.

**NOTE**

If you create your pages, with or without tables, wider than the nominal 640 pixels (from the default 640x480 screen setting) you're going to lose a lot of people. Individuals with 800x600 and higher screen settings are in the minority.

**Table 4.8**    Lists

| TYPE OF LIST | TAG SET | ITEM TAG | SUBITEM TAG |
|---|---|---|---|
| Ordered, or numbered lists | <OL></OL> | <LI> | |
| Unordered, or bulleted lists | <UL></UL> | <LI> | |
| Definition lists | <DL></DL> | <DT> | <DD> |

```
<H3>M.N.P. PART 3 </H3>
<UL>
<LI><A HREF="mnp3.html#photonselectrons">PHOTONS AND ELECTRONS</A>
<LI><A HREF="mnp3.html#quantumphysics">QUANTUM PHYSICS</A>
<LI><A HREF="mnp3.html#theelectronwave">THE ELECTRON WAVE</A>
<LI><A HREF="mnp3.html#protonneutron">THE PROTON/NEUTRON WAVE</A>
<LI><A HREF="mnp3.html#atomicwaves">ATOMIC WAVES AND ANTIMATTER</A>
</UL>
<H3>M.N.P. PART 4 </H3>
<UL>
<LI><A HREF="mnp4.html#electronwaves">ELECTRON WAVES</A>
<LI><A HREF="mnp4.html#neutronwaves">NEUTRON WAVES</A>
<LI><A HREF="mnp4.html#forces">FORCES: STRONG, ELECTROMAGNETIC, WEAK
AND GRAVITY</A>
<LI><A HREF="mnp4.html#stabilityparticles">STABILITY OF PARTICLES</A>
<LI><A HREF="mnp4.html#emg">ELECTRICITY, MAGNETISM AND GRAVITY</A>
<LI><A HREF="mnp4.html#chargemagnetism">CHARGE AND MAGNETISM</A>
</UL>
```

**Figure 4.9**  List combined with links and text.

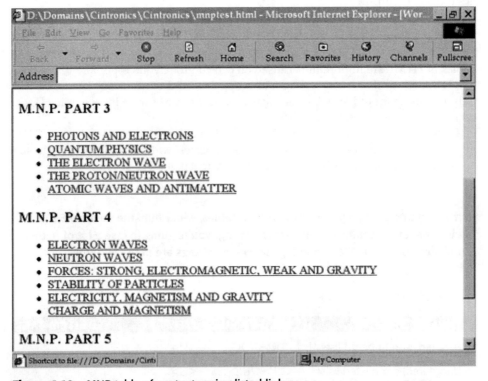

**Figure 4.10**  MNP table of contents using listed links.

Table rows and columns are constructed using the element TR at the start of each row, and within each row a series of one or more TD elements for each column. How does the table know how many columns it has? The browser has to do a reality check by reading the whole table in and then doing its best to format the output.

More than just a grid with fixed-size pigeonholes, table rows and columns are flexible. Row and column elements can be expanded using the ROWSPAN and COLSPAN attributes. For example if we had a table with two columns and five rows we could make the top row one single wide element by using "COLSPAN=2". Conversely, if we want the entire left-hand column to be a single element we can use "ROWSPAN=5". The important thing is to make sure you're counting your rows and columns correctly.

Finally, you can set the width of each element by using the WIDTH attribute. This can get difficult and it's easy to incorrectly format tables by giving the browser a mixed-up pixel count. Your table will increase to twice your screen width or reduce to the top-left quarter of the screen. To fix this, you'll need go through and recount. Some HTML editing programs such as FrontPage do a good job of managing these table cell widths.

Figure 4.11 illustrates the table layout for another one of the Phunmen, Malibu Bob.

Bob's page is set up as a 7 row 2 column table. Row 1 spans 2 columns and contains the Phunmen banner graphic and Bob's name in large Courier type. In row 2 column 1 we have Bob's quote and we find that the column 2 element is going to span the next 5 rows. This creates space for Bob's picture. The next 4 rows only have one element in each because the second element is still working off of the ROWSPAN=5 cell. Finally we have one more row with an empty column 1 and the copyright statement in column 2, which you will notice contains two special characters: the u with the two dots above as &uuml, and the copyright symbol as &copy;.

In this table we have specified all of the cell widths, leaving the cell heights to the browser. We could specify WIDTH= and HEIGHT= if we wanted to.

Malibu Bob's page with grid lines and span elements added for show is shown in Figure 4.12.

Tables can also be nested with tables inside of tables. All this means is that we take one cell and place another table in it, using all the table tools we have already discussed. In this short line of HTML, we see that after the cell tag we start right off with another table. In this case, the width is 100 percent of the cell width (not the whole screen), which you can either specify or leave to the browser.

```
<TD><TABLE WIDTH=100%>. . .</TABLE></TD>
```

Table 4.9 lists attributes that apply to the table as a whole, and Table 4.10 lists attributes commonly applied to individual cells.

There are many options for tables. Those listed are the most common and useful, although your application may require options that most wouldn't have use for. For example, there are unconventional *user agents* (Web browsers) that would interpret table elements in different ways, such as for the visually impaired (using big type), and there is a lot of talk about how to interpret visual content for nonvisually oriented user agents (translating into audio), or for foreign languages (some of which do not read left to right, top to bottom, or have an alphabet).

```
<TABLE WIDTH="100%">
  <TR>
    <TD WIDTH="640" COLSPAN="2"><IMG SRC="images/littlephun.GIF"
                            WIDTH="254" HEIGHT="77">
    <FONT FACE="Courier New" SIZE="+4"> <B>Malibu Bob</B></FONT>
    </TD>
  </TR>
  <TR>
    <TD WIDTH="106" ALIGN="CENTER"><FONT FACE="Courier New">
    <B>RADICAL WAVES, DUDE!</B></FONT>
    </TD>
    <TD WIDTH="534" ROWSPAN="5"><IMG SRC="images/malibubob.JPG"
                            WIDTH="491" HEIGHT="699">
    </TD>
  </TR>
  <TR>
    <TD WIDTH="106" ALIGN="CENTER"><FONT FACE="Courier New">
    <B>Malibu Bob<BR>$119.95</B></FONT>
    </TD>
  </TR>
  <TR>
    <TD WIDTH="106" ALIGN="CENTER"><B><FONT FACE="Courier New">
    <A HREF="betterbuyit.htm">Order Malibu Bob</A></FONT></B>
    </TD>
  </TR>
  <TR>
    <TD WIDTH="106" ALIGN="CENTER"><FONT FACE="Courier New">
    <A HREF="meetthephunmen.htm">Back to:<BR>
    Meet the Phunmen</A></FONT>
    </TD>
  </TR>
  <TR>
    <TD WIDTH="106"></TD>
  </TR>
  <TR>
    <TD WIDTH="106"></TD>
    <TD WIDTH="534"><HR>
    <P>Ph&uuml;nmen &copy; Bezanis 1997 and Patent pending!</P>
    </TD>
  </TR>
</TABLE>
```

**Figure 4.11** Table-driven aliens for sale.

**NOTE**
I suggest reading the HTML technical report on HTML 4.0, which you can find at
www.w3.org/TR/REC-html40/ under the W3C library at www.w3.org/TR.

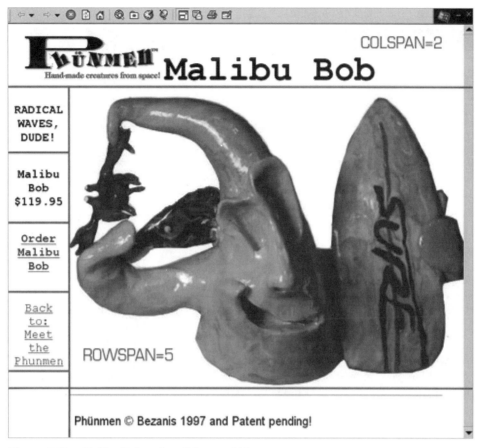

**Figure 4.12**  Malibu Bob pulls a fish out of his ear.

**Table 4.9**  Table Attributes

| TABLE ATTRIBUTES | COMMENTS | PARAMETERS |
|---|---|---|
| ALIGN= | Controls alignment of contents of table. | "left, right, center, justify" |
| BGCOLOR= | Sets background color for the whole table. | See color guide |
| BORDER= | Sets a border for your table and its cells, which is created by the browser. | # of pixels; "0" removes any border |
| BORDERCOLOR= | Sets color for the border around the table. | See color guide |
| CELLSPACING= | Sets spacing between cells (outside of cells) | # of pixels |
| CELLPADDING= | Sets padding around the content of each cell (this is still within the cell). | # of pixels |
| WIDTH= | Sets width for the table. | # of pixels or percent |

**Table 4.10** Individual Cell Attributes

| CELL ATTRIBUTES | COMMENTS | PARAMETERS |
|---|---|---|
| ALIGN= | Controls alignment of contents of cell. | "left, right, center, justify" |
| BGCOLOR= | Sets background color for the cell. | See color guide |
| COLSPAN= | Spreads cell over multiple columns. | # of columns |
| ROWSPAN= | Spreads cell over multiple rows. | # of rows |
| VALIGN= | Sets vertical alignment, best for scrunching content to one end of the cell, especially the top. | TOP, MIDDLE, BOTTOM |

## Fonts in HTML

The FONT tag in HTML is a simple but powerful tag with only three attributes, as shown in Table 4.11.

With the FACE attribute we have the freedom to specify any font, but we are constantly warned in Web design classes that we have to use the lowest common denominator because not everyone has every font. The only thing you can be certain of is that everybody has Arial, Courier, and Times on the PC, and Helvetica, Courier, and Times on the Mac. So our freedom is sacrificed for compatibility. Dynamic HTML has an answer for this which we'll discuss later in Chapter 5.

The FACE attribute can take one or more fonts in a list and it will apply the first legitimate font found; for example:

```
FONT FACE=Glacier,Arial,Helvetica,"Sans Serif".
```

This last typeface is a last resort that offers a choice of serif or sans serif and instructs the browser to pick the default typeface of that category. If the name of a typeface is more than one word, you must put it in quotes so the browser can parse the font name properly.

The SIZE attribute gives the option of setting the font size based on the 1 through 7 default browser determined sizes. You have seen this earlier as +4 (which means 4 sizes bigger than before). You can choose +1, 1, or –1, which will increase, set at, or decrease the font size to the specified size index 1 through 7.

**Table 4.11** Font Attributes

| FONT ATTRIBUTE | DESCRIPTION | PARAMETERS |
|---|---|---|
| COLOR= | Sets font color | See color guide |
| FACE= | Sets font face | Any *available* font |
| SIZE= | Sets font size | +n, n, -n (where n=1 through 7) |

## Images in HTML

The IMG tag has three important attributes, which are listed in Table 4.12:

- SRC=*"image file url"* gives the image filename and location.
- The set of HEIGHT= and WIDTH= attributes specify the exact size of the image. If you omit these while in a table, the image may not display the way you want it to. If these do not match the exact image size, the image will be stretched or compressed to fit.
- ALT= specifies a string of text to display in place of the image while it is loading, if it cannot be found, or when a low-bandwidth turkey has turned off image display in his or her browser.

## TIP

**If you want to put a comment in HTML, frame it with <!-- and --> and the browser will ignore it.**

```
<!-- Do not ever ever change these table cell sizes!!! -->
```

**These comments can span any number of lines.**

## Frames in HTML

If you think that you've never seen an HTML frame, you just don't know that you have. Frames divide the screen into sections, each one running off of a separate HTML

**Table 4.12**   IMG Attributes

| IMG ATTRIBUTE | DESCRIPTION | PARAMETERS |
|---|---|---|
| ALIGN= | Shifts the image left, right, or center. Tables should really be used to do this instead. | "left, right, center, justify" |
| ALT= | Specifies alternate text. Make this meaningful, please! | Anything at all |
| BORDER= | Sets border width. | # of pixels |
| HEIGHT= | Sets image height. | # of pixels |
| HSPACE= | Sets horizontal elbow room (whitespace to left and right of image). | # of pixels |
| SRC= | Image file path and name. | The image itself |
| VSPACE= | Sets vertical elbow room. (whitespace above and below image). | # of pixels |
| WIDTH= | Sets image width. | # of pixels |

## JPEG, GIF, AND ANIMATED GIF

Putting images on the Web can be a confusing task if you haven't figured out what these formats mean and what they're good for.

JPEG means Joint Photographic Experts Group and is a format that is better suited to photographs. JPEG provides for variable image compression, which trades decreasing image quality for decreasing file size. This means you can take an image and make it very small.

Making an image very small, however, sacrifices a lot of the image quality. The good news for Web designers is that the quality you get with a really small JPEG image is still good enough for Web graphics. We're not creating 1200 dpi images for magazine quality printing. In fact, the image resolution for the Internet is only 72 dpi.

Adobe Photoshop allows you to set the image compression on a JPEG file at a value from 0 to 10 when it is saved as shown in Figure 4.13. Not all programs let you do this. Some give a three-value choice of low, medium, or high. Some don't ask at all. Graphics Workshop for Windows, a shareware graphics conversion program I use a lot, allows you to set JPEG quality from 1 to 100. Check out this program at www.mindworkshop.com.

GIF stands for Graphics Interchange Format. A GIF file can have an background that is transparent, meaning you can have images that block out only their outline and not just the usual square box. GIF is best used for nonphotographic artwork and does not offer any compression options like JPEG does. Plain GIF format images download from the top down at full quality. You can also save files in interlaced format to have the effect of increasing image quality as the download continues, which I prefer to see when I'm Web surfing.

Animated GIFs simply take a series of GIF images and string them together in a format that will display each image for a certain time period and then move on to the next one. Alchemy Mindworks also makes GIF Construction Set for Windows (which I also use a lot) that allows you to create animated GIFs down to the millisecond delay.

Note: GIF89a is a GIF format that allows one color to be specified as *transparent*, for purposes of hiding the background and so your image is not always square. You can't put these into an animated GIF because they may not all have the same color specified as transparent. You can, however, make the animated GIF into a GIF89a by specifying a transparent color after building the animation, if you have a program that allows you to do so.

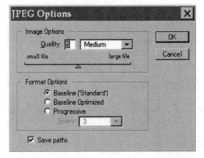

**Figure 4.13**   Adobe JPEG compression options.

document. This can be useful for maintaining consistency of a sidebar menu display or a top or bottom line banner section. There are a lot of interesting ways frames can be used; however, frames will keep search engines from finding anything on your site. To find out why, go to a site with frames and view the source. (View menu, display source). You will see about five lines of code that do nothing but declare the frame element and reference the Web page containing the frame markup.

You can directly type any frame page filename into the location bar on your Web browser and have it come up as an entire page on its own. View the source and you'll find all the content that has been hiding in the anonymous frame.

The following is a example of the entire body of a homepage created with frames. Where's the content?

```
<FRAMESET COLS="22%,78%">
<FRAME SRC="frameleft.html" NAME="frameleft" SCROLLING=YES>
<FRAME SRC="frameright.html" NAME="frameright" SCROLLING=YES>
</FRAMESET>
```

## Forms in HTML

Forms are important and are big business. After all, anything useful we do on the Internet, especially when it comes to searching and spending money, requires that a form be filled out and posted.

The FORM tag has two essential elements: ACTION gives the name of the script the data is to be sent to for processing, and METHOD gives how it is to be sent, which is the difficult part of the form.

The following is the skeleton of the form used at www.prolotherapy.com to send the results of a book and video order form to my order e-mailbox. This would be a minimal use of FORM that would send an empty result.

```
<FORM ACTION="cgi-bin/fmail.pl" METHOD="POST">
<INPUT TYPE="SUBMIT" NAME="Submit1">
<INPUT TYPE="RESET" NAME="Reset1">
</FORM>
```

These two specific INPUT TYPE statements use the HTML keywords SUBMIT and RESET, both of which create default buttons on the screen. The RESET button clears the form and starts again at the top. The SUBMIT button wraps up the content (assuming there was any) and sends it to a PERL script called fmail.pl, which is of course in my site's cgi-bin directory. I don't have to do anything more with HTML to make that happen.

There are two options to the METHOD tag: GET and POST, both of which send data, which makes GET a little confusing at first. GET sends the data the way you see search engines work. If you do a view source on the Yahoo! homepage you will find the lines (not quite next to each other):

```
<form action="http://search.yahoo.com/bin/search">
<input size=30 name=p> <input type=submit value=Search>
```

The *search!* button is really a SUBMIT button labeled "Search." A search engine query submitted for "Joe Satriani" will send the following line to the search engine, which also displays in your locator window:

```
http://search.yahoo.com/bin/search?p=Joe+Satriani
```

As you can see, the GET method took the ACTION URL and added a "?", the input line name "p=", and the search text entries on the end separated by a "+". This is exactly what is submitted to the search engine to get your results and it is up to the receiving program to figure out what to do with this information.

GET is the simpler method of form data transmission. POST is a little more complicated, so first let's take a look at more of the options we have available with the FORM tag. The GET and POST tags will both have their workings laid wide open in Chapter 9, "Perl & CGI."

We'll discuss the following tags:

- INPUT
- TEXTAREA
- SELECT

The INPUT tag creates boxes for input. There are several types of input we can ask for.

TYPE = HIDDEN input is information we want sent along with the form that the user does not see or enter. This can be anything we want and may mean something to us or to the processing script.

The following example form (from the entry form mentioned earlier) gives three hidden elements: the e-mail address to where the script is to send the form data after processing, the subject that shows up on our e-mail subject line, and the Web page to link to after the data is processed (in this case, a thank-you-for-your-order notice).

```
<INPUT TYPE="hidden" NAME="recipient" VALUE="Websales@prolotherapy.com">
<INPUT TYPE="hidden" NAME="subject" VALUE="Prolotherapy book order">
<INPUT TYPE="hidden" NAME="thankurl"
VALUE="http://www.prolotherapy.com/prolothanks.htm">
```

It is the NAME and VALUE field pairs that are sent to the script. This information is not in a friendly human-readable format and looks more like the GET submission without the URL. It is up to the script to format this information in an e-mail-friendly format.

TYPE = TEXT input creates the simple visible input text box. Instead of a VALUE attribute, these boxes have a SIZE. The text input is not limited to this many characters, this just creates a box big enough to show that many. Again, a set of NAME and VALUE pairs are sent to the script from each text box.

```
Name             <INPUT TYPE="TEXT" NAME="name" SIZE="40">
Address          <INPUT TYPE="TEXT" NAME="address" SIZE="40">
City, State, Zip <INPUT TYPE="TEXT" NAME="citystzip" SIZE="40">
e-mail address   <INPUT TYPE="TEXT" NAME="username" SIZE="40">
Telephone number <INPUT TYPE="TEXT" NAME="phonenumber" SIZE="12">
```

The use of *username* as the e-mail address is one standard that has emerged. Most scripts I know of will take this and put it in the from category in the e-mail, so you have somewhere to reply to. If this is not specified, you may get an e-mail from, literally, No-Email-Given@nowhere.none, and you won't know who sent it.

TYPE = PASSWORD input works the same way as TYPE = TEXT, indicating only stars to the user (but the script sees all).

TYPE = RADIO input creates a bullet selection. These have an additional attribute called CHECKED and if present, this is the radio button that starts out selected. The user can only pick one with the same NAME, and that one will have the VALUE assigned to the NAME and sent.

```
Credit card type
<INPUT TYPE="RADIO" NAME="creditcard" VALUE="visa" CHECKED>Visa
<INPUT TYPE="RADIO" NAME="creditcard" VALUE="mastercard">Mastercard
<INPUT TYPE="RADIO" NAME="creditcard" VALUE="amex">American Express
```

TYPE = CHECKBOX input creates a little box to check. In this case, the VALUE represents the data that will be sent if the box is checked. Unchecked boxes will not have a NAME/VALUE pair sent. Like the radio button, several checkboxes can have the same name, in which case multiple pairs with the same name will be sent. If you don't specify any value for the box you will receive "on" as the default.

The TEXTAREA tag gives a two-dimensional area for text entry and has none of the preceding special options. It has the necessary NAME attribute and ROWS= and COLS=, which specify the dimensions of the box in character units.

The SELECT tag creates a static or pull-down list of multiple items from which the user can select one or more. This is a pair tag with starting and ending elements.

The starting tag attributes are NAME, SIZE, and MULTIPLE. SIZE gives the number of rows to show, not the number of rows allowed. You can have any number of rows and if they exceed the SIZE, the list becomes a pull-down list (for a size of 1) or scrolling list (for a size > 1). The MULTIPLE tag allows the user to select more than one option, but will not work for a pull-down menu.

For each selection in the list we have the OPTION tag. This tag will also have the SELECTED attribute stated if the page is to load with that option selected as a default. The following example will give us a pull-down menu of any number of Phunmen.

```
<SELECT NAME="phunmen" SIZE=1>
<OPTION>Boris
<OPTION>Malibu Bob
<OPTION>Mr. Bigwig
more options go here
</SELECT>
```

## NOTE

**Use tables to format forms! This makes it easy to give the form a uniform and even look with rows and columns matched and lined up.**

Figure 4.14 is the result of the prolotherapy.com order form with tables, entry boxes, and all elements in place.

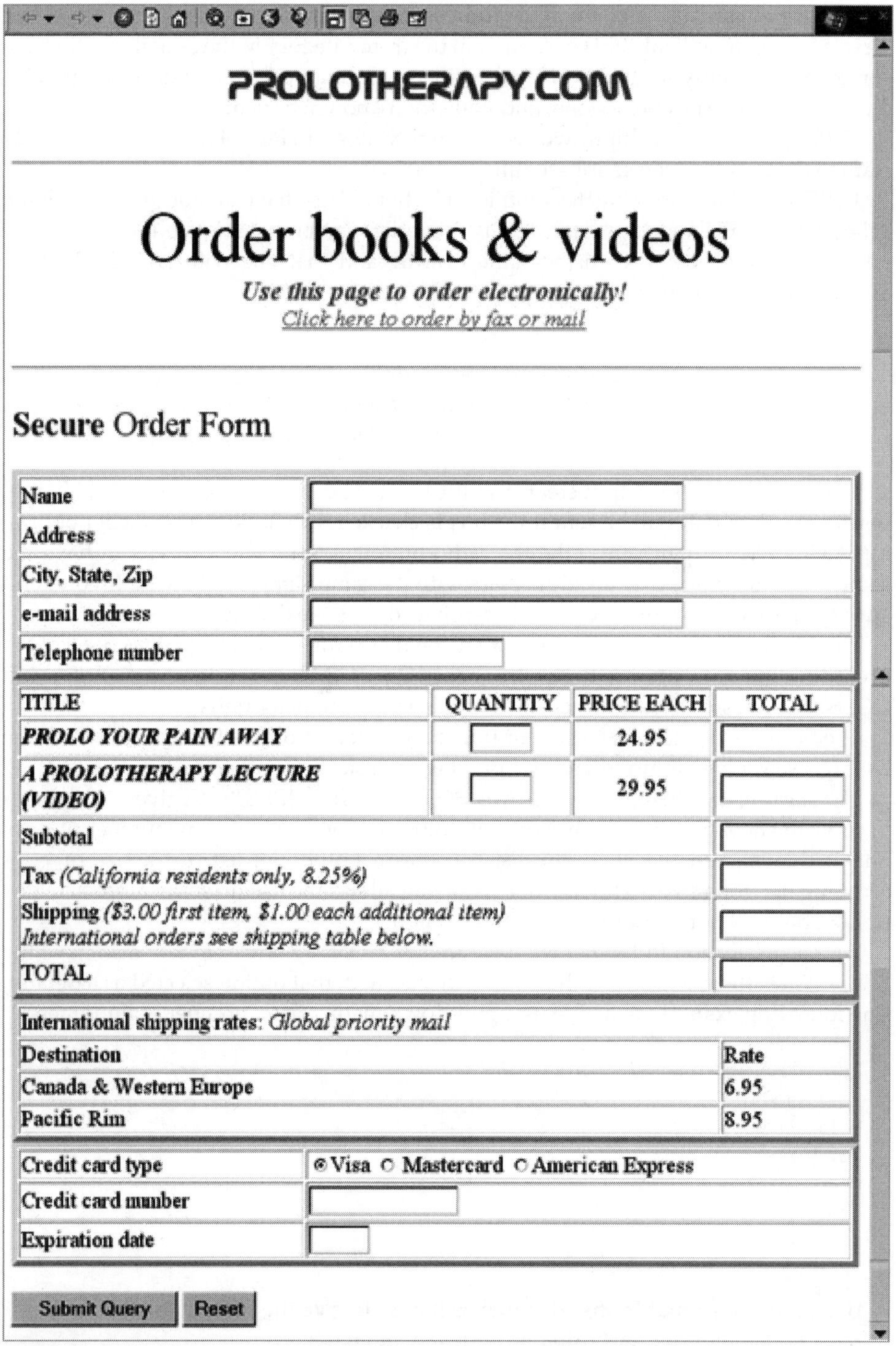

# PROLOTHERAPY.COM

# Order books & videos
*Use this page to order electronically!*
*Click here to order by fax or mail*

## Secure Order Form

| Name | |
| --- | --- |
| Address | |
| City, State, Zip | |
| e-mail address | |
| Telephone number | |

| TITLE | QUANTITY | PRICE EACH | TOTAL |
| --- | --- | --- | --- |
| *PROLO YOUR PAIN AWAY* | | 24.95 | |
| *A PROLOTHERAPY LECTURE (VIDEO)* | | 29.95 | |
| Subtotal | | | |
| Tax *(California residents only, 8.25%)* | | | |
| Shipping *($3.00 first item, $1.00 each additional item)* *International orders see shipping table below.* | | | |
| TOTAL | | | |

| International shipping rates: *Global priority mail* | |
| --- | --- |
| Destination | Rate |
| Canada & Western Europe | 6.95 |
| Pacific Rim | 8.95 |

| Credit card type | ⦿ Visa ○ Mastercard ○ American Express |
| --- | --- |
| Credit card number | |
| Expiration date | |

[ Submit Query ]  [ Reset ]

**Figure 4.14**   An order form in working order.

You can see that the first five lines are standard TYPE = TEXT boxes, the credit card selection gives a radio button selection, and the SUBMIT and RESET buttons are last.

Figure 4.15 illustrates the result this form would give if it were it filled out and posted by our late president Franklin Roosevelt. The e-mail header contains hidden fields from the form, such as the subject. The original e-mail was sent to Websales@ prolotherapy.com, which is set up to auto-forward the e-mail to the order desk and the sender's e-mail address is taken from the *username* entered.

Then the name and value pairs are sent along, some are empty, finalized by the SUBMIT value.

```
Sender: Websales@prolotherapy.com
Date: Mon, 8 Jun 1943 16:47:37 -0400
Message-Id: <194306082047.QAA09348@cintronics.com>
From: frankr@whitehouse.gov
Reply-To: frankr@whitehouse.gov
To: orderdesk@prolotherapy.com
Subject: Prolotherapy book order

Below is the information submitted on Jun-8-43 16:47 EST
------------------------------------------------------------

name:  Franklin Roosevelt
address:  1600 Pennsylvania Ave
citystzip:  Washington, DC 20001
username:  frankr@whitehouse.gov
phonenumber:  202 467-5200
hauserqty:  1
hausertotal:  24.95
videoqty:
videototal:
subtotal:  24.95
tax:
shipping:  3.00
total:  27.95
creditcard:  visa
ccnumber:  1234123412341234
ccdate:  3/44
Submit1:  Submit Query
```

**Figure 4.15**    Posted form received in the mail.

### Adam Denning, Microsoft

Adam is a very nice British guy who works in one of the leading-edge areas of Microsoft, XML technologies. Adam is also a really really busy guy, so I was lucky to get an hour in his schedule (every now and then during the interview his e-mail notification would go off, giving a pleasant-sounding "bing").

After we met, Adam took me for a coffee at the Starbucks station inside one of the vast Microsoft cafeterias, teeming with employees slightly after 1 P.M. The attendant made me a top-quality cappuccino while Adam and I got to talking about the interview. Then he paid for the coffee with one wave of the hand using his Microsoft ID card like a Mobil speedpass and we returned to his office through the maze of security doors through which we had come. I don't personally know what it's like to work at Microsoft, but it seems they provide a great deal of services to their employees.

Adam is also a very fast talker, so this interview reads about double the length of others! (Look out, I'm becoming British! Wouldn't an American have said, "twice the size?") Some of the stuff we talk about here refers to technologies studied in future chapters, so you may want to come back later and read this again!

*So Adam, I know that you're involved with XML. I really don't know any more than that!*

I'm the group program manager of the team responsible for delivering something called MSXML, which is a DLL [Dynamic Linked Library, a .DLL file is full of subroutines/methods that can be called by another program, such as the IE5 browser in this case] that ships currently inside IE5, and we will feature inside new versions of the operating system, which provides a lot of basic XML functionality. So it provides parsing, for example, it provides object model, and it provides all the other facilities that we believe are essential as the basic infrastructure of XML. It's the first step along a path. Well, it's the second step along the path because in IE4 the very first steps were laid out by providing very simple parsing. In IE5 we've done a lot of extensions and the raw capacity that we didn't have before is now there, and to some extent this will work on the server, too. The next step forward is to fulfill the vision of what XML is.

*I know that IE4 has some kind of XML capability, and I can see that IE5 probably has a lot more XML in it, but since there isn't any real XML on the Web except as a curiosity, where are things really at right now?*

Where they're at right now is that people are interested in understanding what XML gives them. They're all over the work, but nobody's really sure yet what it means to them. So we try to clarify that. We have our own particular vision of what XML is. So when XML was first created it was seen as a way of marking up documents, seen as a way of simplifying SGML so that people could understand what a document's semantics were. So they could say who the author was, where it was written, about whom the document relates, and all stuff like that, information about, and what not. And that's certainly plausible, we can certainly do that, but that's a relatively subset interest, in fact. If you think about a document, what is a document with markup? It's unstructured data. It contains random data marked up in a random way with no structure applied to it. What does a database give you? A database gives you structured records. There is therefore a continuum all the way from unstructured documents all the way through structured records, which people will want to represent data in. They are already constraining themselves either to the fully structured or fully unstructured because there is no good means to describe information in any other way. What XML does, though, is it allows you to now think of data in the way that it should truly be represented rather than in the way that you have constrained it to be represented. (bing) So rather than being forced into rows you can now begin to have hierarchies as you see fit. You have those hierarchies being sparse and irregular, which is how real data actually is. So now you can begin to represent information and move information in the way that it actually exists in a person's mind or on a machine, or how it should exist.

*That was one of the first things I saw when I learned about XML at Web98. It was being explained and I said, "what you're really talking about is a database communication system or something." And of course to them it was obvious, like, yeah, so what else is new? But it's surprising for some people. So what does Microsoft want to do with XML?*
What we want to do is allow it to be used to represent data that are used where they are accompanied by why their use is important, to allow the data to be moved from server to middle tier to client [a tier is a server between the client and the server that the client is ultimately connected to as in a large corporate intranet] as appropriate, to have transformations performed upon it, to display it when appropriate, to do whatever you choose to do with it and then send back the changes that you made.

So to make it, as you say, the database for the Web, is . . . I think of your typical application that uses data. It speaks to a database, gets information, displays it in a form, allows you to change it and sends it back again. That now moves on to the point where you can do that across multiple tiers and so forth. But they still typically rely upon permanent connections between machines. The Web clearly changes a lot of that, because now ephemeral [short-lived] connections between two machines is also the idea, meaning that in fact some of these things may not happen now, they may happen the next time you connect. So then what XML allows you to do is effectively begin to treat information as being something that is ultimately sent to be stored somewhere, but nevertheless can be manipulated easily and uniformly at any part of the cycle that you choose to, and then be batched up as necessary for whatever applications you have.

*Is the intention to replace, like, current object-oriented serialization of data or is it just supplemented? [Serialization means to save or transmit the current state of an object, meaning the contents of its properties and data space, as a stream of data that can be used to reconstruct it at a later time or at the other end of the communication line. This is discussed later on.]*
I would say supplemented. Replacement's an interesting word because I think a lot of people still need traditional ways of positioning objects. So what does XML give you that you don't already have? It allows you in fact to do something more interesting. Supposing you were to (bing) define an object which persisted itself as XML. And then the receiver of this object in traditional systems . . .

*By persisted you mean?*
Saves its state. Serializes.

*So you're saying it's always there as XML, or it communicates itself as XML?*
Either of those. Either of those is fine.

*So the word persisted, I've heard that in relation to database stuff and I don't know really what it's supposed to mean.*
It's a very good phrase, because it's used for everything. In the database sense it means that information is stored and can then be retrieved. In the object sense it means that the current state of an object is converted into some data format which is then parsed into something else which can understand it. Typically the thing which understands it is a mirror copy of the object which created it. So, therefore, a persistent format for an object needs to be enough information to allow something else to recreate the sense that the object first had. Doesn't have to be the same object, could be another object that understands the semantics of the original object, so that it can recreate the appropriate stuff, but without having to have the exact same code base, which is a very useful thing in the Web system.

*So you're saying the idea of XML is to use it as a tool?*
That's one of the uses, it's not the only use by any means. We see the corporate world, or the world in general as wanting to take information from a number of disparate sources. So let's imagine we are making and selling cars, for example, and we have a number of suppliers of parts for our cars, like engines and transmissions and whatever else. And we have database on each of these company's products, and they're all in different formats defined by these vendors. (bing) So let's collect information from each of these places and tie that together in some meaningful way and then send it to people who then decide which parts to order or which parts to incorporate. So it might even be something where you have different suppliers for the same thing.

It's a very common requirement to take data in different formats from different places, and produce a format which is effectively a logical view over that, so it's the view that you or your application wants rather than that which the vendors provide, and then allow you to use that as the medium of transmission between yourself, and the middle tier, and the clients that you have whatever they intend to do with the data. So in some respects it's like a hallucination. It's like if you want data, where the data is actually persisted elsewhere, so it's a logical view over the data rather than being the data itself. Each little part of it comes from different places. So this is what XML is good for, it can represent anything you choose to represent. It's very flexible. It also has the virtue that it's extensible so if you wanted to, say you already agreed with this person that the format of the data was right in that way and then there's somebody else who now says, "I want exactly the same stuff but I want you to tell me a little bit more," or "I want to augment it in some way," you can do that. You can add new fields, you can add whatever you choose to add without breaking the representations you already have.

*So you see XML being more of a communications tool than a storage tool?*
Right now. I think that in the future it may become storage. That's an interesting question, because what are the requirements of storage? The first is efficient storage. The second is efficient query. And the third is efficient and transactionable updates. [A transaction is a communication cycle for data updates that involves fail-safe processing to ensure its completion.] All of those problems are very hard for what is essentially a text-based format.

*In a traditional database the data purpose and properties are defined separately from the data itself, but in XML that's no longer true, right?*
Partially true. I think the main issue with storage is that just like with object-oriented storage the problem you get in to is that it's very easy to optimize a regular relational database with regular relational data. But when the data starts getting irregular, how do you create an index, for example? How do you easily identify something you need to update? I'm not a database expert but already I can see that there's problems there for storing XML in a way that would then be equivalent to SQL [System Query Language, a standardized database access language]. So I think that's somewhere else. I think that someday that probably will happen but it isn't this year's goal or even next year's goal.

*But what's the idea with IE5, what applications do we see out there in the near future?*
What IE5 does is it lets you do a lot of the things that we've already espoused XMLs virtues for, in a way that a lot of this part of the story [talking about the car supplier example] now can be realized. So we provide ways of receiving XML, parsing it therefore rephrasing it through the object model, to some extent querying it; you can transform it, you can change it from the way it is to the way you want it to be. One thing you want to use that for, for example, is to display it, so you can transform it from XML into HTML, for example.

*Does IE5 support XSSL [XML Style Sheet Language]?*
It does.

*So you could receive a fully marked-up XML document and you really wouldn't be able to tell the difference if you didn't know it was XML?*
From the browser point of view, yes. So there, for example, is IE5 showing two pieces of information, but if we look at the source for that, it is in fact XML. [Adam shows me that the page currently displaying on his workstation has XML source]. So, as you can see, you can manipulate it in any way.

*XML almost seems simpler than HTML.*
Yes, because it separates data from content. That's the whole key thing, really. I mean, what you saw in the XML file is purely content. There is nothing in there at all telling you about how to present this. Then when you go to the XSSL, this is actually an XSSL document but it contains a lot of HTML.

*I know that I heard something about how the browser takes XML and actually internally converts it to Dynamic HTML.*
That is an implementation we've done, yes it does do that because the browser itself only understands HTML.

*Is that the way IE5 is done then?*
Yes. We do actually convert.

*Is there a future for Dynamic XML, too?*
That's an interesting question. Dynamic XML implies that there are suddenly semantics to XML that don't currently exist. So that means that somebody somewhere would have to define and get agreed upon a set of standards on how you're going to include script, for example, in XML. There's no XML script type as there is an HTML script type. The whole

dynamism of Dynamic HTML is performed through script. So I don't know the answer to that question, I really don't. I think the future holds something unknown to virtually everybody and we will program off in different directions and see what takes.

*I'm sure this stuff is where broadcasting was in 1925. No moving pictures.*
I think that's probably true. Of course you must bear in mind the British had been transmitting radio for three years at that point. [Adam now shows me more stuff on his workstation and returns to the car supplier example]. So we have these groups of companies, or people, etc., who want some root information. We already know there are standards for UI, the user interface, as HTML, so we're happy with that, so why should we change that? There is a standard way of actually accessing data, which is to use the URL, but there's no definition for how it comes back to you. Right now it comes back to you as HTML, which is fundamentally useless. It means you've got to go and try to find the information, and if they change the page you've got to change your code. So that's what we want to achieve where XML becomes the standard for data and HTML is the standard for display.

*Basically a browser standard for data handling?*
Right, not just browsers though, because it's also interesting to consider people being sent XML from a large database. Right now that involves conversion from record set format into XML, for example, but it's nevertheless plausible. They're collecting that information, doing whatever they want to do with it, and shipping off bits as appropriate to other people. So it isn't just for those people who are using a browser to see data as you return it, but also for those people who want to retrieve information in any other way. So we're trying to say that it's the universal data format. It's key also that there are two things about that. That means it's data itself, so it is purchase orders, or whatever it happens to be. It's also information about Websites. Now Website is a bad term. People think of Websites as providers of pages.

*It's starting to become an inadequate term.*
Yes. We would really like people to start thinking of their Websites, or whatever you want to call it, as providers of information.

*Because when I keep saying "Web page," it's like, well, that's not what I want to say. It's variable, sometimes it's active, stuff like that.*
Right, exactly. Web page is no longer an appropriate term. It's information that may or may not end up being displayed. So what I'm saying here is I'm trying to define the relationship between XML and HTML. We don't believe that one replaces the other. We believe that one is about display, one is about data.

*Sure, but if you use XML with style sheets, who needs HTML, except maybe for some tables or something?*
Well, there are things that you can't really easily do with XML and style sheets, like what happens if the information is just displayed, it doesn't have any content that you'd want to save.

*That's true, there is some HTML you need, but a lot of it, about half of it, could be tossed.*
That's possibly true. It depends on where the world wants to go with that. If you look at the XSL [meaning the style sheet; Adam's reaching, this is a term that has no acronym yet], there clearly includes a lot of HTML in this case to produce HTML's output.

*Well, there you go, maybe HTML will end up in the style sheet, maybe that's the best place for it.*
So I described this before. XML's purpose in life is to represent data. And because it's text-based format it's totally flexible, you can represent data all the way from structured to unstructured and there is a continuum all the way through. Can I talk briefly about DTDs?

*Yeah, I talk about them, too.*
The main thing I'm saying about DTDs is what they allow you to do is to define the structure of the document. But they are in a somewhat arcane language. They are not extensible. There are some restrictions on what you can represent with a DTD. Therefore the W3C's looking to, replace is a bad word, looking to augment DTDs with a new thing called XML schema, which is the idea of containing the same information a DTD would hold but in XML itself.

*It seems everything in the DTD boils down to text, so it seems it should be more than that.*
Absolutely. In fact, as of today . . . [Adam shows me the XML document object model].

*Oh, wonderful, another document object model!*
Well, that's now become a recommendation, so that moves up to recommendation as of today. It's the same one as the HTML one, essentially, give or take. The paper defines both. The thing that's now a recommendation defines both. And the low level, the level 1 I think we call it, or the core, that is effectively the same. So there are some little extra bits of HTML.

*Do you work with any developers who are developing some kind of XML applications?*
There are a whole bunch of people doing XML work inside Microsoft. Outside Microsoft we do have quite a few large companies.

*Is there really any XML out on the Web yet?*
There's a little bit here and there, but this is used actually for other purposes. This is used for two technologies here. CDF and OSD [see below]. CDF is Channel Description Format, which is an XML grammar that lets you define when a Website should be updated by the client, so for offline browsing and so forth.

*Is that about IE4 channels? Is that what we're talking about?*
Yes. Open Software Distribution is something that we did in connection with a couple of other companies. It was destined to become a big thing and I don't know what's happened to it recently, but essentially what that allows you to do is to define how and when to upgrade the software on your system. So if you went to download, for example, Excel from the Web, what this would do is say, "go to this Website automatically behind the scenes and check it out and if there's a download this is what you have to do, follow these steps." So it's a great way of making a whole company have the same version of software, for example. It's only used in relatively small ways right now.

*What might the developers be thinking? To me it seems like XML will eventually replace HTML, for the most part, with the exception of page structuring rather than display. The style sheet will take over what it looks like. The HTML is for where it goes and how it flows, and the XML is really all the information itself. It seems like XML*

*will take over 80 percent of the structure of HTML, and at this point you could see
everything being done on the Web in XML, with style sheets and a little markup and
in fact being used to store a great deal of smaller databases. These days, if you have
a file that's less than a megabyte, it could be read in and analyzed in half a second,
so it's like you don't need a relational database for something that size. So for other
than larger databases you could use XML to store Word documents, to store Internet
information, to store anything the average user would have.*

It's entirely plausible, yes. We can't dictate what happens, we can only point people in
paths and they choose to follow these paths or not. I think everything that we've said are
all perfectly plausible, so all we can do is put things out there to enable people to do
things and see which ones they adopt and then focus on those.

*Microsoft's always been in the position of being the 800-pound gorilla who can say,
you put the product out and if people like it they use it and if they don't they won't
but there are certainly no barriers to putting it out there. So I'm trying to see, what's
the idea?*

I do believe that representation of data is the most important use for XML, and therefore
that does imply that you will separate the data from the implementation. That implies
that the user interface is going to be built up rather than being static. So the XML doesn't
contain presentation information that you can refer to. How the results are represented is
not dramatically important, really. Maybe that it can be presented. I do believe it's very
important that you can change the way it's presented.

If I just have a plain XML file, which doesn't contain any reference to a style sheet,
then what you see is the data. You can apply a CSS to that and change some things in
certain ways but you couldn't fundamentally change the structure of what you get versus
what you see; they are the same. What XSL does, on the other hand, is it allows you to
change the structure. So that if the XML data you receive has to be translated into
something (bing) before you display it, then you obviously have a lot more flexibility. You
can change entirely the way that it looks compared to how you receive it, so you have a
lot of flexibility as far as structure goes. A simple example of that would be if you were,
for example, selling stock then you might want to see less of the information that would
be sent to you than if you were a broker. So you would have different style sheets for
different people.

*How did you come to be in this position?*

I've been at Microsoft for 6 1/2 years, and I've done a few different things.

*So 6 1/2 years ago Microsoft was in a position of what, just releasing Windows 3.1,
no Internet?*

No Internet. The world had not heard of it, well many parts of the world had heard of the
Internet but not many people. I actually joined first as, Microsoft has a division called
Microsoft Consulting Services, whose purpose in life is to go and help major clients
implement Microsoft technologies, and I joined that first of all. I was there for a couple of
years and then I came to Redmond. I was in the U.K. [United Kingdom] first. When I first
came here I was program manager for MFC [Microsoft Foundation Classes] in the C++
group. Then that led to various things like OLE [Object Linking and Embedding] controls,
which are now ActiveX controls. It led to something called ATL which is a programming
library for C++ developers to create COM [Component Object Model] objects and various

other bits and pieces. And after a lot of work, I was probably there for 18 months to two years, we began to focus in the C++ team more and more on the enterprise, what it meant if somebody who wants to build enterprise applications in C++, what did we need to give them as opposed to the traditional customer in C++ who was the independent software vendor. And so we began to think about that and we actually finally released the Visual C++ product for the enterprise, which contained some of the things that we believed enterprises would need. And that's developed further since I left. But I then moved over to work on the IE team, and my job was basically to make everybody want to use DHTML.

*Was that a decision you made or did you just end up there?*
That was a decision I made. I was bored of being on the C++ team. I was more interested in Dynamic HTML, I thought it was the cutting edge, so I moved to that. I was there for a little while and then I decided what we really needed to do, I worked with another person, was focus on letting people debug their browser-based applications. So we wrote a script debugger for IE to use IE to develop applications using script and still be able to debug them and therefore make the development environment more pleasant.

*Is that the product that is being released now?*
We released it about a year ago, same time as IE4 pretty much.

*I talked to someone else at Microsoft the other day and he said they were releasing this big new improved script debugger.*
Oh, in Visual InterDev. They've taken what we did and made it radically better. So we just kind of got the idea out and got it happening and other people took it on and did the work. So after that was done, that was in September of last year, I was thinking about what happens next, and there's a guy named Adam Bosworth who works at Microsoft, very influential person, knows a lot of stuff, he's always having radical ideas. And one of his radical ideas was that XML was going to be important. So he decided that he wanted to create a team that developed the basic fundamentals of what's required to use XML, and he asked me to join him and so I did. And so I'm here. And XML has indeed become the big think he predicted it would and so I was very glad to be involved.

*Sure, it's just getting started really. One idea I had a while ago was about search engines. The task of indexing is left entirely up to the search engine. The information that the user provides is unreliable and completely unstructured. Do you see XML figuring in there somewhere? I was thinking of adding search engine tags to the language.*
I'm sure it could. I'm not involved in the search engine work at all, but it's very, very logical that it should.

*So coming from a pretty solid Dynamic HTML background, what do you see for XML?*
The first thing I want to do is make sure that what we perceive as the vision for XML is the correct one. If it is the correct one, then some of these things will have to happen. If it isn't the correct one, then we'll have to think, what is? So I could imagine people defining how script fits into XML and therefore you get a Dynamic XML kind of concept. There is as far as I know no work going on in that area right now in the W3C. I could be wrong but I don't believe there is.

*I suppose you could always form your own committee.*
We have to convince them it's worthwhile first.

*If we were to lean towards scripting in XML, and as a person who worked in the Dynamic HTML area in Microsoft, is there any leaning toward JavaScript or VBScript either way?*

That's the virtue of the architecture we have. We have this active scripting architecture that allows you to plug in any language you choose. It doesn't matter. We provide an object model and you can program it with anything from JavaScript to VBScript to Visual Basic to C++ to Java to PERL to Python to anything. We provide absolutely no barrier to any language, so we don't care what you use. We provide a set of interfaces to allow you to control us. (bing) Active scripting happened in IEEE and it's just developed since then.

*Is active scripting related to ActiveX scripting?*

Same thing.

*As a Microsoft employee, would you have any advice for anyone else who's thinking of working here?*

Be excited about what you do.

*Are there a lot of people who apply?*

We have a hard time finding people. We have to go overseas sometimes (chuckle).

*So Microsoft needs people?*

We have, I forgot exactly how many, it's about 2,500 vacancies.

*Really?*

I believe so. (bing)

*What do you see yourself doing a year from now?*

I was asked that question yesterday. I still don't know.

*How far in the future can you see? Six months?*

Three months. I know that in three months' time I'll still be doing what I'm doing, and my first goal in life is to ship Explorer 5. Once that's happened then I'll think about what happens next, but I do believe I would start thinking now about what we do next with XML.

*What exactly do you do?*

That's a very hard question. My role in life is to make sure that we're delivering the right XML components at the right time with the right quality through IE. And that everybody knows about what we're doing and why it's important and that we listen to customers.

*So you're a researcher?*

No, I'm responsible for making sure this product ships.

*How do you do that?*

By driving people.

*Do you whip programmers?*

Some of that! I try not to, I try to make people autonomous and a lot of people here, one of the key things about Microsoft is that people have pride in their work and want to do the necessary stuff.

*Do you test products? Do you test IE5?*
Sure, I use it every day. I build applications using technology that you could call ad hoc testing. XML applications, DHTML applications. And I present at PDCs (professional developers conferences), I explain our strategy to higher-level people, I talk to customers about what they want to do, and I manage people. Think of it as a software house inside Microsoft. Each product group is its own self-contained product, and self-contained company actually in which we have to define what we're doing, make people want it to be done, get it to happen, find somewhere to ship it, and do it. So that's what we do.

*So we'll be seeing your product in IE5. Is there a release date?*
First half of '99.

*Anything else we're going to see in IE5 that's dramatically new?*
Not that I can talk about!

*Thanks, Adam!*

# Summary

There is plenty more I could say about writing HTML, but without knowing how to write applets, scripts, and all the other Web technologies discussed later in the book it wouldn't be very helpful. We'll cross those bridges when we build them. In this chapter we've discussed what markup languages are about, why we need them and what they're good for, and learned how to write useful code in HTML. There is no substitute for experience so I urge you, if you do not have one, to go out and write yourself a homepage right now.

**CHAPTER**

**5**

# Dynamic HTML

Now that you know HTML, it's time to take a step up the ladder to Dynamic HTML. You've seen Web pages that move? This chapter is where you find out how to do that. By the end of this chapter you'll be able to create Web pages that move. You'll be able to write DHTML and create Web pages that interact with the user.

Dynamic HTML is not a new language, but a combination of languages and features that create an unprecedented synthesis of Web programming versatility. If that sounds like a mouthful, here is what Dynamic HTML is all about:

$$
\begin{array}{r}
\phantom{\times}\textit{HTML} \\
\times\ \textit{JavaScript} \\
\times\ \textit{Style Sheets} \\
\hline
\textit{Dynamic HTML}
\end{array}
$$

The key to Dynamic HTML is the word *Dynamic*.

## DEFINITION: DYNAMIC
**Force or energy in motion; has its roots in the Greek word for power.**

Dynamic HTML is a strong force hitting the Web. I've seen more books come out on DHTML since I started writing this one than in the entire previous history of the universe. This is a technology with a future, and a big one.

Up until now, Web pages have remained static, unchanging sites that many designers have tried to liven up by using animated GIFs, frames, and other reaches toward interactive content. Dynamic HTML brings dynamic content to the Web by giving you the capability to change the appearance and/or the content of a Web page interactively based on the viewer's actions.

We've already studied HTML, and the next chapter explores the full power of JavaScript. In this chapter we're going to take a thorough look at an enhancement to HTML called *style sheets* and get an introduction to JavaScript as it is used in DHTML. The key to making HTML dynamic is the style sheet.

# Style Sheets

Style sheets are an addition to HTML that allow you to separate display properties from structure. Although the structural elements of HTML are generic and not very descriptive, we can add a kind of descriptiveness in the way we use the style sheet.

The following code illustrates an outline of a simple style sheet.

```
<STYLE TYPE="style sheet type">
BODY {body display attributes}
P {P tag display attributes}
A {A tag display attributes}
</STYLE>
```

Although a style sheet should be valid if placed anywhere in the document, my Web editor says a style sheet will work only if placed between the HEAD and BODY sections of the page. This is because a style sheet is only effective if placed before the element to which it applies.

Style sheet elements are contained between the <STYLE></STYLE> tag set, and the STYLE tag has an attribute that declares the document as a certain type of style sheet. This example would be declared as a *cascading style sheet*, which is explained later in this chapter.

The body of the style sheet attaches specific display attributes to specific HTML tags. Although in this example we are saying that all P tags will have a specific display attribute, it is just as easy to create different sets of attributes for different P tags by assigning names to the P tags (or any tag).

We can pull all of the display properties out of the HTML code, such as FONT FACE, SIZE, COLOR, Bold, Underline, even BODY BACKGROUND and BGCOLOR. In short, any tag that describes the display properties of the page is moved to the style sheet.

Figure 5.1 illustrates the homepage for www.prolotherapy.com, which uses a style sheet. The background is white, the Prolotherapy.com text is purple, and the links are dark green. Through the use of JavaScript, when the user places the mouse over a link it changes to underlined purple. (The mouse is over the first link in this black-and-white screenshot.) The banner font is Times and the link font used is Eurostile, a unique sans serif font.

We're now going to change *only the style sheet*, not any of the content of the page, and see what we can do.

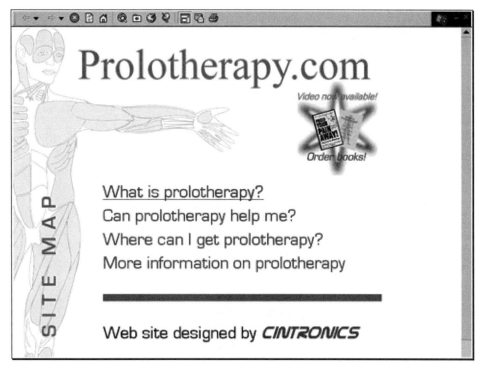

**Figure 5.1**  Markup, Prolotherapy style.

Although Figure 5.2 is shown in monochrome, the background is changed from white to pink, the banner and links have been changed to italicized Times, and the links are now in red. This may not be a drastic change in style, but now let's take a look at the third example.

In Figure 5.3 I've risked my reputation as an award-winning Web designer. I've changed the background image (this, too, is defined in the style sheet) to a repeating Leonardo da Vinci classic with a dark gray background color, leaving my text images barely readable. I've changed the banner font to PowerLine (in yellow) and the link font to white Keypunch with the selected link to underlined black. Finally, the bottom line is a combination of a pink "Site designed by" and light green "Cintronics" in Physics Alpha and Physics Beta, respectively. I realize that it's unlikely anyone would have these fonts on his or her computer, but Dynamic HTML has another promising feature called *dynamic fonts*, which we'll discuss later in this chapter.

## Cascading Style Sheets

In the case of cascading style sheets, the cascade involves multiple sets of style tags set up in a succession of stages where each stage accumulates from one to the next. The term *cascading* refers to the hierarchy of style attributes that are applied to an HTML tag.

Style definitions can actually be placed in three locations: inline styles, embedded styles sheet, and linked style sheet.

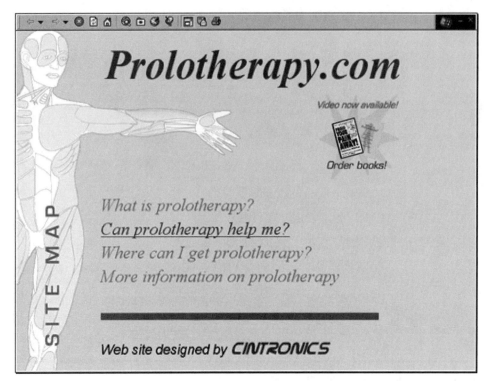

**Figure 5.2**   Variation on a theme.

Inline styles can be applied to individual tags in the BODY section of the page by using the STYLE= attribute within the tags themselves. Most HTML tags now accept this attribute. Even though this is not part of a separate style sheet, it is called a style sheet because it is done in style sheet fashion. For example:

## FONTS, STYLES, AND TYPOGRAPHICAL JARGON

The world of typography is now digital. A lot of this terminology comes from the old way of doing things. Today's electronically typeset newspapers seem miraculous compared to the way things used to be done.

The following is a list of typographical terms in order to help understand the language of layout:

**Basic Terms:**

**Typeface.** A design for a set of characters, such as Times Roman.

**Font.** Typeface + specific properties of the typeface such as size, slant, weight, pitch, etc., such as *12-pt bold italic Times Roman.*

**Font family.** Set of fonts composed of a typeface with various properties.

**Subordinate Terms:**

**Ascender.** The part of lowercase characters above the body, as in b, d, f, h, k, l, t.

**Baseline.** The line that could drawn along the base characters on a line (baseline).

**Descender.** The part of the character below the baseline, as in g, j, p, q, y.

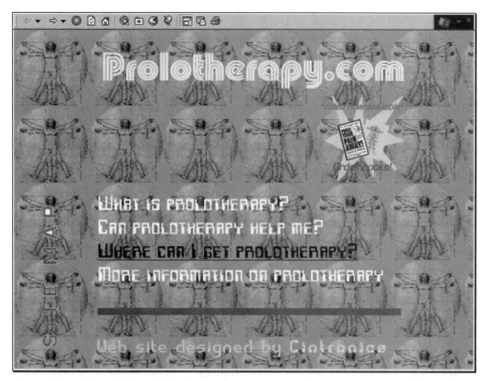

**Figure 5.3**   Style sheet run amok.

```
<P STYLE="font-size:18pt; font-style:Arial,Helvetica">Designed by</P>
```

An embedded style sheet is a set of styles enclosed by a set of STYLE tags. For example:

```
<STYLE>style sheet attributes</STYLE>
```

**Italic.** A slanted typeface (careful, don't say font!).

**Kerning.** Spacing between characters, also the act of adjusting that space.

**Leading (line spacing, pronounced "ledding").** The space between baselines, from the element lead. Blocks of mechanical type used to be cast from molten lead.

**Monospace, or fixed pitch.** All characters are given the same horizontal spacing.

**Pica.** A unit of measurement, 6 picas per inch (or 12 points per pica).

**Pitch.** Characters per inch. Pica at 10cpi and elite at 12cpi are found on typewriters. *(Careful, don't confuse the horizontal 10cpi pica pitch with the 6cpi vertical pica height!)*

**Point.** A unit of measurement, there are 72 points per inch.

**Proportional spacing.** Each character is given different horizontal spacing as needed.

**Sans serif.** Typeface without serifs, as in "Arial and Helvetica are sans serif."

**Serif.** Decorative tag on the end of a letter, as in "Times is a serif typeface."

**Weight.** Heaviness of the line, such as bold, extra bold, light, narrow.

**X-height.** The height of a lowercase x.

A linked style sheet can enclose a style list in a separate style sheet file which we link to in the HEAD section. For example:

```
<LINK HREF="prolotherapy.css" REL=STYLESHEET>
```

Cascading style sheets can be viewed as a series of waterfalls. At the top is the inline style. The browser looks to see if an inline style has been declared for the element. If there is none, the job falls to the embedded style sheet. If there is none, the job falls to the linked style sheet. If there is none, the browser uses the default display attributes.

This means that you can have all three types of style sheet markup in the same document. The linked style sheet can be used to declare a base format for an entire Web site (or a portion of a Web site), the embedded style sheets can override certain styles in the individual page, and the inline styles have the last word.

Cascading style sheets have their own specification currently called CSS1 and CSS2. We'll be using CSS1 in this chapter. The CSS2 recommendation has recently been released, but it does not yet have the implementation to make it useful.

# Using JavaScript to Make HTML Dynamic

JavaScript brings the capability to write an interactive program to HTML. This is done by applying the features of the JavaScript language to the content of the HTML document. It is the style sheet's link to HTML tags that makes what you might call "programming the style sheet" possible.

This comes in the form of dynamic positioning, dynamic content, and events. Cascading style sheets seem static, but when you link style sheets to JavaScript and *events*, style sheets start changing on the fly! *Dynamic positioning* allows you to tell the browser exactly where to put a block of content without using tables. When you link dynamic positioning to JavaScript and events, these blocks can start moving!

*Dynamic content* lets you take a single block of content anywhere in a page and link an event to JavaScript that can update, replace, or remodel it at any time.

JavaScript is dynamic!

## Events

When we're running JavaScript in a Web browser, we receive information on what the user is doing with the mouse and keyboard. This is called *monitoring events*. Table 5.1 lists some of the events we can use.

Any of these events, particularly those that happen with the mouse or in a form, can trigger us to perform a function with JavaScript. Some functions we can perform are:

- Calculating the total amount of an order and displaying the results for the buyer's approval
- Changing the display characteristics of elements defined in a style sheet
- Allowing the user to move things around on the page

**Table 5.1** Some Useful Events

| JAVASCRIPT EVENT | EVENT DESCRIPTION |
|---|---|
| ONMOUSEMOVE | When the mouse is moved |
| ONMOUSEOVER | When the mouse is moved over an element |
| ONMOUSEOUT | When the mouse is moved off of an element |
| ONCLICK | When a mouse button is pressed |
| ONCHANGE | When data is entered in a form field |

- Moving elements around on the page without asking the user
- Triggering changes on page content based on a timer

We have seen how we can change the display characteristics of elements defined in a style sheet on the www.prolotherapy.com homepage. This is done through JavaScript using the ONMOUSEOVER and ONMOUSEOUT events. We'll be taking a look at the other possibilities later in this chapter.

In languages like Java we would have to perform special functions to monitor events like ONMOUSEOVER and ONMOUSEOUT, but because JavaScript is running in the Web browser, this is already taken care of for us. All we need to do is write *ON"EVENT"* and our JavaScript function will automatically occur.

## Using Events with Style Sheets

Events are linked together through what is called the *Document Object Model* (DOM). The DOM was originally created by Netscape for the purpose of using JavaScript, also invented by Netscape. Since then, the DOM has been expanded to give access to an entire document.

For the purposes of instruction, we'll use JavaScript throughout this chapter. To cause an event to trigger a JavaScript function to access a CSS element, the following steps need to occur:

1. A style sheet is written.
2. The target HTML element is given a NAME attribute.
3. The activating HTML element (which may be the same as the target HTML element) is given an EVENT attribute that calls a JavaScript function.
4. The JavaScript function is written to modify the DOM element with the NAME attribute.

In order to explain how this works we need to go through each of these steps. A full explanation of JavaScript is discussed in Chapter 6, "JavaScript."

## Writing Style Sheets

Embedded style sheets begin with the <STYLE> tag. The TYPE attribute should be declared but the default type is "text/css", giving us <STYLE TYPE="text/css">.

## CSS, Scripting, and the Document Object Model

Document Object Model (DOM) is a formidable acronym. This model is a way to get at the elements of a Web page in a scripting program running in the Web browser. It allows us to modify content and/or style characteristics of a specific tag in the page like we did in the menu example shown earlier.

Let's take this one word at a time.

Model. A model is a specified structure that we can follow.

Document. A document is a Web page loaded in the browser window.

Document Model. The document model is a structure applied to a document loaded in the browser.

Object. The browser allows a document to be viewed as an object that has properties.

Document Object Model. The Document Object Model is a structure that gives object properties to a document loaded in the browser.

The CSS specification includes the DOM as a method of dynamically changing style characteristics in Dynamic HTML. The DOM can also be used to dynamically change content in the Web page. Since scripting languages are the only programs we can run that have the privileges to affect the browser, they are responsible for using DOM to dynamically change Web page content.

The DOM is a hierarchical structure based entirely on HTML tags. The original DOM was included with the original version of JavaScript. It was a smaller object model mainly meant to provide access to link and form elements. For example, you could examine the text the user entered in a text box before the form was submitted, or you could change the URL of a link in response to a button the user clicked. It has since been expanded to include every part of the HTML document. Since the original model was simpler, we'll briefly use it as an example to show how it works.

At the top is the *document* object, which contains all other objects. The second level separates into three groups: *anchor*, *link*, and *form*. The notation for these groups is always in object property format: *document.anchor*, *document.link*, and *document.form*.

The anchor and link groups stop there and include whatever respective tags are found in the document. The form group moves on to include six third-level groups: *text*, *textarea*, *radio*, *checkbox*, *select*, and *button*.

In order to reference specific tags, the tag must be given a name, which is an attribute we can add to any tag. We write our tag like this, for example:

```
<INPUT TYPE="TEXT" NAME="TOTAL" SIZE="10">
```

We can access the content of this text box by using the object property *document.form.text.total.value*.

Access to all elements gives us CSS as an essential component of DHTML. Through scripting with the expanded DOM, we can write code that actively changes content, like:

```
document.form.text.total.value = (price * quantity) + tax;
```

The actual style declarations have a single format. This consists of the element followed by the declaration. Figure 5.4 illustrates the style sheet for Figure 5.3.

Each element is followed by a set of curly braces containing elements in pairs. These pairs can be formatted in one of the options listed in Table 5.2.

```
<STYLE TYPE="text/css">
BODY {background-image:url(images/davincit.gif);
  background-color:#AAAAAA}
A {font: 18pt/24pt Keypunch; text-decoration:none; color:white;
   letter-spacing:.75pt}
P.cintron {font: bold 18pt/24pt PhysicsAlpha; color:#FFCCFF;
         letter-spacing:2pt}
A.cintron {font: bold 18pt/24pt PhysicsBeta; color:#AAFFAA;
         letter-spacing:3pt}
.prolo {color:white; font-style:bold italic; text-decoration:none}
.prolobold {color:black; font-style:italic bold;
          text-decoration:underline}
#banner {font: bold 42pt Garamond,Serif; color:white}
</STYLE>
```

**Figure 5.4**   Style sheet source.

This style sheet illustrates three different ways of declaring styles based on the Document Object Model.

The first type of style declaration using the BODY and A tag declarations shows how to use the tag format to associate display properties with elements. There's also an example of a style sheet URL that gives the path and filename for the background image. Quote marks are unnecessary for the parameters unless the font name contains a space. Colors can use the 16-color name or an RGB triplet. This example uses a light gray background by assigning the three primary colors the same value.

## NOTE
**The P tag is assigned a light green, which I achieved by starting with white (#FFFFFF) and pulling back the green value (#FFCCFF) a bit. The A tag is assigned a light purple color by taking white and pulling back the red and blue values.**

The second type of style declaration uses a CLASS. In this case, we are declaring a class called *cintron* that assigns specific display properties to specific tags in the *cintron* class. Both tags are assigned an 18-point font size with 24-point line spacing. The fonts and letter spacing are slightly different to give the resulting effect.

The *.cintron* tags are now members of the class *cintron* and their properties can now be changed using the *cintron* class as a whole or by using their individual *cintron.tag*

**Table 5.2**   Style Sheet Format Options

| METHOD | FORMAT |
|--------|--------|
| By tag: | tag {name:property; name:property;} |
| By class: | tag.class {name:property; name:property;} |
| By id: | #id {name:property; name:property;} |

objects. There are two other classes declared here, the *prolo* and *prolobold* classes. Not assigning a specific tag to each would make these properties apply to all tags declared with the respective CLASS attribute.

The third type of style declaration is an ID declaration. These are similar to the CLASS declaration but do not apply to individual tags, only to members of the ID declaration group. These are prefixed with the pound (#) sign as shown.

In the body of the document the DOM allows us to assign three different attributes to an HTML tag that apply CSS elements to the content: NAME=, CLASS=, and ID=.

The NAME= attribute gives that specific tag a handle in the DOM. This is illustrated in the sidebar *CSS, Scripting, and the Document Object Model*.

The CLASS= attribute tells the DOM to apply a style class to the content of the HTML tag elements. In Figure 5.4 we define the class *cintron*:

```
P.cintron {font: bold 18pt/24pt PhysicsAlpha; color:#FFCCFF;
          letter-spacing:2pt}
A.cintron {font: bold 18pt/24pt PhysicsBeta; color:#AAFFAA;
          letter-spacing:3pt}
```

which will be applied to the A and P tags defined as members of the cintron class:

```
<P CLASS="cintron">Web site designed by
<A CLASS="cintron" HREF="http://www.cintronics.com">Cintronics</A>
</P>
```

This gives us two advantages. First, both these tags have related content that is reflected by their group membership in the cintron class. Second, we can use JavaScript later to change their style attributes as a group or individually by type of tag.

The ID= attribute is the same as the CLASS attribute without the tag distinctions. The ID *banner* is declared using the # sign as:

```
#banner {font: bold 42pt Garamond,Serif; color:white}
```

which will be applied to the tag *P* defined as a member the *banner* class:

```
<P ID="banner">Prolotherapy.com</P></TD>
```

which causes the text to be so displayed. We can also use JavaScript to interactively change display properties of all members of the *banner* ID.

Names, Classes, and IDs all have to follow the DOM.

## Microsoft DOM

The entire DOM would be impossible to explain in this chapter. This simplified DOM shows you what you need to know to get started writing scripts under the MS IE DOM. Figure 5.5 shows that all parts of the DOM are included in the *document* object.

The *all* object is particular to Microsoft and gives access to all objects in the document regardless of how else they may be represented. The *all* object can be used as a

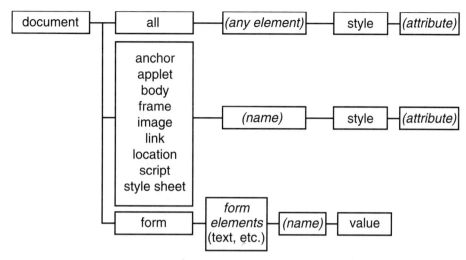

**Figure 5.5** Simplified MS IE DOM.

shotgun technique to hit whatever tag you're aiming at without having to know exactly what type of tag it is. But if you want to be more specific, and you should, the next set of elements cover everything from *anchor* to *stylesheet* by type of element. The *form* element, however, has its own schema due to the need to represent the many different types of elements within the form. This gives the form element numerous *child* elements to include all the elements that can fall within the FORM tag.

The cintronics.com menu, illustrated in Figure 5.6, has a two-layer display engine. The entire HTML document is about three times the size shown, however, the portions irrelevant to this example have been stripped from the illustration. The page is divided into three sections: STYLE, SCRIPT, and BODY.

```
<HTML>
<HEAD><TITLE>Cintronics - a vision for the future</TITLE>

<STYLE TYPE="text/css">
.menushow {visibility="visible"}
.menuhide {visibility="hidden"}
</STYLE>
<SCRIPT LANGUAGE="javascript">
function showmenu(menu) {
   document.all(menu).className="menushow";
}
function hidemenu(menu) {
   document.all(menu).className="menuhide";
}
</SCRIPT>
```
*Continues*

**Figure 5.6** Cintronics menu dynamo redux.

```
</HEAD>

<BODY BACKGROUND="cintronics/images/darkglyph.GIF">
<DIV ONMOUSEOVER="showmenu('professional')"
     ONMOUSEOUT="hidemenu('professional')">
  <IMG SRC="professional.GIF" ID="pro" ALT="professional" WIDTH="108"
   HEIGHT="36" ONMOUSEOVER="redimg();" ONMOUSEOUT="blueimg();">
    <DIV ID="professional" CLASS="menuhide">
    ("professional" menu goes here)
    </DIV> </DIV>
<DIV ONMOUSEOVER="showmenu('scientific')"
     ONMOUSEOUT="hidemenu('scientific')">
  <IMG SRC="scientific.GIF" ID="sci" ALT="scientific" WIDTH="108"
   HEIGHT="36" ONMOUSEOVER="redimg();" ONMOUSEOUT="blueimg();">
   <DIV ID="scientific" CLASS="menuhide">
   ("scientific" menu goes here)
   </DIV> </DIV>
<DIV ONMOUSEOVER="showmenu('philosophic')"
     ONMOUSEOUT="hidemenu('philosophic')">
  <IMG SRC="philosophic.GIF" ID="phi" ALT="philosophic" WIDTH="108"
   HEIGHT="36" ONMOUSEOVER="redimg();" ONMOUSEOUT="blueimg();">
    <DIV ID="philosophic" CLASS="menuhide">
    ("philosophic" menu goes here)
    </DIV> </DIV>
<DIV ONMOUSEOVER="showmenu('artistic')"
     ONMOUSEOUT="hidemenu('artistic')">
  <IMG SRC=" artistic.GIF" ID="art" ALT="artistic" WIDTH="108"
   HEIGHT="36" ONMOUSEOVER="redimg();" ONMOUSEOUT="blueimg();">
    <DIV ID="artistic" CLASS="menuhide">
    ("artistic" menu goes here)
    </DIV> </DIV>
<DIV ONMOUSEOVER="showmenu('personal')"
     ONMOUSEOUT="hidemenu('personal')">
  <IMG SRC="personal.GIF" ID="per" ALT="personal" WIDTH="108"
   HEIGHT="36" ONMOUSEOVER="redimg();" ONMOUSEOUT="blueimg();">
    <DIV ID="personal" CLASS="menuhide">
    ("personal") menu goes here
    </DIV> </DIV>
  </BODY>
```

**Figure 5.6**   *(Continued)*

This page consists of five sets of menus, each with two pairs of <DIV></DIV> tags. The DIV tag creates an arbitrary division of the document that we can address through the DOM by assigning each DIV section an ID attribute. In each menu section of this page, we have one set of outer DIV tags that include the menu banner and content, and one set of inner DIV tags that include only the menu content. When the mouse is moved over the outer DIV area, the menu is displayed. When the mouse is moved away, the menu disappears again. This is done by using the *visibility* CSS attribute, which has only two possible values: *visible* and *hidden*. These are two very simple attributes, and we will be going over attributes as a subject later in this chapter.

The first thing you will notice is that in the style sheet there are two classes defined: *.menushow* is assigned only the *visibility=visible* attribute, and *.menuhide* is assigned only the *visibility=hidden* attribute.

Next we have two JavaScript functions, one to show a menu by assigning the *.menushow* class to the object whose ID is passed, and the other to hide a menu by assigning the *.menuhide* class to the object whose ID is passed. The passed variable is named *menu*, which shows up in the *document.all(menu)*. This causes the browser to refer to the DOM to locate all elements with an ID equal to the value in the *menu* variable. This could also be done using a literal by writing *document.all("professional")*, but then we would need five times as many functions, one for each menu.

In the body of the document the outer DIV element is assigned two events. ONMOUSEOVER calls the JavaScript function *showmenu* and passes the ID of the inner DIV element. Since we want all menus to start out as hidden, the inner DIV elements are all declared members of the *menuhide* class, which will be assigned when the page is loaded. The other event assigned is ONMOUSEOUT, which calls *hidemenu*.

You may notice that the outer division IMG element also has two events assigned whose JavaScript functions are not shown in the preceding example. These events cause the menu banner images to swap when the mouse is passed over them. A blue image is inactive and a red image is active (*active* meaning the mouse is over the image). Figure 5.7 illustrates the *redimg()* function because *blueimg()* is just like it; the only difference is that each image name does not have an x at the end.

In Figure 5.7 we introduce a shortcut to typing the entire DOM string for each element two times in each statement. The first line assigns to the variable *coolpix* the DOM address of the IMG statement that triggered the event that called this function. JavaScript is very forgiving, so we do not have to declare this variable before using it.

The variable srcElement is a property of the event function of the JavaScript language. The DOM address of the tag is automatically contained in the *srcElement* object

```
function redimg() {
  coolpix=window.event.srcElement;
  if (coolpix.id=="pro")
     {coolpix.src="cintronics/images/professionalx.GIF";}
  if (coolpix.id=="sci")
     {coolpix.src="cintronics/images/scientificx.GIF";}
  if (coolpix.id=="phi")
     {coolpix.src="cintronics/images/philosophicx.GIF";}
  if (coolpix.id=="art")
     {coolpix.src="cintronics/images/artisticx.GIF";}
  if (coolpix.id=="per")
     {coolpix.src="cintronics/images/personalx.GIF";}
}
```

**Figure 5.7**   Hot image swapping.

and we assign this to the *coolpix* variable. All we have to do at this point is to compare *coolpix.id* with one of five possible calling IDs and assign the matching tag's SRC attribute a new value.

Let's say this function was called by the IMG tag with the "pro" ID, and that this image is the second IMG tag declared in the document. Behind the scenes the browser keeps all such elements in arrays so they can be identified by their position in the document. In JavaScript, arrays start at element 0, so the second element would be referenced as element 1. The browser will use its internal representation of the DOM for this document to translate the reference *coolpix.id* to the full address *window.event.IMG[1].id*, which equals *pro*.

All of this technical slavery gives us the effect we get when the browser immediately redisplays the changed element with its new SRC attribute.

# Netscape DOM

The challenge with Navigator is not so much finding the right name for the element, but in grappling with the differences in the way the model is implemented.

To translate Figure 5.8 into an effective Navigator version, the change in DOM attributes is small, but the design philosophy is very different.

## Microsoft, Netscape, JavaScript, VBScript, and DOM

Currently there are two versions of the DOM, one for Netscape Navigator and one for Internet Explorer. These are similar but are different enough that if you want to use all the features of JavaScript, you have to write in two versions, one for each browser. Depending on what your scripting is meant to do, you may be able to write only one version. We'll discuss examples of both cases in this chapter.

Each new version of a browser includes more features, meaning more backward incompatibility for the future. Currently, DHTML is ineffective for either browser earlier than version 3, and has difficulty below version 4, which has bugs and inconsistencies with the way the specification says that CSS is supposed to work with JavaScript/JScript. Version 5 of both Explorer and Navigator promises to comply with the new JavaScript standard ECMAscript, which will be explained in Chapter 6.

Fortunately, these browsers are free so people do not have to pay to keep up. Unfortunately, downloading these browsers requires patience and a little bit of know-how, not to mention the fact that many low-end users may be completely unaware that their Navigator Version 2 is an antique.

When scripting for Explorer, you can use either JScript or VBScript. With Explorer, some of the features of Dynamic HTML, such as Dynamic fonts, require installing ActiveX controls. Dynamic fonts are supported by both scripting languages but ActiveX is a Microsoft technology not supported within Navigator.

There is a second type of style sheet called *JavaScript Style Sheets* (JSSS). JSSS also conforms to the CSS specification, but is only supported by Navigator. CSS-type style sheets can be directly translated to JSSS-type style sheets and back, but JSSS supports only the Netscape DOM. We will be looking at JSSS in this chapter.

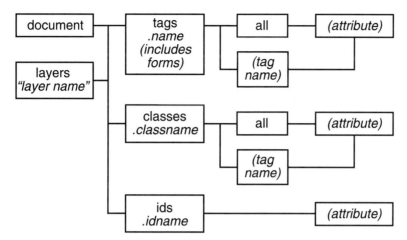

**Figure 5.8**    Simplified Netscape DOM.

When programming for Navigator you are limited by the fact that the browser will *not* update the display without reloading the whole page, and we do not want to do this just to change the color of some text. We have recourse in this case, however, because there are two exceptions: the IMG and LAYER elements.

The <LAYER></LAYER> tag set is an HTML element not supported by Microsoft, but it is essential because it is the only tag in Navigator that will react to events and change a text display. The relevant attribute to the LAYER tag is VISIBILITY (either *hide* or *show*), which work in the same way as the Explorer *hidden* and *visible* attributes.

Since we cannot dynamically change text in Navigator, we have to create a separate copy of each area we want to display in the form of a LAYER element. Each area will be initially declared as *hide* or *show*, and we then use events to call scripts that will swap these like a slide show.

Figure 5.9 is a simple example of how we would use layers to create a popup menu of film directors and their movies. The main menu on the left will need to be a layer if

**Figure 5.9**    Thinking in layers.

we are going to use it to trigger events. We can position this layer at the upper left-hand corner (TOP=0 LEFT=0) and this layer will always be visible.

Next we create four other invisible layers. These can all be put in the same location at (50,200) or they can be staggered so the top line is always next to the director. Finally, we use the ONCLICK event to trigger which layer to make visible. As part of the ONCLICK event we can access the exact coordinates of the click to determine which layer to display.

Figure 5.10 shows how the cintronics.com menu translates to layers.

```
<HTML>
<HEAD><TITLE>Cintronics - a vision for the future</TITLE>

<STYLE TYPE="text/css">
BODY {bgcolor:black}
A {font: 10pt Arial,Helvetica,"Sans Serif"; text-align: center; color:
white; text-decoration:none}
</STYLE>

<SCRIPT LANGUAGE="javascript">
function proshow() {
  document.layers["promin"].visibility="hide";
  document.layers["promax"].visibility="show";
  return true;
}
function prohide() {
  document.layers["promin"].visibility="show";
  document.layers["promax"].visibility="hide";
  return true;
}
function scishow(){same as proshow() using "sci"}
function scihide(){same as prohide() using "sci"}
function phishow(){same as proshow() using "phi"}
function phihide(){same as prohide() using "phi"}
function artshow(){same as proshow() using "art"}
function arthide(){same as prohide() using "art"}
function pershow(){same as proshow() using "per"}
function perhide(){same as prohide() using "per"}
</SCRIPT>
</HEAD>

<BODY BACKGROUND="cintronics/images/darkglyph.GIF">
<IMG SRC="cintronics/images/vision.GIF" ALT="a vision for the future"
WIDTH="590" HEIGHT="83">

<LAYER NAME="promin" VISIBILITY="show" ONMOUSEOVER="proshow()" TOP=165
```

**Figure 5.10**  Cintronics layered menu engine.

```
LEFT=12 WIDTH=120>
<IMG SRC="cintronics/images/professional.GIF" ALT="professional"
WIDTH="108" HEIGHT="36">
</LAYER>

<LAYER NAME="promax" VISIBILITY="hide" ONMOUSEOUT="prohide()" TOP=165
LEFT=6 WIDTH=120>
<IMG SRC="cintronics/images/professionalx.GIF" ALT="professional"
WIDTH="108" HEIGHT="36">
("professional" menu goes here)
</LAYER>

(scimin/scimax menu goes here)
(phimin/phimax menu goes here)
(artmin/artmax menu goes here)
(permin/permax menu goes here)

</BODY>
</HTML>
```

**Figure 5.10**   *(Continued)*

The first thing we change is the style sheet. We are not going to use this to assign the *hide* or *show* values to the *visibility* attribute. We are going to initialize this value in the LAYER tag and use JavaScript to directly access the LAYER visibility attribute through its DOM reference.

I have created five sets of functions, one for each menu. I could have made two functions with variables, but the end result would have been the same amount of code, and I believe this would run faster as it is more direct. Each function reverses the visibility attributes on each set of menu layers. I have only shown one set of functions since they are the same outside of the NAME references.

Finally, within the BODY each menu has two layers, one with the blue colored banner only *"promin"*, and one with the red banner and full menu listing *"promax"*. The *promin* layer is initialized as visible and the *promax* layer as hidden. Both menus have the same TOP and LEFT attributes. Actually, there is a six-pixel difference here, which is a result of trial and error. The red and blue versions of the menu images did not overlap, so I adjusted the coordinates so the swapping wouldn't create a shifting image.

Notice that on the *promin* layer the ONMOUSEOVER event triggers displaying the *promax* layer, but there is no ONMOUSEOUT event. That's because once the layer is shifted, event control has passed to the new layer! On the *promax* layer we have ONMOUSEOUT to display the *promin* layer but not ONMOUSEOVER because the mouse is already over.

Again, only one set of menus is shown here since they are all the same except for the named variables and coordinates.

# CSS Style Attributes

This section gives a breakdown of the most common and useful CSS attributes. These attributes are broken down into categories as they are applied to fonts, backgrounds, and text, and are followed by a section on *Events*.

## Fonts

### Font family {font-family: *font1, font2, "font 3"*}

This attribute replaces the HTML FONT tag, and in the same way a list of fonts can be given. If a font has whitespace in the name it must be enclosed in quotes. The generic font names *serif*, *"sans serif," cursive, fancy*, and *monospace* are always a last resort. Dynamic fonts may end up replacing this tag in turn.

### Font size {font-size: 24pt}

This attribute replaces the HTML SIZE tag and offers a lot more options. There are actually several ways to declare the font size, but I see no reason to use anything other than point size. If you're going to go to all the trouble of creating specific sizes, why start using unusual units of measure? Points are typographical standards.

### Font style {font-style: italic}

This attribute replaces the HTML I tag, and offers two additional options: *oblique* and *normal*. Why declare normal? You could dynamically italicize, though it's bad design. Bold and italic are often used together, but don't confuse bold with italic; italic is a style, bold is a weight.

### Font weight {font-weight: bold}

This attribute replaces the HTML B tag and offers a new scheme of line weight. In addition to the choices of *normal* and *bold,* you can also pick a number between 100 and 900.

### Font variant {font-variant: small-caps}

This attribute offers the option you see with the usual *normal* alternative.

### Line height {line-height: 36pt}

This attribute is a new and useful option that will set the line height, or leading.

### Font {font: italic bold 24pt/30pt Arial}

This attribute is a very useful all-in-one tag that allows you to declare *style, weight, size/height,* and *font* at one time. Although you don't have to use all of them, elements must occur in the order shown.

### Text-decoration {text-decoration: underline}

This attribute replaces several HTML tags including U, STRIKE, and BLINK. BLINK is a Netscape-only tag. Options include *none, underline, overline, line-through,* and *blink.*

In this case, *none* is more than window dressing as you can use it to turn off automatic underlining of links and use your own scheme.

Color    {color:red}
           {color:#RRGGBB}
           {color:rgb(255,255,255)}

These attributes are the color options using text, hex, and decimal RGB triplets.

# Backgrounds

### Background color {background-color:white}

This attribute replaces the HTML attribute BGCOLOR= and can be used with BODY, or LAYER, TABLE, and TD/TR table elements to set colors for partial areas of the screen.

### Background image {background-image:url(file.gif)}

This attribute replaces the HTML attribute BACKGROUND= and can be used in the same places as background-color. The following are a few positioning attributes not available in HTML:

### Background repeat {background-repeat:repeat-y}

This attribute offers three new options to keep the background image from uncontrollably reproducing itself. These are *no-repeat*, *repeat-x*, and *repeat-y*. No-repeat displays the image once, which is useful for full-screen background images. *Repeat-x* causes the image to be repeated only in the x-direction, useful for backgrounds that appear to spring from the top of the screen. *Repeat-y* causes the image to be repeated only in the y-direction, useful for the vast majority of background images that run along the left side of the screen.

### Background attachment {background-attachment:fixed}

This attribute is a new option where *fixed* specifies that the image will not move when the page is scrolled. We are so used to the scrolling effect that it can be a bit disorienting when the background is set to *fixed*. *Scroll* is also available, but is the default option.

### Background position {background-position:*horizontal vertical*}

This attribute allows you to set the origin point for the background image, offering horizontal options such as *right*, *center*, and *left*. The vertical attribute is optional with *top*, *center*, and *bottom*. This does not work properly in versions 4.

### Background {background: white url(happy.gif) repeat-y scroll left top}

This is another shotgun command that sets all the background attributes at once in a specific order: *color*, *image*, *repeat*, *attachment*, and *position*.

# Text

### Word spacing {word-spacing: 10pt}

This attribute allows you to insert extra spacing between words, and is best expressed in point size. *Normal* is the default.

### Letter spacing {letter-spacing: 3pt}

This attribute allows you to insert extra spacing between letters, and is best expressed in point size. *Normal* is the default.

### Text align {text-align: justify}

This attribute replaces the HTML tag CENTER and attribute ALIGN=. Options include: right, center, left, and justify (filling the line, as in word processors), which doesn't always work.

### Text indent {text-indent: 50%}

This attribute can be expressed as a measurement (such as points) or as a percentage of the line width. It applies to the first line of a block of text. Be sure to check your justification; don't make the mistake of setting an indent over text that is not left-justified.

# Events

In versions 3, there are only three events supported by the Explorer and Navigator browsers: ONLOAD, ONBLUR, and ONFOCUS.

Versions 4 support the following events. There are additional events supported by either browser but they are not the same events so they are not listed here.

| | |
|---|---|
| ONLOAD | When the document has finished downloading (not necessarily displaying) all the page content from the server. |
| ONFOCUS | When the cursor is moved into a FORM element, it receives focus. |
| ONBLUR | When the cursor is moved out of a FORM element, it goes "out of focus." |
| ONCHANGE | When text, text area, or select box content has been changed, after ONBLUR. |
| ONMOUSEOVER | When the mouse is moved over the area defined by an HTML element. Used with ONMOUSEOUT. |
| ONMOUSEOUT | When the mouse leaves an area defined by an HTML element. Used with ONMOUSEOVER. |
| ONMOUSEDOWN | When a mouse button is pressed, along with ONCLICK. |
| ONMOUSEUP | When a mouse button is released, after ONCLICK. |
| ONMOUSEMOVE | When the mouse is moved, this event is triggered for every pixel the mouse moves across. Because this is a high-overhead |

event, it should only be accessed in a script, where the browser's Event object is used to access all the information on where the mouse was moved to. It would be rare to keep track of where the mouse is on the screen. Usually ONMOUSEOVER or ONCLICK are sufficient.

| | |
|---|---|
| ONCLICK | When any mouse button is clicked you can use the browser's Event object to find out which button and what combination of *shift*, *ctrl*, and *alt* was also pressed. This is best used to execute a script at the user's request in combination with the FORM tag BUTTON attribute. |
| ONKEYPRESS | When a key is pressed, you can use the browser's Event object to find out which key and what combination of *shift*, *ctrl*, and *alt* was also pressed. |
| ONKEYDOWN | When the key goes down, along with ONKEYPRESS. |
| ONKEYUP | When the key goes up, after ONKEYPRESS. |
| ONSUBMIT | When the SUBMIT button is pressed in a form. The ONSUBMIT event goes in the FORM tag, not the BUTTON tag. |
| ONRESET | When the RESET button is pressed in a form. The ONRESET event goes in the FORM tag just as the ONSUBMIT event, not in the BUTTON tag. |

## NOTE

**In Explorer you can trigger an event off of any HTML tag, but with Navigator, events can only be triggered within a LAYER or link (A) tag.**

## Dynamic Fonts

*Dynamic fonts* is a great idea that does not seem to be getting the attention it deserves. Not that anyone is against them, it's just that nobody's using them. I suspect a large part of the problem is that few people have bothered to find out how to create a dynamic downloadable font.

Portable Font Resources (PFRs) are automatically supported by Navigator and can be added to Explorer by a one-time ActiveX control download. Truedoc, at www.truedoc .com, sells a dynamic font creating program. To help you get started with dynamic fonts, Truedoc has provided several PFR files online where you can link to its dynamic fonts at no charge. You can't have the fonts and they won't work if you copy the files from your cache, but you can use them all you want. Figure 5.11 illustrates Truedoc's dynamic fonts.

None of the fonts shown in the truedoc.com homepage are GIFs, not even the snow-capped "Look ma, no GIFs!" display. These are all PFR files downloaded with the page and displayed by the browser. You can swipe them as text. They are not images.

There are two steps to using these fonts:

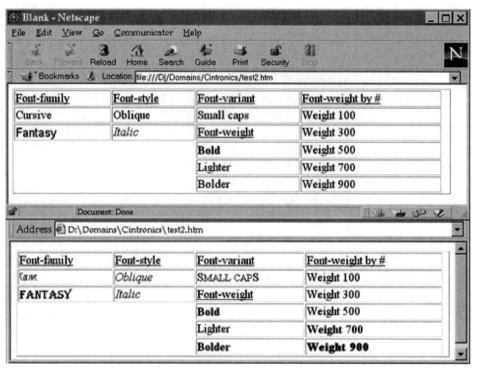

**Figure 5.11** Dynamic fonts in action.

1. You pick the font resource you want to use and reference it through links in the HEAD section of your page using the code like this, for example:

```
<LINK REL="fontdef" SRC="http://www.truedoc.com/pfrs/AmeriGarmnd.pfr">
```

2. You declare the FONT tag in your page or via CSS. For example:

```
P {font-family:"AmeriGarmnd BT"; size:3; color:black}
<FONT FACE="BakerSignet BT" COLOR=red SIZE=6>
```

## JavaScript Style Sheets

With Navigator version 4, Netscape released its own version of CSS1 called *JavaScript Style Sheets* (JSSS). JSSS are much like CSS Style Sheets. JSSS was written to specifically follow the Netscape DOM. But then again, since Netscape wrote Navigator, JSSS was written so Netscape's implementation of CSS would also support its DOM. The result? Two ways you can write a style sheet.

At developer.netscape.com Netscape claims, "CSS is static, JSSS is dynamic." Well, the truth is, it seems you can write your code either way and it comes out just as dynamic. Nevertheless, the two models are different enough to merit an explanation.

```
<STYLE TYPE="text/css">
BODY {background-image: url(images/Musclesb.GIF)}
P {font: normal 18pt/24pt Eurostile, Arial, Helvetica}
A {font: normal 18pt/24pt Eurostile, Arial, Helvetica;
   text-decoration:none; color:#006400}
</STYLE>
```

**Figure 5.12**    A little bit of CSS.

Let's take a look at the difference between the two. Here's a BODY style declaration in CSS and JSSS. In CSS we see our familiar TAG {attribute: value}. In JSSS, instead of having two ways to declare a style (one in the style sheet or HTML STYLE attribute and another in the JavaScript code), we only have one way. In JSSS we declare the style in the same way we would normally modify it in the JavaScript code.

```
CSS:  BODY {background-image: url(images/Musclesb.GIF)}
JSSS: tags.BODY.backgroundImage="images/Musclest.GIF";
```

The attributes are the same except for their punctuation. The CSS hyphen becomes a JSSS capitalization, so in CSS the *background-image* attribute becomes *backgroundImage* in JSSS. Then again, *color* is still *color* since it has no punctuation.

Figure 5.12 is a piece of a CSS format style sheet that we'll translate into JSSS. This declares the BODY background image as shown earlier, and declares default styles for the P and A tags.

In JSSS this becomes more wordy, and in fact we try to cut down on this wordiness by using the *with* statement to replace the beginning of these long DOM strings. For example, as shown in Figure 5.13, the first *with* statement allows us to write *fontSize=* instead of *tags.A.fontSize= .*

```
<STYLE TYPE="text/javascript">
tags.BODY.backgroundImage="images/Musclest.GIF";
with (tags.P) {
  fontSize="18pt";
  lineHeight="24pt";
  fontFamily="Eurostile,Arial,Helvetica";
  }
with (tags.A) {
  fontSize="18pt";
  lineHeight="24pt";
  fontFamily="Eurostile,Arial,Helvetica";
  color="teal";
  textDecoration="none"
  }
</STYLE>
```

**Figure 5.13**    A little bit of JSSS.

The first thing we have to do is declare the style sheet as JSSS using the *STYLE TYPE="text/javascript"* declaration.

Next we move on to declare the font attributes. JSSS does not have the all-at-once CSS font statement so we declare the attributes one at a time using the next best thing, the *with* statement.

As you have seen, there are compatibility issues with writing DHTML for both browsers. Not only do the two browsers support slightly different features and have completely different DOMs, but they also have different features that are badly supported or downright buggy. A solution is needed to this schizophrenic technology!

# Browser DHTML Compatibility

In perusing the Net, there is a lot of talk about XBDHTML (Cross-Browser Dynamic HTML). XBDHTML is either code that will work on both browsers (having to settle for the lowest common denominator), or having two versions of JavaScript functions in your document. Visual editing tools that claim to produce DHTML to work in both browsers are not yet online.

Even with XBDHTML and visual development, the browsers themselves are not perfect, so development against the CSS spec does not necessarily guarantee success. For example, in the cintronics.com menu example in Figure 5.6 when the layer menu model is accessed it works, but if you take the mouse and move it quickly across the menu a few times, you can make all of the layers visible. The point is that the ONMOUSEOVER works but the ONMOUSEOUT does not always do its job.

In reviewing the browser DHTML properties charts at style.webreview.com, you can see that not a single one of the browser versions are fully compliant with the program. Perhaps with versions 5 many of these inconsistencies will vanish, but I'm sure that just as in the past, versions 5 will introduce more of the same cross-browser incompatibility. Our standard of coding will have to improve over time.

# The Future of DHTML

The Netscape Web site promises version 5 will give full compliance with CSS1, but how is not explained.

The Microsoft Web site promises many improvements for DHTML in Explorer version 5, including some elements that are *proposed extensions* to CSS2. Does this mean that they are up for CSS3 status?

It's clear that DHTML is a hot technology that is going places fast. And our challenge is in keeping up.

**INTERVIEW**

*Garth Bruce, Microsoft*
   Garth's official job title is "Microsoft Technical Evangelist," which is a pretty interesting job title, don't you think? In fact, all the guys in Garth's team are Technical Evangelists.

This means they go around spreading the word about Microsoft technologies, and they do a lot of public relations work, traveling to trade shows and working with developers. These guys even work with companies that are putting out products that compete with Microsoft, if those products are based on Microsoft technologies (which pretty much any product that runs under Windows is).

I wanted to speak with Garth about Dynamic HTML, since that's his specialty, hoping to shed some light on where this technology is going. These guys are way up in the ozone, so prepare yourself for a thoroughly technical and insightful talk straight from the top.

*So Garth, what is the Developer Relations Group all about?*
The real emphasis is based on the fact that we frequently release a lot of new technologies. Our goal is to assist developers on implementing the new technologies. There is little or no documentation when you're running through pre-beta and beta cycles. It's important, when the product's released, to have industry support for the new technologies. We also collect feedback on the products during the beta cycles from the companies that are developing demanding, real-world applications.

*So you're here to assist people with getting familiar with new technologies?*
Right. To clear the roadblocks and help ensure their products are successful is another way to put it.

*To you, a new technology would be what?*
Good question. The next version of Internet Explorer has new technologies that I'm evangelizing. You might think "Internet Explorer? That product has been around for years!" Each new version of IE has had significant enhancements, more so than other MS products given the rapid evolution of the Internet. For example, we've added many new features to conform to recently released industry standards; i.e., W3C XML standard.

*HTML's an old technology, so to speak, and IE5 is a new technology, so where does Microsoft come in as far as authoring tools?*
We do have several different tools that fall into many categories. Visual Interdev is a programmer-centric HTML authoring tool; Front Page is a Web page designer-centric HTML authoring tool. In the recent past I worked closely with the competitors of those two products to support them in actually creating a better product—go figure.

You can't get away with just an HTML authoring tool anymore.

That's right. You need site management, database integration, support for various languages, etc. A lot of the companies I work with, like NetObjects for example, have a complete Internet application solution, which includes business logic components on a server and client-side presentation authoring tools, and the management software to tie it all together.

*Now that's an interesting point because you have the client and the server sides. On the client side you have HTML, scripting, CGI, maybe some applets, and on the server side you have more HTML, with possibly Active Server Pages, more scripting, more Java in the form of servlets. So you have client- and server-side development?*
You bet. If you're going to leverage the Internet in your application then you need to develop an n-tier or DNA-based application which includes the client- and server-side components.

*Yeah, there sure are a lot of authoring tools coming out, faster than even the technology changes. Does that mean that you have to be familiar with all the technologies?*

DRG evangelists are required to have a strong breadth of Internet technologies, but most of us will specialize in a area, such as client-side technologies. I focus on the Internet Explorer and the associated technologies and those associated technologies on the server that drive the client. I can help vendors at a high level on the server-side technologies and drill down into details on the client-side technologies. If one of the vendors I'm working with needs detailed information on our server-side technologies then I'll ask a fellow DRG evangelist or a project team member who specialized in those technologies to help me. There are a lot of great, innovative companies in the market space that have outstanding Internet authoring tools.

The same for other new technologies like XML and XSL. XML and XSL are usually generated on the server and then interpreted and displayed on the client using the technologies in the browser. The more technologies I understand and know in depth, the more value I am to the vendors I help.

*Specifically, if some developer calls you up, what would they say? If they said, "I'm trying to write an engine that will translate JavaScript into VBScript. What do I do with function X?" What would you do?*

Well, hopefully I'd have some knowledge of what they were looking to do, given if they've called me and not developer support, then they know my area of technology expertise. If I can't answer them immediately then I'd probably send an e-mail  to the appropriate person on the project development team for the answer. We work closely with the product teams to get detailed technical information and in return we provide them customer feedback.

So you're more of a coordinator, you know where to find things out.

Yeah, that's another highly valued skill of an evangelist. When I quickly deliver information to a vendor it reduces their product's time to market or when I can coordinate a developer lab to assist several of their project team developers it increases the quality of their product.

*Is DHTML your specialty?*

Yes. DHTML is a very efficient and easy way to build a distributed applications user interface. Mere mortals can quickly create effective UI using DHTML. If you think about why you use Hot Metal Pro you could throw that Web page together in a hurry, and if that Web page can become the actual user interface for your application, then you'd be done at that point, wouldn't you? So if you think about what a C++ developer goes through putting that UI [user interface] together, and what a VB programmer goes through, and what an HTML programmer goes through, DHTML is a quicker way to do that, and it's scalable to millions of Internet users.

It definitely is, but in my battle with Dynamic HTML, my first challenge was to overcome the dual object model, and I ended up writing three versions of several Web pages. One for Netscape, one for Microsoft, and one for "other" that doesn't have any Dynamic HTML. I was really curious about IE5, if there's any change.

Yeah there is, and we've taken your point to heart. The IE5 development team is working hard to make it much easier for developers like yourself to author a single page and have it work on multiple versions of browsers from multiple vendors. IE5 does this in several ways; one of the primary ways is called Behaviors. Briefly, a behavior is an easy way to extend the richness of a Web page by adding specific functionality on a page. Behaviors can take advantage of specific browser features without breaking down level browsers. You can also add your own tags using XML, which older browsers will ignore.

I did look at it but I didn't really spend a lot of time figuring it out.

In addition to providing great backward browser compatibility, behaviors allow you to simplify and extend the functionality of your application or Web page. For example, you can separate out what would be considered a developer's responsibility for coding script for, say, connecting to a remote database to populate a table. The designer can then integrate the behavior in one simple line and not be worried about messing up the script somehow, like if they just happen to delete a tag or move something around. Oh, and one more thing, this isn't any new syntax, it's all familiar HTML so designers don't have to learn anything new. It's an important component of IE5.

*I think it's important, too!*
Two other things customers told us were direly important in regard to IE5 were reliability and performance. The development team has been working hard on both of these issues. The team's goal is to have IE5 be the most reliable and fastest browser available. I know we're going to impress a lot of people when it's released.

*Let me throw this question out to you. If Microsoft wanted to, could you go and rewrite the script engine in Navigator because it's open source? Is there any interest in that?*
There's a group called ActiveScripting.org. They've actually taken the Mozilla source and, it's what they call Mothra. I guess Mothra is a sometimes friend, sometimes opponent of Godzilla. So anyway, they built this version of Mozilla that hosts Active Scripting engines. The guys who did this happen to be VBA [Visual Basic Application] licensing partners and they've been writing script engines as their business for years. They really like Active Scripting and so they went off and did this because they thought it would be fun and the source was just sitting right out there and they could just go do it. So I've certainly heard of folks who are working with the Mozilla source who essentially integrate IE technologies into it. We find that we have plenty on our plate already just dealing with IE and don't feel any need to go off and be messing with Mozilla.

We don't have any problem with those technologies being integrated with Mozilla or Navigator; there just isn't much of a business model for us to be the ones to go do it. There are lots of people who have worked with IE because of the way it's componentized. They're familiar with how to work with that and they can integrate that with Mozilla, and I think that's just swell.

*Is IE open source enough where someone could take it and do that?*
We've just chosen to go down a different road where, rather than providing the source code, we worked to define a set of binary interfaces that people can use instead to integrate, and essentially we see that we're the folks who are responsible for delivering the correct behavior in the components. And if other people want to go off and use those components, I mean the whole reason you use a component is you don't want to write the functionality in the component. So we find that's a more supportable model, that it's also a higher performance model and we just feel that we can control our own development work better than we can act as the integrator for changes that people around the world are making.

*I remember when I was working on mainframes, third-party code was not as common and was very likely to crash from time to time, but the OS was very ironclad and kept applications running in their own memory space, like with NT today, and so even if they did crash it didn't affect anything else. But in the PC world you have this third-party code everywhere so the challenge is to make it crash-proof or "minimally crashful."*
I like that. Minimally crashful. That's cool. Trademark that one.

*Then there's the Mac. It very rarely bombs, but they do run tighter control on their OS . . .*
We've been working with the testing folks, and the folks who sell test tools like Rational Software and Omega Technologies, how do you test these kinds of applications. And the browser interestingly is one of the earliest and best supporters of a technology called active accessibility, which initially was defined to expose the state of UI elements for people who were using Braille readers and screen readers and stuff like that, the blind who have voice synthesizers telling them what's going on on the screen. Well, it turns out that exactly that same technology is a great way for a test tool to be able to reach into an application and find the state of all the UI elements. So using things like that, the tools available to test these kinds of applications are progressing very quickly. If you look at Rational's Web test tool, they have that ability to run a page, run the client-side script for a while, and then stop it and go in and check and see if everything's in the state it should be. What's selected, what's in the input fields, those kinds of things. So again, the focus of the browser, far beyond just viewing pretty pictures on the Web, is being a platform for these kind of distributed applications. It takes a lot of infrastructure to pull that off.

*I was looking at internationalization and to me that's the thing that really goes off the deep end. It's hard enough to design a page for text that goes right or left, then there's text that goes up and down, hieroglyphs, and then what do you do for a blind person?*
Have you seen the IE5 demo where people are entering different characters and doing spell checks against different characters? There are some great demos coming for you.
    Internationalization is great. On NT5 for example, assuming you have the proper fonts installed, which is reasonable if you're working with multiple languages anyway, I could fire up Office and I could have the Japanese UI turned on for Office while everything else is in English UI. So IE takes advantage of that when it's running on NT. Even on Win 98, you can go to a site which has Russian, Arabic, Kanji, all on the same page and it displays all of it. It's there now in NT5 beta 2.
    If you can get to the next PDC [Professional Developers Conference] we're going to have three solid days minimal of content on this kind of stuff. Our goal is to make your head explode with all the information you come away with. Come let us explode your head.

*What happened at the last PDC?*
There were quite a few announcements, but the big announcements came from the XML and XSL groups.

*To me XML is like the electric car. It's a great idea but where's it going? Right now XML is used internally in some Microsoft products but you never see that. So to the developer who's developing this kind of stuff it's more obvious. But what is it to somebody out there who's designing for clients?*
I agree with your point, most end users will never directly handle XML but most developers will in the near future. The more complexity we can remove from the

development effort, the faster companies can get products to market. In the case of the Web, for people who are doing HTML development, they will begin to integrate XML and XSL into their pages with the next generation of browsers. By the end of 1999 most HTML page authoring tools, and most RAD tools, will support it.

There are various levels of client integration for XML. IE4 currently leverages XML for CDF and Databinding. IE5 goes much farther in allowing you to embed XML directly into your HTML page as data or as new tags to extend the functionality of the browser in a standards-based way. Now the browser companies don't have to invent new HTML tags that will conflict with other browsers, and older browsers simply ignore the new XML tags they don't understand.

### *Really, how would that work?*
To the HTML author, XML is easy to digest. The syntax is almost identical and it works with existing HTML standards. For example, I can create a new tag in my HTML page using XML that adds a formatted footnote to the bottom of my page. Inside my new XML footnote tag I can use all the wonderful formatting properties of CSS, just as I can with HTML tags.

### *What about Dynamic XML?*
That's a good one, Dynamic XML. Another term for you to trademark. When you said that, I thought "that's XSL." The XSL, or as I think of it, "HTML style sheets on steroids," is similar to the concept of Cascading Style Sheets in Dynamic HTML. Remember, DHTML is HTML + Script. The script is what makes the HTML "dynamic," or its ability to change how the HTML is presented given user requirements or actions. XSL also allows me to change how XML is presented to the user but on a broader scale. For example, I could use XSL to display the XML data to a user in HTML 4.0, or older HTML 3.2, or even a Word document format. Data on a page rarely changes, or I shouldn't say "rarely changes," but it's usually predetermined by some database, and the only thing that really changes is who your client is or who you're presenting to. Is it an old Win 3.1 machine, is it a Windows 98 machine, is it a Mac, is it a Unix box, or maybe WebTV? So XSL can easily provide a template for the XML data to output to a particular platform. The support in IE5 is 100% compliant with the W3C standards. So that's a huge win, I think, for everybody in the industry.

### *That's always a win when somebody follows the standards!*
We've added a few convenience routines to our XML implementation in IE5 to make it easier to do some of the more complex things, again saving developers a lot of time and effort.

It's the fact that they're there always makes somebody mad because it's such a temptation to use them but they don't follow the standards.

Standards issued from most standards organizations provide a foundation and are meant to be built on given additional company integration and customer requirements. In 1996 we signed a pledge with the industry and W3C. The pledge states we are committed to working with the World Wide Web Consortium (W3C) to implement W3C-approved standards. To date, Internet Explorer has the most complete support for W3C standards and we will continue because our customers are telling us it's important to them!

### *This really makes we wonder. If people start going to XML and the HTML starts fading away or going to the style sheet, is there any dynamic provision in XML?*
No, it's just data.

*I mean if I want to put JavaScript in XML, XML has a Document Object Model, right? So if we put the JavaScript in there, would it work?*

XML simply describes application data and provides a set of standard methods for working with it; HTML defines similar methods for viewing information or data. JavaScript, VBScript, or other programming languages, provide the glue or logic to integrate the data into the user interface. XML is flexible enough such that you could insert script code into an XML structure and then interpret it on the client, but that's like driving a thumbtack into the wall with a sledgehammer.

*I guess it's just something we just haven't done yet. Has anybody done this?*

Someone may have, I haven't been closely watching what's currently been happening in the XML world. Production-quality XML and XSL parsers and tools are just now becoming readily available. IE5 beta 2 is a major release for use in support of XML and XSL so many people are just now beginning to grasp the capability of the technologies. There are some really compelling and enlightening examples on the Microsoft XML Web site.

*Do you think they'll call it Dynamic XML?*

That's probably overloading the word *Dynamic* a bit.

*I'm trying to figure out what drives this market because Microsoft does all this work in creating a new browser, and then it's free. And then there's all this work in XML research and all that, and it doesn't make any money either. It has to make money for somebody in some way?*

The business model is a bit mysterious at first glance, but if you take into account all the products inside Microsoft that leverage these foundational technologies then it makes perfect sense. They [the IE team] really pioneered the new forms package behind Dynamic HTML.

*The forms package?*

Yeah, it's termed *forms* package because we have various fundamental ways to display an application's user interface. IE was one of the first applications to create a Web-based display rendering engine, named WebBrowser Control. Later we added the DHTML Editing control. Several other applications in the company are now leveraging those base technologies, for example Microsoft Money99 and Encarta. Money99 was one of the first applications that use the WebBrowser control extensively. If you have Money99 you know the interface has a friendly and familiar Web look and feel. There are a slew of other companies that have done the same thing; e.g., AOL, Quicken, Eudora, Lotus Notes. Why write all the code to parse, manage, and display Internet content in your application when we provide the development components to you for free? The story is similar for XML. XML is a new fundamental technology that most applications, and other vendors in the industry, can benefit from. So the profit comes indirectly from improving our existing applications. The Office 2000 development team is now using XML extensively for persistence of document data and other functionality.

*It sounds like XML is going to take over the universe.*

I don't think so; it's still a young technology.

*I know, that's what's scary about it. It's just getting started and you're starting to throw it in all these applications.*

Yeah, it does have many advantages and I think we'll definitely see more people exploit it in the future. What HTML did for universal information display, XML will do for universal information transfer and access. Besides, the computer business wouldn't be any fun if it didn't change every few months, right?

It sounds like nobody's going to have to write a display interface anymore, they can just use the browser engine, you can almost see somebody writing a version of Microsoft Word using IE5 and DHTML.

It may be a few more years before we actually see a major application like Office that is based on DHTML exclusively. The technologies in IE have opened a lot of new doors for developers but there are still several challenges. The decision to use DHTML depends on your application's requirements. If you application is an n-tier or Internet-based then DHTML is the road to take. If your application is localized to a single machine or LAN then using existing win32 APIs are the route to take.

*With IE5, someone now has a choice between going the Dynamic HTML route with JavaScript and HTML, or they can go and start learning XML and XSL. If you were going to be a programmer, what would you do?*
I think a lot of people in the industry are in wonderment about this one. The key to remember is that HTML is the descriptive language for displaying information. The "Dynamic" part is primarily JavaScript. JavaScript, VBScript, PERL, or whatever, is what brings the static HTML pages alive. The page changes given user actions; i.e., JavaScript changes the HTML. XML is a completely different critter. It doesn't have anything to do with how the information is displayed to the user, it is simply a way to describe data, that when used with HTML, will be displayed. XSL, much like CSS, provides advanced formatting of the XML data like filtering, rearranging, sorting, etc. So, the technologies aren't mutually exclusive, they are designed to work together.

*So what you're talking about is, the trend is toward making data available dynamically from distributed sources. It's like, you have your static Web page which always displays the same thing. Then you have some more sophisticated sites where you go and retrieve data from a single fixed database. And then now, what we're talking about here especially with XML, is now we're starting to make things, as you say, Internet aware, to where you can write a site that will go out and exchange information with different sites and present that to the user on a dynamic level and in a way where they could change the way it's presented without having to write more than one application on the other end. So Internet awareness is providing dynamic data presentation in  distributed software.*
Excellent summary. So now you have XML, which is a rich way to describe data, Dynamic HTML, which provides the rich display, and JavaScript, which provides the programming logic. Those are the essence of any application; all based on open industry standards. With those basic pieces I can build a highly functional distributed application. It's a unique type of application that we've never had before. Take eTrade for example. They're an online investing site. They offer current information on stocks and mutual funds, informative articles, I can set up a portfolio with them, and I can even refinance my house loan, all online. Is this an application? You bet! Did I have to drive across town to buy the application and go through a time-consuming install before I could run the application on my computer? Will I have to upgrade this application on my system in a few months when there's a new release or bug fixes? Can I use someone else's computer and still use this application with all my data? Can I use this application from practically anywhere in the world from most computers? If I replace or upgrade my computer tomorrow, will the app still work? I think you get the idea.

*What do you see yourself doing in two years?*
I've been an evangelist less than two years and I've been having so much fun I really haven't thought about my next adventure. I'll definitely stay in the computer industry; I'm addicted to the excitement of the never-ending change treadmill.

*How about one year?*
Still working for Uncle Bill, probably evangelizing Windows 2001.

*Do you think that the two (Win NT and Win 98) are going to merge?*
Yeah, the development teams merged some time ago so there is a single code base going forward.

*Like Win NTX?*
We always seem to get stuck with these naming issues. We just introduced the new naming for our future operating system, it's called Windows 2000. Go figure. For the individual technologies our marketing department likes the word Plus a lot. For example, COM is becoming COM+ so you'll probably see more of that naming style.

*Well, thanks, Garth!*

# Summary

We have seen in this chapter that Dynamic HTML is a huge subject, involving:

- Cascading Style Sheets and the CSS1 and CSS2 specifications. These have become languages in their own right, and the future does not look to hold any simplification of these standards.

- The Document Object Model as issued by the W3C and its different implementations by Netscape and Microsoft, which are likely to change in the next few releases.

- Dynamic fonts, a DHTML component so new and easy to use perhaps people are puzzled by why there aren't two or three conflicting specifications bouncing around.

- JavaScript, a small part of which we've examined to discuss DHTML. Although the structure of this language is not likely to change much, the methods it provides to interact with the DOM will. You can go a lot farther with JavaScript than we have in this chapter, and we'll discuss JavaScript in more detail in the next chapter.

# INFORMATIVE SITES!

*www.Webreview.com*
*style.Webreview.com*
**Web Review is a great online magazine!**

*developer.netscape.com/javascript*
*developer.netscape.com/dhtml*
**Netscape DevEdge online.**

*www.microsoft.com/sitebuilder* (go to site map, or directly to):
*www.microsoft.com/sitebuilder/siteinfo/sitemap.asp* (then click on Workshop:
DHTML HTML & CSS)
**Microsoft Site Builder network (DHTML section).**

*www.w3.org/TR/*
*www.w3.org/stylesheets*
**W3C Technical Reports (includes CSS1 and CSS2 specifications).**

*www.rhoque.com* (Reaz was a Web98 speaker)
*www.dhtmlzone.com*
*www.ruleWeb.com/dhtml*
**Dynamic HTML power sites!**

*www.truedoc.com*
*www.hexmac.com*
**These sites are all about dynamic fonts!**

# JavaScript

Now that you've learned Dynamic HTML, you know that the dynamic part depends on scripting languages, of which JavaScript is the top contender. Scripting goes way beyond Dynamic HTML, however, and there are plenty more things you can do with JavaScript.

In this chapter you're going to learn how to use JavaScript. Although I can't teach everything about JavaScript in a couple of dozen pages, this will get you going, and going, and going! With Dynamic HTML you're not really using the full power of JavaScript. You can set a property here and there with a statement, but there's just so much more to programming!

By the end of this chapter you will not only know JavaScript but you will have learned a true programming language, complete with all the elements that make up such a language. We'll be seeing some pretty amazing stuff that can be used to make the Internet really work for you.

## What Is JavaScript?

JavaScript is a scripting language that has moved a long way toward qualifying as a full-fledged programming language. Although I keep hearing claims that JavaScript has nothing to do with Java, it's certain that the Java language was in mind when JavaScript was originally designed. JavaScript was first released under the name Live-Script by Netscape with its 2.0 browser. But all speculation aside, JavaScript contains a bit of many languages and if nothing else, JavaScript and Java both sprung from the same object-oriented soil. The efficient string handling of PERL, the object functionality of C++ and Java, and the scripting heritage of Unix all have a bit of their DNA in JavaScript.

JavaScript can be described as a simplified form of Java that depends on the browser to supply a lot of the high-powered functionality that a language like Java has. The browser's JavaScript engine makes it unnecessary to write sophisticated event-handling routines, oversee the translation of variables from one type to another, or write a whole series of methods to do all the normal housekeeping required to ensure the simplest of functions work reliably. This makes writing JavaScript a much easier job than writing in languages that chastise you for your every missing punctuation mark or variable declaration.

If JavaScript keeps improving by leaps and bounds as it has the last few years, Java's reign will be threatened, or at least squeezed out of some of the territory it now occupies.

## Differences between Java and JavaScript

JavaScript and Java are both programming languages. Java came first and is definitely more sophisticated, but the gap is closing. Aside from the earlier discussion about writing JavaScript, here are the basic differences:

**JavaScript is stored on the host machine as source text.** Java is stored on the host machine as compiled bytecode (a form of *object code* as discussed in Chapter 2, "How Does the Internet Work?").

**JavaScript is compiled and run as the page is loaded by the browser.** Java is compiled from interpretive bytecode to client native code through the Java Virtual Machine and run only after the applet has fully loaded.

**JavaScript has limited ability to store cookies on the client machine.** Java is restricted from any access to the client file system.

**JavaScript can control a Java applet.** A Java applet cannot control JavaScript.

**JavaScript running on the server is called *server-side* JavaScript.** Java programs running on the server are called *servlets*.

**JavaScript running on the client is, well, just plain JavaScript.** Java programs running on the client are called *applets*.

**JavaScript can interact with the DOM to make HTML dynamic.** Java is, again, restricted to running inside its own sandbox.

As far as Web builders are concerned, the primary functional difference between these two languages is that JavaScript can act within the browser, and will soon be able to dynamically change any element on the Web page. Java is destined to remain a restricted application. It is very fast and high powered, but is encapsulated to perform specific tasks under tight security.

**ECMASCRIPT**

Netscape started it, but in early 1997 it gave the job of updating JavaScript to the European Computer Manufacturers Association (ECMA), a European organization founded in 1961. The ECMA has started technological standards committees in the same manner as our W3C.

Standard ECMA-262 was released in June 1997. This ECMA Standard defines the ECMAScript scripting language. The originating technology for this ECMA Standard is JavaScript. ECMAScript is JavaScript.

Microsoft and Netscape are committed to supporting the standards as released by ECMA.

We will go over the elements of JavaScript starting with data types, then move on to expressions, statements, and functions. We'll also discuss how JavaScript works inside Web browsers and see examples of how to put all of this to work.

# Data Types

Data types can be declared as constants or variables. Technically, constants are simply assigned and variables are declared using the *var* keyword. One of the forgiving features of the language is that it will work either way.

Elementary data types are types of data, such as numbers or character strings, whose basic functions are built into the language runtime. It would be too much work for programmers to have to define assignment, addition, subtraction, and so forth, for basic data types in every program, so elementary data types are provided.

The truth is that even object data types can have basic functions included as part of the language, but the difference with these is that they are still treated as objects with properties, and so you can extend their functionality.

## Elementary Data Types

JavaScript has only a few data types: Boolean, number, string, Array, and Object. The first three are elementary and the last two are object data types.

**Boolean**   result = true; var result = false;

This data type gives the expected values *true* and *false*. Internally, these may or may not be represented as 1 and 0. The important thing is that we use the literals *true* and *false* to represent this data type.

**Number**   c = 186282; var x = 0;

All numbers are represented as floating point. On most computers, floating-point numbers are stored in two parts: the number value (which is called a *mantissa*), and an exponent value. The mantissa is stored without a decimal point and is assumed to be a decimal number whose value is between 1 and 10 (if not 0), such as 1.23456789. The exponent is the exponent of 10 to multiply the number by. For example, the speed of light would be represented as 1.86282E+05 (you can actually write it this way), which means $1.86282 \times 10^5$. In JavaScript you can use numbers as small as $10^{-300}$ to as large as $10^{+300}$.

| | |
|---|---|
| **String** | **today = "Friday"; comment = "I said, '15% is enough!'"; var blanks = "";** |

The word *string* must come from the expression "to string together." Strings are, well, strings of 0s or more characters. You can have up to a megabyte-long string, but it's hard to find a reason for one more than a few hundred characters long.

There are many special aspects to strings. For example, if your string is in double quotes you can only have single quotes inside the string, and vice versa. Any other characters are valid. There are always exceptions, however, and with strings there is a set of special characters called *escape sequences*. Escape sequences are used in two ways. First, the \ character is used to include the next character in the string; for example, "I said, \"Quotes are OK!\"". Second, they are used to represent characters that can't be shown; for example, the line break sequence \n as in, "I'm a poet,\nand I don't know it". Table 6.1 lists the more common JavaScript escape sequences.

## Object Data Types

Elementary data types are elementary because they occupy a single predictable memory location. More sophisticated data types require methods to implement them and so are created as objects. Remember, objects have properties (data with attributes) and methods (functions).

Object data types are created (or *instantiated*, which means we are creating an *instance* or occurrence of the object) with the *new* keyword. In JavaScript we have two object data types: Arrays and Objects.

**NOTE**
Object data types are capitalized!

**Table 6.1**  JavaScript Escape Sequences

| SEQUENCE | FUNCTION |
|---|---|
| \ | Interpret the next character as part of the string |
| \\ | Backslash |
| \n | Newline (depends on OS: DOS = carriage return+line feed, Unix = line feed) |
| \r | Carriage return |
| \t | Tab |
| \xFF | Hexadecimal character FF |

**Arrays**
```
var days = new Array
("Monday","Tuesday","Wednesday","Thursday","Friday");
var months = new Array(12);
channel[13] = "UPN";
```

Because of the flexibility of arrays, the Array data type is created using the Array object. An array can be created simply by initializing the values as in the previous example, which creates a five element string array. Arrays can also be created by declaring how many elements they have as in the second example, which is declared as an empty array with 12 elements.

Array elements start at 0, so a 12-element array would have elements 0 through 11 and would be referenced by subscript using square brackets (e.g., days[1]). In the third example, we create a 14-element array by initializing only the last element.

Arrays can also be created as a property list. This is a 3-element array referenced by strings instead of subscript numbers.

```
name = new Array(3);
name["first"] = "johnnie"
name["middle"] = "b"
name["last"] = "goode"
```

This gives us the flexibility of referencing each element in any of three ways.

```
name["first"] = "johnnie"
name[0] = "johnnie"
name.first = "johnnie"
```

Finally, all arrays have a length property that makes the size of the array accessible; for example, name.length is equal to 3 in the previous array. The following array would give a result of 3.

```
arraysize = name.length
```

Again, remember that this array has elements [0], [1], and [2]. This gives us an easy way of adding to the array. To add the sixth day of the week to the previous example we could code:

```
numdays = days.length
days[numdays]="Saturday"
```

**Objects**
```
thingamabob = new Object;
layerx = new Object (passlayer);
```

There are two reasons to create objects. First, creating an object from scratch that can then be assigned properties. This would most likely be done to create a database type of structure. Second, to make a new reference to an existing object that has been passed by a function call.

There is a lot more to describing objects than there is to other data types. Then again, in JavaScript there is a lot less to explaining objects than in other languages. Objects in JavaScript are straightforward because the JavaScript engine handles the hard stuff (like creating the object and declaring its specific properties) automatically. What applies to objects here also applies to objects in other languages, but you just have to do more to make it work the way it's supposed to.

Creating an object is as simple as shown. You can apply properties to the object just by doing it, you don't have to declare them in advance. The following four statements create an object, assign it two properties with initial values, and associate a function with the object, which then becomes a method of our object. Notice there is no () in the object-function association.

```
president = new Object
president.lastname = "Clinton"
president.firstname = "Bill"
president.testimony = grandjury
```

We can do much more with this. These next statements create room for even more data by creating objects and arrays inside the object.

```
president.wife = new Object
president.wife.firstname = "Hillary"
president.wife.testimony = grandjury
president.staff = new Array();
president.staff["vice president"] = "Al Gore"
```

You could even enclose the preceding statements in a new function that will initialize all this for you by calling it with the initial values instead of assigning them manually.

```
function president(lname,fname,wname,vpname) {
this.lastname = lname
this.firstname = fname
this.testimony = grandjury
this.wife = new Object
this.wife.firstname = wname
this.wife.testimony = grandjury
this.staff = new Array();
this.staff["vice president"] = vpname
}
```

What's this all about? I mean *this! This* tells the function that *this* property belongs to whatever object has called the function and not a specific named object. *This* can also be used in another function to access properties set in previous functions, like the preceding example.

Writing the function in this way enables you to create several instances of information and even invoke methods on this data. Here we'll call the function to create a new *president* object called *pres48th* and then use some of its methods to get some sensitive information.

```
var prez48th = new president("Clinton","Bill","Hillary","Al Gore")
secrets = prez48th.testimony()
moresecrets = prez48th.wife.testimony()
var prez49th = new president(??? ...)
```

Adding a final function makes this script work.

```
function grandjury(){
    return ("sshhhhh! ");
}
```

Figure 6.1 shows the whole set of script functioning with only this object-oriented code. This script reveals some very important points about how JavaScript runs in a Web browser.

There are two script sections in Figure 6.1: the script in the head and the script in the body. Further, some of the script in the head is inside of functions and some is not.

```
<HTML>
<HEAD><TITLE></TITLE>
</HEAD>
<SCRIPT>
function President(lname,fname,wname,vpname) {
    this.lastname = lname;
    this.firstname = fname;
    this.testimony = grandjury;
    this.wife = new Object;
    this.wife.firstname = wname;
    this.wife.testimony = grandjury;
    this.staff = new Array();
    this.staff["vice president"] = vpname;
}
function grandjury(){
    return ("sshhhhh!");
}
var prez48th = new President("Clinton","Bill","Hillary","Al Gore")
secrets = prez48th.testimony();
moresecrets = prez48th.wife.testimony();
</SCRIPT>
<BODY>
<SCRIPT>
document.write ("<H1> Secrets! </H1><BR>" + secrets + "<BR>");
document.write ("<H2> and more secrets! </H2><BR>" + moresecrets);
</SCRIPT>
</BODY>
</HTML>
```

**Figure 6.1**  Presidential programming.

The script in the head section is compiled and executed before the browser gets to the body section. This makes all of the properties of the *prez48th* object available to the body at the outset. Technically, the statements in any script section should come after the functions. If they were first, the browser would not know what functions they refer to. Browsers are forgiving, however, and will execute the script anyway (at least in this case).

The script in the body section takes the place of any HTML and creates the HTML for the page. If you load this page and then select View, Source, you get all of the above, except the SCRIPT section in the body is replaced with:

```
<BODY>
<H1> Secrets! </H1>sshhhhh!<BR><H2> and more secrets! </H2>sshhhhh!
</BODY>
```

Now we'll move on to more about JavaScript, including how to write statements.

## Operators

An *operator* is a symbol that describes a mathematical operation to be performed on one or more variables. Every language has operators, and since mathematics is a universal language, they're all pretty much the same. The only variation you will find involves exactly which symbols are used and which of the more complex ones are supported.

JavaScript supports the usual operators.

**Arithmetic operators** include plus (+), minus (–), multiply (*), divide(/) and remainder (%). This last is used to leave the remainder after a division, as in (9 % 4 = 1).

**Comparison operators** include equals (= =), not equals (!=), less than (<), greater than (>), less than or equal to (<=), and greater than or equal to (>=). Relational conditions are always put in parentheses, as in (a != b).

**Logical operators** include and (&&), or ( | | ) and not (!), and are always put in parentheses, as in (!a && b).

**Assignment operators** include equals (=) and the combination arithmetic operators illustrated in Table 6.2. The special double plus (++)and double minus (– –)operators can be used in expressions where the value of the variable is evaluated as part of a larger expression. The position of the operator determines whether the variable is evaluated before or after the addition or subtraction is done. ++x would increment x and then evaluate it. x++ would evaluate x and then increment it. We'll take a look at how this is used when we discuss looping later in this chapter.

## Evaluations

Operators are used to create expressions which, after evaluation, are assigned to variables or used to test conditions.

**Table 6.2**   Assignment Operators

| OPERATOR | EXAMPLES | EQUIVALENT |
|---|---|---|
| = | x = y | |
| += | x+= y | x = x + y |
| -= | x-= y | x = x - y |
| *= | x*=y | x = x * y |
| /= | x/=y | x = x / y |
| %= | x%=y | x = x % y |
| ++ | x++ | x = x + 1 |
| | ++x | |
| -- | x-- | x = x - 1 |
| | --x | |

Variable expressions are assigned using parentheses to control the sequence in the same way we studied these algebraic properties in high school, such as:

```
a = (b * (c + d);
a += b / (c * d);
a -= (b + c)/((d++ / e++) - (f * g));
```

The addition operator can also be used with strings to *concatenate* them. The presidential script example shown earlier is an example of this, where the *document.write* statement puts out a concatenated string of HTML code, also shown earlier.

Conditional expressions are all boiled down to a single *true* or *false* value and are evaluated using the same parentheses controls as variable expressions.

```
if (a < b)
while (a < 10 && b != 0)
test = (a != 0  && (b > 100 || c = "start"))
```

There is a special conditional operator that works like this:

```
x = a ? b : c
```

This first tests a, and if true assigns b, otherwise c, and can be implemented with a full combination of expressions:

```
x = ((a == 0 || b != 0) ? (c * d) : (e / f))
```

# Statements

There are only a few basic statements in JavaScript. These can be broken down into if statements, loop statements, and conditional statements.

## If Statements

if         **if (condition) statement; else statement;**

The *if* statement is present in its usual form, with or without the *else*. If *else* is present it only needs a semicolon on the same line as the if, one of the few places a semicolon is required. This statement, like any JavaScript statement, can be laid out with as much or as little whitespace as desired. If a block of statements is to be executed as part of an *if* or *else* condition, it must be included in curly braces.

```
if (a < b) c = d;
if (a < b) c = d; else d = e;
if (a < b)
  { statement block };
if (a < b) {
  statement block
}
else {
  statement block
};
```

## Loop Statements

No matter what form they come in, loop statements are written within the context of these conditions:

- A starting, or initial, condition
- A condition that changes before or after the loop is executed
- An evaluation of conditions as to whether the loop should be executed a first time or a next time
- A section of one or more statements that is repeated

for         **for (initial condition statements; repeat condition test; condition change statements) {statements}**

The for statement is in predictable format and contains three evaluations separated by semicolons. The initialization segment is optional and can contain one or more assignment statements. The repeat condition test segment is required. The condition change segment is optional and can contain one or more assignment statements.

```
for (test=0; test < 1000; test++)
for (;timeleft!=0;)
```

The first example will execute with the value of *test* starting at 0, incrementing *test* by 1 after each repetition until *test* reaches 1000. The value of *test* can be changed inside the loop, but if this is done it should be done carefully to make sure the loop does not repeat indefinitely. This type of situation is known as an *infinite* loop. The second example will execute as long as *timeleft* is not 0, but is the same as the next type of loop statement.

**while**         **while (repeat condition test) { statements }**

The while statement simply repeats the loop as long as the test is passed.

**do**            **do { statements } while (repeat condition test)**

The *do* loop is the same as the *while* loop, except that the condition is tested after the loop is executed, which guarantees at least one repetition of the loop.

**break and continue**

These are statements that can go inside loops that modify the execution sequence. Break causes the loop to be terminated. Continue causes the loop to skip the remainder of statements and go immediately to the next repeat condition test.

The following example keeps the Web browser captive until an image loads or until about 60 seconds passes, whichever comes first. There are other ways to do this, but this example illustrates the *break* and *continue* statements. *Complete* is a property of the *image* object that tells when the picture is done loading.

```
for (timeleft = 60000; timeleft < 0; timeleft--) {
    if (!mypicture.complete)
        continue
    else
        break
}
```

# Structure

When we talk about *structure*, we're talking about how the code is formatted. More specifically, we mean what symbols and spaces are used to define where statements begin and end, and how they are physically placed. This gives structure to the language in the same way shelves and bookends give structure to literature. I know some people who like to leave their books laying all over the floor, but you certainly wouldn't be able to find one as easily, and with code, well just forget about ever being sloppy.

JavaScript, like all languages, has specific rules that apply to its structure.

- JavaScript must always occur between <SCRIPT> and </SCRIPT> tags.
- JavaScript functions and blocks of statements are enclosed in curly braces { }.
- JavaScript evaluation expressions are always enclosed in parentheses ( ).
- JavaScript array elements are indicated using square brackets [ ].

- There are two types of comments, single-line start with //. Multiline start with /* and end with */.

- HTML comments <!-- and --> are not recognized by JavaScript, and in fact are used to hide JavaScript from nonscript-handling browsers, but not from script-savvy browsers.

- JavaScript statements can end with a semicolon, but if you don't put one in, the browser will not give you any grief, unless its assumption of where the semicolon should go is incorrect.

# Writing JavaScript

We are now going to study three working JavaScript programs on the Web, all illustrative of very basic and important things JavaScript was intended for.

I will explain everything that happens in these examples and bring to your attention elements of JavaScript that are not contained in the element listings seen previously for lack of space. There is a lot to this language, and to just dump it all out in front of you like a set of Tinkertoys isn't going to do much good. This is enough to get you started and make you dangerous.

A full reference book on JavaScript is recommended, but only after you get your feet wet. These books contain listings of hundreds of functions (many of which you will never use) and all kinds of ins and outs to the language (many of which you will either never run across or which should be avoided anyway).

**NOTE**
My philosophy is, if you are going to write code that is safe, efficient, and as generic as possible, you should not get involved in trying to hack around language nooks, crannies, and quirks. Be mainstream. Stay in the crosswalk. Don't cross against the light.

## Browser Detection

One of the first things you have to do to provide cross-browser compatibility is to determine what browser the user is running so you can avoid script error messages, browser crashes, and bad-looking pages.

Running JavaScript on a 2.0 browser is not worth the time, since only Netscape supports it and the original DOM is very slim. Running JavaScript on a 3.0 browser is risky at best because of the huge disparity of features supported, difference in implementations, and difficult browsers.

In Figure 6.2, we detect three pieces of information:

- Whether the browser is Netscape, Microsoft, or something else

- What version of the browser we are running

- The operating system the browser is running under

The main target of this browser detection program is the browser version. I only want to run JavaScript on version 4 or higher of Explorer or Navigator. The results are displayed to impress the user, then based on what is found, I jump to one of three pages. One for Navigator 4 and above, one for Explorer 4 and above, and one for anything else.

```
<HTML>
<HEAD><TITLE>You are now being abducted by Phunmen!</TITLE>
<STYLE TYPE="text/css">
BODY {background-color:black}
P {text-align:center}
</STYLE>
<SCRIPT LANGUAGE="javascript">
<!--
//IE4="mozilla/4.0 (compatible; msie 4.01; windows 98)"
//NS4="mozilla/4.01 [en] (win95; i)"
//NS3="mozilla/3.0c-nnic30 (win95; u;)"
function detect(){
 var browser = navigator.userAgent.toLowerCase()
 this.version = parseInt(navigator.appVersion)
 this.namever = parseFloat(navigator.appVersion)
 this.ns  = (browser.indexOf('mozilla') != -1) &&
            (browser.indexOf('compatible') == -1)
 this.ie  = (browser.indexOf('msie') != -1)
 this.unk = (!this.ns && !this.ie)
 this.ns4up = this.ns && (this.version >= 4)
 this.ie4up = this.ie && (this.version >= 4)
}
who = new detect();
//-->
</SCRIPT>
</HEAD>
<BODY BGCOLOR="BLACK">
<SCRIPT LANGUAGE="javascript">
<!--
 if (who.ns4up)
   document.write
        ('<META HTTP-EQUIV="Refresh" CONTENT="10;URL=indexns.html">')
 if (who.ie4up)
   document.write
        ('<META HTTP-EQUIV="Refresh" CONTENT="10;URL=indexie.html">')
 if (!who.ns4up && !who.ie4up)
   document.write
        ('<META HTTP-EQUIV="Refresh" CONTENT="10;URL=indexok.html">')
   document.write("<FONT FACE=Arial,Helvetica SIZE=+2 COLOR=white>");
   document.write("<CENTER><P>")
```
*Continues*

**Figure 6.2**    Browser radar tower.

```
    document.write("<HR><BLINK>NOW ENTERING PH&uuml;NSPACE</BLINK><HR>")
    document.write ("<A HREF='indexok.html'>
                      <IMG SRC='images/saucer.gif' BORDER=0></A><BR>")
    document.write("<FONT SIZE=+1 COLOR=blue>BROWSER DETECTED: ")
if (who.ns)
    document.write("Netscape<BR>")
if (who.ie)
    document.write("Explorer<BR>")
if (who.unk)
    document.write("Unknown!!!<BR>")
document.write
    ("VERSION DETECTED: " + parseFloat(navigator.appVersion) + "<BR>");
document.write("OS DETECTED: ")
if (who.win)
    document.write("WINDOWS")
if (who.os2)
    document.write("OS/2")
if (who.mac)
    document.write("MAC")
if (who.unix)
    document.write("UNIX")
if (who.vms)
    document.write("VAX/VMS")
document.write("<HR>")
document.write("<FONT COLOR=red>")
if (!who.ns4up && !who.ie4up){
    document.write
      ("Explorer or Navigator versions 4 or above are recommended<BR>")
    document.write
      ("for viewing this fun fun fun JavaScript-active site!!!<BR>")
} else
    document.write("<BLINK>JAVASCRIPT ACTIVATED</BLINK>")
 document.write("</P></CENTER></FONT>")
//-->
</SCRIPT>
<NOSCRIPT>
<META HTTP-EQUIV="Refresh" CONTENT="10;URL=indexok.html">')
<FONT FACE=Arial,Helvetica SIZE=+2 COLOR=white>");
<CENTER><P>
<HR><BLINK>NOW ENTERING PH&uuml;NSPACE</BLINK><HR>
<A HREF='indexok.html'><IMG SRC='images/saucer.gif' BORDER=0></A><BR>
<FONT SIZE=+1 COLOR=blue>HUMANS DETECTED
</NOSCRIPT>
</BODY>
</HTML>
```

**Figure 6.2** *(Continued)*

The SCRIPT tags immediately enclose a set of comment tags to hide the JavaScript from any nonscript-savvy browsers. Since this is the INDEX page where everyone visiting the www.phunmen.com Web site will land, we have to be ready to handle any browser that comes along. The comment tags hide the script from the HTML engine but not from the JavaScript engine. And conversely, the final comment tag is preceded by a JavaScript comment tag so this comment won't be misinterpreted as a JavaScript string!

The next few lines give an example of the strings that are returned when different browsers are queried for their identification. Odd, but even Explorer says *Mozilla*. It also identifies itself as *MSIE* and gives the correct OS. We're not distinguishing between Windows 95 and 98 here, so both browsers give us enough information to determine that we're running under Windows.

```
IEv4 = Mozilla/4.0 (compatible; MSIE 4.01; Windows 98)
NSv4 = Mozilla/4.01 [en] (Win95; I)
NSv3 = Mozilla/3.0C-nnic30 (Win95; U;)
```

The *detect* function will take the string returned by the browser and *parse* it (meaning break it up and analyze the pieces) to determine everything we need to know about our JavaScript environment.

Browsers that cannot read JavaScript will be left with an extremely abbreviated version of this page consisting of the HTML code within the NOSCRIPT tag pair. This code displays a default detection page advising the viewer to upgrade his or her browser and jumps to a non-JavaScript homepage. JavaScript-savvy browsers will ignore the markup within the NOSCRIPT tags. Explorer will also ignore the unsupported BLINK tag.

The first thing we do is access the user agent identification string by using the built-in browser property *navigator.userAgent*. We then remove variations in representation by converting it to lowercase using *toLowerCase*, a method of the String object. To make our life easier, strings, like arrays, are not declared as objects but are handled as objects within JavaScript, giving us many built-in methods like this one to manipulate them.

Next, we use the *parseInt* and *parseFloat* methods on the *navigator.appVersion* browser property. These parsing functions are built-in JavaScript methods. JavaScript has a great deal of built-in methods available to use that we do not have to take any special measure to include in our programming. These two mathematical methods will return the first valid string within the string that fits the *integer* and *float* formats, respectively. This means that when Explorer returns "4.01" the *integer* will be 4 and the *float* will be 4.01. These can also be used to validate user input in forms that we'll discuss in the next example.

Another string method used here is *indexOf()*. This method searches one string for another string inside of it, which we'll call a *substring*. If the substring is found, it returns its starting position within the string with 0 (the first character). If the substring is not found, the function returns −1.

This script is a good example of a lot of *if* statements with conditional expressions. There are a lot of *if* statements and assignments based on conditionals such as *x = (expression)*.

After we are finished with everything inside of the function, we then have to call the function as a first action so we can base our Web page activity on the results. This is done by one line within the script:

```
who = new detect();
```

The code that will detect the OS is not shown here. That is because there are a lot more OSs than browser versions so it would add more than another whole page to the code, and it's just more of the same *if this, if that*. The full version can be viewed online. Better yet, the guru on browser detection can be found online at developer.netscape.com.

Once inside the BODY of the document, we don't waste any time getting back to JavaScript. A series of *document.write* statements, another built-in JavaScript function, write out HTML markup that displays the result of our browser radar script and executes a META tag to wait 10 seconds and then jump to the appropriate page.

In any case, we end up with a browser that displays a page without JavaScript errors or invalid markup. The result as seen on a JavaScript-savvy browser is shown in Figure 6.3. The spaceship is an animated GIF that wobbles back and forth as it scans the ground. The top and bottom lines will flash when viewed with Navigator, and after 10 seconds the page will automatically jump.

## Form Validation

The next JavaScript implementation we are going to study is an exercise in validating user input. Specifically, we will be checking numerical input and using the result to calculate fields or give error messages where appropriate. This particular script works in both Navigator and Explorer.

The code we will be reviewing has had its table tags removed so we can see the forest for the trees. Because of this, the layout is not obvious. Figure 6.4 illustrates the layout of the page so we can follow along with the script as shown in Figure 6.5. Sections not dealing with this study have been removed from the page and the code (specifically the credit card entry section and shipping charge table) so we are only left with what is relevant. You can see the entire form online at www.prolotherapy.com.

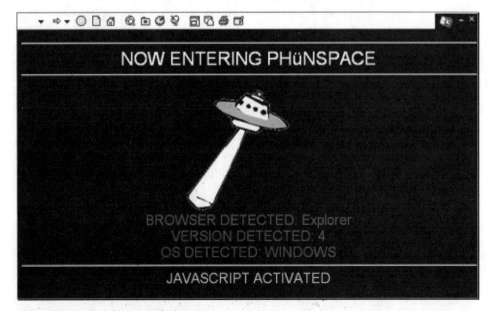

**Figure 6.3**   Alien browser detector.

Unlike the previous script, this is powered by events. The events we will discuss are accepting the quantity for two items to be ordered, and computing totals fields. The script will compute the totals for each item, subtotal all items for the purchase, take a guess at the shipping amount, and add it all up into the totals box. The events driving HTML attributes are shown in bold.

Let's start with the form rather than the functions. This FORM object is named *orders* by giving it the *NAME=orders* attribute. It has five text entry fields that trigger events. Remember, there is no such thing as numerical data entry in forms, only text.

These text fields use the ONBLUR event to trigger field validation and the ONFOCUS event to trigger field computation. You will recall that ONFOCUS is triggered when the cursor is placed in a text box and ONBLUR is triggered when another field gets focus. The reason ONCHANGE is not used here is because a user can leave a quantity field unchanged, which in this case could mean blank, and so the event will not be triggered. This would work if we were not also interested in controlling which text box the browser gives focus to next!

In Figure 6.4 the user starts by entering his or her personal information and then moves on to the items he or she has come here to order.

The first event occurs when the user exits the first quantity field. The ONBLUR event calls the function *valhauser()*. The first thing you see is the mysterious statement:

```
with (document.orders) { statement block }
```

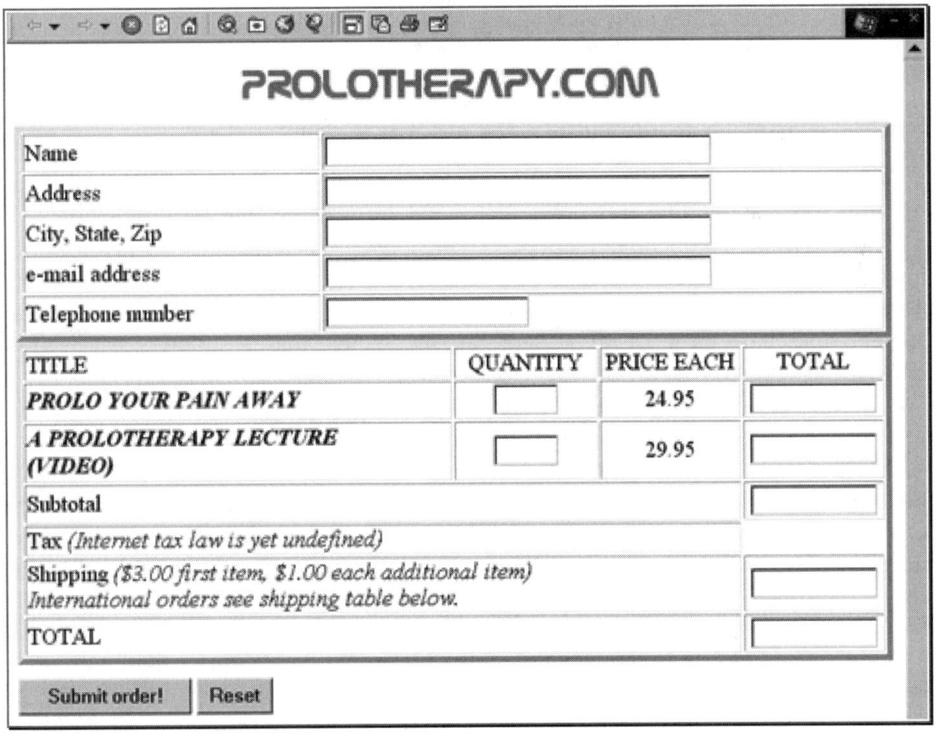

**Figure 6.4**    Form input faced by the user.

*With* is a special type of statement specific to objects. It puts the enclosed statement block at a certain level in the DOM (like the DOS *change directory* command) so we don't have to type the entire DOM address for every property in the *with* statement block. In this case, it saves us from typing lengthy addresses such as *document.orders.hausertotal.value.*

The first action we take in our validation function is to check and see if nothing was entered, in which case we set the value to 0 so our number-checking function will not fail.

Next, we use a new variation on the *parseInt* and *parseFloat* functions that has a second argument. This argument sets the *number base* for the integer or float parsing functions. This is important because these functions will also handle *octal (base 8)* and *hexadecimal (base 16)* number parsing, which we definitely do not want. Base 10 it is. I also use an *or* ( || ) condition to provide for the instance that 0 was entered, because when the results of the *parseInt* and *parseFloat* functions are evaluated as a Boolean expression, 0 will be interpreted as *false*, giving us an *alert* message.

An *alert* statement displays an *alert* message, which is a little input box that appears on the screen that displays a message to make the user click on the OK button.

## NOTE
**To see how an alert message works, go into your browser location window and type:**

```
javascript: alert("surprise!")
```

**The secret is you can type any JavaScript statement into the location bar and have it execute instantly. If you have a document loaded, it can act on the document content. To see your browser's userAgent ID, type:**

```
javascript: document.write(navigator.userAgent)
```

**The *document.write* statement will cause the browser to automatically open a new document window and display the result as the only content.**

Our field validation functions use the built-in browser object property *.value,* which gives the string value of a text field. Text fields are not declared as objects but, like everything else in the document, are part of the DOM. When the browser loads a document, it builds an object that represents the structure of that document. This object becomes the DOM as applied to that specific document and includes every variable, element, and character in the document. So any element that is not an object itself is still a property of this document super-object, which reigns above all it can see.

If the validation of the data entered is passed, we perform the calculation to set the value of the total field on the current line to the result of the computation, which is automatically displayed by the browser when it is assigned. We then bypass entry of the totals field by calling the *focus()* method (another built-in browser object function) to set the next data entry field. If the validation fails, we display an alert message, clear the value of the text field by setting it to spaces, and give focus back to that field. The second data entry line is the same as the first, except in this case, if validation passes, it calculates the subtotal and then gives focus to the shipping field.

There is one fail-safe in the subtotals field. Normally the subtotals field would be bypassed, but if the user elects to put the cursor in the subtotals field, the ONFOCUS event will again call the subtotal calculation function. We could put more validation functions in here to make this fancy, but it's really not necessary.

For example, we could add events to the item totals fields on each line to recalculate the line totals if they are ever given focus. Further, in these functions and in the subtotal calculation function, we could use ONFOCUS events to force focus to go on to the next field. This would prevent the user from entering anything in any of the line totals or subtotals fields. But since this form is pretty simple and not subject to much abuse, it's more work than it's worth. If we were dealing with a complex form with many lines and calculations, such a set of functions could save a lot of time in checking user input. Finally, the only reason we go to all this trouble is so the user doesn't get upset when we charge his or her credit card for some amount other than what it should be because he or she goofed up. So ask yourself, "did I add up five fields or did I add up six?"

When the shipping field ONFOCUS event is triggered, *calcship()* is called to estimate shipping based on a domestic order, charging $3 plus $1 for each item above 1. Instead of writing long lines of code to check to see if nothing was ordered, I set the value to 0 if it comes out less than 3 because if both quantities are 0, the result of the shipping calculation will be $(3 + (0 + 0 - 1)) = 2$. This also brings to mind the possibility that the user entered negative numbers in the quantities. This is another case where I don't bother because, if the user is here to make trouble, it's really a pretty desperate way to waste his or her time and mine. My main concern is to help the user who is here to buy something.

At the shipping field, ONBLUR event *valship()* is called in case the user has decided to enter a value in the shipping field. If validation is not passed, the field value is reestimated and focus is returned to the shipping field so the user gets the chance to reenter the data.

Finally, the totals field ONFOCUS triggers the final *calctotal()* function call, adding everything up. Figure 6.5 illustrates the form input.

```
<HTML>
<HEAD>
<TITLE>Prolotherapy Order Form</TITLE>
</HEAD>
<SCRIPT LANGUAGE="javascript">
function valhauser(){
  with (document.orders) {
    if (hauserqty.value=="")
       hauserqty.value = "0";
    if (parseInt(hauserqty.value,10)||hauserqty.value=="0") {
      hausertotal.value = parseInt(hauserqty.value,10)*24.95;
      videoqty.focus();
    }
    else {
      alert(hauserqty.value + " ?");
      hauserqty.value = "";
      hauserqty.focus();
    }
  }
}
```

*Continues*

**Figure 6.5** Form input faced by the programmer.

```
function valvideo(){
  with (document.orders) {
    if (videoqty.value=="")
        videoqty.value = "0";
    if (parseInt(videoqty.value,10)||videoqty.value=="0") {
      videototal.value = parseInt(videoqty.value,10)*29.95;
      calcsubtotal();
      shipping.focus();
    }
    else {
      alert (videoqty.value + " ?");
      videoqty.value = "";
      videoqty.focus();
    }
  }
}
function calcsubtotal(){
  with (document.orders) {
    subtotal.value = parseInt(hauserqty.value,10)*24.95 +
                     parseInt(videoqty.value,10)*29.95;
  }
}
function calcship() {
  with (document.orders) {
    shipping.value = 3 +
      (parseInt(videoqty.value,10) + parseInt(hauserqty.value,10) - 1);
    if (shipping.value < 3)
      shipping.value = 0;
  }
}
function valship(){
  with (document.orders) {
    if (!parseFloat(shipping.value)&&shipping.value!="0") {
      alert (shipping.value + " ?");
      calcship();
      shipping.focus();
    }
    else
      total.focus();
  }
}
function calctotal(){
  with (document.orders) {
    total.value = parseInt(hauserqty.value)*24.95 +
                  parseInt(videoqty.value)*29.95 +
                  parseFloat(shipping.value);
  }
}
```

**Figure 6.5** *(Continued)*

```
</SCRIPT>
<BODY>
<IMG SRC="proloanim.gif">
<FORM ACTION="cgi-bin/fmail.pl" NAME="orders" METHOD="POST">
<INPUT TYPE="hidden" NAME="recipient" VALUE="Websales@cintronics.com">
<INPUT TYPE="hidden" NAME="subject"   VALUE="Prolotherapy book order">
<INPUT TYPE="hidden" NAME="thankurl"
 VALUE="http://www.prolotherapy.com/prolothanks.htm">
Name             <INPUT TYPE="TEXT" NAME="name"      SIZE="40">
Address          <INPUT TYPE="TEXT" NAME="address"   SIZE="40">
City, State, Zip<INPUT TYPE="TEXT" NAME="citystzip" SIZE="40">
e-mail address  <INPUT TYPE="TEXT" NAME="username"  SIZE="40">
Telephone number<INPUT TYPE="TEXT" NAME="phonenumber">
(table stuff removed, table header row follows:)
TITLE   QUANTITY   PRICE EACH   TOTAL
(table stuff removed, first row:)
PROLO YOUR PAIN AWAY
<INPUT TYPE="TEXT" NAME="hauserqty" SIZE="5" ONBLUR="valhauser()">
24.95
<INPUT TYPE="TEXT" NAME="hausertotal" SIZE="12">
(table stuff removed, second row:)
A PROLOTHERAPY LECTURE (VIDEO)
<INPUT TYPE="TEXT" NAME="videoqty" SIZE="5" ONBLUR="valvideo()">
29.95
<INPUT TYPE="TEXT" NAME="videototal" SIZE="12">
(table stuff removed, subtotal row:)
Subtotal
<INPUT TYPE="TEXT" NAME="subtotal" SIZE="12" ONFOCUS="calcsubtotal()">
(table stuff removed, tax row:)
Tax (Internet tax law is yet undefined)
(table stuff removed, shipping row:)
Shipping ($3.00 first item, $1.00 each additional item)
International orders see shipping table below.
<INPUT TYPE="TEXT" NAME="shipping" SIZE="12" ONFOCUS="calcship()"
                                             ONBLUR="valship()">
(table stuff removed, total row:)
TOTAL
<INPUT TYPE="TEXT" NAME="total" SIZE="12" ONFOCUS="calctotal()">
<INPUT TYPE="SUBMIT" VALUE="Submit order!" NAME="Submit1">
<INPUT TYPE="RESET" NAME="Reset1"></FORM>
</BODY>
</HTML>
```

**Figure 6.5**    *(Continued)*

## Animation

In our final example, we're really going to fire up the flivver (an old car with a crank; no I'm not that old) and use Dynamic Positioning.

## MATH IN JAVASCRIPT

The JavaScript object gives us easy access to complex mathematical algorithms.

Math is an object because it has properties in the form of mathematical constants such as PI, and methods such as sin(), cos(), etc. The following table lists the properties that have a full 18 significant digits.

Built-In Properties and Methods of the JavaScript MATH Object

| PROPERTY | VALUE |
|----------|-------|
| E | 2.718 |
| LN2 | 0.693 |
| LN10 | 2.302 |
| LOG2E | 1.442 |
| LOG10E | 0.434 |
| PI | 3.1415…etc. |
| SQRT1_2 | .707 (root $\frac{1}{2}$) |
| SQRT2 | 1.414 |

| METHOD | DESCRIPTION |
|--------|-------------|
| abs(n) | Absolute value |
| acos(t) | Arccosine (1/cos) |
| asin(t) | Arcsine (1/sin) |
| atan(t) | Arctangent (1/tan) |
| ceil(n) | Next integer above n |
| exp(n) | $e^n$ |
| floor(n) | Next integer below n |
| log(n) | Log e(n) |
| max(a,b) | Larger number |
| min(a,b) | Smaller number |
| pow(a,b) | $a^b$ |
| random() | Between 0 and 1 |
| round(n) | Splits at <.5, >=.5 |
| sin(t) | Sine |
| sqrt(n) | Square root |
| tan(t) | Tangent |

You should prefix these properties and functions with *Math*, as shown in the code examples. Invalid numbers are two intrinsic (built-in) constants: NaN and Infinity.

NaN (Not a Number) is a constant you will get if you execute an invalid calculation such as total = "hello" * 9.95, which doesn't work. User input is especially relevant here, which is why we use functions like parseInt and parseFloat.

*Infinity* means just that and results in a divide by 0 or multiplying numbers too large to compute, which should never happen.

Use if statements and validation functions to ensure your math doesn't go bonkers.

This example is a masterpiece in JavaScript. It selects an image and a vertical coordinate at random, and then walks the image across the screen as illustrated in Figure 6.6. Since this is just a still picture, the arrow has been added to show the motion. Images are alternated flying left to right, then right to left.

We will be looking at both Explorer and Navigator versions of this animation script.

The script starts off with an array of the names of 43 different GIF files. Again, only the code relevant to this animation is shown. All the JavaScript is of course included, but the only HTML you see is what is relevant to the IMG tag we are going to animate. In this case, all that is missing is the HTML table with the images and text you can see in Figure 6.8. The whole page is online at www.phunmen.com.

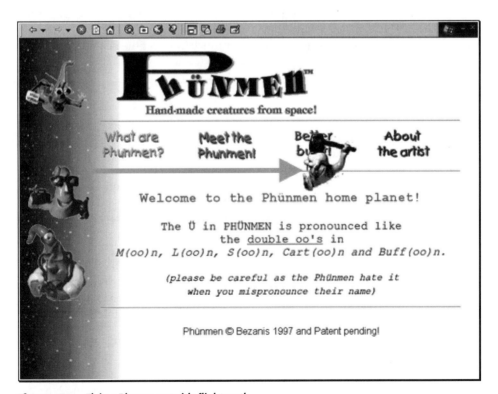

**Figure 6.6** Flying Phunmen with flight path.

The main *phunexec* function is automatically started when the page loads as a result of the BODY event ONLOAD="phunexec()". The *phunexec* function starts the show and calls the *phunmotor* function, which runs the show. *Phunmotor* selects the image using the *selectphun* function, sets the direction variables, then calls the *flyphun* function to perform the animation. *Phunmotor* repeats ad infinitum.

The image we are going to animate is named *whatphun*, and is declared in an IMG tag with a blank SRC attribute that will be filled in by *selectphun*. The first thing each of these functions does is to set the *phun* variable equal to the value of the address of the *whatphun* image in the DOM. This is similar to using the *what* statement described earlier.

```
var phun = document.images.whatphun;
```

Since I create the variable *phun* to represent an image (which is technically an object since it has properties), I can add my own properties to it at will. First, I add the *xdir* property to represent the current image direction, in *phunexec*. Next, we use the *setInterval* function to set a timer that will start the *phunmotor* function in 20 seconds. *SetInterval* is a built-in JavaScript function that accepts a JavaScript command followed by a delay time in milliseconds.

```
setInterval('phunmotor()',20000);
```

The *selectphun* function uses the official random-number generator in the JavaScript *Math* object to get a number between 0 and 42, the range of image subscripts in the *phunmen* array. The *Math.random* function generates a random number between 0 and 1. Multiplying this by 42, then using the *Math.floor* function to get the next integer down, gives us an integer between 0 when *Math.random()* = 0, and 42 when *Math.random()* = 1.

```
phunnum = Math.floor(Math.random()*42);
```

Using this random index, we set the *phun.src* attribute to the path of the source image by concatenating of the image path with the filename. We then set the *phun .visibility* attribute to *show* just to be sure.

*Phunmotor* continues by adding properties for the starting point, ending point, number of pixels for each move, and a random value for the vertical position. You have to use Cartesian coordinates for this. Here's a refresher in 100 words or less: The x-axis goes from 0 on the left edge of the screen to a positive value equal to the screen size on the right edge of the screen. The y-axis goes from 0 at the top of the screen to a positive value at the bottom of the screen. The reason the (0,0) origin is at the top left is because that is the only predictable place you can put it. Web pages can always scroll off the bottom or to the right, but at load time the document is always oriented to the upper left.

The style properties *posTop* and *posLeft* are built-in properties of the image object initially set in the IMG tag STYLE attribute. These specify where the top-left corner of the image is placed.

```
STYLE="position:absolute;TOP:125px;LEFT:1000px"
```

There are two options for the position property, *absolute* and *relative*. In Dynamic Positioning, we can place an element either at an absolute coordinate position, or at a position relative to a prior position declaration. Further, there is no rule that elements cannot be positioned over other elements. Personally, I see little use for relative positioning, but plenty of use for absolute positioning, if only because relative positioning is harder to work with and is subject to compounding errors made in the positioning it is done relative to. The measurements are in pixels.

In JavaScript we can actually move the image to a position that is not on the screen! I don't want the image to stop while a part of it is still showing, so allowing for a display size of up to 600 × 800, this script moves each image from an x-axis value of below −100 to over +900. Each move changes the image position by 20 pixels simply because testing shows this to look the best. To add a bit of fun we randomly select a new y-axis value for each new image so you never quite know where the next one will come from.

```
phundate = new Date;
phun.style.posTop=(phundate.getSeconds())*10;
```

This could have been done using *Math.random*, but these statements show how the *Date* object can be used. Every time we initialize *phundate*, the new *Date* object assigns the date and time down to the seconds. We then use the *getseconds* method of the *Date* object to get a "random" number between 1 and 60 and multiply this by 10 to get a y-coordinate between 1 and 600. The *Date* object has more methods for year, month, day, hour, minute, and so forth. How do you think those Web sites update the time so efficiently?

We now enter the *flyphun* function, the heart of this matter. This is the easiest part. All we need to do is set the *whatphun* style attribute *posLeft* to the new location.

```
phun.style.posLeft += phun.xinc;
```

All that is now left is to see if we've reached the landing zone. If not, we set a timer to call *flyphun* again in 200 milliseconds. This is not really a *reflexive* call where the procedure calls itself. We are setting a timer to execute the procedure, which the browser takes over and handles for us.

```
setTimeout("flyphun()",200);
```

Figure 6.7 is the full Explorer code listing.

```
<HTML>
<HEAD><LINK HREF="phunmen.css" REL="STYLESHEET">
<TITLE>Phunmen home planet</TITLE>
<SCRIPT LANGUAGE="javascript">
phunmen=new Array("bifft.GIF","bigalt.GIF","bobbyt.GIF",
                  "borist.GIF","burtt.GIF", "bustert.GIF",
                  "clintt.GIF","dannyt.GIF","doctort.GIF",
                  "doriangrayphunt.GIF", "elsont.GIF",
```
                                                              *Continues*

**Figure 6.7**   Flying Phunmen, Explorer style.

```
                        "erniet.GIF","frankt.GIF","fredt.GIF",
                        "gabrielt.GIF", "garyt.GIF","howardt.GIF",
                        "ivant.GIF","larryt.GIF","malibubobt.GIF",
                        "mannyt.GIF","miket.GIF","mortyt.GIF",
                        "mrbigwigt.GIF","mrcongenialityt.GIF",
                        "mrfriendlyt.GIF","mrgreenbuckst.GIF",
                        "mrperfectiont.GIF","mrretentivet.GIF",
                        "mrshankst.GIF","mrspinklet.GIF",
                        "nelsont.GIF","ralpht.GIF","randyt.GIF",
                        "reggiet.GIF","rickt.GIF","rockot.GIF",
                        "salesjoet.GIF","spiket.GIF","symoret.GIF",
                        "tonyt.GIF","victort.GIF","wallyt.GIF");
function phunexec() {
  var phun = document.images.whatphun;
  phun.xdir = "right";
  setInterval('phunmotor()',20000);
  phunmotor();
}
function phunmotor(){
  var phun = document.images.whatphun;
  selectphun();
  phundate = new Date;
  if (phun.xdir=="right"){
    phun.style.posLeft=-150;
    phun.style.posTop=(phundate.getSeconds())*10;
    phun.xinc=20;
    phun.xend=940;}
  if (phun.xdir=="left") {
    phun.style.posLeft=1000;
    phun.style.posTop=(phundate.getSeconds())*10;
    phun.xinc=-20;
    phun.xend=-140;}
  flyphun();
  if (phun.xdir=="right")
    phun.xdir="left";
  else
    phun.xdir="right";
}
function selectphun(){
  var phun = document.images.whatphun;
  phunnum = Math.floor(Math.random()*42);
  newimage = "images/" + phunmen[phunnum];
  phun.src = newimage;
  phun.visibility = "show";
}
function flyphun(){
  var phun = document.images.whatphun;
  phun.style.posLeft += phun.xinc;
```

**Figure 6.7**   *(Continued)*

```
    if (phun.xinc > 0 && phun.style.posLeft < phun.xend)
        setTimeout("flyphun()",200);
    if (phun.xinc < 0 && phun.style.posLeft > phun.xend)
        setTimeout("flyphun()",200);
}
</SCRIPT>
<BODY BACKGROUND="images/space.GIF" ONLOAD="phunexec()">
<IMG NAME="whatphun" SRC="" HEIGHT="100" WIDTH="100" BORDER="0"
STYLE="position:absolute;TOP:125px;LEFT:1000px">
</BODY>
</HTML>
```

**Figure 6.7**   *(Continued)*

Now it's time for a paradigm shift, by which I mean a change in the way we look at the world, as we move on to explain what we have to change to make the Navigator version work.

The first and most basic change is what we are animating. In Navigator we have to declare our moving object as a layer, since Dynamic Positioning can just be done with this single tag. As in the menu examples we have seen earlier, the Navigator DOM only permits us to dynamically update properties of a layer.

```
<LAYER NAME="phun" VISIBILITY="hide">
<IMG NAME="whatphun" SRC="" HEIGHT="100" WIDTH="100" BORDER="0">
</LAYER>
```

The IMG tag is the same, except now it has no STYLE and is enclosed in a LAYER whose *visibility* is initialized to *hide*. Now when our functions want to locate the animation object in Navigator's version of the DOM, we have to reference the LAYER by its NAME attribute instead of going directly to the image.

```
var phun = document.layers["phun"];
```

Then in *selectphun()* we select the image file as before, but now we are using Navigator's DOM so we also have to set the *visibility* to Navigator's *show* instead of Explorer's *visible*.

```
phun.document.images["whatphun"].src = newimage;
phun.visibility="show";
```

Navigator's positioning properties are also different than in Explorer. We change the values of *xpos* and *ypos* instead of *posTop* and *posLeft*. Also, testing the movement in Navigator gives us a better result if we set the pixel increment to 15 instead of 20.

And, finally, to move our little friend instead of simply changing style properties we have to call the LAYER object *moveTo()* method.

```
document.layers["phun"].moveTo(phun.xpos,phun.ypos);
```

These changes don't look so difficult, and all my hard work looks easy once it's over. The truth is, if you get a conceptual understanding of the way each DOM works, it will be easy.

Future DOM structures promise to expand on both the different types I have explained so there will be plenty of use for what we have discussed. Figure 6.8 illustrates the Navigator code listing.

```
<HTML>
<HEAD><LINK HREF="phunmen.css" REL="STYLESHEET">
<TITLE>Phunmen home planet</TITLE>
</HEAD>
<SCRIPT LANGUAGE="javascript">
phunmen=new Array(same as above);
function phunexec() {
  var phun = document.layers["phun"];
  phun.xdir = "right";
  setInterval('phunmotor()',20000);
  phunmotor();
}
function phunmotor(){
  var phun = document.layers["phun"];
  selectphun();
  if (phun.xdir=="right"){
    phun.xpos=-150;
    phun.ypos=(phundate.getSeconds())*10;
    phun.xinc=15;
    phun.xend=990;}
  if (phun.xdir=="left") {
    phun.xpos=1000;
    phun.ypos=(phundate.getSeconds())*10;
    phun.xinc=-15;
    phun.xend=-150;}
  document.layers["phun"].moveTo(phun.xpos,phun.ypos);
  flyphun();
  if (phun.xdir=="right")
    phun.xdir="left";
  else
    phun.xdir="right";
}
function selectphun(){
  var phun = document.layers["phun"];
  phunnum = Math.floor(Math.random()*42);
  newimage = "images/" + phunmen[phunnum];
  phun.document.images["whatphun"].src = newimage;
  phun.visibility="show";
}
```

**Figure 6.8**   Flying Phunmen, Navigator style.

```
function flyphun(){
  var phun = document.layers["phun"];
  document.layers["phun"].moveTo(phun.xpos,phun.ypos);
  phun.xpos += phun.xinc;
  if (phun.xinc > 0 && phun.xpos < phun.xend)
    setTimeout("flyphun()",200);
  if (phun.xinc < 0 && phun.xpos > phun.xend)
    setTimeout("flyphun()",200);
}
</SCRIPT>
<BODY BACKGROUND="images/space.GIF" ONLOAD="phunexec()">
<LAYER NAME="phun" VISIBILITY="hide">
<IMG NAME="whatphun" SRC="" HEIGHT="100" WIDTH="100" BORDER="0">
</LAYER>
</BODY>
</HTML>
```

**Figure 6.8**    *(Continued)*

## INTERVIEW

*Eric Byunn, Netscape*
   Eric is the Group Product Manager for Netscape Communicator and came to Netscape straight out of Stanford Business School. I'm talking with Eric to find out more about Netscape's plans for the future of JavaScript. I believe it's always best to go straight to the source, and since Netscape was the source of JavaScript that's where I went.

*What exactly is it that you do, Eric?*
I've been at Netscape for about two and a half years now. I came on board during the Navigator 3.0 development cycle, and have been working on Navigator and Communicator ever since.

*What exactly do you with Communicator, JavaScript, and Dynamic HTML?*
I'm part of the team that helps set the direction for these products and technologies, develop them, and push them forward. We go and talk with developers and customers and see what kind of demands there are, what kind of market needs there are; we work on developing them, and then turn around and try to communicate to the world exactly what it is that we've done.

*Is there anything exciting going on in the world of JavaScript and Dynamic HTML right now?*
Yeah, absolutely. First of all there are a couple of interesting worlds. As you know, Dynamic HTML is really an umbrella name that refers to several different technologies. All of those technologies now, at least the first level, have become W3C recommendations. Most recently the Level One DOM has become a recommendation. So a lot of the activity here at Netscape is focused on creating fully compliant implementations of that at the same time that we are continuing to work with the W3C on the next level of innovation in that space.

The reason why it's pretty important for us to get to a point where there are fully compliant implementations is that we have not seen the kind of adoption of Dynamic HTML that we'd like to see and that we'd expect given the promise and the benefits of Dynamic HTML. That is driven primarily because the implementations from all of the browser vendors have not been fully standard, partially because the standardization process has not been complete. But now that we have at least first level specs on all these various standards, it's certainly our responsibility, and something that we're very heavily involved in doing, coming up with fully standard implementations of it. In turn, developers who want to write to those standards will be confident that users will be able to see exactly what they intend.

*I've had experience with that thing they call XBDHTML, a seven-letter acronym.* It's good stuff for what it is, but it would make a lot more sense if you didn't have to jump through any hoops to make it work in all the browsers, if it just inherently did because they supported the same standard. And that's the point of standardization, and that's the point of our effort. So that's, in the short run, one of the things we're working on.

At the same time we want to push the concepts behind Dynamic HTML forward, because it's all about making it easier for developers and making it easier for users to view highly interactive dynamic content. So from the perspective of the developer you want to do everything with more abstractions and more concepts so the developer doesn't have to do a lot of very low level meticulous and tedious coding, that's always open to bugs and that sort of thing.

And at the same time for the end user, we want to do it in such a way that they get very rich performance despite the fact that their connection to the server may be somewhat limited in bandwidth or the server may be resource constrained just because of the load that's on it. So we want to be able to allow for fewer round trips to the server and to increase the end user's experience. That was the original rationale behind these technologies and there's obviously a lot further that we can go in pushing that forward.

An example of that is a proposal that we made to the W3C called Action Sheets which is a step for taking a lot of the dynamic scripting and separating that out from the document. Much as cascading style sheets do that for style, action sheets do that for action. So that's something that is currently where we're pushing innovation in the Dynamic HTML space, and because we do feel that standards are so important we started that process by submitting a proposal to the W3C.

That's a formal proposal to the W3C so the W3C watchers [that's you, the reader!] can go and look at it. And realistically it will probably evolve, as it goes through the standardization process. Other interested parties will contribute their ideas, and then we'll work on an implementation that can be fully standard. So there are definitely a lot of innovation going on there.

Also in the pure JavaScript language itself, they're working on things enhance the programming language itself to make it easier for developers.

*There's plenty to JavaScript, the challenge is not that it lacks features. It's first of all understanding how to make the DOM work, and then of course the cross-browser problem.*
When a lot of people think about JavaScript they think about the DOM and how it hooks into the browser and having more control over the browser and having more items that

are directly addressable to the script both in the document, which is the DOM, and within the browser itself, which is another area that we're working on.

*You said Level One DOM, what does that mean, really?*
The W3C has taken all the things that people talk about with DOM and broken that into some basic levels. One of the very first things they did was they split the DOM effort into several different levels. It's a very similar concept to CSS1 and CSS2, so that some of the more basic things are in the earlier levels and then the more complicated things are at the higher levels.

*When the DOM first came out it was Netscape's idea originally, supporting the A tag and the IMG tag, and then Microsoft kind of took it and ran with it and made it apply to just about everything and we haven't had compatibility since.*
According to the W3C's Web site (at http://w3.org/DOM/Activity), Level 0 is the kind of functionality that was in IE 3 and Navigator 3, which is the last time that we had really reasonably solid compatibility. And then Level 1 talks about having access from a scripting language to a document, be it an HTML or an XML document, so that you can manipulate the document itself using the DOM. Level 2 allows you to manipulate the style sheet and to manipulate the style information, as well as, it will most likely define an event model to capture events. And then they anticipate some further levels in the DOM but they're not there yet.

So Level 1 is a W3C recommendation, so they're done on that, and Level 2 is starting. So given that the only commonality at the current time is Level 0, it will take a lot of work to fully implement Level 1, so we're off doing that work.

*Is the Mozilla project mostly responsible for maintaining the Communicator?*
We have published all of our Communicator and Navigator source code publicly, and the public shepherd of that is Mozilla.org. They're the open source arm of Netscape. At the same time we continue to have a full-fledged development team here within Netscape working on that open source code.

We, Netscape, are committed implementing DOM level 1, regardless of the level of 'Net contribution. Now at the same time, we're definitely getting contributions from the 'Net in helping us do that implementation and we're also getting a lot of support in terms of testing to make sure that we do have a fully compliant DOM and fully compliant style sheets and fully compliant HTML 4.

*So will this be in Navigator 5?*
Yes, it's all planned for version 5.

*When I went to Microsoft, it seems every person I talked to, no matter what I was talking about, ended up talking about XML. And you mentioned XML. Several things strike me when I think of XML, I could ask you a whole bunch of questions but where would you start?*
I would start with a couple of general caveats about XML. One is that XML is a very important technology going forward and it has a lot of promise, basically to help promote data and information interchange in a much richer way than HTML. However, it alone is not the answer to the world's problems. Definitely in some areas the hype has run ahead of the actuality. Coming back down into technology, exactly what is going on, Netscape has one of the first working shipping applications of XML, which is that if you've used the "What's Related" feature in Communicator 4.5, or in 4.06, that feature is actually powered by XML.

What the feature does is that if you're looking at a particular site it gives you some other pages that are related to  the page you're looking at in case you want to look for some other information on it. So if you're looking at the Netscape home page and you click the "What's Related" button it will tell you more information, give you some links to other places at Netscape, and also links you off to the Internet and all sorts of other different places.

*So how does XML figure in there? Does the browser send and receive XML?*
The way that XML figures into there is that the information that is all of those related links is sent back to the browser using XML. In particular we're using an XML application. XML is a W3C recommendation, and there's a W3C working draft for something called Resource Description Framework, or RDF, which is an XML application. The information in "What's Related?" is transmitted in an XML format, and the particular format that it's transmitted in is RDF. So we're actually using that there.

Going forward, in Communicator 5 we do a couple different things with XML I talked about XML before in relation to the DOM, and the Level 1 DOM talks about how you refer to an XML document. The way we display XML documents is using cascading style sheets. My understanding is that Microsoft is also are going to be implementing that.

*I know IE displays XML as Dynamic HTML, when the browser processes XML stuff it translates it to Dynamic HTML since that's what the browser is designed to do as a display engine.*
That's the way the browser internally handles it, but from the content developer's perspective it's given to the browser as an XML file. But unless the XML file also has along with it a corresponding style sheet, there's no way to display it. If you think about HTML, HTML contains the structural information and style information. Like the bold tag, that's style information. Or the paragraph tag, that tells you both that logically it's a separate section, but it also tells you to put a space between it and the next paragraph.

XML is powerful specifically because it only provides contextual information. It provides no style information. So to display XML you have to have some sort of style sheet to get the style information. Netscape has really been promoting use of CSS at least until XSL gets further along in the standardization process. I know that both Netscape and Microsoft are both actively involved in the working group that's working on XSL, but I believe at the point it is formally a working draft and I believe that it will probably undergo significant further change before it's finalized.

*So the $64,000 question becomes, is there a place for JavaScript in XML or XSL?*
Netscape absolutely thinks so. The DOM  applies to XML and is a recommendation. That actually defines how JavaScript, or another scripting language but Netscape believe strongly in JavaScript, can talk to the document. The DOM inherently is just a set of interfaces between the document and some sort of programming language. It's an access method. And within Netscape our primary language for using that access method is JavaScript, given that a lot of programmers know how to write it, it's standardized by ECMA and it really is the de facto language of the Web. So we continue to invest heavily in JavaScript and in this case using JavaScript with XML documents using the DOM.

So XML and documents and scripts work through the DOM. For data, JavaScript can talk to data elements as well out of XML. And for data we primarily use RDF as a particular application of XML, but JavaScript has the capability to work with that as well.

*I was looking at translating a Dynamic HTML Web page into XML. And I found that with XSL you have to take the content and assign a rule to it, and the rule will have the HTML formatting in it. The problem is I end up writing the whole thing over again in XSL, so I'm not really writing a "rule" because I'm having to just put the HTML in the style sheet just the way it was, and at this point it's not a rule that is generally applied, it's just making it apply to specific instances as it did before.*

Translating DHTML pages to XML and XSL verbatim is possible, but as you noted, this doesn't really get you any benefits from using XML. Action sheets are one part of the formula that can make the use of XML more effective. Used in conjunction with standard CSS, they allow you to factor event-based behavior in addition to presentation-related style. The key to using XML, CSS, and action sheets is still the ability to factor a document into repeating and reusable components. If there is a one-to-one correspondence between elements in your XML and rules in your XSL, there's little advantage in using these technologies.

*So tell me about action sheets. Is that two specifications?*

Action sheets is a single proposal to the W3C and it would conceptually apply to both. Syntactically they look very much like CSS, so they have the same kind of bracket structure, and then you would define the actual JavaScript procedure or the actual event within that context.

*So we're attaching an event to a tag or a piece of the DOM, the same way that style sheets do? So if we stuck with HTML we could now split the document out into four files. Your core HTML, the style sheet, a scripting file and an action sheet. And then with XML we could do the same thing.*

Exactly right.

*It's interesting to try and get your mind around what people are doing. I keep trying to get, what are these people thinking about, what's behind everything they're saying, because they have some kind of philosophy which has been going on in their space which they work in and which has now become invisible to them because it's part of their operating basis. I'm sure Netscape has their own philosophy going on here.*

The fact that we're using XML for the "What's Related" feature is just an indicator of where we're headed. I think when we get to 5.0 you will see internally to Communicator and also within our Netcenter Portal site that we'll be using XML all over the place as an internal tool within the product. So we can switch a lot of data communication methods within the product to XML and we'll also be converting a lot of the user interface towards XML and HTML.

*It's good to try and make it as easy as possible for your development people to minimize the amount of custom c code or whatever that goes into writing the browser and depend as much as possible on Internet standard formats to manipulate content, even within the program itself. As far as Netscape goes, you're primarily Internet oriented—what I wonder is what Netscape's idea is of the future Internet-wise. It seems that the bulk of Netscape's business is in the server area now, is that right?*

Actually we have two business views that we derive revenue from. One is the sale of servers and services to large enterprises. Then we also have the Netcenter Portal site, which is the place you can go for services and tools to help you use and navigate the

'Net. So it has channels, it has personalization, it has lots of content, it helps you search. So we do derive business around that, much like Excite or Yahoo! or any of those companies do.

The theme there is that Netscape's entire focus is on the Internet in general, and specifically within a business context on something we call the Net Economy, which is where really fundamental business processes and the way business operates is being transformed by the presence of this ubiquitous Internet. And we are building products and services, whether they be on Netcenter or on the Enterprise software side, that enable a company to participate in this Net Economy.

*What's your idea of where the future is going? I know everything's going to be faster and bigger and better and ...*
Maybe smaller. In terms of software size, amount of information that has been downloaded from a particular page. Smaller is sometimes better, bigger is sometimes better. I generally think it will be better and more information will flow and more activity will happen over the 'Net and the 'Net will continue to transform the fabric of business.

*What seems to be happening is even though we're standardizing certain programming technologies, they're having to increase bandwidth to accommodate content such as multimedia and things like that. So things like JavaScript are pretty standard at this point and we're just figuring out how to integrate them to make the development more standard and simple and at the same time opening it up to newer things. As far as JavaScript, are there any plans for this?*
Within the pure language space, it's continuing to develop. There is a follow up to ECMA-262 that I believe is in process. In addition, there is much innovation and new development on its way in the areas of Dynamic HTML and how JavaScript relates to the browser, the document, and Web applications.

*Thanks, Eric!*

# Summary

In this chapter we have reviewed the language that makes Dynamic HTML impressive. These features needed to be presented separately because of the huge scope of JavaScript. Even so, there is still a great deal more you can learn to do in this language.

Hopefully you have learned what JavaScript is, how it works, and you have a starting point from which to use it. JavaScript will be discussed again later in the book when we talk about programming tools that are emerging for languages like Java and JavaScript.

There is no Web site reference section for this chapter because the relevant sites were listed in Chapter 5, "Dynamic HTML." Visit these sites again, you may see some things that didn't mean much before.

Search the Web and see what JavaScript is doing out there.

# Visual Basic and VBScript

The usefulness of Visual Basic (VB) can be summed up in two letters: E Z! Visual Basic is a full-fledged programming language and is an excellent place to start doing real programming. It's easy to learn, easy to use, and it does not compromise on features. You can write standalone applications in VB, just like in Java, that do not need a Web browser to run. You can also write the Microsoft version of applets, ActiveX controls, in VB. ActiveX controls are explained in Chapter 3, "Programming, Scripting, and Applets."

There are pros and cons to selecting Visual Basic, which we'll discuss shortly, but that's true for any language.

VBScript is a scripting language just like JavaScript. Whereas Java and JavaScript are similar but not alike, VB and VBScript are nearly identical. VBScript is a stripped down version of VB. In this chapter we are going to write a program in VB, take the code and paste it into the SCRIPT section of a Web page, and perform slight modifications on it to make it work as a script.

We are also going to see the parallels between VBScript and JavaScript by translating some of the scripts we've written in JavaScript into VBScript.

## Pros and Cons of VB and VBScript

There are three sides to consider when looking over the pros and cons of VB/VBScript programming.

**Writing non-Internet VB applications.** At this moment, VB is a Microsoft-specific operating-system-dependent language. Even if VB is available for a Mac or for a Unix OS, it still must be compiled to native code, and as such, you would at least have to have one version of your VB program compiled for each OS in which you want it to run.

**Writing ActiveX controls in VB.** There is no such thing as a VB applet. This is because, unlike Java, there is no such thing as a "VB Virtual Machine" (although there was at one time a claim by one software company to have written one). Although ActiveX controls can do some pretty cool things, ActiveX controls are Windows-only. In order to have a "Mac ActiveX control," we would have to compile our VB ActiveX source program to Mac native code.

**Writing VBScript.** Currently only Internet Explorer has a VBScript engine. Running VBScript in Navigator will only give you a blank stare when the browser skips right over your <SCRIPT LANGUAGE="VBScript"> tag set. Or, if you just write <SCRIPT>, Navigator will try to interpret your VBScript as JavaScript, which goes over like heavy metal at a swing dance. With the Mozilla open source project, Microsoft could very well step forward and add a VBScript engine to Navigator.

# Writing Visual Basic and VBScript

There is not a special editor made by Microsoft for VBScript. However, since VB and VBScript are similar, it is possible to write a program in VB and convert it to VBScript. I'll show you how to do this later in the chapter.

Visual Basic is a Microsoft licensed technology, and is currently in Version 6 release. VB comes in several different flavors.

VB 5 offers the Control Creation Edition, which allows you to write VB programs and ActiveX controls. It's free, but it has several limitations. Programs can be run from the VB CCE but it will not compile them for distribution, meaning you can't create a standalone executable. You can even write an ActiveX control (a program that runs like an applet), but again it takes more know-how to actually make it distributable.

VB 5 and 6 both offer the Learning Edition, which is a step up from the Control Creation Edition. It's not free (it costs less than $40), but it includes a full set of manuals and a great help file. Both versions also offer the Professional Edition, which would be the usual package for an individual to buy and is priced at less than $500. The Enterprise Edition is meant for company/corporate use and goes for a hefty $2,000. If you're a student or teacher, the Professional Edition comes in an Academic flavor, which is less than $100. It's still a full-strength Professional Edition but is simply not upgradeable to the Enterprise Edition.

Unlike the scripting languages, VB has been around for several years and has a lot of sophisticated add-on products and tools that you can get from Microsoft and other vendors to enhance its functionality. These include ActiveX controls and ActiveX control writing applications, database creation and programming tools, and much more.

# What Kind of Language Is VB?

The VB *Integrated Development Environment (IDE)* is an incredible program writing tool. What makes it easy to write VB is just the thing that it has in common with scripting languages, and which in fact characterizes all modern windows/GUI programming: the event-driven program.

In the days of DOS and before GUI, programs were menu driven. The user was presented with a selection and would enter the text (whether numbers or letters) to go on to the next step. Further choices were governed by pressing control keys like Return, Escape, Control-this, and Alt-that. All of these keyboard events had to be explicitly coded into each and every text input subroutine in order to work.

This is no longer the case. Today's programs are decentralized, transfer of control being handled by the system through the use of events. We don't have to have a menu saying, "if this and if that go here or go there." We don't have to have function key handling statements programmed into every text entry line saying, "if this key then abort the routine, if that key display the choices," and so forth. Events take care of this for us.

In event-driven programming, like in scripting, we have a series of functions, methods, or subroutines (depending on the specific language), and these are represented on the screen by graphical user controls. The user activates that control through a mouse click or function key, and that function, method, or subroutine magically activates without having to have a central branching routine to decide what to do with the mouse click or function key. It's all invisible to the programmer.

What we are going to be doing in writing VB is using the VB toolbox to drag and drop controls onto the screen. We'll then need to write little bits of code to handle events associated with each control. There are two controls that have to be given special attention because they are different: the FORM control and the GENERAL control.

The FORM control is a container for all the controls on the form and it can also be assigned events. Remember the ONLOAD event from DHTML? In VB, the FORM control has this event, which activates when the program starts, and more events that we can apply to the form as a whole. This makes the FORM control the closest thing we have to a main procedure that has a say over all the other controls.

The GENERAL control is only used to declare global variables, meaning data that can be accessed by all functions. We'll be taking a closer look at this control later in this chapter.

## What Makes VB so Easy?

When you write HTML code, whether you use an HTML editor or not, you don't need a compiler. (If you want to review the role of a compiler in programming, look back at Chapter 3.) You test HTML code by simply loading it right into the browser. The same is true for JavaScript.

But when you get to full-fledged languages like VB and Java you have to get your hands on a software package that will compile the programs you write. Without the VB compiler you can't run your VB programs. Although VB is not free, when you buy a VB package you not only get a compiler, you get a VB editor that has evolved into the best thing since papyrus. That's what makes VB so easy. You don't have to write any GUI code! All the user interface programming is drag and drop so the only code you have to write is specific to the task. And what's more, since the GUI code is written for you, the GUI side always works.

VB is easy because you can learn the language while writing programs. Because VB code editors use fail-safe drag-and-drop screen elements, your programs will run from the moment you create them, no matter how brief they may be.

## Writing VB

Figure 7.1 illustrates the Microsoft Visual Basic IDE program screen. When you start VB the most important window on your screen is the form window. The following list explains the uses of this and other VB windows.

**IDE window.** This window is VB itself and includes the menubar, toolbar, and all the other windows including the control coordinates toolbar that shows exactly where controls are located on the screen.

**Project window.** This window holds your form and any other forms (such as popup windows) that you may generate in your program.

**Form window.** The form window represents the user interface. You can drag and drop controls onto the form, select controls to edit their properties, and double-click them to edit their event code.

**Toolbox.** These are the drag-and-drop controls. The selection of available controls varies based on the edition of VB you are using and how you may have customized it.

**Project explorer.** This window shows the filenames and hierarchy of the forms and other code modules in your projects.

**Code window.** This window is where the event subroutines are written.

**Property window.** Every control has properties like color, name, and location, and every property of every control can be set in the property window. This includes a little help at the bottom of the window to remind you what the property is used for because we already have enough things to remember in a day.

When you start VB, the first thing it asks you is what kind of project you want to create. For our purposes, a *standard EXE* is all we need. Even though we can't use this project outside of the development program, for learning purposes we don't need to. Position the windows in a way where you can see the form window, toolbox, and property window all at the same time. We don't need to see the project explorer and code windows at this point.

If you scan through the menubar and toolbar you will see many options. All the options we need right now are already on the screen in the form of the toolbox and property window, and many of these are actually duplicates of what you see in the menubar and toolbar.

Before we begin programming, let's take a look through the toolbox and see what our options are.

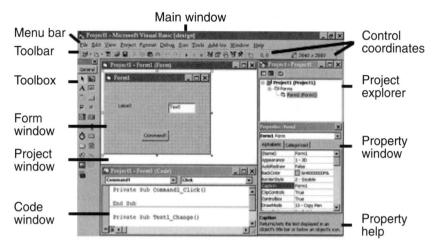

**Figure 7.1**  Microsoft Visual Basic for Windows.

# VB Toolbox

There are two ways to put controls on the screen. You can either double-click them to make them appear in the middle of the form and then move them to where you want them, or you can single-click them and put the cursor on the form to click and drag the controls to the size and location you want.

These controls all appear how they look in the toolbox and several of them appear just the same as their HTML FORM counterparts. Here they are, not quite in the same order they appear in Figure 7.2. As we go through each control, try it out on the form.

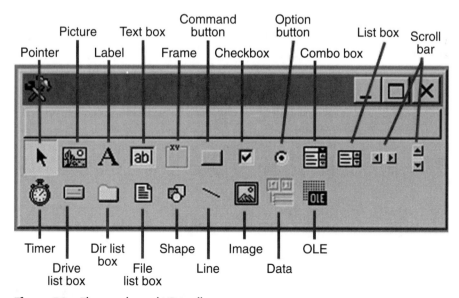

**Figure 7.2**  The unadorned VB toolbox.

**The pointer control.** This needs no introduction.

**The label box.** This control puts plain text on the screen. When you first put a control on the screen, VB gives it a generic name. You can see how this works in Figure 7.1 where there are three controls: a label box *Label1*, a text box *Text1*, and a command button *Command1*.

**The text box.** This control puts a user input box of any size on the screen.

**The command button.** This control puts a button on the screen that can be given a color and even a graphic image background. All control attributes are set in the properties window, which we'll look at next.

**Checkbox.** This control puts a checkbox on the screen. Checkboxes, like option buttons, can be grouped using the frame control. Responses to box checking must be controlled through event code.

**Frame.** This control is used to group controls, especially option buttons where only one in the group can be set.

**Option button.** This control is just like the HTML radio button. If you have only one set of option buttons in the form, you don't need to put them in a frame. Otherwise, frames will automatically limit each set of framed options to one selection.

**Line.** The simplest of all controls, this is just as it says, a line.

**Combo box and list box.** These controls have several options that we'll discuss later in this chapter.

**Drive list, dir list, and file list.** These controls are higher-level controls that allow you to select a drive, directory, or file. There is a better option for these that we'll go over later in this chapter.

**Scrollbars.** These controls will put a horizontal or vertical scrollbar on the screen, but all you get is the box with the slider. Any effect these have has to be programmed into the control's CHANGE event.

**Shape.** With this control, you can select from any of several shapes, all of which are simply ornamental.

**Image and picture.** We'll go over using these controls later in this chapter as well.

**Data.** This control is not available in the CCE but it is present in the Learning Edition. It is a more advanced control that adds database interfaces to packages such as Microsoft Access.

**OLE.** This is another advanced option that places controls that can interface with other applications.

## Using the VB Toolbox to Create an Application

First, start a new project or delete everything from the form you've been using.

Next, put a label box across the top of the form. Now go to the property window and select the *Caption* property. Remove the *Label1* caption and add *Warp Drive Calculator*.

Notice how VB replaces the label caption with every keystroke. When you program *Change events* in a *text box* control, VB will activate the change event for every keystroke. Click on the form background area so you can change the form caption to *Star Fleet*.

Now add three more labels in a single column below, and add a text box next to each label. Change the label captions to *Distance in light years, Warp factor,* and *Travel time in days.* Go to the *font* property and choose your preference by clicking on the ellipsis (…) in the *font* property entry. Go to the *text* property for the input boxes and remove the default text.

Next, add two command buttons to the bottom of the screen. Change the caption for one to *&Calculate* and the other to *&Reset*. The & creates an *Alt-* shortcut key using the next letter. We could have called the second control *Clear*, but this would have conflicted with the *Alt-C* shortcut for *Calculate* unless we captioned the button as *Clea&r*, which creates the less obvious *Alt-R* shortcut.

We can also add an ampersand to the start of the first two label boxes as *&Distance* and *&Warp*, but now we have a problem because we want the program to jump to the text box, not the label. To set this up we go to the *TabIndex* property. The text box *TabIndex* must be 1 greater than the label *TabIndex*. Set the *TabIndex* for all the boxes on the form so if we tab through the form it will go from top to bottom and not jump around.

Finally, move all these controls around on the screen and resize them to make it look good. If you want, put a line control here or there to embellish the screen, and change its *BorderColor* property by clicking on the down arrow in its property entry. Notice you can select from *Palette* or *System*.

We can also change the *ForeColor* property for the *Warp Drive Calculator* label to red and the *BackColor* for the form itself and all the labels to light blue. Here's a little trick: Click on one label to select it, then shift-click on the other two so all three are selected at once. Now when you change a property, it will change for all three at the same time. We can change the *BackColor* for the command buttons to gray as well. To do this you have to set their *Style* property to *Graphical*.

Now press *F5* or the *Play* button on the toolbar to run the project and Tab through the fields. Try the *Alt* key shortcuts or enter data. You can see all the controls highlight, the cursor moves around, and data appears in the text boxes, but the command buttons don't do anything—the event code to respond to our commands still has to be written.

What we have should now look something like Figure 7.3. Your project box will look different because I actually wrote this as an ActiveX control, but it runs the same as an EXE. I also have the project and form saved under the names *Warpexe* and *Warp*.

Notice the VB title now says we're in run mode. Since our program doesn't do anything yet, we want to exit. We have three ways to stop the program. First, we can use the media player type *Stop* control on the toolbar. Or second, click the *Close box* on the StarFleet window. Third and better yet, we can add an *Exit button* to our program.

If we add an *Exit* button to the form, then we need to set the button's *Cancel* property to true. This assigns the *Escape* key to this button. Only one button can have *Cancel* as *true*, so don't try to fool VB! If you set another one to *true*, this one will automatically turn *false*.

Now we're going to program our first event! Double-click the *Exit* button. The code window appears and lands you right in the *Click* event. Type *End*—that's it. Close the box, run it, and press escape. Wow!

We'll come back and finish this program later. First, let's explore VB some more.

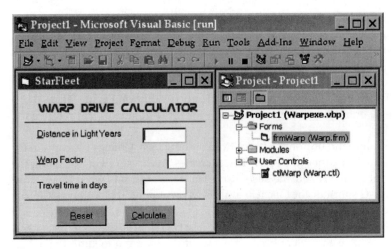

**Figure 7.3**   VB in action.

# Properties

As you have seen from the preceding exercise, every control has a fairly long list of properties that are specific to its function. These are viewed and changed in the VB properties window and if you look near the top of the window you will see two tabs. Click on these tabs and you will see that the property list can be viewed in two ways, alphabetically and categorized.

When you view by category the properties fall into these categories:

**Appearance.** These properties include captions, background and foreground colors or images, borders, and whether the control is hidden or visible.

**Behavior.** These properties include what happens to the control itself when it is clicked, dragged, dropped, scrolled, sized, tabbed, typed, and so forth. The control can also be set as enabled or not.

**Data and DDE (Dynamic Data Exchange).** This is used to link controls to databases.

**Font.** This property sets the font for controls that use fonts.

**Position.** This property can be used to fine tune the placement and size of the control. Default measurements are in twips, of which there are 1,440 to the inch.

**Scale.** For pictures only, this property controls how the picture is sized in the control. You can program event code to load and swap picture files and these controls decide how they will be displayed. The image and picture controls are the same basic control, but the picture control has a lot more property settings.

**Misc.** Anything other property, mostly specialized tabs by control. TabIndex is included here as well as the ToolTipText property, which sets the text that is displayed after the cursor is put over a control for a few seconds. Read the property help captions to see what these do.

Table 7.1 contains a list of the property controls for the most frequently used controls. The best way to see what these properties do is to read the property help and test them. But we'll go over a few of the major ones here.

**Name.** Every control has a name, and you'll be using this property in event code as a handle to the control just like in Dynamic HTML. It is suggested that you give a name to the control that starts with a three-letter abbreviation of the type of control followed by a descriptive name. In the Warp Drive control shown earlier, some of the names I gave to controls are *frmWarp*, *lblDistance*, and *txtDistance*.

**Cancel.** As mentioned earlier, this control enables the Escape key for one command button in the form. Must be accompanied by an *End* statement in the *Click* event to exit the program.

**DisabledPicture and DownPicture.** These controls specify what image to display when a command button is disabled and depressed, and can be used with the *Picture* property. The *Style* property must be set to graphical.

**Enabled.** This control enables and disables the control. Like many of these properties, this can be dynamically set from within the event code, allowing you to turn controls on and off depending on what's going on.

**Font.** This control gives a menu of font face, style, size, and effects.

**LargeChange.** This control is for scrollbars only. The meaning of the scrollbar is entirely based on the properties set for it, which include *Max*, *Min*, *SmallChange*, and *LargeChange*. The max and min determine the values at each end of the bar. When you click on a scrollbar you can click the arrows at either end, which moves the scrollbar a *SmallChange* interval, or the space between the box and the arrows, which moves the scrollbar a *LargeChange* interval. The current location of the scroll box, which can also be set as an initial value and when changed activates the *Change* event, is in the *Value* property.

**Locked.** This control can be set for a text box to prevent the user from changing the content.

**PasswordChar.** This control sets a character that will echo when input is entered in a text box.

**Picture.** This control specifies a background image for the control. See also *DisabledPicture* and *DownPicture*.

**SmallChange.** See *LargeChange*.

**TabIndex.** This control sets the order of focus for controls when the tab key is pressed and can be used with shortcut keys to jump to text boxes where the text box *TabIndex* is set to 1 greater than the label *TabIndex*.

**ToolTipText.** This control displays a hint box when the cursor is left over the control.

**Value.** The status of an option button, checkbox, or scrollbar.

**Visible.** Allows you to hide and show controls.

**Table 7.1** A Sample of VB Control Properties

| | LABEL | TEXT BOX | COMMAND BUTTON | OPTION BUTTON & CHECKBOX | SCROLLBARS, H & V | IMAGE | PICTURE |
|---|---|---|---|---|---|---|---|
| Name | ✓ | ✓ | ✓ | ✓ | ✓ | ✓ | ✓ |
| Alignment | ✓ | ✓ | | ✓ | | | ✓ |
| Appearance | ✓ | ✓ | ✓ | ✓ | | ✓ | ✓ |
| AutoRedraw | | | | | | | ✓ |
| AutoSize | ✓ | ✓ | | | | | ✓ |
| BackColor | ✓ | ✓ | ✓ | ✓ | | | ✓ |
| BackStyle | ✓ | | | | | | |
| BorderStyle | ✓ | ✓ | | | | ✓ | |
| Cancel | | | ✓ | | | | |
| Caption | ✓ | | ✓ | ✓ | | | |
| ClipControls | | | | | | | ✓ |
| Default | | | ✓ | | | | |
| DataField | ✓ | ✓ | ✓ | ✓ | | ✓ | ✓ |
| DataSource | ✓ | ✓ | ✓ | ✓ | | ✓ | ✓ |
| DisabledPicture | | | ✓ | ✓ | | | |
| DownPicture | | | ✓ | ✓ | | | |
| DragIcon | ✓ | ✓ | ✓ | ✓ | ✓ | ✓ | ✓ |
| DragMode | ✓ | ✓ | ✓ | ✓ | ✓ | ✓ | ✓ |
| DrawMode | | | | | | | ✓ |

**Table 7.1** Continued

| | LABEL | TEXT BOX | COMMAND BUTTON | OPTION BUTTON & CHECKBOX | SCROLLBARS, H & V | IMAGE | PICTURE |
|---|---|---|---|---|---|---|---|
| DrawStyle | | | | | | | ✓ |
| DrawWidth | | | | | | | ✓ |
| Enabled | ✓ | ✓ | ✓ | ✓ | ✓ | ✓ | ✓ |
| FillColor | | | | | | | ✓ |
| FillStyle | | | | | | | ✓ |
| Font | ✓ | ✓ | ✓ | ✓ | | | ✓ |
| FontTransparent | | | | | | | ✓ |
| ForeColor | ✓ | ✓ | | ✓ | | | ✓ |
| Height | ✓ | ✓ | ✓ | ✓ | ✓ | ✓ | ✓ |
| HelpContextID | | ✓ | ✓ | ✓ | ✓ | | ✓ |
| HideSelection | | ✓ | | | | | ✓ |
| Index | ✓ | ✓ | ✓ | ✓ | ✓ | ✓ | ✓ |
| LargeChange | | | | | ✓ | | ✓ |
| Left | ✓ | ✓ | ✓ | ✓ | ✓ | ✓ | ✓ |
| LinkItem | ✓ | ✓ | | | | | ✓ |
| LinkMode | ✓ | ✓ | | | | | ✓ |
| LinkTimeout | ✓ | ✓ | | | | | ✓ |
| LinkTopic | ✓ | ✓ | | | | | ✓ |

*Continues*

**Table 7.1** A Sample of VB Control Properties *(Continued)*

| | LABEL | TEXT BOX | COMMAND BUTTON | OPTION BUTTON & CHECKBOX | SCROLLBARS, H & V | IMAGE | PICTURE |
|---|---|---|---|---|---|---|---|
| Locked | | ✓ | | | | | |
| MaskColor | | | ✓ | ✓ | | | |
| Max | | | | | ✓ | | |
| MaxLength | | ✓ | | | | | |
| Min | | | | | ✓ | | |
| MouseIcon | ✓ | ✓ | ✓ | ✓ | ✓ | ✓ | ✓ |
| MousePointer | ✓ | ✓ | ✓ | ✓ | ✓ | ✓ | ✓ |
| MultiLine | | ✓ | | | | | |
| Negotiate | | | | | | ✓ | ✓ |
| OLEDragMode | | ✓ | | | | ✓ | ✓ |
| OLEDropMode | ✓ | ✓ | ✓ | ✓ | | ✓ | ✓ |
| PasswordChar | | ✓ | | | | | |
| Picture | | | ✓ | ✓ | | ✓ | ✓ |
| RightToLeft | ✓ | ✓ | ✓ | ✓ | ✓ | ✓ | ✓ |
| ScaleHeight | | | | | | | ✓ |
| ScaleLeft | | | | | | | ✓ |
| ScaleMode | | | | | | | ✓ |
| ScaleTop | | | | | | | ✓ |

**Table 7.1** *Continued*

| | LABEL | TEXT BOX | COMMAND BUTTON | OPTION BUTTON & CHECKBOX | SCROLLBARS, H & V | IMAGE | PICTURE |
|---|---|---|---|---|---|---|---|
| ScaleWidth | | | | | | | ✓ |
| ScrollBars | | ✓ | | | | | |
| SmallChange | | | | | ✓ | | |
| Stretch | | | | | | ✓ | |
| Style | | | ✓ | ✓ | | | |
| TabIndex | | ✓ | ✓ | ✓ | ✓ | | ✓ |
| TabStop | | ✓ | ✓ | ✓ | ✓ | | ✓ |
| Tag | ✓ | ✓ | ✓ | ✓ | ✓ | ✓ | ✓ |
| Text | | ✓ | | | | | |
| ToolTipText | ✓ | ✓ | ✓ | ✓ | | ✓ | ✓ |
| Top | ✓ | ✓ | ✓ | ✓ | ✓ | ✓ | ✓ |
| UseMaskColor | | | ✓ | ✓ | | | |
| UseMnemonic | ✓ | | | | | | |
| Value | | | | ✓ | ✓ | | |
| Visible | ✓ | ✓ | ✓ | ✓ | ✓ | ✓ | ✓ |
| WhatsThisHelpID | ✓ | ✓ | ✓ | ✓ | ✓ | ✓ | ✓ |
| Width | ✓ | ✓ | ✓ | ✓ | ✓ | ✓ | ✓ |
| WordWrap | ✓ | | | | | | |

# Writing VB Event Code

VB is a full-fledged language and to write event code we have to be able to write using the VB language. This chapter will give you an introduction to get you started writing useful code. I will also bring to your attention the parallels between VB and VBScript where they occur.

To start, when you double-click a control, the *Code window* activates. The code window has three boxes. The top-left window shows the current control and allows you to select any control that supports events. The top-right box shows the current event and allows you to select any event supported by the selected control.

The large window contains the code. As you can see, the subfunctions come with the starting and ending statements already present. The event names assigned by VB are formed by combining the control name with the event name, which makes control names important. For our Warp Drive Calculator, this gives us four events: *Form_Load*, *cmdCalculate_Click*, *cmdReset_Click*, and *cmdExit_Click*.

Aside from *cmdExit_Click()*, which we have already written, there are two events with simple code. *Form_Load()* is executed when the program is started, and *cmdReset_Click()* is self-explanatory (as it should be).

```
Dim distance As Double
Dim warp As Double
Dim warpfactor As Double
Dim traveltime As Double

Private Sub Form_Load()
  distance = 0
  warp = 0
End Sub
```

In the preceding example, the *Form_Load()* event is the *general* section, which has no distinguishing marks. It consists only of data declarations that will be invoked at load time. Using the *Dim* statement, variables are declared with explicit data types, something which does not occur in scripting languages.

*Form_Load* first declares itself as a *Private* subroutine, then initializes two variables to 0. This has to do with the concept of *scope*, which will be explained in the next section. This may or may not be necessary, but it's good form.

```
Private Sub cmdReset_Click()
  txtDistance.Text = ""
  txtWarp.Text = ""
  txtTravel.Text = ""
  distance = 0
  warp = 0
  txtDistance.SetFocus
End Sub
```

The *cmdReset_Click()* event clears all the text boxes, referring to them by a means fearfully similar to the Document Object Model from Dynamic HTML. This is because all these controls are Visual Basic objects, and just as we have objects in the document model, we have objects in the VB form. Remember, an object has methods and an object has data so what else could all these properties be about? When you are setting properties you are just defining object data. Visual Basic is an object-oriented language, even if it does seem too easy to program to deserve that title.

Finally, just as in DHTML, it puts the cursor back in the first text box by setting focus.

# Scope

*Scope* is defined in the dictionary as "extent of activity or influence." In programming, scope definitely has to do with extent—it defines in what parts of this code and other associated code we are permitted to reference a specific data variable or a specific subroutine (function or method, for example).

Scope is not very important in scripting languages, but it does have some importance in VB (and is extremely important when you get to sophisticated languages like Java and C++).

Let's take a look at what the options are for scope of reference in VB. Table 7.2 illustrates these for both data and subroutines. These define access as within the subroutine only, outside the subroutine but within the module, and by other programs external to the module but within the project.

This takes a little explanation about declaring data and subroutines.

Projects in VB start with a *form*. A *form* represents a window on the screen and you can write multiple forms if you want to have multiple windows. A more generic term for VB code units like forms is *module*, and in VB there are several types of modules. For instance, you can add modules that consist of subroutines that have nothing to do with the screen, such as calculations. When you compile a project in VB, these are combined into a single executable. Still, the whole purpose of this is to use these pieces in different projects.

Data is normally declared using the *Dim* statement. This is a holdover of early programming techniques from the 1950s where data was declared based on its specific size or dimension. The *Dim* statement is the usual way of declaring data in VB. Declaring data inside of a subroutine only allows its use in, or *limits its scope to,* that subroutine. Declaring data in the *General* section of the module broadens its scope to anywhere in that module.

Since we're no longer in the 1950s, we now have the *Public* statement (instead of *Dim*), which is only used in the *General* section and allows data to be used in any module in the entire project.

**Table 7.2**   Scope in VB

| SCOPE | DATA | SUBROUTINES |
|---|---|---|
| Subroutine only | Dim | N/A |
| Module only | General Dim | Private |
| Entire project | General Public | Public (default) |

These relations among data, subroutines, and modules are figured out, or *resolved*, at compile time. Remember, this is all just a bunch of artificial rules written by the authors of VB to give you exact control over what your program is doing with data.

# WARNING!
**Data variables can be used without any declaration in VB. This means that if you declare a variable in one place whose scope does not reach to another place, and then mistakenly try to use that variable in that other place, VB will create a doppelganger variable that has nothing to do with the original!**

In VB there are both *subroutines* and *functions*. The difference is this: *Functions* return an argument, *subs* don't. Hearken back to Chapter 3 and you will recall that a method can represent a data value. This is how *functions* work in VB. Both *subs* and *functions* can accept passed values, but *subs* act like the classic program subroutine and *functions* act like the modern method. For example, if you look at the two subroutines listed earlier, neither accepts or returns an argument.

```
Private Sub Form_Load()
Private Sub cmdReset_Click()
```

These subs can be called in two ways. First, you can simply use the subroutine as a statement. Second, you can use the *Call* statement. These two options are equivalent. If the *Call* statement is not present, the parentheses around the arguments are not used, although they must always be present in the declaration as in the preceding example.

```
cmdReset_click
Call cmdReset_Click()
```

Functions may be called in the same way as subs, or as part of an assignment or conditional statement in order to do something with the value that is returned. As an example we have the special VB statement *MsgBox*. These three function calls will all work.

```
intKey = MsgBox("Warp what?",vbQuestion,"The Captain wants to know ...")
Call MsgBox("Warp what?",vbQuestion,"The Captain wants to know ...")
MsgBox "Warp what?",vbQuestion,"The Captain wants to know ..."
```

This statement, an enhancement to the Warp Drive Calculator, appears when the user enters an invalid number for the warp factor. It displays a message and may return the value of the key typed in response, giving the user a choice of ENTER for OK and ESCAPE for Cancel. Because this VB function can send back the key value as an *integer*, the function is declared with the *integer* data type. Although we can't look at this specific function because it's built into VB, it would look like this:

```
Function MsgBox(Msg as String,Opt as Integer,Title as String)as Integer
```

This function statement creates references to four different pieces of data. The three that are being passed are either not Public or are part of another module. They have their data types explicitly declared so there is no mistake about what kind of data is being passed. The function itself returns an *Integer* for the value of the key pressed. The function is Public (which is the default) and, because it certainly is not part of our module, it resides somewhere in the VB runtime. The second *option* parameter is explained in the intrinsic function section later in this chapter.

The moral of the story is: Every piece of data and subroutine or function in VB has a specifically defined scope and type. Now that we've bridged the subject of data types, it's time to get more deeply involved.

# VB Data Types

Why assign data to specific types? All the data just ends up as a string of memory locations inside the computer anyway. Languages like VBScript work without having to say whether they're dealing with numbers or strings.

The purpose of declaring variables with specific data types is to provide each one with a set of rules that will be followed in its use. In higher-level languages, this speeds up processing and ensures correct results. You wouldn't want an ICBM to have an erroneous destination entered, because it could end up blowing up the wrong city! This may be a morbid example, but it demonstrates just how important bug-free programming can be.

We introduced data types in Chapter 6, "JavaScript," and yes, it's true that VBScript does not use them. Although internally VBScript must deal with specific data types, it does not allow you to declare them so it takes upon itself the task of figuring them out as it goes. JavaScript is only slightly different in this respect since, even though a data type can be explicitly declared, VBScript and JavaScript can transform a variable into another data type at any time.

In addition, both VB and VBScript include a default data type that is used to hold variables of any data type. This catch-all data type is called *variant*. It can be *explicitly* declared in VB, but is *implicitly* assigned to variables not declared with any other data type.

The VB data types are listed next. Remember, these data types are declared with *Dim* or *Public*.

**Boolean.** True or False. These words are constants in VB and can be used to assign values. For example, blnHungry = True.

**Byte.** Numeric values from 0 to 255. These values are good for small positive numbers like error codes.

**Currency.** Currency is a cross between Integer and Double, giving a double precision number with four fixed decimal places. It holds numbers from nearly $+10^{15}$ to $-10^{15}$ ($\pm1$ quadrillion) plus the four decimals. Aside from this, the currency data type does not affect how the numbers are calculated or displayed. To display a value as currency, use the VB Format function. This will format a string based on the Currency tab of your Regional Settings in the Control Panel. For example, txtBigMoney = Format (curBigMoney,"currency").

Test this data type using the Chapter 7 VB Currency project that you can find through the companion Web site at www.wiley.com/compbooks/cintron.

**Date.** Holds a date and a time. You can choose to use either or both parts, and VB is very smart about what you're doing with this data type. There are quite a few built-in functions in VB for doing date arithmetic, an otherwise slavish task for even the keenest of programmers. The year is four digits and date, like Currency, complies with international data representation.

Test this data type using the Chapter 7 VB Date project that you can find at the companion Web site at www.wiley.com/compbooks/cintron.

**Double.** Double-precision floating point, from approximately $+10^{300}$ to $-10^{300}$ with 14 decimal places.

**Integer.** An integer from $2^{15}$ to $-2^{15}$ ($\pm32,767$).

**Long.** Long is to integer what double is to single, a double-precision integer from $+2^{31}$ to $-2^{31}$ ($\pm2,147,483,648$). In case you're wondering how 31 is twice 15, what we're looking at with long is a binary combination of two 16-bit integer variables. Integer is internally represented as a 2-byte (or 16-bit) number, where 15 of these is the number and 1 is the sign. When we add 16 more bits, we don't need the sign again, so we get a 31-bit number with a 1-bit sign stored as a 4-byte number. If you take the time to figure it out, you will see that all these data types are based on byte counts.

**Object.** Same thing as in JavaScript. All controls and forms are objects; objects hold data and methods.

**Single.** Single-precision floating point, from approximately $+3.4 \times 10^{38}$ to $-3.4 \times 10^{38}$ with six decimal places.

**String.** Character strings. These can be up to almost $2^{16}$ (just over 65,000) characters long.

**Variant.** The default data type as described previously, variant can be any data type.

Okay, and now the $64,000 question: What's missing from all this? The answer is *Arrays*.

We're in high-level language land now, and arrays are not a data type in VB. *All data types can be arrays.* All you have to do is include the element count after the variable name. For example, *Dim strDays (7) as String*.

To round out our study of subroutines, functions, and data types, let's take a look now at the full event code for the Warp Drive Calculator in Figure 7.4.

```
Dim distance As Double
Dim warp As Double
Dim warpfactor As Double
Dim traveltime As Double

Private Sub Form_Load()
  distance = 0
  warp = 0
```

**Figure 7.4**  Warp Drive event core.

```
  End Sub

  Private Sub cmdReset_Click()
    txtDistance.Text = ""
    txtWarp.Text = ""
    txtTravel.Text = ""
    distance = 0
    warp = 0
    txtDistance.SetFocus
  End Sub

  Private Sub cmdExit_Click()
    End
    Unload Me
  End Sub

  Private Sub cmdCalculate_Click()
  If Val(txtDistance.Text) <= 0 Then
    intKey = MsgBox("What kind of a helmsman are you?", vbQuestion,
                    "Performance Review")
    txtDistance.SetFocus
    Exit Sub
  End If
  If Val(txtWarp.Text) <= 0 Then
    intKey = MsgBox("Warp what?", vbQuestion,
                    "The Captain wants to know ...")
    txtWarp.SetFocus
    Exit Sub
  End If
  If Val(txtWarp.Text) >= 10 Then
    intKey = MsgBox("I'm givin her all I got, Cap'n!", vbOKOnly,
                    "Engineering here!")
    txtWarp.SetFocus
    Exit Sub
  End If

  distance = txtDistance.Text
  warp = txtWarp.Text
  warpfactor = 2 ^ (warp - 1)
  traveltime = Format(((distance / warpfactor) * 365.25), "###,###.##")
  txtTravel.Text = traveltime

  End Sub
```

**Figure 7.4** *(Continued)*

First we have our *general* section data declarations, the *Form_Load*, *cmdReset_Click*, and *cmdExit_Click* subroutines. This last declaration has an additional statement, *Unload Me*, which ensures the form is removed from memory after the *End* statement, not important in the learning environment but is otherwise. Then we get to the meat of the form, the *cmdCalculate_Click* subroutine.

This subroutine uses the *Val* function (remember, VB functions return values) to check and see if a valid number was entered in the *txtDistance* input box. We can't go a negative distance, and 0 means that either 0 or an invalid number was entered. So if the value returned is negative or 0, a message box is displayed, focus is set back on the offending input box, and *Exit Sub* terminates the subroutine. The same thing is done for the *txtWarp* input box, which is also checked to see that we don't exceed warp 9.9.

Why don't we check the user input in the input box *change* events? Because VB triggers a *change* event for every keystroke and we may get an error if we check before the whole entry is completed. We could also check for erroneous entry at the *LostFocus* event, but if the user simply tabs across the box, an error will still be generated, so it's easier and cleaner to put it all where it is. These error handlings are further than we've gone before in checking data and make the program a lot more user friendly, even downright fun.

Finally, a VB *format* function with a *format string* is used to ensure our output always has two decimal places. Notice the VB caret "^" used as the exponent operator where $2 \wedge (\text{warp} - 1)$ gives you $2^{(\text{warp}-1)}$.

# VB Operators

VB supports a standard set of assignment and comparison operators (see Table 7.3). Languages differ slightly in some of their operators, but in VB the two to remember are *not equals* as <> and string *concatenation* as & or +. The VB logical operators are AND, OR, and NOT.

# VB Statements

VB offers five different types of loops and two types of if statements: the standard *If* and a very flexible *Case* statement.

**Table 7.3**  VB Assignment and Comparison Operators

| ASSIGNMENT | | COMPARISON | |
|---|---|---|---|
| + | Add | = | Equal |
| - | Subtract | <> | Not equal |
| * | Multiply | > | Greater than |
| / | Divide | < | Less than |
| ^ | Exponent | <= | Less than or equal |
| &,+ | Concatenate | >= | Greater than or equal |

# Looping

In loop statements VB uses *Loop* and *Next* instead of *End*. Recall from the discussion of loops in the previous chapter that they consist of four parts:

- A starting, or initial, condition
- A condition that changes before or after the loop is executed
- An evaluation of conditions as to whether the loop should be executed a first time or a next time
- A section of one or more statements that are repeated

**Do While ... Loop**     **Do While** *(condition) (statements)* **Loop**

The *Do While Loop* tests the conditional expression at the beginning of each loop and will execute the loop *while* the condition is true.

**Do Until ... Loop**     **Do Until** *(condition) (statements)* **Loop**

The *Do Until Loop* tests the conditional expression at the beginning of each loop and will execute the loop *until* the condition is true.

**Do ... Loop While**     **Do** *(statements)* **Loop While** *(condition)*

The *Do Loop While* tests the conditional expression at the end of each loop and will execute the loop *while* the condition is true.

**Do ... Loop Until**     **Do** *(statements)* **Loop Until** *(condition)*

The *Do Loop Until* tests the conditional expression at the end of each loop and will execute the loop *until* the condition is true.

**For**          **For intCount = intStart To intEnd Step intIncrement (statements)**
              **Next intCount**

The *For* loop is in its easiest form in VB. It loops a counter from a starting quantity to an ending quantity by a specific increment. The *Step intIncrement* part is optional; if it's missing, the default increment will be 1.

# If and Case

**If ... Then ... Else**     **If (condition) Then (statements) ElseIf (statements) Else**
              **(statements) EndIf**

The VB *If* statement has a couple of special components. The only required parts are *If*, *Then*, and *Else*. The *ElseIf* statement is optional and allows you to avoid having to use nested *Else ... If* pairs that need their own *EndIf*, you can use just one *EndIf* at the end of the last clause. Finally, an *ElseIf* cannot follow an *Else*.

**Select**     **Select Case (expression)**
          **Case: (literal, Is relation, or range) (statements)**

> Case Else (statements)
> End Select

The *Select* statement is very flexible, yet simple. An expression is evaluated, followed by a list of possible *Case* results and statements. *Case Else* is executed if none of the other cases is true. *End Select* ends the *Select* statement.

The *Select Case* expression can be any expression that gives a numerical or string result, such as *1600* or *Pennsylvania*. The *Case* options can be literals or a range of literals, such as *1000 to 1999* or *"A" to "Z"*. They can even be relations, such as *Is > 999* or *Is >= "A"*. They can also be a combination of all three!

Here is an example. The *Case* options are evaluated in order, and only the first true result is executed.

```
Private Sub cmdTest_Click()
Dim intTest As Integer
intTest = Val(txtEnter.Text)
Select Case intTest
  Case 0:           lblPhase.Caption = "Newborn"
  Case 1 To 12:     lblPhase.Caption = "Child"
  Case Is < 20:     lblPhase.Caption = "Teenager"
  Case Else:        lblPhase.Caption = "Adult"
  End Select
End Sub
```

# Advanced VB Controls

There are several advanced controls in VB, and being advanced controls they have a lot to offer. In this short introduction I will introduce these and show you what they are capable of, but there is a lot more to their full capabilities.

**Timer.** The *Timer* control is extremely useful and simple, too. The timer has a location on the form but is invisible when the program is running, and there are only two properties that control its actions: *Enabled* and *Interval*. The timer will trigger a *Timer* event every *Interval* milliseconds for as long as it is enabled. That's all there is to it. Check out the timer function using the Chapter 7 VB Artman project available at the companion Web site at www.wiley.com/compbooks/cintron.

**List Box.** The *listbox* control displays a list of items from which the user can select. As with all VB controls, it's up to you to fill the box with selections and to do something with the selected items. The list items are added and removed with two list box object methods: *.AddItem and .RemoveItem*, which end up in the *.List* array property.

When an item is selected, the array index of the current selection is indicated by the *ListIndex* property, which holds only one value at a time. If you want the user to be able to select more than one item you have to code the *Click* event to respond when a selection is made. If no selection is made, *ListIndex* will be –1.

**Combo Box.** The *Combo box* is a more sophisticated version of the list box and there are actually three kinds of *combo boxes* you can create by setting the *Style* property to *0 for Dropdown Combo*, *1 for Simple Combo*, and *2 for Dropdown List*. The best way to see this is to create a form with all three. Then add a text box and command button and add an item from the text box to all three boxes when the button is clicked.

There are two hints to this. First, the *simple combo* box can be dragged down to any size and displays the list at the same time as the selection. Second, both *dropdown* types are the same except for one thing: With both *combo* types you can rewrite the routine to accept input from the selection part and add it to the list part, but with the *list* type you cannot accept user input.

**Common dialog box.** The *Common dialog box* is the epitome of sophisticated controls and offers four highly sophisticated types of *Common dialog box*. Being such a highly evolved control, it's not even in the toolbox. This comes from the *Components* selection on the *Project* menu. Selecting this option bombards you with a list of dozens of controls you can add to your program. You'll get the idea of how to do this by the end of this chapter. Go down the list to the *Microsoft Common Dialog Control* and select this box. No, the control has not appeared on the form, it has appeared on the toolbar. Now you can drag and drop this onto your form. Like the Timer control, this control appears on the form but is invisible to the user.

The function this box performs is controlled not by a property, but by calling one of its methods. There are five methods, and each one creates an entirely different control from this single object.

**ShowOpen.** The complete windows file open function with drive, directory, and all the bells and whistles found in your standard windows File Open dialog box. The file selected is returned in the *FileName* property for the control.

**ShowSave.** Same as ShowOpen except that the Save title and button are used instead of Open.

**ShowPrinter.** The complete windows printer selection with printers, properties, and all the options found in your standard windows Print dialog box. The printer selected is not returned, but anything sent to the printer automatically goes to the right place.

**ShowFont.** The complete font selection window. Attributes of selected fonts are returned in the various Font… properties.

**ShowColor.** The complete color selection window. Color is returned in the *Color* property.

# Adding Advanced VB Controls to a Program

Let's use the Microsoft Active Movie control to write our own Media Player program. Figure 7.5 illustrates the multimedia controls in VB.

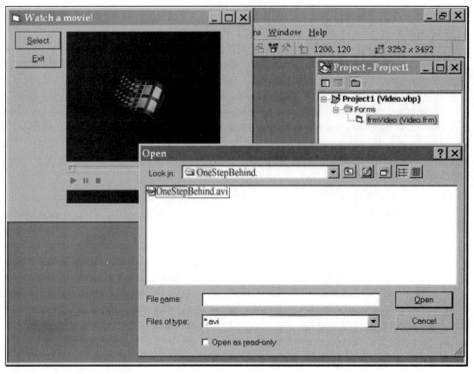

**Figure 7.5** Multimedia controls in VB.

First, open a new form and add the *Common Dialog Box* and *two Command Buttons*. Label one button *Select* and the other one *Exit*. Then go back to the *Components* window and select the *Microsoft Active Movie Control* and add this to your form. Make it really big so it won't cut off the picture.

Now run it and see what happens.

Aside from setting the usual properties for these buttons, add the Click event shown next, which assigns the *FileName* property <u>output</u> from the *Common Dialog Box* to the *FileName* property <u>input</u> to the *Active Movie Control*!

```
Private Sub cmdSelect_Click()
  CommonDialog1.ShowOpen
  ActiveMovie1.filename = CommonDialog1.filename
End Sub
```

That's all there is to it! It couldn't have taken more than five minutes to put this together.

This control is actually an ActiveX control and can be used in a different way to create a Web page with the Active Movie Player, which we'll see at the end of this chapter.

Figure 7.6 shows the Active Movie Player, Common Dialog box and all.

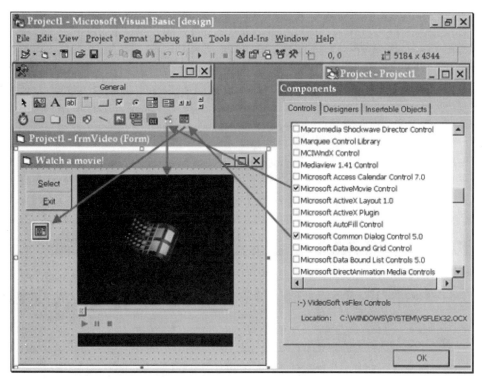

**Figure 7.6**   Five-minute movie player.

# Intrinsic VB Functions

Do I have to tell you *intrinsic* means built in? VB has tons of intrinsic functions that would take pages and pages to list. The most commonly useful functions are these few which have had only brief mention up until now: *Val*, *MsgBox*, and *InputBox*.

**Val**          **number = Val(string)**

This function translates text input into a numeric variable. If the variable data type supports a decimal point, this will also be translated. *Val* will handle any string it is given and as long as the first character is numeric, it will return a valid number value. The first nonnumeric, nonblank character ends *Val*'s attempts at translation.

**MsgBox**     **number = MsgBox (prompt,option,title)**

We've seen this one a few times. *MsgBox* displays a small window with a *title*, *prompt*, *graphic symbol*, and *buttons*. The only required field is *prompt*. The *option* controls what buttons and symbol display, and will default to the OK button alone and no symbol.

As in some binary option setups, this control accepts multiple options as a combination of binary values. This also introduces several VB *intrinsic variables* that are made available because they are easier to remember than list data values. This list of options can be combined using either the intrinsic names or the numbers they represent. For example, giving the option as *vbYesNo + vbQuestion* might be wordy but it's a lot easier than remembering *4* is *vbYesNo* and *32* is *vbQuestion*. Further, putting down an option as *36* may not be as easy for someone else who comes along to figure out as it is for you eidetic polymaths.

Table 7.4 lists MsgBox calling options and Table 7.5 lists other MsgBox button values returned.

**InputBox**     string = InputBox (prompt,title,default input)

This function displays a small window with a *prompt, title, text box*, and the *OK* and *Cancel* buttons. The only required field is *prompt*. The *default input* is displayed in the

**Table 7.4**   MsgBox Options

| BUTTON OPTIONS | VALUE | RESULT |
| --- | --- | --- |
| vbOKOnly | 0 | Display OK button only |
| vbOKCancel | 1 | Display OK and Cancel buttons |
| vbAbortRetryIgnore | 2 | Display Abort, Retry, and Ignore buttons |
| vbYesNoCancel | 3 | Display Yes, No, and Cancel buttons |
| vbYesNo | 4 | Display Yes and No buttons |
| vbRetryCancel | 5 | Display Retry and Cancel buttons |
| ICON OPTIONS | VALUE | RESULT |
| vbCritical | 16 | Display Critical Message icon (an *x*) |
| vbQuestion | 32 | Display Warning Query icon (a *?*) |
| vbExclamation | 48 | Display Warning Message icon (a *!*) |
| vbInformation | 64 | Display Information Message icon (an *i*) |

**Table 7.5**   Return Values from MsgBox

| RETURN OPTIONS | VALUE | BUTTON |
| --- | --- | --- |
| vbOK | 1 | OK |
| vbCancel | 2 | Cancel |
| vbAbort | 3 | Abort |
| vbRetry | 4 | Retry |
| vbIgnore | 5 | Ignore |
| vbYes | 6 | Yes |
| vbNo | 7 | No |

text box when it appears. If *OK* is clicked or *Enter* is pressed, the text in the box is returned. If *Cancel* is clicked or *Escape* is pressed, an empty string is returned.

There are plenty more built-in VB functions, so if you're serious, you need to dig in and learn all about VB!

## INFORMATIVE SITES!

**www.devx.com**
**The Development Exchange is a technical site with tons of data for developers on VB and more.**

**msdn.microsoft.com/vbasic**
**Microsoft Visual Basic includes everything Microsoft has to offer on Visual Basic.**

**comp.lang.basic.visual.***
**Visual Basic Newsgroups offer several newsgroups on VB—pick and choose!**

## Translating VB to VBScript

In this section we're going to take the VB Warp Drive Calculator and turn it into VBScript. This involves five easy steps and shows you just how alike these languages are, and what's more, how you can avoid having to write an ActiveX control by using VBScript! Figure 7.7 is an example of VB code morphed into VBScript.

1. Copy the VB code to VBScript.

2. Remove the VB language elements that are not part of VBScript.

3. Change the VB language elements that are different in VBScript.

4. Write the HTML document, translating the VB form controls to HTML FORM elements.

5. Shift the VB object references to the browser DOM.

```
<HTML>
<HEAD>
<TITLE>Warp Drive Calculator in VBScript</TITLE>
</HEAD>

<SCRIPT LANGUAGE="VBScript">
Dim distance, warp, warpfactor, traveltime
Sub frmWarp_Load
  frmWarp.txtDistance.focus()
  distance = 0
  warp = 0
```
*Continues*

**Figure 7.7** VB converted to VBScript + HTML.

```
End Sub
Sub btnReset_Click()
  frmWarp.txtDistance.value = ""
  frmWarp.txtWarp.value = ""
  frmWarp.txtTravel.value = ""
  distance = 0
  warp = 0
  frmWarp.txtDistance.focus()
End Sub

Sub btnCalc_Click()
  If not IsNumeric(frmWarp.txtDistance.value) Then
    intKey = MsgBox("What kind of a helmsman are you?", vbQuestion,
                 "Performance Review")
    frmWarp.txtDistance.focus()
    Exit Sub
  Else
    If frmWarp.txtDistance.value <= 0 Then
    intKey = MsgBox("What kind of a helmsman are you?", vbQuestion,
                 "Performance Review")
      frmWarp.txtDistance.focus()
      Exit Sub
    End If
  End If

  If not IsNumeric(frmWarp.txtWarp.value) Then
    intKey = MsgBox("Warp what?", vbQuestion,
                 "The Captain wants to know ...")
    frmWarp.txtWarp.focus()
    Exit Sub
  Else
    If frmWarp.txtWarp.value <= 0 Then
      intKey = MsgBox("Warp what?", vbQuestion,
                   "The Captain wants to know ...")
      frmWarp.txtWarp.focus()
      Exit Sub
    Else
      If frmWarp.txtWarp.value >= 10 Then
        intKey = MsgBox("I'm givin her all I got, Cap'n!", vbOKOnly,
                     "Engineering here!")
        frmWarp.txtWarp.focus()
        Exit Sub
      End If
    End If
  End If

  distance = frmWarp.txtDistance.value
  warp = frmWarp.txtWarp.value
```

**Figure 7.7**    *(Continued)*

```
   warpfactor = 2 ^ (warp - 1)
   traveltime = (distance / warpfactor) * 365.25
   frmWarp.txtTravel.value = traveltime

End Sub
</SCRIPT>
<BODY ONLOAD="frmWarp_Load()">
<FORM NAME="frmWarp">
<TABLE BGCOLOR="#80FFFF">
<TR>
  <TD COLSPAN="2" ALIGN="CENTER" WIDTH="300">
    <FONT FACE="Arial" COLOR="#D24400">WARP DRIVE CALCULATOR</FONT>
    <HR COLOR="#FF0000"> </TD>
</TR>
<TR>
  <TD WIDTH="200" ALIGN="RIGHT">
  <FONT FACE="Arial">Distance in light years</FONT></TD>
  <TD WIDTH="100"><INPUT TYPE="TEXT" NAME="txtDistance" SIZE="5">
</TD>
</TR>
<TR>
  <TD WIDTH="200" ALIGN="RIGHT"><FONT FACE="Arial">Warp factor</FONT>
</TD>
  <TD WIDTH="100"><INPUT TYPE="TEXT" NAME="txtWarp" SIZE="5"> </TD>
</TR>
<TR>
  <TD WIDTH="200" ALIGN="RIGHT">
  <FONT FACE="Arial">Travel time in days</FONT></TD>
  <TD WIDTH="100"><INPUT TYPE="TEXT" NAME="txtTravel" SIZE="10"></TD>
</TR>
<TR>
  <TD WIDTH="300" COLSPAN="2" ALIGN="CENTER"><HR COLOR="#FF0000">
    <INPUT TYPE="BUTTON" NAME="btnReset" VALUE="Clear"
     ONCLICK="btnReset_Click()">
    <INPUT TYPE="BUTTON" NAME="btnCalc" VALUE="Calculate!"
     ONCLICK="btnCalc_Click()">
  </TD>
</TR>
</TABLE>

</FORM>
</BODY>
</HTML>
```

**Figure 7.7** *(Continued)*

We'll go through this now in more detail.
Start in the Warp Drive project by opening the code window.

1. Select all the code, top to bottom, and copy and paste it into an HTML document between a set of <SCRIPT language="VBScript"></SCRIPT> tags.

2. Remove the data types from the variable declarations. This also allows you to factor them into a single declaration. Remove the *cmdExit_Click* subroutine since we aren't going to use the *Exit* button, at least not in the way it's used in the VB program.

3. Make a few changes to account for changing VB events to DHTML events and differences in VB and VBScript. First, change the *setfocus* calls to *focus()*. Then change the *Val* calls, since there is no *Val* function in VBScript, to the intrinsic function *isNumeric* (see the VBScript listing). We didn't use this function in VB because it is not as good as *Val*, but on the other hand, VBScript does a better job with *isNumeric*. This is not a huge leap of genius, I reached this conclusion by running simple tests on the few available options.

We're almost done, only two steps left. This next step is actually the most work, but again it is easy.

4. The VB controls have to be rewritten as HTML *FORM* components. In fact, we might as well create the whole HTML document right now. To do this I created a simple table with five rows and two columns, three text input boxes, and two buttons. The *FORM* tag is given the *frmWarp* name from VB. The *INPUT* elements were all given the same names as their VB control counterparts, and *ONCLICK* events were added to the button *INPUT* types to call the VBScript subroutines.

Event code calls are automatic in VB, but not in HTML. The actions in this specific step are shown in the code snippets shown next. You may begin to realize that the lion's share of the work here is in writing the HTML document structure and making it look nice, not on translating the VB control objects.

```
<BODY ONLOAD="frmWarp_Load()">
<FORM NAME="frmWarp">
<INPUT TYPE="TEXT"   NAME="txtDistance">
<INPUT TYPE="TEXT"   NAME="txtWarp">
<INPUT TYPE="TEXT"   NAME="txtTravel">
<INPUT TYPE="BUTTON" NAME="btnReset" VALUE="Clear"
       ONCLICK="btnReset_Click()">
<INPUT TYPE="BUTTON" NAME="btnCalc" VALUE="Calculate!"
       ONCLICK="btnCalc_Click()">
```

5. The final step is to change the VB object model code to Explorer DOM references. This really is very easy. All we have to do is add *frmWarp* to the beginning of each reference and change references to the VB *text* and *caption* properties to the DOM *value* property. For example, txtDistance.Text becomes frmWarp.txtDistance.value.

That is it! If it seems a little difficult, look it over again, or just do all the steps yourself, and you'll realize it's a lot easier than starting from scratch. Take a look—you've written a whole VBScript document, top to bottom, mostly based on cut-and-paste from a drag-and-drop VB program! You can see the result in Figure 7.8.

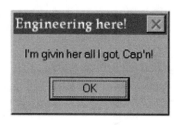

**Figure 7.8** Warp Drive Calculator in VBScript.

# Using ActiveX with VBScript

What's been said about ActiveX controls so far is that ActiveX is a Windows-specific technology, and that ActiveX controls are downloadable, executable components that are permanently installed on the user's machine and so are available to any application that cares to use them.

If you stopped to smell the roses in the VB component exercise shown previously you will have noticed that there are quite a few ActiveX controls, already installed on your computer, and possibly even unknown to you.

As I see it, the main hurdle with ActiveX controls on the Internet is that every time one is downloaded it asks the user if it is OK to install. This makes using these controls on Web pages distracting. ActiveX controls installed as part of the VB IDE are different. Many of them install with the VB IDE without having to check with you first, and they can be distributed with software you write. Either way, until somebody writes a useful "VB Virtual Machine" or some ingenious equivalent, these are Windows-only programs.

Adding ActiveX controls to Web pages is actually easy. Each one has an extremely-long-impossible-to-remember-and-difficult-to-type identification number. ActiveX controls can be found all over the Internet. You can spend hours searching for and gathering them like nuts for the winter.

The free download from Microsoft called the *ActiveX Control Pad* is really easy to use and allows you to create an HTML document with ActiveX controls in much the same manner as the VB CCE allows you to drag and drop ActiveX components into your VB form.

Figure 7.9 illustrates the ActiveX Control Pad adding a control. You can't actually make the *Edit* menu and the *Insert ActiveX Control* Box display at the same time, this is a picture doctored for educational purposes, sort of a time-lapse screen capture.

In the *Insert* box we see a list of potential ActiveX controls, just like in VB, with the *ActiveMovie* player selected. You can also see the HTML button code added to allow the user to enter the filename, as shown in Figure 7.10.

When you select a control, all HTML code is automatically sucked right into the HTML document, and the properties can be edited in a property window just like in VB.

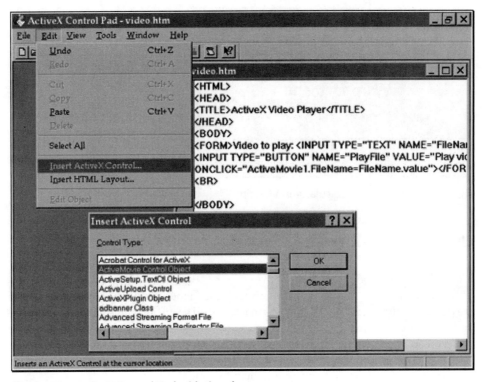

**Figure 7.9** ActiveX Control Pad with time lapse.

The HTML OBJECT element contains the ActiveX control and its properties. How this tag is used in HTML will be discussed in the next chapter in the section on Java Applets. Here is a good look at the exact code used to put this control in the Web page, without all 57 parameters.

```
<OBJECT ID="ActiveMovie1" WIDTH=238 HEIGHT=252
 CLASSID="CLSID:22D6F312-B0F6-11D0-94AB-0080C74C7E95">
    <PARAM NAME=parameter VALUE=value>
    (repeat ad parametrum)
</OBJECT>
```

The only vital parameter we need be concerned with in this *OBJECT* element is the filename, which is shown as selected in the property window. We have a few different options with this and other properties. We can hard-code it into the *PARAMETER* tag, or we can get input from the user in a text box. Using the DOM and DHTML, we can dynamically set the Active MoviePlayer *FileName* property.

In this particular HTML document this is accomplished by embedding a line of script in the *ONCLICK* event for the *Play video!* button.

```
<FORM>Video to play: <INPUT TYPE="TEXT" NAME="FileName"><BR><BR>
<INPUT TYPE="BUTTON" NAME="PlayFile" VALUE="Play video!"
ONCLICK="ActiveMovie1.FileName=FileName.value"></FORM>
```

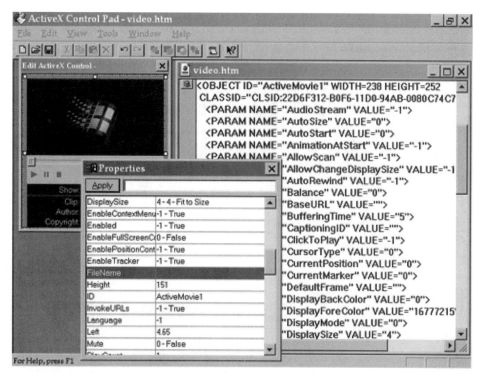

**Figure 7.10**  ActiveX Control Pad ActiveMovie Control properties.

In case you're wondering how setting only the *FileName* property makes the movie play, it doesn't. We also have to set the *AutoStart* property/parameter to 1.

Figure 7.11 illustrates this control in action. The active code just shown can be seen in the HoTMetaL PROWeb editor. The guy in the picture is psychic detective Miles A. Far, Third Eye who is tracing the entry point to an alternate universe.

---

**VB, VIRTUAL MACHINES, AND VAPORWARE**

The possibility of a VB Virtual Machine is a bit up in the air right now. It's not too much of a stretch to imagine such a thing, and I have seen reference to it in two places:

- A software company claimed to have written one in early 1997.
- In an interview with the Microsoft VB5 team, this possibility was mentioned, although not in the same context. It is most likely that the *VBRUN200.DLL* component that ends up in the Windows directory on Windows computers that run VB code is referred to by Microsoft as the *VB Virtual Machine*. Whether or not there are going to be versions for every OS is unclear at this time.

Undoubtedly, VB has a big future, and somewhere along the line a VB Virtual Machine will show up.

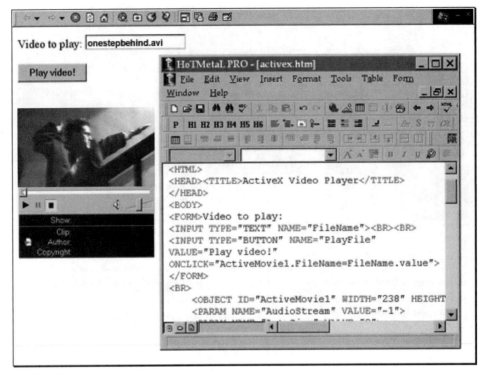

**Figure 7.11** ActiveX ActiveMovie activated.

# INFORMATIVE SITES!

*msdn.microsoft.com/scripting*
**Microsoft Scripting Technologies includes not only VBScript, but JScript and DHTML, scriptlets, and much more!**

*www.sitebuilder.net*
**Welcome to unauthorized Site Builder that includes more information on scripting from independent sources.**

## INTERVIEW

*Peter Plamondon, Microsoft*

Peter Plamondon is Garth Bruce's manager (Garth has an interview in Chapter 5, "Dynamic HTML"). His official title is Group Program Manager, Developer Relations Group. He's in charge of all the guys that help software developers work with Microsoft technology. As a result, he seems to know something about everything.

Garth and Peter are also *technology evangelists*, because their job involves a lot of public relations, public speaking, and promoting the technologies Microsoft has developed to outside developers. We'll be talking about what that involves.

I had originally got together with Garth to talk about Dynamic HTML, and I did, but because of Peter's technological multiplicity and evangelistic mission, the interview diversified into the things that Peter is working on these days, and since he's the main man, I followed his lead.

*So, Peter, you're a manager then. What do you do?*
Herd a whole bunch of these technology evangelist cats around! We've got better than a dozen folks on the Windows DNA architecture at the moment.

*DNA means Distributed Network Architecture?*
I think so! I've seen the press report their interpretation of what it stands for so many times I kind of lose track of what the official one is, but certainly the distributed network part is really the key. Our notion is it's distributed, it runs on a network, it's an application framework. I've also seen it as Distributed Internetworking.

We look for different technology leverage points, where we have some new technology coming out that perhaps needs a little bit of assistance to get that kind of jumping off initial adoption. Or maybe it's something that the benefit of which is not immediately obvious, or more forward looking (as in it's hard to justify under what our quarterly performance is going to be when we report to Wall Street this quarter, you've got to take a little farther view). So one of the things that we do is just keep the technology in front of people, and one of the things we're focused on right now is the technology underpinnings of the DNA application framework.

If I want to write a distributed application, maybe I've chosen to follow the Internet model, with a browser-based user interface for that minimal install. The application is downloaded through the Web server and the HTML user interface is much like the kinds of things that you see at amazon.com, or something like that. What we are doing here is talking to folks who are in a position to start investing in those technologies now, about how do you take something that today might be a client/server application and transform it into this n-tiered, distributed, scalable, browser-based kind of application.

*You mean blow it out?*
Yeah, exactly. What if, heaven forbid, your app is really successful and now instead of getting 10,000 people coming to your site every day you've got a million? Darn. So those kinds of things are what we're looking at. Our audience is software developers rather than press and analysts and folks like that. Folks who are looking for technology solutions to the problems that they're grappling with, looking to adopt this kind of framework and we go off and just make sure they've got the information that they need, help them get answers to their questions and things like that.

*You mentioned forward looking applications, things that might not look like they're worth investment or whatever, today. There certainly is probably a lot of that on the Internet.*
Yup. I know part of the challenge is there are so many offerings from so many companies and being able to spend the time looking at all of them and understanding the strengths and weaknesses of them all is a very daunting task. But it's one that our product groups because they're competing with those others, and many of those guys are career-long guys that come from other companies and wanted to take another swing at it here. So in some sense, what we're taking out to the developer community that we're talking to is the distillation of all of those careers around a particular technology, and our focus is always on making those technologies very simple to use.

That's a message that somebody has to go and take out and talk to people and help folks understand the business case around taking a technology, completely re-architecting it and applying it in this manner. Why would you do that? How does the technology work with the various Microsoft technology pieces that I could incorporate into solving that?

*It sounds like you've learned a great deal.*
Oh, every day!

*Just last week I was looking into installing a storefront, and it seems virtually impossible for a small operation to do this on their own. All I have to do is get the right scripts and install them, and the supplier is making it into this huge project.*
Microsoft's got a product strategy, this notion of identifying things that lots of people want to do, and then making it very easy for them to do it. If you could imagine, going down the road to when e-commerce becomes something that, like, every corner flower shop has their e-commerce site up. You can imagine that you'd see something like the Site Server Commerce Edition priced at a point that's very attractive for a small operation and as part of that consumer package you'd have that credit card arrangement already there, so maybe to facilitate that Microsoft becomes the credit card consolidator. I don't know anything about this space, I'm just projecting how our business works, but either we become the consolidator or we find a partner who says, OK, anybody who buys Commerce Edition, they're pre-approved in this process to run the little wizard, we give you back some magic cookie or something like that, and boom, you're online, you can take credit cards. That's just our business model. Find things people want to do and make it real easy.

*Like selling a package for a couple hundred bucks?*
Yeah, I sure hope so.

*I spent last week struggling with trying to get a Web host to send a secure e-mail. But all the technologies are like that to some degree. I know that some people need to have it installed turnkey, but all I want to do is post a CGI form!*
You ought to be able to go out on the Internet and offer your services or your products and clock money. That ought to be easy. How do you go off and solve your business problem, right? You've got products, you're able to deal with credit cards and if you could just get this stuff together on the Internet and fill out the credit card form and take the credit card number and send it to the right place.

Did you know that through a technology called active debugging, that lets a script engine, well, pop the stack [this is a programming term used in a conversational way, meaning put this thought on hold for a minute]. IE3 shipped with VBScript and JScript, so now we have this problem where gee, if you only have one script language life is really easy, you just wire that sucker into the browser and life is good. Well right away we have two, so we said OK, we either hack these two things in there somehow or we define an interface which lets us plug some arbitrary script engine into the browser. So we did that, that was called active scripting. It's a set of interfaces that let you interface a random script engine into the browser. That was swell, but most of the time when I start writing scripts they don't work. So now what do you do? The browser doesn't know anything about debugging and there's no kind of IDE [Interactive Development Environment] around this language and what do I do?

So we define another set of interfaces called active debugging. These interfaces let you take something like the script debugger, which is a free download off our Web site, and a script engine, which supports the right interface. So essentially we're talking about just the host and the engine know how to talk the same protocol. And now you can be debugging the scripts that you're writing. So for example, our VBScript and JScript already support this. There's two Perl scripts that do. For Perl there's PScript from MKS and there's, I can't remember the names of the products. There's activestate.com and mks.com, they each have a Perl engine that supports this. They're working on active debugging, I don't know if they actually have the active debugging part shipped.

*What I do is run a script on a local copy of the site, and once I get it working I just translate everything to the Internet and debug that.*
Imagine if you will that you're adding into a page, and it's already got some JavaScript in there and now you're working with Perl. So how do you debug across the two languages? This is actually supported by that technology. I've got a client-side script running but it's interacting with maybe an ASP page over on the server, how do I debug those interactions? It's some very cool stuff.

This is a tool that can be used by anybody. It's not something that we have a big associated cost with. We're giving this out to people, encouraging people to use this, because it is extremely useful in a variety of environments and languages. So go to microsoft.com/scripting and it will lead you off to these interesting things.

*It's mind boggling to try and get your mind around all the technologies. If you're going to work in the industry you have to find the edges and get a grip, and the edges are very open, it kind of just fades off into Jello or something.*
One of the challenges we're looking at with Internet development in general and particularly as we go off and look at applications built around the DNA framework, the problem is, how do we build one of those things? What's the tool that's really good for building what in the past has been a client-server application and now I want it to be a distributed Internet application. Where are the tools for that? The Visual InterDev guys are working on trying to solve that, and that's a Microsoft dev tool. But then we also work with a lot of the people who are competing on kind of tangential development tools to our own. So we work with Borland and PowerSoft and companies like that, Allaire with ColdFusion some people see as a competitor to ASP, and work with just a lot of folks off in the tools market to help them get the information they need so that they can decide whether there's a good business case for them to target our stuff and help them overcome problems.

*So what's the business plan here, if you're working with competitors?*
This really goes back to Windows 3.0 and 3.1 where Borland, for example, wanted to target Windows 3.0 but there were pieces of the Windows operating system that weren't available to distribute. It really was the Windows SDK [Software Development Kit]. So at one point Borland's story was, first you come buy Borland's product and give us some money, and then you've got to go back to Microsoft and you've got to buy the Windows SDK, and then you can finally build an app with Borland's development tools. That was obviously a lousy solution. No customer wants to go out and have to assemble all this stuff by hand from multiple vendors. So to help the Windows developers who chose to use Borland's tools, we want them to be successful to because this is way more about Windows than it is about Microsoft's development tools. We found ways to work with Borland to make that happen, so we have a licensing program that let's them license our SDK so they can incorporate that into their development tools. And we're doing lots of similar kinds of things with the folks doing Internet applications. What are the pieces that they need to redistribute with their products so that their customers get a good

experience? So there's some licensing stuff in there but mostly it's just a matter of getting the information out.

The more tools that target Windows, whether they're our tools or competing tools, the richer the selection that a developer has and the competition between those tool vendors results in just better and better tools for the person targeting Windows. Similarly we've got folks who go off and work with Lotus and IBM and Oracle and folks like that, on e-mail systems that compete with our e-mail systems, databases that compete with our databases. Again, the more products that are out there presenting solutions to customers and competing amongst themselves to see who's got the better product, the better and more successful a platform Windows is. I can imagine going into a new company and saying hey, you should hire several dozen people and you should give them a whopping big budget and they're going to go off and do a whole bunch of stuff that you can't tie to revenue. Isn't that a great business model?

But Bill is a big believer in evangelism. Steve B. is a big believer in evangelism. Over the years we've had the opportunity to demonstrate that this is a really good business proposition for Microsoft although you can't draw a direct correlation between our activities and revenue.

*So you're talking about evangelism. What is that? What is technology evangelism? Putting out the word about technology?*

Yup. For example everybody on my team has some kind of technology focus. Garth's been doing DHTML one way or another for a couple years, so when somebody wants to dig in to DHTML, Garth's the guy who's specializing in deep knowledge on DHTML. I've got another guy who's been very focused on Java VM and low-level Java programming issues. We have some technology focus for each person, but then the team has objectives for working with certain targeted software developers to adopt certain things.

We make up this laundry list of, what are the characteristics of a good DNA application? It's supposed to be used in a distributed environment, it's supposed to have its user interface be delivered over HTTP, consist largely of DHTML, have interactivity through scripting, have some kind of security. I'm kind of thinking of the corporate intranet model, or I'm a salesman on the road and I'm using virtual private networking to get into the corporate network, something like that. So we end up with this, kind of points of light—different things an application should do. And then we go off and sit down with a company who is interested in doing that kind of thing and we say OK, let's talk about your application, and which of these technologies makes sense, and when you're going to ship it. And we basically come up with this deal that says you're going to write an app that has these kinds of characteristics because that's what you've decided you want to do, and we're going to help you do that, and in return once you've done that we're going to help you get some visibility for that.

We've got folks who talk to press and analysts a couple times a week every week, forever! We've got to have something to tell them because we've got this call schedule so what are we going to tell them this week? We're always looking for things we can talk about like case studies of people who have adopted our technologies and have a good business case for it, glad they did it and their products have been around because they've done it. So we talk about that. We do various kinds of speaking opportunities at conferences and there's a bunch of things like that we do to get some visibility for the folks who have survived those early days of some new technology.

There's nothing like dropping alpha release bits on somebody's desk to really punish them. But for a lot of folks, a lot of times their strategic differentiator is that they get involved very early with technologies and they make that early adoption. One of the things that distinguishes them from other vendors is those folks love to get in there at the alpha stage and just suffer, and submit bug reports and stuff. We want to be sure that those folks have that opportunity, and when they come out the other side and know that life was not an oncoming train, that really was the end of the tunnel, we want to be sure that the world hears about the good work they've done.

### What is Windows DNA architecture?

We're still going through the politically correct naming exercise. The notion of DNA architecture is rather than the monolithic single computer application that we had ten years ago, or the two-tiered, client-server application that we've had over the last five years, that instead you have the n-tier application whose key characteristics are scalability. That is probably one of the biggest ones. The other is flexibility on the client presentation side. So, as you can imagine, we have a set of technologies that we think people ought to use in implementing this architecture.

From the DRG [Developer Relations Group] perspective, I'm going to talk HTTP between the client and the server, so here you use Internet Information Server or some other Web server to dish up Dynamic HTML content as the application user interface. Now the application that I'm running is essentially a browser window and then the application in the DHTML that's being presented in the browser window. From things like amazon.com today we already know about filling in forms and searching and things like that.

But what about the guy who works for an insurance company who would like to be able to download to his notebook all the relevant insurance data? Then he goes off and sits down in your living room and tries to sell you a whole bunch of insurance, takes this data and presents it in an Excel table and switches it all around to try to show you the best or optimal insurance policy for you to buy. And then wouldn't it be dandy if he could also take the order there, even though he's not hooked up to anything, and post that order, close the deal and walk away? Then we he hooks back up to the corporate network through the phone in the hotel room, then that order goes through and he gets back the confirmation number, sends off the confirmation letter, all that just happens there.

Now you need to have disconnected support. That's the model that I live with all the time. I take my notebook home and do work, I get on the airplane and go someplace else and do work. Disconnected is just a reality of the way people work anymore, or a large number of people anyway. So we have a product, Microsoft Message Queue Server or MSMQ, which lets you do exactly that. It lets you take some work and package it up essentially as a message, you could almost think if it as an e-mail message. So there on the client machine it represents my finished work. It sits there and waits and once I dial in and get connected to the server again it says OK, I'm hooked up now, I go ahead and fire that thing down. So when the client side shoots that message down to the server then it goes ahead and completes all that activity just as if you've been wired into the network the whole time.

### What is a DNA application? What does DNA mean to Microsoft?

It means that people are shipping applications that can be much more successful in the kind of operating environment that people are facing today. They want to take their business logic that is running on a variety of servers. They want to have that scale consistently. They want to be able to expose that to their customers and their business partners. Part of DNA is just thinking differently about application architecture. It says that rather than having one application server I may have a whole bunch. Maybe I have so many people hitting my site, like amazon.com, that I just have a whole bunch of servers to handle the load.

*Is DNA something that is already figured out and set at this point?*
Yeah ... in the technological sense it is. We know the technology components that contribute to an application that has this kind of structure. The thing that we're still wrestling with is the clearest way to describe this to people. So we're trying on different presentation approaches to see which ones seem to work best.

*So is it the plan then that this is going to be a standard for the future?*
Yeah. This is going to be the kind of application development architecture that our development tools target essentially by default. Again, this notion that maybe I write my business logic in COBOL, deploy it as a component, and then I generate my user interface. And maybe that user interface is emitted as VB [Visual Basic], maybe it's emitted as Dynamic HTML. And you know Microsoft, we have to provide 6, 8, or 100 different ways of doing things just to keep everybody confused. People's needs are different so the nature of the solution they need is different as well and we try to deal with that. That's one of the things we do best.

*Thanks, Peter!*

# Summary

Visual Basic, being a full-fledged language, has many more features than we can possibly discuss in one chapter. Hopefully, this has been a good introduction to what a full-fledged language is, what it can do, and how you go about writing in the language.

If you want to be a serious VB programmer, I suggest you get the Professional edition and continue your study. There are many VB code writing tools out there, but because VB is a Microsoft copyright, there is only one place you can get a compiler. With the release of VB version 6 there is no doubt VB is going to only get bigger, better, and more Internet capable.

There are several large areas of VB applications out there of which we barely scratched the surface, such as ActiveX, database, and scripting. Microsoft is even starting to use VB and VBScript to play a role in dynamically creating content from Active Server Pages.

There are several ways you can get more involved in the technology of Visual Basic:

- Magazines, such as the *Visual Basic Programmer's Journal*
- The VB trade show, VBITS (Visual Basic Insider's Technical Summit)
- Visiting VB-related Web sites, some of which are mentioned in this chapter

# Java

The most important feature of Java is that it is designed to run on any platform, and when we say *platform* we mean a particular machine running a particular OS. Sun is a manufacturer and Solaris is its Unix OS, which gives us the Sun Solaris platform. There is also the DEC Alpha platform, Mac OS 8, and PC Windows (in this case, a generic manufacturer). In this chapter, we'll be covering:

- Important facts about what Java is and what it's used for.
- How applets are linked to Web pages.
- How Java is different from other languages, and how you can understand Java.
- The basics of learning the Java language.

## What Is Java?

Java was created by Sun Microsystems, initially conceived as a language that would run in consumer appliances! The crew that invented Java tore apart everything from VCRs to videogame players to find a common denominator they could work with. They came up with a language that could actually be used in any appliance with a CPU chip, bare-bones OS, and Java VM all built in.

It is the Java VM, or Virtual Machine, that makes Java a universal language. As mentioned in Chapter 7, "Visual Basic and VBScript," there is currently no cross-platform

VM for Visual Basic; it remains a Microsoft proprietary language. If you're running VB on the client, the client must be running Windows. If you're running VB on the server, the server must be a Microsoft server. Not so with Java. Java will run on any platform because Java VMs have been written for every OS under the sun.

Java was created by Sun but has been licensed for implementation across the board, and this includes Microsoft. However, unlike HTML and DHTML languages, Sun still maintains creative control over just what goes into Java and what does not. The creativity conflict has resulted in a lawsuit currently in progress between Sun and Microsoft. It seems that Microsoft, in usual form, has made some improvements to the language. Microsoft claims this is within its contract agreement and that it's just making things easier. Sun can't revoke Microsoft's license because the contract is limited to financial damages, so the argument is now worth about $35 million.

Nevertheless, Java continues to carry the world (at least the Internet world) on its shoulders. Microsoft has released a new version of Visual J++ that integrates Java development into its Visual InterDev product. There is a plethora of Java development tools on the market for every purpose imaginable, and every month the trade journals carry announcements of more new releases.

Java is a multimedia, multipurpose language. Java is a programmer's language. The basics are easy enough to learn, but there are so many applications that can be done with Java that you could spend years becoming an expert in the language.

Writing Java with visual drag-and-drop development tools is possible, but then you're not really learning Java. On the other hand, it's impossible to try to teach you Java in 25 pages. So what we're going to be looking at is what Java is used for, how you can use it, and get you oriented to what Java is so you can go out and learn it for real. There are a lot of books out there on Java, and most of them assume you're ready to jump in head first. It's really best to learn Java by finding out what you're jumping into first.

## What Is Java Used for?

When Java was first released in 1994, the buzz was all about Java *applets*. The word *applet* is a term for small application. Java made it possible for the first time to put a program into a Web page and run it. Java was first, before Dynamic HTML and JavaScript, and before we knew what was happening, we were bombarded with cute little graphic applications in the form of animations and games that could interact with the user.

Since that time, applets have moved on to higher purposes. Java applets now interface with databases running on Internet servers ready to deliver up-to-the-minute information in text or graphical formats. Java applets are also being used for educational purposes to illustrate concepts in ways the user can interact with scientific and mathematical information.

Java is also going on to serve an important function on Web servers. In fact, it appears that Java is taking over a lot of functions that used to be accomplished by other programs. Java *servlets* are the counterpart of applets running on more and more Web servers in a client/server capacity to serve up information as mentioned earlier and illustrated in Figure 8.1.

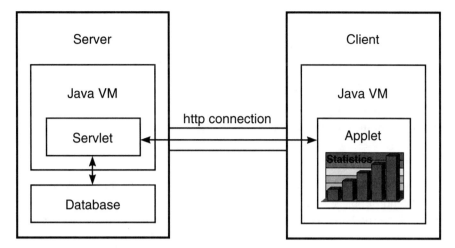

**Figure 8.1**  Java client applet to Java server servlet.

Servlets are also more efficient than the CGI scripts they are replacing because the servlets stay running on the server. With CGI scripts, every time a request is made, the server has to initiate the CGI compiler, translate the program, then load the compiled version before even beginning to service the request. A Java servlet stays up and running and ready to respond with no such overhead. Last but not least, the two Java programs do not have to be running on the same platform.

Java can also be used to write standalone programs, just like Visual Basic. The Java Virtual Machine can run independently of a Web browser to support standalone applications. A lot of major corporations and government agencies are turning to Java as a multiplatform solution for their internal data processing needs.

Whether on the Internet or an intranet, Java is being applied to applications that include multimedia, database, e-commerce, cryptography, and even network management. Java is most certainly on track to becoming a central technology around which all networking will evolve. The main challenge to Java implementation is in speeding up the Java VM to compete with languages that compile to native code, such as C++. This is being worked on in the form of better compilers, streamlined Java VMs, and building the Java VM into hardware at the chip level.

# Putting Java Applets in a Web Page

In HTML version 3, the *APPLET* tag was added to allow you to embed applets in Web pages, but with version 4 this tag has already been deprecated in favor of the new *OBJECT* tag. These tags have a lot of similar attributes, the *OBJECT* tag being the more general. We're going to take a look at both tags, since there will probably be a lot more *APPLET*s out there than *OBJECT*s (for a while at least).

Here is the bare minimum for an *APPLET* tag:

```
<APPLET CODE="Warp.class" WIDTH="200" HEIGHT="150"></APPLET>
```

It includes the *CODE* attribute, which specifies the executable Java program, and the *WIDTH* and *HEIGHT* attributes give a size for the applet window.

Java-compiled programs, whether applets or executables, are called *class files*. The *CODE* attribute is case sensitive. Even though there is no HTML in this example, the *APPLET* tag is paired for a reason. Any HTML put between the tags will be executed if for some reason the applet cannot be run. This allows us to provide alternative content for a non-Java or Java-disabled browser.

Here is a bare-minimum *OBJECT* tag for the same applet:

```
<OBJECT CLASSID="java:Warp.class" WIDTH="200" HEIGHT="150"></OBJECT>
```

The only difference in this case is the attribute *CLASSID*, which also allows us to specify what kind of object we are dealing with; in this case, a Java object. In dealing with Microsoft products, I have come to expect a certain level of predictable funny business leaning toward the consumer's advantage. In this case, I called a bluff on Microsoft's browser and simply changed the *APPLET* tag to *OBJECT* without changing any of the attributes. Guess what? It worked exactly the same! *In fact, it even worked when the starting tag said OBJECT and the ending tag said APPLET.* This should tell you something about Microsoft's design philosophy.

Figure 8.2 is an interesting illustration of how Navigator and Explorer handle both of these tags with the same applet. There are four versions of the applet here, two for Navigator and two for Explorer.

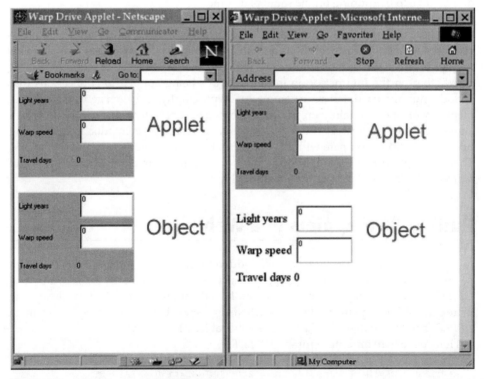

**Figure 8.2** Applets versus objects.

This version of the Warp Drive applet has been given minimal functionality to serve as the simplest possible example of Java programming. This is the exact same applet running in all four copies, based on the exact tags shown earlier. The Applet and Object words were added to this screenshot for your benefit and were not part of the original markup. In this demonstration you will notice that Microsoft has once again come through where the Explorer *OBJECT* version has unexpectedly given the applet an enhanced display.

Let's take a look at the full *APPLET* and *OBJECT* specifications in HTML.

# Writing APPLET Tags for Java

Here's the format for the *APPLET* tag:

```
<APPLET CODE="class file name"
 CODEBASE="uri"
 WIDTH=#pixels HEIGHT=#pixels
 HSPACE=#pixels VSPACE=#pixels
 ALIGN="left,right,center"
 ALT="description"
 NAME="reference name"
 ARCHIVE="URI,URI,URI. . ."
 STYLE="style attributes"
 ID="id"
 CLASS="class">
<PARAM NAME="name" VALUE="value">
 (repeat for all parameters)
 alternate non-Java HTML code
</APPLET>
```

Each of the *APPLET* attributes is explained next.

### CODE = "class file name"

This attribute specifies the Java class filename either with or without the full URI path. The official term for the URI path is *base URI*. The base URI can alternately be given in the *CODEBASE* attribute. If no URL is present it will default to the current path. Its equivalent in the *OBJECT* tag is *CLASSID*.

### CODEBASE = "uri"

This attribute specifies the base URI for the applet, and may contain the directory name but not the Java class filename. It is also used in the *OBJECT* tag.

### WIDTH = #pixels and HEIGHT = #pixels

These attributes specify the screen width and height of the applet. It is also used in the *OBJECT* tag.

### HSPACE = #pixels, VSPACE = #pixels

These attributes specify the amount of space to give the applet. These are standard HTML attributes and will cause other HTML elements on the page to be distanced from this element. They are also used in the *OBJECT* tag.

### ALIGN = "alignment"

The *ALIGN* attribute can be used to position the applet just as any HTML element that accepts alignment control. It is also used in the *OBJECT* tag.

### ALT = "description"

This attribute specifies a text string to display in place of the applet. See *OBJECT STANDBY* attribute.

### NAME = "reference name"

This attribute gives a name to this particular running applet. Java methods are available to send and receive data between applets on the same page using the *NAME* attribute to identify each other. This is different than the way applet/servlet pairs communicate.

### ARCHIVE = "URI,URI,URI. . ."

This attribute specifies a list of files that will be preloaded by the browser. These may include things like images and other Java class files. Preloading reduces wait time for applets that will be calling on other resources during their execution. It is also used in the *OBJECT* tag.

The *APPLET* tag also accepts these attributes from DHTML: *STYLE, ID,* and *CLASS*.

*PARAM* is another element that goes with the *APPLET* tag. This special element will be discussed after we go over the *OBJECT* tag since it is enclosed as a separate tag within the *APPLET* or *OBJECT* pair and is equally important to both of them.

## Writing *OBJECT* Tags for a Java Applet

Here's the format for the *OBJECT* tag:

```
<OBJECT CLASSID="class file name"
 CODEBASE="uri"
 WIDTH=#pixels HEIGHT=#pixels
 HSPACE=#pixels VSPACE=#pixels
 ALIGN="alignment"
 STANDBY="description"
 CODETYPE="mime type"
 ARCHIVE="URI,URI,URI. . ."
 STYLE="style attributes"
 ID="id"
 CLASS="class"
 ONevent="script code"
 (repeat for all events)>
<PARAM NAME="name" VALUE="value">
 (repeat for all parameters)
 alternate non-Java HTML code
</OBJECT>
```

Each of the *OBJECT* attributes is explained next.

### CLASSID = "class file name"

This attribute specifies the Java class filename either with or without the full URI path. The official term for the URI path is *base URI*. The base URI can alternately be given in the *CODEBASE* attribute. If no URL is present it will default to the current path. Its equivalent in the *APPLET* tag is *CODE*.

### CODEBASE = "uri"

This attribute specifies the base URI for the applet, and may contain the directory name but not the Java class filename. It is also used in the *APPLET* tag.

### WIDTH = #pixels and HEIGHT = #pixels

These attributes specify the screen width and height of the applet and are used in the *APPLET* tag.

### HSPACE = #pixels, VSPACE = #pixels

These attributes specify the amount of space to give the applet. These are standard HTML attributes and will cause other HTML elements on the page to be distanced from this element. The *ALIGN* attribute can be used to position the applet within the larger space provided for it. They are also used in the *APPLET* tag.

### ALIGN = "alignment"

The *ALIGN* attribute can be used to position the applet just as any HTML element that accepts alignment control. It is also used in the *APPLET* tag.

### STANDBY ="description"

This attribute specifies a text string to display in place of the applet. See *APPLET ALT* attribute.

### CODETYPE = "mime type"

This attribute tells the browser what kind of object is contained in the *CLASSID* attribute, so the browser will be able to handle it properly or, more importantly, *not* handle it in an inappropriate manner.

In case you haven't been keeping up, *MIME* means *Multipart Internet Mail Extension*. There are many MIME types, and there are currently two parts to a MIME type; hence the term *Multipart*. We already know why they relate to the Internet. This term originally was intended to identify file types for *Mail* attachments so they could be properly opened at the receiving end, and this idea is an *Extension* to HTML.

MIME has come to do more than identify mail attachments; now it's used to identify content types for just about anything that's sent over the Internet. There are eight basic MIME types: *application, audio, image, message, model, multipart, text,* and *video*. We've seen these used particularly in CSS and scripting to identify the type of style sheet and script language to the browser. Here it identifies what kind of applet is used.

There are dozens of MIME subtypes; in fact, it would take pages to list them all. Even though the Java applet subtype is specified in the HTML 4 specification, it's not listed in the W3C MIME type reference document. The complete MIME type for a Java applet is *application/java-archive*.

**ARCHIVE = "URI,URI,URI. . ."**

This attribute specifies a list of files that will be preloaded by the browser. These may include things like images and other Java class files. Preloading reduces wait time for applets that will be calling on other resources during their execution. It is also used in the *APPLET* tag.

The *OBJECT* tag also accepts these attributes:

**From DHTML:** STYLE, ID, and CLASS.

**Event handling:** ONCLICK, ONDBLCLICK, ONMOUSEDOWN, ONMOUSEUP, ONMOUSEOVER, ONMOUSEMOVE, ONMOUSEOUT, ONKEYPRESS, ONKEY-DOWN, ONKEYUP.

# PARAM Tags

Java applets are run under the auspices of the Java VM under the tight security of the so-called *sandbox*. This means that the applet cannot read from or write to any storage device on the user's computer. This cuts Java off from any and all interaction with the user's computer; however, the applet can still interact with the browser in any of about three different ways.

The first of these is the *PARAM* tag. The *PARAM* tag sends information to the Java applet, and in order to do this the tag has its own attributes.

Here again is the simple format of the *PARAM* element:

```
<PARAM NAME="name" VALUE="value">
```

**NAME = "name"**

This attribute specifies the name of the parameter that must berecognized by the applet.

**VALUE = "value"**

This attribute specifies the value of the parameter named in the *NAME* attribute.

These values are the equivalent of strings entered as arguments to a DOS-style command line. Here is an example of the Warp Drive Calculator, with parameters added for font and color. The parameters are passed from HTML to the Java applet using a combination of the *NAME* and *VALUE* attributes. What these parameters are called and what they do is entirely up to the applet programmer.

```
<APPLET CODE="Warp.class" WIDTH="200" HEIGHT="150">
<PARAM NAME="font" VALUE="helvetica">
<PARAM NAME="color" VALUE="blue">
</APPLET>
```

The applet must be programmed to get these values from the browser based on their names, and this is accomplished in Java via a simple method called *getParameter*, which we'll discuss later in this chapter.

# Writing Java Programs

The first thing you need to do is download the latest version of the Sun JDK, or Java Development Kit, which is free via Sun's Java site at java.sun.com/products.

Install this kit and you're ready to write, compile, and run Java! Using the Sun JDK, we can write Java using any text editor or word processing program, but we have to compile at the command line. We're not doing drag-and-drop programming here because this is about achieving a real understanding of Java programming.

To compile a Java source file, simply type *javac className.java* at the command prompt.

Java executable files, whether applets or not, all have the *.class* extension and are called *class files*. Java is a hard-core object-oriented language, so a class file contains *methods* and *data*. The applet file listed next is called *Agent.java* and compiles to *Agent.class*. This applet, being only five lines long, is very simple. It was written to display a property from the user agent, which we have been introduced to in Chapter 5, "DHTML," as a technical name for the browser.

```
import java.awt.*;
public class Agent extends java.applet.Applet {
  public void paint(Graphics g) {
    String userAgent = System.getProperty("java.vendor");
    g.drawString(userAgent,10,15);
  }
}
```

Figure 8.3 shows the exciting output of this applet, revealing the vendors of the Java VM for each particular browser.

Each line of this short applet is significant and merits a section of its own. We'll start with the *import* statement, which explains the concept of using *libraries* of prewritten code for a specific purpose.

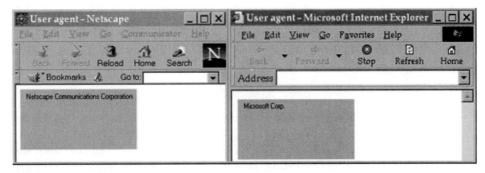

**Figure 8.3**    UserAgent mania.

# INFORMATIVE SITES!

*java.sun.com*
**At the Sun Microsystems Java site, you can download the Sun JDK and get the latest Java news.**

*msdn.microsoft.com/visualj*
**At Microsoft Visual J++, you can download the Microsoft Java SDK and get the latest on MS Java.**

# Java Libraries

Like many high-level languages, Java comes with *libraries* of prewritten code that you can use to great advantage to write high-level programs. To explain what these do, let's go back to the days before Windows and the GUI interface. Actually, we don't have to go that far back, DOS and Unix are both alive and well.

Let's say we want to open a window on the screen to create a graphical user interface, display a graphic, or do something in a graphic way. Where do we start? Before the days when this was built in to a language like Java, we would have to start by doing a mathematical calculation to locate where our image was to appear on the screen. Then we would have to write a loop to display a spot of color, pixel by pixel, to draw our image.

Now we wouldn't want to have to do that for every button, background, label, and input box that we need to display. That would drive us insane and we would quit programming, move to Montana, and take up sheep shearing. To spare us this mental anguish, Java gives us preprogrammed code delivered in files called *packages* that contain *class libraries* that will do this GUI stuff for us. So the first thing we do in our applet is to make one of those libraries accessible to our program. We do that with the statement:

```
import java.awt.*;
```

Figure 8.4 shows the relationship of components of the Java applet to the Java language libraries, and includes several graphical notes on structure that we'll discuss now.

AWT (Abstract Windowing Toolkit) is a class library that provides the applet with several methods needed to display in a graphical fashion. The Java AWT is full of methods that can be called upon. The *graphics* library in the *java.awt* package contains the method *drawString* that is used in the applet. We could import just this part of the package by typing:

```
import java.awt.graphics;
```

The asterisk found in "java.awt.*" gives us the full range of methods without having to know which section of the library they come from. In fact, we can import from any number of class libraries just by listing them in *import* statements. Why don't we just

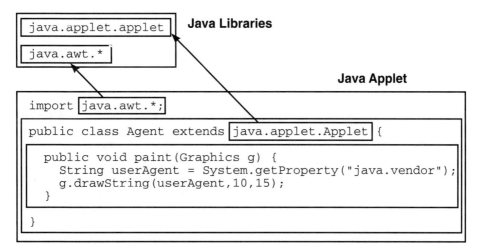

**Figure 8.4** The components of Java.

import all these libraries all of the time? There are quite a few of them, and the number keeps growing. Which libraries we import depends on what our program is supposed to be doing, and besides, it's possible that methods could have the same name in different libraries.

The Sun JDK comes with a set of packages containing several sets of class libraries that are guaranteed to be universally found on all Java platforms.

These are:

| | |
|---|---|
| **java.lang** | Java core language classes that do not need an explicit *import* statement |
| **java.util** | Miscellaneous classes |
| **java.io** | Classes for all kinds of input and output |
| **java.net** | Networking classes |
| **java.awt** | Abstract windowing toolkit for GUI elements |
| **java.applet** | Classes that provide graphical support for applets |

Next, in order to explain the meaning of *extends* in the class declaration statement, we need to look at the concept of *inheritance*, a mechanism that so many have worked so hard for so long to describe.

# Inheritance

The class declaration in this applet does not stand alone as does a function or subroutine in Visual Basic, it comes with a modifier, *extends*. What it extends is a class library, *java.applet.Applet*. What's the difference between importing and extending?

Let's go back to the pre-GUI concept of a simple program with no GUI capability. What does it do and how? It's supposed to get some data and draw it on the screen but it has no external methods available to it. Now we start at the first line and import the *java.awt* class libraries. This makes methods available to do all kinds of graphical drawing things. But on what? There's no window, no graphical slate on which to start scribbling. We are still at the point at which all we have is this applet program and some external methods.

What is it? When we load this program into a Web browser, what does it represent? Why should the browser do anything with it at all?

In Java, like in the Document Object Model, you have a hierarchical structure of objects. At the top is the generic object *Object*. This is a class with methods that apply very broadly. Just like we are all a subset of the *human* class, every Java program is a subset of the *Object* object. This is where the object-oriented basis of Java begins.

From there on down, Java objects start diversifying. If we were programming a network or i/o application like a servlet that never displayed anything on a screen, we might have an object that represents a network connection to a client or an i/o connection to a file. An applet is by definition a graphical application, so Java diversifies the *Object* class into an object that is a graphical unit on the screen called a *Panel*. This *Panel* object contains methods and properties that draw things on the screen.

These Java class library extensions of the *Object* class define what kind of functionality the Java program, class, or object represents. In all cases, these are still *Objects* that *inherit* the methods and properties of the basic Java *Object* class that resides in the *Java.lang* class library. All Java programs are a *subclass* of the *Object* class, and the *Object* class is a *superclass* of all Java programs. A program is a class is an object.

The *Applet* class of the *java.applet* class library is defined as a subclass of the *Panel* class, so what we end up with in an applet is a class that *inherits* the methods and properties that draw things on the screen. When we add buttons, labels, and images, all we have to do is say *paint* and we can do all the painting we want without drawing a single pixel. In fact, we have access to several GUI methods without having to write them ourselves.

Figure 8.5 shows the relation of every method and object in this tiny Java applet to Java class libraries. To sum up, the *java.lang* package is automatically available to all Java classes. The Applet class file consists of the code in the box labeled Java Applet. The import statement causes all methods in the *java.awt* package to also be accessible to the methods in the applet. The applet extends the class *java.applet.Applet* so that it can inherit applet functionality and the GUI methods that class library provides through its inheritance from the *Panel* class. The class itself is named *Agent* and declares only one method of its own, *paint*. The *paint* method *overrides* the *paint* method provided by the *java.awt.Graphics* class library and operates on the *Graphics* object passed to it. It also uses the *drawString* method from that class library. We'll take a look at overriding in the next section.

This little applet also calls methods from *java.lang*. The obvious one is *System.getProperty*, which retrieves the property from the browser called *java.vendor*. The other one is *String*, which is a data type but not a simple data type like *Integer* or *Boolean*. Strings have methods and properties of their own, which makes them objects. As an object provided by the Java runtime, it has to come from somewhere, and that place is *java.lang*. You could of course argue that data types like integers and Booleans also deserve to be objects, since we do things with them just like we do with strings. The hard-core object-oriented language fans would agree with you! But either because some programmers are sentimental and like to stick with tradition or because it's just downright easier to do, the simpler data types are kept simple and not treated as objects.

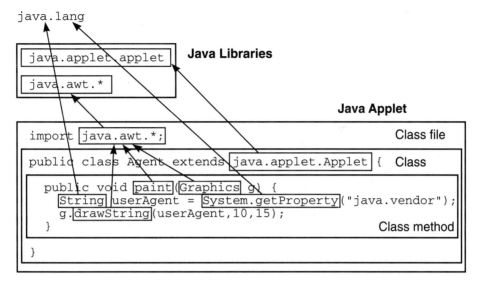

**Figure 8.5**   Unified Java theory.

However, there are many data types that are treated as objects, and the criteria for this is usually that the data type resembles something that was built out of something else, just as an object is built of properties. A string is built of characters and if you've ever had to program around strings without having friendly string methods in the language, you know it's difficult to continually loop character by character to move, compare, or simply validate the contents. String deserves to be an object to make an easier time of it for all of us.

Also in this simple applet appears the passed object *Graphics*. The *Graphics* object, customarily named *g*, is automatically given to the *paint* method to allow the applet to apply its graphical methods. After all, when we're drawing something it has to be drawn somewhere, and that somewhere is a *Graphics* object.

Last but not least, *void* means the method does not return a value, and *public* is similar to its counterpart in VB.

We've now covered just about every last keyword in this applet, but not every last concept in Java. As you have seen, nothing is taken for granted in Java. Everything has to be done explicitly. We do have the capability to call upon numerous class libraries that do a lot of work for us, but we still have to know exactly which methods we are using and what they do. In fact, there are entire books full of descriptions of these class libraries. The Java class libraries described earlier are known as the *core Java API*, or *Application Program Interface*, and there are plenty more APIs available.

## Writing Java Applets

An applet is a special kind of Java program. Because it inherits from the class library *java.applet.Applet* it is not written to be run standalone. The full hierarchy that governs an applet starts with the *Applet* class, which inherits from the *Panel* class, which inherits from the *Container* class, which inherits from the *Component* class, which, like all Java classes, inherits from the *Object* class.

This is not some royal hierarchy. Just because an applet is four rungs down the ladder doesn't mean everything *within* an applet is five rungs down the ladder. The purpose of the hierarchy is to define properties and methods that govern the appearance and behavior of a specific object in the Java entity. An applet can have a *Component* such as, for example, a *Button*, which is an object that inherits directly from a *Component*. The truth is, the farther down the hierarchy an object is, the more methods and properties it gathers from the levels above. The top levels have the broadest and simplest objects, while the lower levels have the most specific and functional objects. This is why *applet* is actually near the bottom. Figure 8.6 demonstrates some of the more relevant objects in the Java hierarchy.

When the browser sees the *<APPLET>* or *<OBJECT>* tag, it creates a *Panel* object and loads the Java class file. The applet, appearing as a square box, certainly looks like a panel. The browser calls one of its own classes that is in turn programmed to call specific methods, at specific times, expected to be found in the applet.

Even if these methods were not originally programmed into the applet, when it was compiled, Java put dummy methods into the applet based on the applet's inheritance from the *Applet* superclass where these methods are defined. These dummy methods don't do anything except be there when the browser calls them to satisfy the requirements of an Applet object. But when these methods are present in the applet, they are said to *override* the methods in their superclass.

This brings us to what is called the life cycle of an applet. There are five methods that are always called in an applet. You may include all or none of them, but of course if none are present, nothing will happen. You at least need to have *paint()* to draw something on the screen. What is in these methods is up to you.

*init()*     This is called when the applet is loaded and provides for initialization of variables and other setup.

*start()*    This is called when the applet is first displayed and whenever it is made visible. It allows you to start *threads*, which continue to run for the life of the applet.

*paint()*    This draws the screen as we have seen. This is called whenever the applet is made visible, and whenever else the programmer wants to draw something on the screen.

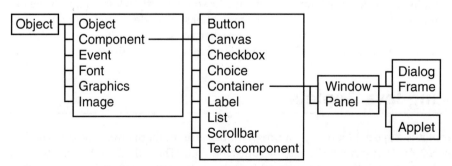

**Figure 8.6**   Cross section of java.applet.Applet hierarchy.

*stop()*  This is called when the applet is hidden or terminated, and provides for terminating threads.

*destroy()* This is called when the applet is terminated and cleans up, removing things from memory we don't need anymore before unloading.

The *init()*, *start()*, and *paint()* methods are called when the applet starts. Thereafter, you can call the *paint()* method as many times as you like, and *start()*, *paint()*, and *stop()* may be called again as required. When the applet is terminated, *stop()* and *destroy()* are called. The automatic calls are done by the browser because this Java program inherits from *Applet*, which defines this behavior for applets.

Figure 8.7 shows an applet that implements all of these methods. This applet displays a flashing message, much like an animated GIF but driven by a Java *thread*. The message alternates "I need a …" with "(point at me!)", and when the mouse is placed over the body, the appropriate medical specialist is named.

This applet is an exercise in the five central applet methods, the use of *threads*, and the use of an event-driven mouse handler. That's really a lot of Java.

# Threads

A thread is not something new. At any one time, a computer is doing several things at once. This is called *multitasking* and has been around since the 1960s. Each of the specific tasks that is being performed can be called a *thread*. One of the definitions for *thread* in the dictionary is "a train of thought," or "a pervasive recurring element." The former can be applied to e-mail-type threads, the latter to program-type threads. A thread handles a specific task that is expected to recur; otherwise, we would only have to do it once.

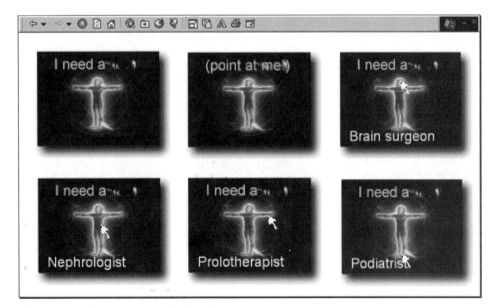

**Figure 8.7** The Artman applet in action.

In this applet the thread does something extremely simple: It displays the alternating text. Still, in order to perform this simple task we need to invoke the *start* and *stop* methods and one more method we haven't talked about, the *run* method.

# Interfaces

The class declaration for this applet not only includes *extends java.applet.Applet* but a new concept, *implements Runnable*. The *implements* statement defined an interface for our Java program. The concept of an interface is not that different from the concept of an inheritance. When you study Java in depth you will read about how the C++ language allows for *multiple inheritance*, where a program can inherit methods and properties from more than one superclass, but how Java only supports *single inheritance*, and that the interface is a way for a Java program to add to its inheritance structure. This is all true, but does not really explain how it works, only that it gives you the capability to do certain things with it such as what is being done here.

In this case, we are implementing the *Runnable* interface that provides the *run* method that will give the applet a continuously running procedure. In a regular Java program, you must have a *main()* method, but there is no provision for this in an applet. If you write a *main* method into an applet it will not be recognized as anything special.

The *Runnable* interface comes from the *java.lang* class library, but an interface can be written by anyone. Let's say you're given the job of writing a suite of Java programs that will display video across a network. You want to enforce that a specific set of methods are used in all programs implementing the *Video* interface. That's what an interface is for. When an interface is implemented it means that the program must have its own version of every method defined in the interface. There is more to this, which requires more space than we have here, but the bottom line is, that is how an interface works. Implementing the *Runnable* interface means we *must* put the *run* method into our applet. This enables our applet to be run, as illustrated in Figure 8.8.

```
import java.awt.*;

public class artman extends java.applet.Applet implements Runnable {

 Image nakedman;
 Image nextimage;
 Graphics nextgraphic;
 Thread ineeda;
 Font arial = new Font("Arial",Font.PLAIN,24);
 String ineed1 = "I need a . . .";
 String ineed2 = "(point at me!)";
 String headera, headerb, footera, footerb;
 String specialist = "";
```

**Figure 8.8** Science becomes art.

```java
String otherguy = "";

public void init() {
    nakedman = getImage(getCodeBase(),"images/artman.GIF");
    nextimage = createImage(size().width,size().height);
    nextgraphic = nextimage.getGraphics();
}
public void start() {
    if (ineeda == null) {
        ineeda = new Thread(this);
        ineeda.start();
    }
}
public void stop () {
    if (ineeda != null) {
        ineeda.stop();
        ineeda = null;
    }
}

public void run() {
    while (true) {
        headera = ineed1;
        headerb = ineed2;
        repaint();
        pause(3000);
        headera = ineed2;
        headerb = ineed1;
        repaint();
        pause(3000);
    }
}
public boolean mouseMove(Event evt, int x, int y) {
    if (x >= 120 && x <= 127 && y >=74 && y <= 77) {
        specialist = "Optometrist";
    }
    if (x >= 119 && x <= 123 && y >= 66 && y <= 74) {
        specialist = "Brain surgeon";
    }
    if (x >= 116 && x <= 118 && y >= 70 && y <= 75) {
        specialist = "ENT specialist";
    }
    if (x >= 128 && x <= 130 && y >= 70 && y <= 75) {
        specialist = "ENT specialist";
    }
    if (x >= 119 && x <= 127 && y >= 75 && y <= 78) {
        specialist = "Dentist";
    }
```

*Continues*

**Figure 8.8** *(Continued)*

```
    if (x >= 80 && x <= 91 && y >= 79 && y <= 85) {
        specialist = "Prolotherapist";
    }
    if (x >= 156 && x <= 167 && y >= 78 && y <= 84) {
        specialist = "Prolotherapist";
    }
    if (x >= 110 && x <= 134 && y >= 143 && y <= 151) {
        specialist = "Podiatrist";
    }
    if (x >= 115 && x <= 133 && y >= 105 && y <= 113) {
        specialist = "Urologist";
    }
    if (x >= 123 && x <= 132 && y >= 79 && y <= 82) {
        specialist = "Cardiologist";
    }
    if (x >= 114 && x <= 122 && y >= 79 && y <= 92) {
        specialist = "Internist";
    }
    if (x >= 115 && x <= 131 && y >= 93 && y <= 98) {
        specialist = "GI specialist";
    }
    if (x >= 115 && x <= 122 && y >= 99 && y <= 105) {
        specialist = "Nephrologist";
    }
    if (x >= 123 && x <= 132 && y >= 99 && y <= 104) {
        specialist = "Hepatologist";
    }
    if (x >= 115 && x <= 133 && y >= 123 && y <= 132) {
        specialist = "Orthopedist";
    }
    if (x >= 115 && x <= 132 && y >= 114 && y <= 122) {
        specialist = "Vascular surgeon";
    }
    if (x >= 117 && x <= 133 && y >= 133 && y <= 142) {
        specialist = "Vascular surgeon";
    }
    if (x >= 92 && x <= 113 && y >= 79 && y <= 86) {
        specialist = "Physical therapist";
    }
    if (x >= 133 && x <= 155 && y >= 79 && y <= 85) {
        specialist = "Physical therapist";
    }
    if (specialist != otherguy) {
        repaint();
        return true;
        }
    else
        return false;
```

**Figure 8.8** *(Continued)*

```
        }
    public boolean mouseExit(Event evt, int x, int y) {
        specialist = " ";
        repaint();
        return true;
    }
    void pause (int time) {
        try {Thread.sleep(time);}
        catch (InterruptedException e) { }
    }
    public void update(Graphics g) {
        paint(g);
    }
    public void paint(Graphics g) {
        nextgraphic.setColor(Color.white);
        nextgraphic.fillRect(0,0,size().width,size().height);
        nextgraphic.drawImage(nakedman,0,0,this);

        nextgraphic.setFont(arial);
        nextgraphic.setColor(Color.black);
        nextgraphic.drawString(headerb,50,50);
        nextgraphic.setColor(Color.red);
        nextgraphic.drawString(headera,50,50);

        nextgraphic.setColor(Color.black);
        nextgraphic.drawString(otherguy,35,170);
        nextgraphic.setColor(Color.white);
        nextgraphic.drawString(specialist,35,170);

        g.drawImage(nextimage,0,0,this);
        otherguy = specialist;
    }
    public void destroy() {
        nextgraphic.dispose();
    }
}
```

**Figure 8.8**   *(Continued)*

# Running Java Applets

This applet implements all of the methods required by *java.applet.Applet*: *init, start, paint, stop,* and *destroy*. It also implements the *run* method from the *Runnable* interface, the *mouseMove* and *mouseExit* events from *java.awt.Event,* and the *update* method, which is used to call *paint* for a special reason.

The first thing this applet does is to declare its variables and objects. *Nakedman* is declared as an Image object and the *init* method's entire job is to read the image from *images/artman.GIF* in the current directory, which in turn is retrieved using the *getCode-Base* method, and load it into a *Graphics* object named *nextgraphic*.

The *start* method checks to see if the *Thread* object is *null*, or empty, and if it is, it instantiates the Thread. Why do we need to create a *new Thread* if we already declared *ineeda* as a Thread up top? This is because when you declare a variable as an object type, that's all you're doing. You're not creating the object—all Java does is associate the variable name with a type of object. In order to actually create an instance of that object, you have to use the *new* statement. And you can do this more than once, in effect reincarnating the object each time.

The *this* object represents the current object, so when we instantiate a *new Thread(this)* we are creating a Thread object for *this* applet object. *This* is used a lot in Java.

The final statement of the applet's *start* method calls the *start* method of the *Thread* object. The *stop* method does the same thing in reverse, checking to see if the Thread is active and if so, calling the *Thread* object *stop* method and then setting the *Thread* object to null.

The *run* method is the driver for the flashing display. This method uses a *Font* object that is instantiated as a 24-point Arial plain font using *new Font*. The Font object takes three parameters: the font name, font style (which is a built-in Java name), and type size. Curious about how to name a font using Java, I wrote a small applet to display a list of all available font names. We'll take a look at that one later in this chapter.

The *run* method executes an infinite loop, no different from what we've seen in VB and JavaScript. The looping statement *while (true)* will obviously never be false. In each loop, it reverses the two text strings, calls *repaint* to update the screen, pauses for three seconds, reverses the strings, and does it again. There is more to this than meets the eye. To start with, *repaint* is used in place of *paint* to make it easier on the Java VM to keep up with our applet. *Repaint* only issues a request to call *paint* and does not force the screen to be updated at that instant. We'll take a look at the tricks of screen repainting in the next section.

The *paint* method does a lot of clever things to make sure the applet is displayed in a user-friendly fashion. First it uses the *setColor* method to pick a color using another built-in Java value, *Color.white*, to set the color that will be used by any subsequent method call that does painting. In order to get rid of the ugly gray applet background the Java VM always displays, it fills the applet panel using the *FillRect* method with its parameters set to coordinates covering the entire panel, and uses the *drawImage* method to put the da Vinci *nakedman* image on top of this.

Next follows the code to draw the fonts. There is a reason the color is set to black, one string is drawn, the color is set to red, and the other string is drawn. This is because the strings, being fonts directly drawn on the screen and not graphics, have no background. So we have to erase the last one before drawing the next one or we'll end up always seeing both strings on the screen at the same time. The first time that this runs, the second string will be drawn in black, erasing nothing, which will have no effect. This same algorithm is applied to the message at the bottom of the screen, which is erased in black and then drawn in white.

Finally, the entire *nextimage Graphic* object is redrawn by calling the *g.drawImage* method. This painting procedure happens twice in every iteration of the *run* method.

# Animation in Java

Even though this applet is very simple, the methods applied here are the same as would be applied to any Java animation. The way they are applied comes from working out how to display the screen with a bit of trial and error to avoid the pitfalls of computer graphic animation.

To get the idea of how this works, you again have to go back to not assuming anything. Just because we have drawn an image in the applet panel once doesn't mean that, like graffiti sprayed on a wall, it will remain there until being scrubbed off or painted over. Java has three methods that redisplay the applet panel area: *update*, *paint*, and *repaint*.

The *update* method is the top-level method and, like all methods in the hierarchy, has a default method that will be executed if you do not override it. This default *update* method will clear the panel, display the background, and then call *paint*. For this reason, we override *update* with our own method, which will not clear the panel but will only call *paint*. This eliminates getting a flashing background-colored box every time our display is updated. To see the havoc this wreaks on your applet, try leaving *update* to the Java VM. Of course, Java does it this way because something has to be done, and Java doesn't know what your applet is supposed to look like.

The *repaint* method is another default method, but one which we do not need to override. As mentioned earlier, *repaint* only issues a request to the Java VM to call the *paint* method, and that request is only executed by the Java VM if and when it has the time. Normally it would go through with no problem, but in some cases, the system could be busy doing something else. What will happen if these requests get backed up is that only the latest *repaint* will be performed and you will get a jumpy animation. The moral: Write your programs efficiently so these requests will not get backed up.

As you can see, screen updating in Java is something that is not all that automatic. The *artman* applet does two versions of screen repainting, one on its own and the other when the mouse is moved. It's easy enough to update the screen every three seconds, but when the mouse is moved the screen can be updated once for every pixel movement. It becomes clear that if we repaint the screen for every pixel crossed by the mouse, our applet will take on that flashing strobe disco look. There are two ways we deal with this.

The first thing we do is only update the screen when a change is required. Every time we change the *specialist* displayed, we save the string displayed in the *otherguy* variable. So when the mouse is moved and there is no change in *specialist* we don't have to update the display. This is accomplished through the simple statement:

```
if (specialist != otherguy) { repaint();}.
```

The second thing we do is update our screen on the *nextgraphic Graphic* object in an "off-line" mode. This way, the updates are *not seen on the screen* until the *g.drawImage* method is called, updating the screen with everything at once. Loading up an image in an off-screen object before displaying makes the actual screen update occur much faster. You can load up a whole series of images so they are ready to display beforehand, thus making your animation much smoother. The smoothness with which this applet updates its display is the result of applying each and every one of these principles, and the necessity for these animating tricks will become apparent if you take an applet and remove these special handlings.

Note that the *pause* method is not public and as such, it is the only method completely internal to the applet. Every other method is *public* and is called by a superclass. This method calls the *Thread* object *sleep* method as part of a *try … catch* statement. This prevents an error from being *thrown* when another event wakes up the Thread. This would happen if the browser is closed, minimized, or hidden behind another window, in which case the *stop* method would be called and the *sleep* method interrupted.

Java error handling is simple. *Try* executes the code in the brackets following it, and in this case when an exception is *thrown*, the *Catch* statement takes no action because there is no code in the brackets following the *Catch* object. If we wanted, we could put code here to be performed if the *sleep* method was interrupted.

Although the *destroy* method is not necessary, it frees up the memory taken by the *nextgraphic* object and is good housekeeping.

# Programming Events in Java

The speed of today's computers gives us the power to do a lot of processing that would have brought a computer to its knees just a few years ago. Even this small applet adds the load of two additional running processes to the CPU load, that of the *Thread* and that of the *Event* handler.

The *Event* object is always present, and all events that occur in the applet panel are passed by the user agent to the applet for processing. Again, if you do not override the event processing in your applet, nothing will occur. Still, the events are triggered and passed at least to dummy routines. This is very similar to what occurs in scripting languages with the browser's Document Object Model where event handlings are scripted. Internet browsing is an event-driven activity and today's object-oriented programs, of which applets, browsers, and windows are all a part, are event-driven.

The point is that every event is handled at some level somewhere. If not in your applet, then in the Java VM, and if not in the Java VM, then in the browser, and if not in the browser, then by the OS. And there is a mechanism by which the method that does finally handle the event reports that it has been handled. This is the Boolean *return* value. Because it must report on its actions, an event-handling method is declared as a Boolean method and not a void method.

The *mouseMove* method in the *artman* applet overrides the mouseMove event in *java.awt.Event*. The method is passed an *Event* object we call *evt* plus the coordinates where the event took place as integers *x* and *y*. This event-handling method does the simple job of checking the coordinates of the event and setting the *specialist* string based on a range of values. This is how an image map works in Java. It has to be programmed, there is no magic mechanism. Code-writing programs make this easy, but the numbers still have to be there.

The final action the *mouseMove* method takes is to tell the calling routine (the Java VM) whether or not it handled the event passed to it. *True* means the event was handled; *False* means it wasn't. This allows the calling routine to perform an alternate event handling.

```
public boolean mouseMove(Event evt, int x, int y)
{
. . . (event handling code) . . .

if (specialist != otherguy) {
        repaint();
        return true;
        }
    else
        return false;
```

Finally, when the mouse leaves the applet panel, the *mouseExit* method clears the specialist display. This is optional and is performed because I wanted to leave the slate cleared, so to speak.

## Experimenting with Java

It is easy to write little applets that will explore the idiosyncrasies of the Java language. Let's take a look at the applet I wrote to explore the font capabilities of Java.

This applet, as shown in Figure 8.9, initiates an array of font names by calling a method from *java.awt* that extracts a list of fonts from the *toolkit*, an object that contains properties from the current platform. It then performs a loop, with the same syntax as a JavaScript loop, to draw the fonts in the font panel. This is a run-once applet so there are no *init*, *start*, *stop*, or *destroy* methods. In order to make the font list easier to see, I set the display font to larger than the default and give each one 25 vertical pixels of room.

Figure 8.10 illustrates the disturbing results. Despite the fact that I must have at least 200 typefaces on my computer, I have access to only a handful of dubious value.

```
import java.awt.*;

public class Fonts extends java.applet.Applet
{
Font bigFont = new Font("Arial",Font.BOLD,24);

  public void paint(Graphics g)
  {
  setFont(bigFont);
  String[] allFonts = getToolkit().getFontList();

  for (int i = 0; i < allFonts.length; i++) {
   g.drawString(allFonts[i],10,25+(i*25));
   }
  }
}
```

**Figure 8.9**   Java font peeker.

**Figure 8.10**   Thin font resources.

You can write little applets like this to familiarize yourself with Java. Now let's take a look at another aspect of working with Java, which is applet/Web page interactivity.

## How Can HTML Interact with Java?

There are two directions of communication to accomplish: HTML to Java, and Java to HTML. Although Java applets run in the high-security sandbox, there are ways to communicate back and forth.

The first and easiest way is through the *PARAM* tag, which passes values to the applet. The Java program can very easily access any number of these using the *getParameter* method. The names used by *getParameter* must be the same as in the *APPLET* or *OBJECT* tags. Numerical values can be passed as strings and then converted using the numerous built-in conversion routines in *Java.lang*.

```
String param1 = getParameter("paramName1");
String param2 = getParameter("paramName2");
```

But what if the parameters are not always the same? There are several ways to do this little trick using Dynamic HTML.

We know that by using JavaScript we can actively generate the contents of a Web page by having embedded JavaScript statements perform a series of *document.write* statements like these. This could of course only occur at document load time.

```
. . . HTML code . . .
<SCRIPT language="javascript">
document.write ('<APPLET CODE="Warp.class" WIDTH="200" HEIGHT="150">')
IF (condition 1)
  document.write ('<PARAM NAME="color" VALUE="blue">')
IF (condition 2)
  document.write ('<PARAM NAME="color" VALUE="red">')
```

```
document.write ('</APPLET>')
</SCRIPT>
. . . HTML code . . .
```

The second option is much more dynamic. Using JavaScript with Java applets, we can not only send values from JavaScript to Java, but we can even read them back. We can also directly call methods within the applet from JavaScript! Even better—this works in both Navigator and Explorer.

Let's say we want to take the running artman applet, and change one of the strings interactively. We can put a JavaScript function into the Web page that will be activated for an event. This short script sets the value of a string and calls a method within the applet itself.

```
function changeText() {
   newstring="You need a . . ."
   document.artman.setMsg(newstring)
}
```

Then we add a method within the applet to receive the values passed and set the string within the applet to the new value. That is all there is to it. You can even call *paint*, *repaint*, or any other method in the applet from JavaScript!

```
public void setMsg(String newMsg)
{
   ineed1 = newMsg;
}
```

A third and most unusual way would be to load several applets in several different layers (for Navigator) or DIVs (for Explorer) and display each one in response to a specific HTML event. Alternately, it should be possible (like we do image replacement) to replace one applet with another. Perhaps with future versions of Explorer and Navigator, newer and stranger methods will become more plausible.

## How Can Java Interact with HTML?

There are still two directions of communication to accomplish: HTML to Java, and Java to HTML. Going back the other way, there are ways for Java to send information back to the calling page.

The first and easiest way is to implement the method call as described earlier, but to add the object-oriented feature of passing a value back from the method. Here we could return the value of the specialist chosen.

```
public String getMsg()
{
   return specialist;
}
```

Then in the JavaScript we assign that value to a string by calling the method. This scheme of *get()* and *set()* is commonly used in Java to set and get the values of variables in other classes.

```
function getSpec() {
  newstring = getMsg()
}
```

A second way of getting values would be to directly access the Java variable. This is possible in Explorer, but unreliable, and Navigator won't let you do it at all, at least not in Version 4.

A third way allows Java to actually reverse the controls and call JavaScript functions directly! This uses the JavaScript URL *"javascript: statement"* way of testing JavaScript statements through the location box that was mentioned in Chapter 6, "JavaScript." This requires using new methods from the *java.net* class library. The way this works is the exact same way we could use Java to jump to another Web page entirely. Because we are using Java to enter a value into the document URL, we can do anything that would be done by entering a value in the browser's location box. The following applet automatically does this because the procedure is part of the *init* method, and as a sample applet, this is all it does. This method could, of course, be named anything and be executed at any time.

```
import java.net.*;
public class scriptIt extends java.applet.Applet {

  public void init() {
      URL javaUrl;
      try {
        javaUrl = new URL("file","","javascript: javaControl()");
        getAppletContext().showDocument(javaUrl);
      }
      catch(MalformedURLException e) {}
  }
}
```

The applet first declares a *URL* object that comes from the *java.net* class library, and then instantiates the object with the value *javascript: javaControl()*. This line does not work the same in Navigator and Explorer. This is because Navigator will throw a *MalformedURLException* on the Explorer version and vice versa. Navigator seems to recognize the *javascript:* format URL with no help, but Explorer needs to be told it's a *file* type URL, not an *http* type URL.

```
Explorer: new URL("file","","javascript: javaControl()");
Navigator: new URL("javascript: javaControl()");
```

The next line delivers the final blow and puts the URL in the document window. As a result, it executes the JavaScript function that can do anything JavaScript can do.

```
function javaControl() {
  any valid Javascript function
}
```

How is it these two statements that create the new URL are calling the same method but take a different number of arguments? Java offers more than one way to call one method, meaning a method can be declared *more than once* in a class by declaring it with different arguments each time. This is called *method overloading*. For example, in the previous two method calls, the Navigator version calls the method with a single String argument, which executes one version of the method in the URL class. The Explorer version calls the method with three String arguments, which executes a different version of the method. That's all there is to it—the purpose of this is to allow flexibility in class libraries. You don't have to worry about calling the right one, Java figures it out for you based on the arguments.

## Learning Java

To start writing applets, you can download code writing programs from Microsoft and/or Sun, but the ones I've seen won't teach you Java, and they don't really give you what you want without having to learn Java anyway. They just speed up program writing for those who already know Java.

As you may have come to understand from this chapter, Java is not as simple as Visual Basic—you can't click a button onto the screen and then just modify the event code. These drag-and-drop editors will either show you nothing or will dump dozens of lines of inexplicable object-oriented code into program. If you don't already understand Java completely, you won't have a clue. The basics of Java are simple, but as you have seen, you have to do everything explicitly in Java.

Get a good book on Java and get ready to write a lot of little applets to test the water. Then find something to write that is meaningful and go for it.

**INFORMATIVE SITE!**
*www.eckelobjects.com/javabook.html*

## Summary

In this chapter we've taken a look at how Java works and what it can do, but I haven't attempted to teach Java—it's just too big a language. There are a lot of great techniques described here that you can use when you do get into serious Java programming, especially the JavaScript/Java communications.

You can download a trial copy of Microsoft Visual J++ from Microsoft and the Sun Java Studio from Sun, which will last for 30 days. You can also download the Sun Java Workshop, which does not expire, for free.

You can do anything in Java, and the Internet world is increasingly turning to Java for solutions. There are several Java publications you can subscribe to, but these are not entry-level mags! Examples include *Java Pro* and *Microsoft Visual J++ Informant.* Many of the usual Internet monthlies have good articles on Java as well, such as *Dr. Dobb's Journal, Web Techniques,* and *Web Developer.*

CHAPTER

9

# PERL and CGI

PERL (Practical Extraction and Report Language) is a text processing language that runs in the background on servers to deliver up Web content in a fashion that is invisible to the viewer. PERL was invented by a man named Larry Wall as a much improved version of *awk*.

Awk is one of those Unix programs with funny names. If you're at all familiar with Unix, the connection between the names of Unix commands and their purpose is usually buried deep within the geek mind. In this case a, w, and k are the initials of the three guys who wrote the first version of awk back in the 1970s. Awk is still around as a member of the standard Unix command set and is an advanced text processing utility used for things like text search and replacement on a large scale.

The concept of a program to do text search and replacement may seem uninteresting to the uninitiated. The truth is that languages like PERL are extremely sophisticated and can do things in a way you would probably never think of unless you had used it before. PERL was around before JavaScript, VBScript, and Active Server Pages, and was initially responsible for *all* programmed HTML generation—period. PERL is still a competitor for many of these functions, and is still the best or only solution for others.

PERL is used, at least on the Internet, to write CGI scripts. CGI scripts are the programs that process the information submitted in HTML FORM submissions. FORMs can be used for anything from spawning an automatic e-mail to database searches and electronic storefronts. The power of PERL can support any and all of these activities.

CGI (Common Gateway Interface) is a term that was formed in the Stone Age days of the Internet. Back when somebody had to figure out how an HTML document could somehow send a communication somewhere, the term *gateway* cropped up. Recall from Chapter 1, "What Has the Internet Become?," that a gateway is a connection between networks. In this case, the *gateway* is the connection between HTML and the rest of the Internet, the CGI method is the *interface*, and it's *common* because it's not security restricted—anybody can use it.

PERL has its origins in Unix and runs primarily on Unix Web servers. It is still a Unix-centric language, although there are versions available for several other platforms, including Windows. Most servers now and for the foreseeable future are Unix-based, so PERL will be around for a long time. Even though it is inevitable that certain companies writing server packages will push their own proprietary technologies for server scripting, if they don't support PERL there will be a lot of loyal Web authors out there who will go somewhere else to find a PERL-friendly environment for their Web sites.

## Where to Find PERL

Freeware versions of PERL are available at www.perl.com.

There are two ways to install PERL: easy and complicated. The complicated way is to get a C compiler, download the source, read all the docs, and compile the whole thing yourself. There are plenty of docs online, newsgroups, and help you can get if you want to go the distance.

The easy way is to download the binaries (executables) and run the install batch. In fact, this is so easy you can do it in about 15 minutes, during which most of the time is spent unzipping files. The following URL has many freeware versions of PERL for just about any platform.

To download one of them, go to reference.perl.com and select the binaries link.

## INFORMATIVE SITES!
*www.perl.com*

*reference.perl.com*

**The central Web site for the PERL community includes information on everything about PERL, including the preceding downloads.**

## Installing PERL for Windows

To download PERL for Windows (which is really for both Windows and DOS):

1. Select the Win32 freeware version. The ActiveState version is also available and has a load of extra features for the educated PERL user, but it is not free.

2. Download PERL5.00402-bindist04-bc.zip and libwin32-0.12.zip. You can link through the companion Web site or see if there's something newer. You will also need a zip program, such as WinZip, which can be found easily through the companion Web site, or at www.winzip.com.

3. Unzip the *PERL5* file, then run the *install.bat* under DOS. Add the *PERL/bin* directory to your path per the instructions in the *readme.win32* file. Then unzip the *libwin* file and run its *install.bat*.

That's it! You're finished and ready to run PERL.

---

## GNU, FSF, AND HURD

A word of warning about digging into PERL sites.

PERL is one of those languages that is very laconic, meaning concise and precise. Just a few symbols can perform an unbelievable amount of processing, and the authors and heavy users of PERL tend to start thinking this way, and communicate with each other and the rest of the world in this way. When you go to these sites and see strange words full of insider puns and acronyms, realize that it's just the Unix and PERL environment bringing out the worst of the geek clique. If this ever happens to you, and you come to occupy a position responsible for maintaining one of these sites or otherwise disseminating this information, please try to provide at least a FAQ explaining what you mean so others can understand what you are saying!

One of the things you will see is a lot of stuff about GNU, freeware, and copylefted software. This involves you because the version of PERL available for downloading is freeware, and it's not just free software, it can't be altered and sold, sold as part of a package, or in any way profited from. The only charge allowed is the cost of distributing the software.

GNU means "GNU's Not Unix!" It is the project of the Free Software Foundation (FSF), which was founded in order to write a completely "free" operating system that would be compatible with (but superior to) existing Unix systems.

According to Brian Youmans, FSF Office Staff, "I think the pun aspect of the name was important as well. It was meant to be a *G'New* system."

The FSF says, "by 'free,' we don't necessarily mean you will pay nothing to get the software, but it does mean you have certain rights when you have this software..."

- You can copy it.
- You have the source code available to you, so you can modify it and recompile it.
- You can redistribute it with or without changes.
- You pay no licensing fees.

The GNU Hurd is the operating system being written by the Free Software Foundation and its volunteers. It is different from Linux. Linux was written by Linus Torvalds, a Swedish graduate student, and volunteers from around the world; modern "GNU/Linux" systems consist of Linus's kernel combined with parts of the GNU system and other free software. So, most GNU software not only runs on Linux, most of Linux systems *are* parts of the GNU system.

The FSF also says, "We have not yet finished the Hurd; hopefully, it will come into wider use soon, once a few more parts are complete. It is close to being ready for full release; once it is, there will be another free Unix-like alternative. We hope that GNU/Hurd systems will be even more powerful and useful than GNU/Linux systems."

# How Does CGI Work with PERL?

The problem that CGI solves is what to do with user input from an HTML FORM. The solution has been programmed into HTML by means of the FORM tag combined with the SUBMIT button.

The SUBMIT button causes two specific actions to occur:

- The data from the form is placed into *environment variables*. If you don't know what these are, and you've ever used an operating system with a command prompt, these are the variables created with the SET command. In any OS (except the exclusive GUI-only Mac) there is always a SET command for the PATH environment variable in the startup; for example, *set path=c:\dos* or *path=/usr/bin* for Unix.

- The *CGI script* named in the form tag *ACTION="scriptName"* parameter is executed. CGI scripts are written in PERL.

The contents of any and all environment variables are available within PERL to be used as textual data in PERL statements. All you have to do is write a simple reference and it's yours.

```
$ENV{îvariableNameÌ}
```

If you recall from Chapter 4, "HTML, XML, SGML," the discussion on how search engines process user input, this is what we're talking about. The form tag *METHOD* parameter specifies either *GET* or *POST* as the mechanism through which the user input is transferred to the environment variables. Each must be handled in a different way.

## NOTE

**These same functions can be programmed with newer scripting languages such as JavaScript and VBScript, and in fact that is what Active Server Pages, server-side JavaScript, and Java servlets are intended to do. Instead of going through the form tag *ACTION* parameter you could use the *SUBMIT* button to call a VBScript subroutine or a JavaScript function to do all the work. If you wanted to get fancy, you could write a Java applet to put up a fully GUI input screen and process everything through a client-server connection. If this doesn't make you feel like you're starting to get the Big Picture, go back and clear up what you missed!**

The jury is still out on exactly what the best solution is for each specific application. At this point in time, the best solution is the one the Web programmer is the most proficient at (or whatever it takes to get the job done).

# GET and POST

Both methods format the user input data in the same way. The difference between them is in how that data is retrieved by PERL. First we'll go over how the data is formatted.

Recall that HTML form input consists of several different options for user input. These are basically the *text box*, *radio button*, *checkbox*, and *select group*. User input from these options is paired up in a very specific way by combining the *INPUT* tag *NAME* parameter and the contents of the input control. The basic format consists of *name* and *value* pairs for each control in the very simple format *name=value*. Spaces in the *value* side are replaced with + characters and the pairs are all connected, or separated depending on how you look at it, by the & character. Here's an example:

```
name=Bill+Clinton&address=1600+Pennsylvania+Ave&city=Washington&state=DC
```

This string would have been generated by a simple form with four text input boxes and a Net-surfing president.

In order to show how the GET and POST methods work we need to have a CGI script to send the data to. Let's say that the FORM tag with its *method* and *action* parameters is written like this:

```
<FORM METHOD="GET" ACTION="cgi-bin/signup.pl">
```

The *.pl* extension means this is a PERL script and *cgi-bin* is the directory where these are usually located. In Unix, *bin* is short for *binary* (computer slang for executable program). Here we have a *FORM* that will format the user input, load it into environment variables, and transfer control to *cgi-bin/signup.pl*.

## The GET Method

GET is the default CGI method so if no method is specified, GET will be used. When the GET method is executed, the CGI data is formatted in two pieces, separated by a "?".

- The contents of the *ACTION=* parameter
- The formatted user input

This is then used to set the next URL for the Web browser, causing control to be transferred to the script. The formatted user input is also placed in the environment variable named QUERY_STRING from where the PERL script can read it. This is limited to 1024 characters. The whole thing looks like this:

```
cgi-bin/signup.pl?name=Bill+Clinton&address=1600 . . . etc.
```

The user input shown in the preceding code (name=…) would give this result. You can see the GET method in action for yourself at any search engine site.

## The POST Method

After all that, the POST method seems much simpler, and our FORM tag would look like this:

```
<FORM METHOD="POST" ACTION="cgi-bin/signup.pl">
```

POST directs the formatted user input into the *standard input buffer*, which is commonly called *STDIN*. For PERL to access this, it simply opens STDIN and reads the line. The user sees nothing in the location box, and in fact, if you don't do anything with HTML in the PERL script, the user will not even be able to tell that anything happened.

How does this data get transferred from the browser FORM elements to the server? The answer is, HTTP.

Here are examples of actual GET and POST results sent through HTTP to a server.

In Figure 9.1, I'm searching for "bacon and eggs" on Yahoo!, which uses the GET method to encodes the CGI data in the HTTP request.

Figure 9.2 is a POST to www.prolotherapy.com. The CGI data follows the HTTP request. Notice also that the *content-length* and other environment variables are included in the header. For all practical purposes, there is no limit to the size of the POST string.

If you look at the actual CGI string, at the end you will notice there are a lot of % signs encoded in the data. In order to keep from confusing PERL with special characters that have other meanings in the language, these are encoded as hexadecimals. This covers almost anything but A through Z and 0 to 9. Most of the remaining characters are encoded as a hexadecimal value preceded by a % sign, spaces included (especially spaces since it is now possible in several OSs to have spaces in a filename). The few exceptions are "@", "*", "-", "_", and ".".

It is not really necessary to memorize this list, only to include code to translate it so the right characters, not these strings, are processed by the PERL script. It is very easy to do this; in fact, it takes only one line of PERL code to do the whole job! We'll be going into exactly how this is done later on. Right now, we'll discuss how various user input controls feed their results back through CGI, and then we'll go on to actual PERL programming.

# CGI Input Controls

Now we'll check out the various types of input controls. Let's say we're buying a car over the Internet, like the college kid in the Saturn commercial.

**The text box** **<INPUT TYPE=text NAME=model>**

We have already discussed the text box. If the user enters *porsche boxster*, it will be returned as *model=porsche+boxster*.

```
GET /bin/search?p=bacon+and+eggs HTTP/1.1
Accept: image/gif, image /x-xbitmap, image/jpeg, image/pjpeg, */*
Referer: http://www.yahoo.com/
Accept-Language: en-us
Accept-Encoding: gzip, deflate
User-Agent: Mozilla/4.0 (compatible; MSIE 4.01 ; Windows 98)
Host: search.yahoo.com
Connection: Keep-Alive
```

**Figure 9.1** The GET method exposed.

```
POST /cgi-bin/fmail.pl HTTP/1.1
Accept: image/gif, image/x-xbitmap, image/jpeg, image/pjpeg, */*
Referer: http://www.prolotherapy.com/proloordercgi.htm
Accept-Language: en-us
Content-Type: application/x-www-form-urlencoded
Accept-Encoding: gzip, deflate
User-Agent: Mozilla/4.0 (compatible; MSIE 4.01; Windows 98)
Host: www.prolotherapy.com
Content-Length: 330
Connection: Keep-Alive
Extension: Security/Remote-Passphrase

recipient=Websales@cintronics.com&subject=Prolotherapy+book+order&than
kurl=http%3A%2F%2Fwww.prolotherapy.com%2Fprolothanks.htm&name=Dave+Cin
tron. . . (address, order, etc.) . . .
&Submit+order=Submit+order
```

**Figure 9.2**    The POST method exposed.

## NOTE
Hidden input will also be sent through and is a way to pass useful information to your PERL script, such as where an e-mail should be sent or the name of a page or file, so your script can be more generic. PASSWORD input is also sent though with the password intact; otherwise, what would be the point?

**The radio button**     &lt;INPUT TYPE=radio NAME=color
                         VALUE=silver CHECKED&gt;
                         &lt;INPUT TYPE=radio NAME=color VALUE=gold&gt;
                         &lt;INPUT TYPE=radio NAME=color VALUE=white&gt;

The radio box works the same as the text box but uses the value given in the INPUT tag, returning *color=silver*. Since one of the radio buttons is always checked, one and only one value is always returned.

**The checkbox**        &lt;INPUT TYPE=checkbox NAME=tires VALUE=pirelli&gt;
                        &lt;INPUT TYPE=checkbox NAME=radio VALUE=bose&gt;

The checkbox may or may not be checked. If nothing is checked, nothing is returned. If no VALUE is specified, *true* will be used. Otherwise, it works the same as all the others. This set could return *tires=pirelli* for one, and nothing for the other.

**The select box**      &lt;SELECT MULTIPLE NAME=extras&gt;
                        &lt;OPTION&gt;air conditioning
                        &lt;OPTION&gt;leather seats
                        &lt;OPTION VALUE=gps&gt;global positioning system
                        &lt;/SELECT&gt;

The select box will return 0 or more pairs for options selected. If there is no *VALUE* parameter, the value returned will be the text of the *OPTION*. Further, the select box

MULTIPLE attribute permits multiple selections. If more than one option is selected there will only be *one* pair returned, but the value side will have *all* the selections separated by "\0". The selections in the preceding example would return *extras=air+conditioning\0leather+seats\0gps.*

| The submit button | <INPUT TYPE=submit NAME="Buy the car!" VALUE=buyit> |
| --- | --- |

Finally, the Submit button will be included as well and will give you a *Buy+the+car%21 =buyit.*
We'll take a look at the power of PERL now.

# Writing PERL Scripts

PERL is an interpreted language. PERL scripts, like scripts in other interpretive languages, are compiled on the fly when they are run. However, it is not completely essential that you have a PERL compiler yourself to write in PERL. All the commercial Web hosts I've seen provide the service of checking your PERL script online. All you need to do is upload it and log in to your control panel page (or whatever your provider calls it) and validate the script. This is necessary either way because no matter how thoroughly you write the script on your own PC, it will have to be changed at least a little to operate in a server environment.

There are tons of PERL resources online, and tons of scripts that are offered for the taking. But even if you do use exclusively copied scripts, you'll still have to modify them to fit your particular domain name, e-mail addresses, your host's directory structure, and whatever files you are accessing on your server. So it behooves you to understand PERL more than just a little.

## An Example CGI/PERL Translation

To give a quick overview of PERL I'll run through a Web page written to accept CGI input, send it to a CGI script using the POST method, write a PERL script to accept this input, and translate it into an e-mail. The CGI order form for this example is illustrated in Figure 9.3.

### The HTML FORM

The HTML in Figure 9.4 has had the banner display code and JavaScript validation removed for simplicity.

This FORM contains three tables: one for the user identification, one for the product selection, and another for the credit card input. The main reason for having several tables is that each one has a different row format, and this makes it easier to maintain.

The CGI action is given in this FORM tag, which starts near the beginning and does not end until the very bottom of the page.

```
<FORM ACTION="cgi-bin/fmail.pl" NAME="orders" METHOD="POST">
```

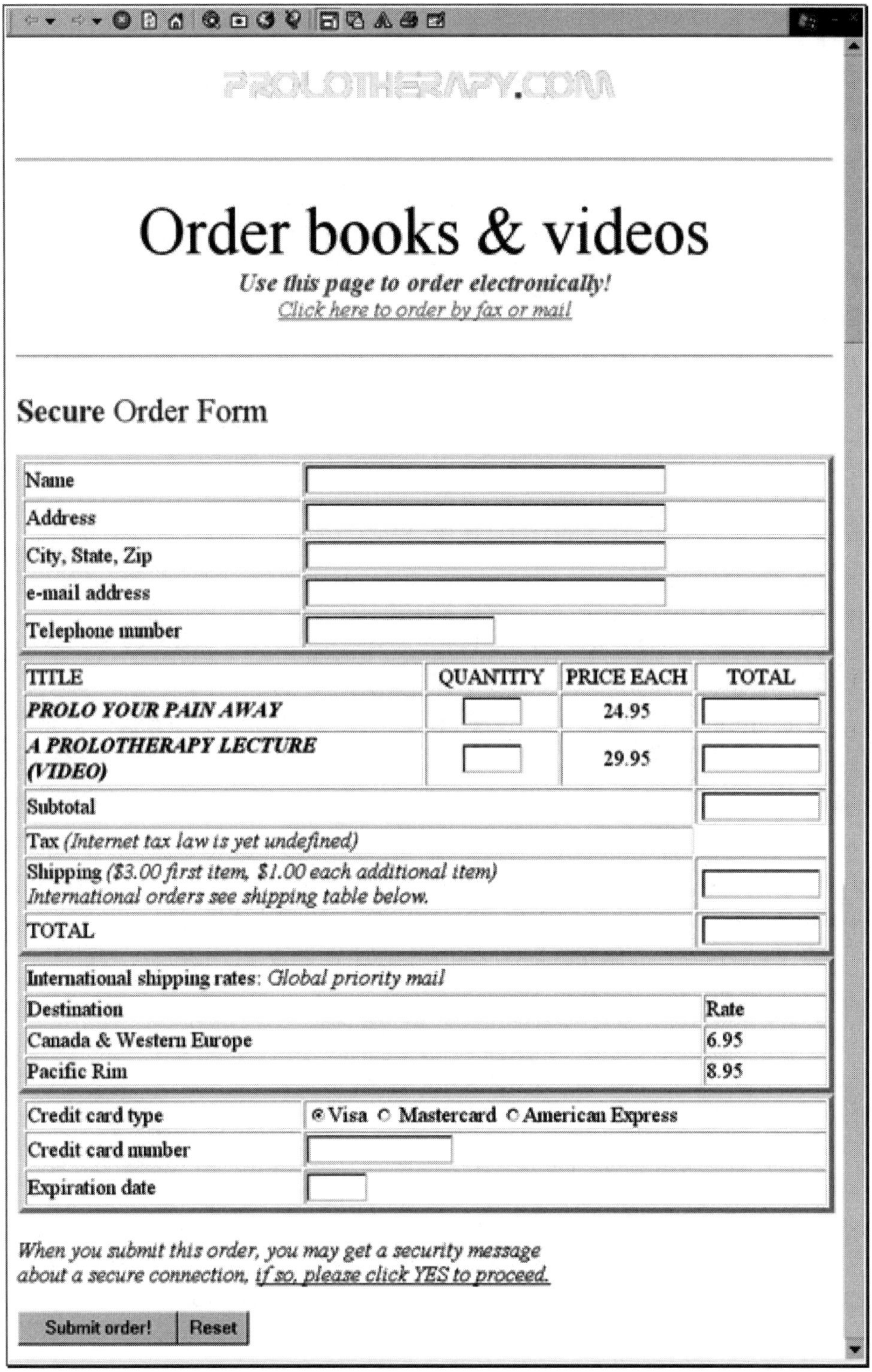

# Order books & videos

*Use this page to order electronically!*

*Click here to order by fax or mail*

## Secure Order Form

| | |
|---|---|
| Name | |
| Address | |
| City, State, Zip | |
| e-mail address | |
| Telephone number | |

| TITLE | QUANTITY | PRICE EACH | TOTAL |
|---|---|---|---|
| *PROLO YOUR PAIN AWAY* | | 24.95 | |
| *A PROLOTHERAPY LECTURE (VIDEO)* | | 29.95 | |
| Subtotal | | | |
| Tax *(Internet tax law is yet undefined)* | | | |
| Shipping *($3.00 first item, $1.00 each additional item)* International orders see shipping table below. | | | |
| TOTAL | | | |

| International shipping rates: *Global priority mail* | |
|---|---|
| Destination | Rate |
| Canada & Western Europe | 6.95 |
| Pacific Rim | 8.95 |

| | |
|---|---|
| Credit card type | ⊙ Visa ○ Mastercard ○ American Express |
| Credit card number | |
| Expiration date | |

*When you submit this order, you may get a security message about a secure connection, if so, please click YES to proceed.*

Submit order!  Reset

**Figure 9.3**  Simple but effective CGI order form.

```
<HTML>
<HEAD>
<TITLE>Prolotherapy Order Form</TITLE>
</HEAD>
<BODY>
. . . banner HTML code . . .
<FORM ACTION="cgi-bin/fmail.pl" NAME="orders" METHOD="POST">
<INPUT TYPE="hidden" NAME="recipient" VALUE="Websales@cintronics.com">
<INPUT TYPE="hidden" NAME="subject" VALUE="Prolotherapy book order">
<INPUT TYPE="hidden" NAME="thankurl"
 VALUE="http://www.prolotherapy.com/prolothanks.htm">
<TABLE WIDTH="100%" BORDER="5">
<TR>
  <TD WIDTH="220">Name </TD>
  <TD WIDTH="420"><INPUT TYPE="TEXT" NAME="name" SIZE="40"></TD>
</TR>
<TR>
  <TD WIDTH="220">Address</TD>
  <TD WIDTH="420"><INPUT TYPE="TEXT" NAME="address" SIZE="40"></TD>
</TR>
<TR>
  <TD WIDTH="220">City, State, Zip</TD>
  <TD WIDTH="420"><INPUT TYPE="TEXT" NAME="citystzip" SIZE="40"></TD>
</TR>
<TR>
  <TD WIDTH="220">e-mail address</TD>
  <TD WIDTH="420"><INPUT TYPE="text" NAME="username" SIZE="40"></TD>
</TR>
<TR>
  <TD WIDTH="220">Telephone number</TD>
  <TD WIDTH="420"><INPUT TYPE="TEXT" NAME="phonenumber"></TD>
</TR>
</TABLE>
<TABLE WIDTH="100%" BORDER="5">
<TR>
  <TD WIDTH="280" COLSPAN="2">TITLE</TD>
  <TD WIDTH="120" ALIGN="CENTER">QUANTITY</TD>
  <TD WIDTH="120" ALIGN="CENTER">PRICE EACH</TD>
  <TD WIDTH="120" ALIGN="CENTER">TOTAL</TD>
</TR>
<TR>
  <TD WIDTH="280" COLSPAN="2"><I><B>PROLO YOUR PAIN AWAY</B></I></TD>
  <TD WIDTH="120" ALIGN="CENTER">
    <INPUT TYPE="TEXT" NAME="hauserqty" SIZE="5"></TD>
  <TD WIDTH="120" ALIGN="CENTER">24.95</TD>
  <TD WIDTH="120" ALIGN="CENTER">
    <INPUT TYPE="TEXT" NAME="hausertotal" SIZE="12"></TD>
</TR>
```

**Figure 9.4**    HTML CGI.

```
<TR>
  <TD WIDTH="280" COLSPAN="2">
    <I><B>A PROLOTHERAPY LECTURE (VIDEO)</B></I></TD>
  <TD WIDTH="120" ALIGN="CENTER">
    <INPUT TYPE="TEXT" NAME="videoqty" SIZE="5"></TD>
  <TD WIDTH="120" ALIGN="CENTER">29.95</TD>
  <TD WIDTH="120" ALIGN="CENTER">
    <INPUT TYPE="TEXT" NAME="videototal" SIZE="12"></TD>
</TR>
<TR>
  <TD WIDTH="520" COLSPAN="4">Subtotal</TD>
  <TD WIDTH="120" ALIGN="CENTER">
  <INPUT TYPE="TEXT" NAME="subtotal" SIZE="12"></TD>
</TR>
<TR>
  <TD WIDTH="520" COLSPAN="4">Tax
    <I>(Internet tax law is yet undefined)</I></TD>
  <TD WIDTH="120"></TD>
</TR>
<TR>
  <TD WIDTH="520" COLSPAN="4">Shipping
    <I>($3.00 first item, $1.00 each additional item)<BR>
       International orders see shipping table below.</I></TD>
  <TD WIDTH="120" ALIGN="CENTER">
    <INPUT TYPE="TEXT" NAME="shipping" SIZE="12"></TD>
</TR>
<TR>
  <TD WIDTH="520" COLSPAN="4">TOTAL</TD>
  <TD WIDTH="120" ALIGN="CENTER">
    <INPUT TYPE="TEXT" NAME="total" SIZE="12"></TD>
</TR>
</TABLE>
<TABLE WIDTH="100%" BORDER="5">
<TR>
  <TD COLSPAN="2">International shipping rates:
  <I>Global priority mail</I></TD>
</TR>
<TR>
  <TD>Destination</TD><TD>Rate</TD>
</TR>
<TR>
  <TD>Canada &amp; Western Europe</TD><TD>6.95</TD>
</TR>
<TR>
  <TD>Pacific Rim </TD><TD>8.95</TD>
</TR>
</TABLE>
```

*Continues*

**Figure 9.4**   *(Continued)*

```
<TABLE WIDTH="100%" BORDER="5">
<TR>
  <TD WIDTH="220">Credit card type</TD>
  <TD WIDTH="420">
    <INPUT TYPE="RADIO" NAME="creditcard" VALUE="visa" CHECKED>Visa
    <INPUT TYPE="RADIO" NAME="creditcard" VALUE="mastercard">
Mastercard
    <INPUT TYPE="RADIO" NAME="creditcard" VALUE="amex">American
Express
  </TD>
</TR>
<TR>
  <TD WIDTH="220">Credit card number</TD>
  <TD WIDTH="420"><INPUT TYPE="TEXT" NAME="ccnumber" SIZE="15"></TD>
</TR>
<TR>
  <TD WIDTH="220">Expiration date</TD>
  <TD WIDTH="420"><INPUT TYPE="TEXT" NAME="ccdate" SIZE="5"></TD>
</TR>
</TABLE>
<INPUT TYPE="SUBMIT" VALUE="Submit order!" NAME="Submit order">
<INPUT TYPE="RESET" NAME="Reset1">
</FORM>
</BODY>
</HTML>
```

**Figure 9.4**   *(Continued)*

There are then three hidden input fields declared: the e-mail recipient, the subject, and the URL for the CGI script to link to after it has sent the e-mail. These could all be programmed directly into the PERL script but are sent this way in order to make the PERL code completely reusable.

If you compare this HTML to Figure 9.3, you'll see exactly how these tables format the INPUT boxes in a user-friendly fashion. Also notice that the WIDTH attributes add up to 640 for each row, ensuring that this display will format in the same predictable manner for any user.

If we pull all the CGI code out of the page, we get a list of input boxes as shown in Table 9.1.

## *Processing Input with PERL*

Let's see how PERL deals with this input. The PERL script we are going to examine is called *fmail.pl*, and converts the CGI information received into an e-mail message that is sent to the selling party to be filled. Figure 9.5 contains the entire script.

To begin with, all PERL scripts must start with a line giving the location of the server's PERL compiler. This is one thing that usually does not change.

**Table 9.1** CGI Name/Value Pairs

| NAME | TYPE | VALUE |
| --- | --- | --- |
| recipient | hidden | Websales@cintronics.com |
| subject | hidden | Prolotherapy book order |
| thankurl | hidden | http://www.prolotherapy.com/prolothanks.htm |
| name | text | |
| address | text | |
| citystzip | text | |
| username | text | |
| phonenumber | text | |
| hauserqty | text | |
| hausertotal | text | |
| videoqty | text | |
| videototal | text | |
| subtotal | text | |
| shipping | text | |
| total | text | |
| creditcard | radio | visa \| mastercard \| amex |
| ccnumber | text | |
| ccdate | text | |
| Submit order | submit | Submit order! |
| Reset1 | reset | *(not transmitted)* |

```
#!/usr/bin/PERL

$mailprog = '/bin/sendmail';
@months = (Jan,Feb,Mar,Apr,May,Jun,Jul,Aug,Sep,Oct,Nov,Dec);
@tstamp = localtime(time);
#tstamp = ($sec,$min,$hour,$mday,$mon,$year,$wday,$yday,$isdst)
$date = $tstamp[3] . "-" . $months[$tstamp[4]] . "-" . $tstamp[5];
$date .= " " . $tstamp[2] . ":" . $tstamp[1];

read(STDIN, $buffer, $ENV{'CONTENT_LENGTH'});
```
*Continues*

**Figure 9.5** PERL CGI to e-mail converter.

```perl
@pairs = split(/&/, $buffer);
foreach $pair (@pairs)
{
    ($name, $value) = split(/=/, $pair);
    $value =~ tr/+/ /;
    $value =~ s/%([a-fA-F0-9][a-fA-F0-9])/pack("c", hex($1))/ge;
    $name =~ tr/+/ /;
    $name =~ s/%([a-fA-F0-9][a-fA-F0-9])/pack("c", hex($1))/ge;
    $cgiarray{$name} = $value;
    push (@names,$name);
    push (@values,$value);
}

$target = $cgiarray{'recipient'};
if ($target eq "") {
  &safe_die("No Recipient Given!\n");
  }

if ($cgiarray{'username'} eq "") {
    $cgiarray{'username'} = "No-Email-Given\@nowhere.none";
  }

open (MAIL, "|$mailprog -t") || die("Can't open $mailprog!\n");
print MAIL "From: $cgiarray{'username'}\n";
print MAIL "Reply-To: $cgiarray('username'}\n";
print MAIL "To: $cgiarray('recipient')\n";
print MAIL "Subject: $cgiarray{'subject'}\n\n";
print MAIL "Information submitted on $date\n";
print MAIL "-----------------------------------------------------
\n\n";

for ($i=0; $i<=$#names; $i++)
{
  print MAIL "$names[$i]:   $values[$i]\n";
}
close (MAIL);

print "Location: $cgiarray{'thankurl'}\n\n";

# end of main procedure

sub safe_die {
    print "Content-type: text/plain\n\n";
    print @_,"\n";
    exit(0);
}
```

**Figure 9.5**  *(Continued)*

To run PERL scripts on your own computer, this line is not needed because you are running PERL at the command line, like so:

```
c:\PERL5\PERL signup.pl
```

### Declaring Variables

The first thing we do, as in most languages, is to declare some variables. There are no data types in PERL. Internally data is represented as numbers or strings. All numbers are double-precision floating-point; this is explained in the section on VB data types in Chapter 7, "Visual Basic and VBScript," but briefly it means you get a 32-bit number. An array or string can be any size, up to the entire available memory.

PERL is different than other languages in that it distinguishes between types of variables by using the first character of the variable name. $ means a single number or string. @ means an array. # is the comment sign and is not a variable.

In *fmail.pl*, the first line sets the value of *$mailprog* to *"/bin/sendmail"*, a simple and direct declaration, and the second line fills the array *@months* with 12 string values in a special PERL kind of declaration.

The third line calls a PERL function *localtime* and fills the array *@tstamp* with its values, which are shown in the comment line following as (second, minute, hour, day of month, year, day of week, day of year, and daylight savings time flag). The script then formats a string called *$date* as *"dd-mmm-yy hh:mm"* with the values from *@tstamp*. When referencing single array members the nonarray $ is used, so instead of *@tstamp[3]*, it is *$tstamp[3]*. This does not stop PERL from keeping array and nonarray variable names separate. You can have a *$x* variable and a *@x* array whose values will not conflict. Array indexes start at 0.

The "." operator is the concatenation sign in PERL, and as in Java comes in the combination ".=" reflexive assignment version, meaning you can say *somestring .= morestring* instead of *somestring = somestring . morestring*.

The next statement reads in the contents of the message sent by the POST method, which is waiting in the *STDIN* input buffer. Being the default input source, *STDIN* does not have to be opened. PERL can open files and even read directories, but we'll discuss that in the next chapter when we cover PERL database techniques.

The read statement reads one line from the file named in the first parameter into the variable named in the second parameter *up* to the size named in the third parameter. In this example, we are using an environment variable named *CONTENT_LENGTH* which, as you can see in Figure 9.2, is sent by the browser to the server through the HTTP header that delivers the CGI input.

The next section, like the *read* statement, is a very common bit of PERL code that you will see in many PERL scripts and books all over the world. This is the PERL code that breaks down the CGI name/value pairs. This code is where you start to feel the power of PERL. Remember, PERL is primarily a text processing, or string manipulation, language.

### Regular Expressions

The first action is to use PERL's *split* function to blow apart the string at the "&" boundaries, storing the results in the array *@pairs*. It is easy to see the elements of this statement. What may not be obvious is the "/&/" element.

This is what is called a *regular expression*. Regular expressions are an element of many Unix-related utilities and we've even seen these in JavaScript. In PERL they are a science, and there could be many pages dedicated to all the possibilities. In fact, there are entire books written on how to write a regular expression!

An expression, in computerese, is a group of symbols that gives a result. One of the primary definitions of *regular* is, conforming with rules, and this makes sense as it comes from the Latin word for *rule*. A regular expression is just a group of symbols that follows the rules of PERL. But there are a lot of rules. In this case, we have the simplest possible expression between the two slashes, an &. Regular expressions in PERL are used for *pattern matching*, where we create an expression that will match a set of characters in a character string.

There is another regular expression below, as *"%([a-fA-F0-9][a-fA-F0-9])"*. This means the % sign followed by two elements: one instance of a character in any of the ranges *a–f, A–F,* or *0–9* followed by another instance of a character in the same ranges. This matches any instance of an encoded hexadecimal character in the format *%nn*. Regular expressions can get very complex and powerful.

The statement with the *split* function takes the CGI string in *$buffer* and splits it up into several array elements using the & sign as the boundary between elements. The & sign is not included.

## Loops

The next block is a type of loop specific to PERL. The *foreach* statement steps through the array @*pairs*, assigning each value in turn to *$pair*. We could use anything for the $ variable, it doesn't matter; we could say foreach *$shoe* (@*pairs*) if we wanted.

The block itself is enclosed by a { } pair as in all modern languages. Notice that each statement must end with a semicolon, which is not optional in PERL.

The beginning of the block does another split, this time splitting each array element, which represents a name/value pair, on the = sign and performing another PERL specialty, which is to assign more than one variable at a time. The pseudo-array *($name, $value)* is assigned the results of the *split*. Actually, in PERL we don't use the term *pseudo-array*, we use the term *list*.

## Lists

The concept of list is important in PERL. In PERL there are two types of variables: *scalar* and *list*. Scalar means a single value: for example, a point on a scale. $ variables are called *scalar* variables and hold single values. A list is *ordered scalar data* and this is a basic concept of the PERL language. @ variables are called *array variables* and *hold lists*. The ($name, $value) reference shown earlier is a list. The expression (1,2,3) is a *list literal*. () is the *empty list*. When you use the *print* statement to output a group of values, these values form a list. Thinking in these terms will help you get along in PERL.

## Removing Special Characters

At this point in the script we have taken the CGI input string, split it up into pair strings stored in the @*pairs* array, and now we are processing the individual elements of that array, separating the name from the value and placing these in *$name* and *$value*. But these name and value strings are still CGI encoded, so the next thing to do is to remove the special characters.

First we use the *tr*, or *transliteration*, function to replace each + sign with a space. The =~ operator is another PERL-specific reflexive called the *substitution* operator that replaces the source variable with its modified self. This statement also uses regular expressions. The *search* function could have been used here as well, but *tr* is a bit more concise in this case, and speed and precision is what PERL is all about.

Next, we use the *search* function to take the encoded hexadecimal characters and replace them with their ASCII character values, for instance translating "http%3A%2F%2F" back to "http://". The search target regular expression was explained earlier. The replacement value uses an esoteric PERL function to *pack*, into a single character represented by "c", the hex value of *$1*. *$1* represents the match found by the first regular expression in the current statement.

Finally, the g parameter at the end means search globally, replacing all values found in the entire string. The e parameter means replace using the evaluated result of the replacement string (the character), not the literal value of what is in the replacement string *("pack("c",hex($1))")*.

## Hash Arrays

All this done, we create what is called a *hash array* of the *$name/$value* pairs. Normally, arrays are accessed by their element number starting with 0 (e.g., *$names[0]*, *$names[1]*, etc.). *Hash arrays* are given string key values and can be stored and retrieved using string keys (e.g., *$surnames{"george"}*). Internally, hash arrays also have numeric element references and are sorted however PERL is programmed to sort them. The important thing is that you can assign them and read them back using a string value.

The hash array as a whole is referenced using the % sign. You would initialize a hash array using a list of key/value pairs very much like the name/value pairs of the CGI scheme like this: *%cgiarray = (key1, value1, key2, value2, key3, value3)*. Like regular arrays, individual hash array elements are referenced using the $ sign, but unlike regular arrays, use the {} set for index reference.

The next few statements in the script store the name/value pairs in a hash array, and then use the *push* function to store them separately in two normal arrays: *@names* for the names and *@values* for the values. *Push* adds a value to the end of an array. The opposite would be *pop*, and could be written *$last = pop(@array)*, which would take the last array element and assign it to *$last*.

There is a good reason for using separate arrays to store the name/value pairs. We can randomly retrieve the *%cgiarray* hash array values using string keys based on our CGI name parameters, but PERL decides how these are stored, which we have no control over. When we want to send the values back in the same order in which they came in, that won't work. We could name each element by its string key and return them that way, but that's too wordy for PERL. Later on in the script I use a single statement loop to e-mail the name/value pairs back.

Table 9.2 shows what happens if you rely on a hash array to order the name/value pairs for you. There is no telling why PERL puts these hash array keys in this order, but to receive an e-mail back with the data in this order would be useless. Using the *sort* function doesn't get us what we need either, because it just ends up in alphabetical order. These mixed results are shown in Table 9.2.

**Table 9.2**   Hash Ordering

| ORIGINAL | HASH FLAVOR | SORTED HASH |
|----------|-------------|-------------|
| recipient | username | Submit order |
| subject | name | address |
| thankurl | shipping | ccdate |
| name | phonenumber | ccnumber |
| address | recipient | citystzip |
| citystzip | ccdate | creditcard |
| username | total | hauserqty |
| phonenumber | hauserqty | hausertotal |
| hauserqty | address | name |
| hausertotal | thankurl | phonenumber |
| videoqty | hausertotal | recipient |
| videototal | subtotal | shipping |
| subtotal | ccnumber | subject |
| shipping | Submit order | subtotal |
| total | subject | thankurl |
| creditcard | citystzip | total |
| ccnumber | videoqty | username |
| ccdate | creditcard | videoqty |
| Submit order | videototal | videototal |

## Preventing Errors in PERL

Now that the name/value pairs are safely stored in arrays that provide us with two access methods, we can go on and actually do something with them.

First there is a test to see that there is somewhere to send the e-mail. This prevents us from crashing the mail program with no recipient. If there is none, a subroutine call to *&safe_die* is issued to display an error message. In PERL, & is another type symbol meaning the variable name that follows is the name of a subroutine. The *safe_die* subroutine displays an HTML header line followed by the contents of @_, which contains an array of parameters; in this case, one or more error messages passed to the subroutine. After this recipient handling, we check to see if the sender's e-mail address was entered, and if not, replace that with a dummy address to satisfy the requirements of the *sendmail* program.

The word *die* in PERL means to end the program. PERL does not generate errors to the user. If something goes wrong and it can't execute, it will just stop, but there are few things that cause this. Normally, PERL is very forgiving. You can use variables that don't exist or misaddress array elements by going way out of bounds, and PERL will just substitute null values or ignore the statement. The primary type of error is a syntax error that will be found when you first run the script. Get rid of these, and there's very little that can crash a PERL program. The *die* statement allows you to generate an error message to the user.

And now we have arrived at the whole purpose for this script: the mail itself.

### Sending Mail with PERL

First we open a file. Remember, STDIN and STDOUT are the defaults. STDIN comes from either the keyboard for PERL to run at the command prompt, or the CGI string for server-side PERL. STDOUT goes to the display for command prompt PERL or to the user agent for server-side PERL. In this example, we are opening a file and calling it MAIL. This is called a *file handle* and although it makes more sense to do so, we don't have to call it MAIL just because it's e-mail, since what we are opening is named in the second parameter. In this case we are opening a *pipe* to *$mailprog*, declared at the start of the script as "*/bin/sendmail*". The *-t* flag tells *sendmail* to read the recipient addresses from the lines labeled "To:" and "Cc:".

The *|pipe* symbol means we want the output directed to the MAIL *file handle* to go to the input of the *sendmail* program, we don't want to create a file called *sendmail*. To open a file for input, use the < symbol, and for output, use the > symbol. We'll be using these symbols in the next chapter.

Notice that we are using variable names in the middle of strings. PERL calls this *variable interpolation*. Alternately we could end the quotes, name the variable, and start the quotes again, but this is not necessary. PERL checks the contents of a "double-quoted string" for variable references automatically. To keep PERL from doing this you can use a 'single-quoted string,' which will not be interpolated. You can see that every symbol means something to PERL!

Yes, that is an OR symbol between the *OPEN* statement and *&safe_die* subroutine call. The result of the OPEN statement is logically evaluated: If true, the second half is not executed; otherwise, it is.

The *print* statements writing to MAIL are self-explanatory. Each one must have the line terminator character represented by "\n" or the output lines will all run together. The name/value printing loop uses a Java-style control structure to run through the values stored in the matched *$names* and *$values* arrays. The variable *$#array* contains the highest element number of the array.

This all over and done with, we close the MAIL file.

The last thing is to transfer the browser location to a page that says, "Thanks for your order." If we didn't do this the user wouldn't be able to tell that anything had happened. Notice there is no file named in the print statement, so the default goes to STDOUT, which ends up back at the user agent.

# Elements

Now that you've had an overview of how PERL works, we'll go into an in-depth breakdown of the language elements of PERL. I've broken this down into four categories:

- Data types: scalars, arrays, and hash arrays
- Statements
- Regular expressions
- File operations

## Data Types

PERL only supports a few data types, but these are quite enough for PERL. PERL is different from all the other languages that are covered in this book in that there is no provision for any kind of graphical interface. Most input comes from files and data streams, and I only say *most* because it is possible to prompt for user input or accept input directed from the command-line level (although this would not be possible in a server environment).

Table 9.3 lists the basic PERL data types.

PERL variable names are case and type sensitive, meaning *$var*, *$VAR*, *@var*, *%var*, and *VAR* are all different variables. The variable name must start with a letter and may contain any combination of letters, numbers, and the underscore _ character.

**$scalar**          **$string, $number, $array[$n], $hasharray{$n}**

Scalar variables are prefixed with the $ sign and include numeric and string types. Individual array elements are represented using the $ sign as an array represents a list of scalar variables.

Numeric types are internally represented as double-precision floating-point. Numbers can be assigned as integers, fixed-point or in floating-point notation; for example, 186282 could also be written as "1.86282e5".

String types are enclosed in either 'single-quote pairs' or "double-quote pairs." Strings in single quotes are true literals and may only contain two escaped characters using the backslash as the escape, the single quote as \', and, of course, the backslash as a double \\. Otherwise, the backslash is left as is.

Double-quoted strings support a PERL string replacement function called *variable interpolation*. Any variable name found inside a double-quoted string will be replaced by the value of that variable. For example, the first two lines would result in the third line being printed:

**Table 9.3**   Data Types

| FORMAT | DATA TYPE |
| --- | --- |
| $data | Scalar |
| @data | Array |
| %data | Hash array |
| data | File handle |

```
$name = "Mark McGwire";
print "The value of name is $name";
The value of name is Mark McGwire
```

Variable interpolation can be avoided by breaking up the string into parts using the "." string concatenation operator; for example:

```
ÎThe value of $name is Ì . $name; # or,
"The value of $" . "name is $name";
```

If a variable is used that was never defined, a blank or 0 value is substituted. Using the preceding statement as an example would not result in an error but in an empty string, if *$name* were undefined:

```
The value of $name is
```

Double-quoted strings also support a full range of escaped characters, including those in Table 9.4.

The most common use of the escaped character is the newline in the print function, since print will not automatically add newlines to the end of a printed string as in some languages.

```
print "There once was a man from Nantucket\nWho kept all of his cash in
a bucket,\nBut his daughter, named Nan,\nRan away with a man,\nAnd as
for the bucket, Nantucket.\n";
```

### *@array*          **@array**

A list is a collection of scalar data put in a specific order, and an array is a variable that holds a list. Arrays are best explained in terms of lists. A list may contain both string and numeric values, and there are many ways to represent a list. The most basic, (), represents the empty list with no elements.

**Table 9.4**  Escaped Characters

| SEQUENCE | CHARACTER |
|----------|-----------|
| \\ | Backslash |
| \" | Double quote |
| \cX | Any control character; e.g., control-x |
| \e | Escape |
| \n | Newline |
| \t | Tab |
| \xFF | Any hexadecimal character |

A list literal may be composed of a mixture of numeric and string values, scalar variables, ranges (see ".." below), and even other lists. Array assignment may be done by means of list literals. In the following code, the *quote word* function is used to create arrays without typing a lot of annoying quote-mark typing, and a third array is formed from a list of two scalar literals and two other arrays.

```
@rgb = qw(red green blue)
@cmy = qw(cyan magenta yellow)
@colors = ("black, "white", @rgb, @cmy)
```

The list constructor operator ".." can be used to create an integral range of numeric values, meaning that the first number is incremented by 1 as long as it does not exceed the value of the second number. A hospital program might skip the number 13. The last line in the following code would give a range of .5, 1.5, 2.5, etc., through 9.5.

```
@floors = (1..12,14..22);
$x = .5; $y = 9.5;
@halfsies = (.5..9.5); or even (.5..10); and even ($x..$y);
```

PERL is very flexible in how lists can be used on both sides of the equal sign. These statements are all valid ways to assign values:

```
($red, $green, $blue) = qw(red green blue);
($top,$bottom) = ($bottom,$top);
```

Array elements are referenced using the [ ] bracket pair, which may contain a literal, scalar variable, or expression. PERL also flexes its muscles in the possibilities for array indexing. The first statement in the following code switches two array values by using two lists referencing the same array. The second statement accomplishes the same thing by using a technique called *slicing*. A slice of the array is represented by using the format @array[element list].

```
($name[$first],$name[$last]) = ($name[$last],$name[$first]);
@name[$first,$last] = @name[$last,$first];
@name[0,2] = qw(Mark McGwire);
```

The highest element of an array is represented by the $#array variable. PERL also supports a bizarre form of element reference in the form of negative indexes. These count back from the last element starting with –1.

```
@ants[$#ants] = "little one";
@ants[-1] = "little one";
```

Arrays can also be assigned to each other directly and by combining array slicing with array assignment.

```
@array2 = @array1;
@slicearray = (0,2,4,6,8);
@array3 = @array2[@slicearray];
```

*%hasharray*    %hasharray

The word *hash* means to chop into pieces, mix up, or muddle. So why is this called a *hash* array? Hashing is an old programming technique. Originally it meant creating a unique index by mixing up the data in a way that would avoid duplication of results from different inputs. So the original concept behind a hash index was to point to different numerical addresses by starting with a nonnumeric key. Hashing has since been improved from a guessing game to a dependable method of storing and retrieving values based on string keys.

A hash array is a list of string keys and values that are paired together. This gives the advantage of direct element reference without having to search through array values for a match. List literals may be used to assign values to a hash array in a way that is similar to a regular array, the difference being that keys and values are paired in this list. In the following code we assign a list of Christmas presents with quantities to the *%christmas* hash array.

```
$partridge = "a partridge in a pear tree"
%christmas = ($partridge,1,"turtle doves",2,"french hens",3)
```

Individual hash array elements are assigned by using the string key in place of the element number.

```
%christmas{"calling birds"} = 4;
```

Hash arrays and regular arrays can be converted back and forth. When converting a hash to a regular array, the key/value pairs get dumped from the hash one after the other. When converting a regular array to a hash, the key/value pairs are read into the hash one after the other. The first two lines in the following code should read and then restore the hash array with no changes. The third line creates a new hash from three pairs converted from the *@presents* array, and the last two lines copy hash arrays whole hog.

```
@twelvedays = %christmas;
%christmas = @twelvedays;
%favorites=@presents[6,7,15,16,17,18];
%nextyear = %christmas;
%allpresents = (%mypresents,%yourpresents);
```

Slicing hash arrays is easier than might first be considered.

```
@favorites{"golden rings","ladies dancing") = (5,9);
```

Finally, hash keys and values can be extracted separately using the *keys* and *values* functions.

```
@presents = keys(%christmas)
@days = values(%christmas)
```

The *defined()* function returns a Boolean value based on whether the scalar or array element has had a value assigned to it. This particularly allows you to check for instances of a hash array:

```
if (defined(%presents("new car")));
```

# Statements

PERL's simplicity makes a discussion of its most used statements pretty short. These are made up of statements for string and array manipulation, if statements and loop controls, and PERL subroutine calls.

To begin with, PERL supports an extended set of mathematical and string handling operators, and a standard set of comparison operators (see Table 9.5).

PERL has separate comparison operators for numeric and string variables (see Table 9.6).

## String and Array Manipulation

We have already looked at one of the two basic string manipulation functions, *split()* and *join()*. Split returns a list of strings by split from a single string at the separator expression. Conversely, join returns a single string from a list of strings joined together by the *glue* string.

**Table 9.5**   PERL Operators

| OPERATORS | DESCRIPTION |
| --- | --- |
| + - * / | Add, subtract, multiply, and divide. PERL also supports the +=, -=, *= and /= combination operators. |
| ** | Exponentiation. This is an older style exponent operator, as in $e = m * c^{**}2$. |
| % | Modulus. This is standard, as in $10\%3 = 1$. |
| ++ -- | Autoincrement and autodecrement. |
| x | String replication. A PERL specialty, works like this: *test x 5 = "testtesttesttesttest"*. |
| . | String concatenation. *"onomato" . "poeia" = "onomatopoeia"*. |
| .. | Range. Creates an integral list of numbers, as in *1..5 = 1,2,3,4,5*. If used with decimals, will add 1 to the base number while not exceeding the limiting number. |
| =~ | Match. Used with regular expressions for string search and replacement. |
| !~ | No match. Complements the match operator. |
| && and \|\| | Logical AND and logical OR. |

**Table 9.6** PERL Comparison Operators

| OPERATOR | NUMERIC | STRING |
|---|---|---|
| Equals | == | eq |
| Not equal | != | ne |
| Less than | < | lt |
| Less than or equal | <= | le |
| Greater than | > | gt |
| Greater than or equal | >= | ge |

```
@pairs = split (/:/,$cgiinput);
$string = join (";"@statements);
```

PERL contains several elementary functions for array manipulation. The easiest of these include *sort()*, which does an alphanumeric sort, and *reverse()*, which reverses the elements.

```
@array1 = sort(@array2)
@array1 = reverse(@array2)
```

There are four functions to add and remove array elements. These are *push()* and *pop()* for the end of the array, and *unshift()* and *shift()* for the start of the array. When an array element is removed it is typically assigned to a scalar variable.

```
push(@saturn5,$stage3);
$stage3 = pop(@saturn5);
unshift(@shuttle,$booster);
$booster = shift(@shuttle);
```

Hash arrays also have their own functions. Adding to a hash array is different than a regular array so it has no special function. But *delete()* is used to remove hash array elements.

```
delete $nominees("the avengers");
```

The *each()* function is provided for easy looping through hash array pairs.

```
while (($title,$star) = each(%movie)) {
  print "The star of $title is $star\n"; }
```

## If Statements

PERL supports two types of *if* statements. The expected version is *if .. else*, which comes with the additional *elsif* branch.

```
if (expression) { statements };
if (expression) { statements } else { statements };
if (expression) { statements } elsif { statements } else { statements };
```

Opposite to *if* is the PERL extension of *unless,* which will accept *else,* but there is no "*elseunless*".

```
unless (expression) { statements };
unless (expression) { statements } else { statements };
```

In usual form, PERL supports an unusual extension of these statements, which allows us to put the cart before the horse. Again, there is no place for an *else* clause here.

```
statement if (expression);
statement unless (expression);
```

## Loop Statements

PERL supports several forms of loop controls. These are *while, until, do, for,* and *foreach.* The first three give interchangeable versions that test for repetition either before or after loop execution.

```
while (expression) { statements };
until (expression) { statements };
do { statements } while (expression);
do { statements } until (expression);
```

The *for* and *foreach* statements give us scalar and array value iterations, respectively. The *for* loop is exactly the same as Java. The *foreach* is illustrated in the example.

```
For (initial value; test condition; increment) { statements };
foreach $scalar (@array) { statements };
```

There are several statements that modify the sequence of loop execution when placed inside the loop. These include *last, next,* and *redo. Last* will break out of the loop that contains it. *Next* will skip the remainder of the loop and start at the next increment. *Redo* will go back to the start of the loop without incrementing. These statements stand alone and are usually part of an *if* or *else* clause.

There is, however, one exception: nested loops. When you have a loop within another loop the *last, next,* and *redo* statements by default apply to the innermost loop of which they are a part. However, they can apply their action to an outer loop if that loop has a label. This skeleton program shows the power of these statements:

```
LOOP: while (expression) do {
        statements
        if ( condition ) { last }
  POOL: until (expression) do {
          if ( condition ) { next LOOP }
```

```
        statements
        for ($i=0; $i<$j; $i++) {
          if ( condition ) { redo POOL }
          if ( condition ) { next }
          statements;

      }
    }
  }
```

## Subroutines

Finally, PERL supports the use of subroutines. Subroutines are defined with the simple *sub subname* statement. Subroutines can be called in either of two ways: first, by simply prefixing the subroutine name with an & sign as in *&subname*. Second, the conventional *subname()* call format. Subroutines can return values so that subroutine calls can be used in assignment statements, as in *$string = subname()*.

If we were to take the Warp Drive Calculator and call PERL code to perform the calculation function, it would look something like this:

```
$traveltime = &warpdrive;

sub warpdrive {
  $warpfactor = 2 ** ($warp - 1);
  $traveltime = ($distance / $warpfactor) * 365.25;
  return $traveltime
}
```

A subroutine can even return a whole list of values, using all the techniques shown in the section on lists.

## Regular Expressions

Once again, an expression, in computerese, is a group of symbols that gives a result. Regular expressions in PERL are used for *pattern matching*, where we create an expression that will match a set of characters in a character string. These can be used in two types of statements: assignment and comparison. There are usually three components to a statement with a regular expression.

**The regular expression** is usually contained in a forward slash // symbol pair; for example, */target/*. Another symbol can be substituted for slashes by using the letter *m* followed by the preferred symbol; for example, *m!target!*.

**The source string** is the string that will be searched for the expression. If the statement is a comparison, pattern matching will return a true or false result. If the statement is an assignment the source string will have pattern matched sections found in the string, which we could call *substrings*, replaced based on the construction of the regular expression and the type of statement. There are two types of substitution statements, which we'll go over in a moment.

**The operator** binds the source string to the regular expression. Only the =~ match operator can be used in an assignment statement. Both the =~ match operator and its converse, the !~ not-match operator, can be used in comparison statements. The example in the first part of the chapter gives an example of the match operator in string replacement. The following line is an example of using the not match operator to skip lines that begin with a comment mark.

```
if ($string !~ /^#/) { .. statements ..}
```

There are a great deal of symbols that have meaning within regular expressions. Table 9.7 is a table of many string matching options using text and special symbols.

Any or all of these options can be combined in a single expression. The amount of creativity and complexity that can result leaves many programmers scratching their heads to try and figure out what kind of string the writer was trying to match! The moral: Try to keep it simple and throw in a comment line or two to show what you mean. Someday you will thank yourself, maybe even tomorrow.

PERL statements that use pattern matching include *substitution* and *transliteration*. The substitution statement directly replaces instances of pattern matching with the substitution string and is formatted as *s/regular expression/substitution string/options*. This substitution statement globally replaces all + signs with a space.

```
$value =~ s/\+/ /g;
```

The transliteration statement is a simpler version that searches for expressions on a character-by-character basis and replaces them with the respective characters in the substitution string. Each character can be represented by a regular expression. This statement is formatted as *tr/characterlist/characterlist/options*. This statement does the same replacement as in the preceding code.

```
$value =~ tr/+/ /g;
```

The substitution and transliteration statements also take options at the end to modify their function. Table 9.8 lists the more useful ones.

## File Operations

The basic PERL file function is contained in the diamond operator <>. This acts on a file to read in the next line. The default file is *STDIN*, so the operator alone, as in *$line = <>*, will actually return a line from *STDIN*.

The diamond operator returns a string up to and including the line terminator for the OS under which PERL is running. This is not healthy for Web-related string manipulation, as the string *"test"* is not equal to the string *"test\n"*. These functions are called *chop()* and *chomp()*. Chop removes the last character of a string, and *chomp* removes the last character only if it's a newline.

One of these functions was not used in the CGI example earlier in the chapter because the environment variable CONTENT_LENGTH already held the exact length of the string so there was no newline character read in. In the next chapter, we will work with handling newlines when dealing with text format and database searches.

**Table 9.7**    PERL Pattern Matching

| PATTERN | DESCRIPTION |
|---------|-------------|
| abc | Match the character string "abc". |
| . | Match any character except newline. |
| a? | Match zero or one instance of "a". |
| a+ | Match one or more repetitions of "a". |
| a* | Match zero or more repetitions of "a". |
| a{2} | Match exactly two repetitions of "a". |
| a{2,4} | Match between two and four repetitions of "a". |
| a{4,} | Match four or more repetitions of "a". |
| ^ | Match beginning of line, as in the preceding example /^#/. |
| $ | Match end of line; e.g., /money.$/. |
| [a-b] | Match any character within the range a to b. |
| [abcde] | Match any character within the brackets. |
| [^a-b] | Match any character except those in the range a–b. |
| [^abcde] | Match any character except those within the brackets. |
| a\|b | Match a or b. |
| \ | Match the next character literally (do not interpret). |
| \d | Match any digit. Same as [0–9]. |
| \D | Match any nondigit. Same as [^0–9]. |
| \s | Match any space character including newline, tab, return, and form feed. Same as [ \n\t\r\f]. |
| \S | Match any nonspace character. |
| \w | Match any word character including letters, numbers, and underscore. Same as [0–9a–zA–Z_]. |
| \W | Match any nonword character. |

**Table 9.8**    Pattern Matching Options

| OPTION | DESCRIPTION |
|--------|-------------|
| /e | Evaluate right side as an expression (as seen in the pack statement). |
| /i | Ignore case in the search string. |
| /g | Replace globally, find all matches. |

Basic PERL file operations are *open*, *<>*, *print*, and *close*.

When opening a file in PERL a *filename* is associated with a *file handle*. The file handle is the only data type in PERL that has no preceding symbol. It is suggested that all such data types, which include labels as well as file handles, are given uppercase names to avoid conflicts with future modifications to the PERL language. For example, if you name your file handle "data" and PERL comes out with a function "data", your script will become defunct.

There are three ways to open files: for input, output, and to append data to an existing file (as shown in Table 9.9).

The lines in the following code open a file for input, read the lines into an array, close the file, and trim the newlines. The default open method is input. Notice the array combined with the diamond operator reads in the entire file automatically.

```
$filename = "mydatabase.txt";
open(FILE,"$filename");
@lines = <FILE>;
close(FILE);
chomp(@lines);
```

There is always the possibility your script will run into a condition where it cannot open a file. For that purpose, PERL has the *die()* function, which operates off the fact that PERL evaluates the results of an *open* statement to a Boolean value. This way, we can use logical statement structure to create a very brief error handling. The following statements are all equivalent.

```
open (FILE,"$filename") || die "Unable to open $filename"
unless open (FILE,"$filename") { die "Unable to open $filename" }
die "Unable to open $filename" unless open (FILE,"$filename")
```

*Die* will print whatever is passed to it plus a system error message and then exit the script. To exit without a message you can either use *"exit 0"* or *die "\n"* where the newline prevents the system error message from being printed. Another way to control file input in a loop is to use the *while ($line = <FILE>)* control loop.

Finally, PERL is able to both read directories and perform tests on files and directories.

The directory *opendir()* and *closedir()* statement formats are similar to their file statement counterparts. There are also the *readdir()* and *chdir()* statements. This series of statements would open a directory, read the first file, change to the directory, and then open that file. In reality it would be more practical to read through the directory files.

**Table 9.9**    File Access Formats

| METHOD | FORMAT |
|--------|--------|
| Input | open(FILE,"<inputfile"); |
| Output | open (FILE,">outputfile"); |
| Append | open (FILE,">>biggerfile"); |

```
opendir (DATADIR,"/www/home/database");
$nextfile = readdir (DATADIR);
closedir(DATADIR);
chdir ("/www/home/database");
open (FILE,$nextfile);
```

PERL supports many more file functions but these are the most common and useful. Before trying to open a file you might want to make sure it's really a file and not a directory or something else. For this purpose, PERL supports a number of testing functions, all in the format:

```
if (-flag filename) . .
```

Table 9.10 lists some of the file test flags.

**Table 9.10**    PERL File Testing

| FLAG | FILE TEST |
| --- | --- |
| -d | If listing is a directory |
| -e | If file exists |
| -s | File exists, returns file size |
| -z | If file exists but is zero size |
| -T | Text format file |
| -B | Binary format file |

**INTERVIEW**

*Eric Tachibana, PERL guru*

I met Eric at the Web98 show where he was a speaker and the conference authority on PERL. Eric is also the author of www.extropia.com, a personal and professional site offering an archive of CGI/PERL scripts free for the taking. This is no ordinary site, these scripts are so much in demand that there are no less than 16 mirror sites around the globe.

Eric is not just a programmer but a writer, ex-rocker, and philosopher also known as Selena Sol, which is Los Angeles spelled almost backwards. The reason for this and a lot of other interesting things about Eric are available on his Web site.

In addition to his unpublished work, he has published several books in the computer field and has started his own company. Eric recently came back to the States from a year in Singapore. He is definitely an international type Internet all-around kind of guy, like me.

*Do you primarily work with PERL?*

Actually these days I primarily work with Java, but I still keep up with PERL. I would say the stuff that I do for my hobby would be PERL and the stuff that I'm being paid for is Java.

*So does this mean that Java is replacing PERL?*

Oh, definitely not. The one thing to remember about programming languages is that they're just tools, and any good carpenter would have several types of hammers, several types of screwdrivers for the many tasks that they face, so programming languages are just the same. You wouldn't want to nail everything with one hammer, you don't want to get into that situation. It's better to have an understanding of all the different technologies out there and then be able to choose which one is appropriate for the task at hand.

I think that Java certainly has a place in Web applications, particularly in front-end clients, but CGI/PERL is going to be around for quite a long time even with servlets that can be done in Java, the majority of Joe's Fish Store type Web sites are going to use CGI/PERL at least for the next five years because they won't really have the need for that much power, so CGI/PERL is really the best answer for most of the small type businesses and hobbyists on the Web.

Today what people primarily want are Web stores, and they also like simple form processing. I think those are the most today. Definitely the most downloaded and most questions relate to the Web stores and e-commerce.

*In terms of things that people do professionally, it seems that there are a ton of PERL scripts out there already. Do you think there's really much PERL authorship going on or just a lot of borrowing?*

I hope that it's a lot of borrowing and I think there's another thing, that good programmers write great programs and great programmers steal great programs. As far as I'm concerned, the less work that we can do repeating each other's work the more progress we can make, so I hope that people are borrowing like crazy.

*If someone learns PERL, what are they really going to do with it? Are they going to just borrow other people's code or write a little bit of code? Is it worth becoming a super expert in PERL?*

No, I don't think it's worth becoming a super expert in PERL. I think, of course, it depends on who the person is. If they just want to have a Web site with some dynamic functionality then it's better to become a jack of all trades and master of none than master any one thing. But if you have a job and you're at a CGI shop then it's better to become a master of some aspect of it. It depends on what your goals are and your long term career path.

For CGI, so much is available on CPAN that [www.cpan.org is the Comprehensive PERL Archive Network] it would be hard for me to think of a situation where I would have to write some kind of complex program. Most of the hard stuff is written so if I need a tree, there's a tree on CPAN so I don't have to write the tree, I just use the tree. So in a sense it's better to learn how to use modules and libraries to be able to have a good knowledge of the APIs available out there on CPAN and elsewhere.

*You lectured at Web98. How do you get into that kind of a position?*

I've been doing this Web site for quite a while now, and in the end I think a lot of people ended up benefiting from the site, so I ended up getting a little bit of gratification online. That flows from my belief in intellectual property, that you benefit more from giving information away, quality information away for free, and if you do that you will be compensated for your work through the trade, which is probably more valuable in the long run.

*How did this get started?*

The Web site? I guess it was about five years ago now, I was working at the National Institute of Health. I was on the genome project. Shortly after I first started was when Netscape broke off from Mosaic and that was when the Web really hit. I was fortunate enough to be around right when all this took off and I got transferred into this job at NIH kind of unexpectedly. At the time they were using Lotus Notes for their networking and their groupware application, and they really hated it. So my project description was implement everything in Lotus Notes on the Web. At the same time they understood it was a monumental task and they didn't necessarily think that I was going to complete this thing. It was more like let's see if it can be done.

And so I had all their groupware programs, calendars, and databases on Lotus Notes and I used CGI PERL to implicate their functionality on the Web. I started with HTML, and then I went from HTML to PERL and that was a big deal. It went really well. My bosses were very nice to me. They basically just said, here's some money to buy books, and you can have eight hours a day for the next year to just play; this is an important project and we feel that it will take some research and development.

So while I did that I had all the traditional C and C++ programmers there to ask them questions about programming in PERL because I hadn't come from a programming background. In the process I became extremely frustrated with the available information on the most simple things like, how do you install PERL on your own PC? There wasn't any good documentation as far as I was concerned for a person that didn't come from a scientific background.

As I was doing it I achieved different stages. I would finish this program or figure out how to use this library and I would then go back and document it all from the perspective of, I'm a person who has a BA in psychology or history and I need to do this on my Web site. At the same time I was realizing that there is a new breed of computer programmers who are coming out, who have not gone to school for computer programming, but have come to the Web because it is a publication media. And they needed to have technical expertise but they didn't have the jargon they needed in order to understand how to do this. Most documentation is in terms of manpages *[man is a Unix command that will display a help page]*; which as far as I'm concerned are anathema to the normal person.

So I ended up writing all this stuff, and then, as I was trying to figure out the best way to explain it to somebody else, I realized that for me the best way is to learn by example, which is to have the code in one window and have a working example in the other, and then kind of go through the example and the code simultaneously and just look to see what it was. The first one I had done was databases so I put that up on the Web and said, hey, if anyone wants to run a database here's what I did and here's why I chose the particular algorithms I did and if you have some better ideas I'd love to hear them so that I can upgrade myself. And I got both. I got people who said, wow, you saved me two weeks, or two months of work (because it had taken me two months). And I said wow, two months of work was saved. And I also got people who said, hey, you should be using a hash here instead of a two-dimensional array, or they said we appreciate what you did and we have some ways that you can be a better programmer, too.

So it helped me and it helped other people at the same time. Over the years as I continued to write these programs for the government, which of course meant that they were freeware, not only did I make a version for where I was working, but at night I would go home and I would write a generic version that could be used by another person besides NIH but with a similar problem. So that's it, one at a time, one script at a time, and I just kept adding them up. And that's what happened, kind of a grassroots movement, day by day.

*That's interesting what you say about the new kind of programmer. I'm writing this book with the intention of teaching people how to do Web programming pretty much from the ground up and one of the first chapters is, what is programming all about, because I do figure there are a lot of programmers out there who don't need a degree in computer science to program. Anybody can have a computer and anybody can go out and buy or even download software for free and start programming.*
Yeah, to me that's an important philosophical change. The Web is becoming the medium of our life, slowly becoming central to what it means to be a student, employee, lawyer, etc. As we groove into the society it's important that we don't develop a new elite class of people that are able to do things that are essential to daily activities in life that no one else can understand. If that happens then you alienate people.

*But you have to admit that in 20 years the Web is going to be a lot more complex than it is today.*
Well, it could be and it also could be easier. Windows is from a certain perspective more complicated than DOS but at the same time it's easier too. The GUI is a lot easier for the average person to get things done than the command line, and I think that Macintosh and Windows are similar in the goal of designing a GUI. I think those people that were designing that in the 60s had the same goal as I do, which is that we need to make sure that this technology is accessible to everybody and not just people that are trained in the technology. In a DOS and Unix world you need to have training in order to simply get around. With Windows and Mac you just don't need that. All you need is to not be afraid to jump onto that course.

My goal is that I eventually see the Web as becoming a sort of network operating system, and that as many people as possible with as little training as possible can do their daily ritual and perhaps more. They can run their business, communicate with friends, keep track of their calendar. They can do all of the things that you want them to take for granted so the technology doesn't get in the way of their daily affairs. So it will get more complicated but at the same time it can become more simple. It all depends on how you present it and how you explain it.

*In my research on the Internet I haven't really discovered anything else that would do CGI. How would you do CGI using a language other than PERL?*
There's a C and C++ library for that. I'm sure Java, Visual Basic, and every language has one, but it may be difficult to find. PERL is pretty much the de facto standard. As far as I'm concerned there is very little reason to write in anything else.

*The main argument I've heard is that instantiating a PERL script is a lot of work for a server compared to a servlet or something.*
I think that that's a valid point but it depends on scale. For many people's Web sites they're only getting ten hits a day or whatever, so it's not too much of a problem for the server. Of course you can get into a problem when you scale that up for a company that's really getting a lot of hits. In that case you can use Apache or Netscape, which has "mod PERL" or integrated PERL. What happens is the server will instantiate a copy of the PERL interpreter and then that interpreter is always running and will be used for all PERL/CGI

requests. So when you use mod PERL it takes no time at all. It's extreme. When you're used to regular CGI it's blindingly fast. And in a lot of cases they load the whole library with everything so that's all ready to go.

*What are you doing with Java these day?*
I'm doing my own company, and I love Java. It's very fun to program but it's just going to be a long time. It's going to be another five years before the basic infrastructure of Java is in place. I think they need at least another couple of versions of Java and they need to incorporate it into all of the Web browsers. It's still quite a barren landscape, the functionality of Java, so they need to get the foundation. They're going really fast but for the average programmer Java's still a pain. It's slow and there is no such thing as write-once run-anywhere, that's just not the case. Something like a menu or a form validation I don't think you'd have a problem, but you have a compatibility problem when you're writing serious applications.

I think Java is everywhere and that it makes sense for an Internet-based application, and people are using it but generally not for Internet, but for intranet applications. Now there's a definite trend, where you can control the scale of requests.

It's typical that I'm writing a front end to some server, and they don't want it more complicated than a Web page, and probably more complicated than CGI, so the best solution is a Java intranet client. That's pretty much everything I've done in Java is an intranet client. Clients are easy, and I think that's probably where Java is going. Servers are everywhere, and I think at this point all of the hard things have been done. And for me, it's kind of a black box thing. I don't care what language it's in, as long as I have the protocols.

*Do you think the future of a Web page is to be a huge Java application?*
I think it'll just be a mixed bag of technology, but of course some technologies will go by the wayside. I think Java will survive but I suspect that it will be limited to a client and maybe some server-side processing. The way they need to approach it is not attack and conquer but a gradient of change. I don't think necessarily that there is somebody strategizing it, it's sort of a natural evolution and the Web will decide itself what technology it wants.

*One way I look at the Internet is these technologies are in a condition where every time a new version is released a huge chunk of it is changing, even 30 percent. I think we're down below the 50 percent mark, but there's so much change that every magazine you buy has lists and lists of product releases. There are so many products being released, probably a lot of them don't sell too many copies. It seems a constant battle of people inventing new technologies and trying to make enough money to survive. Aside from all the creativity the competition is pretty brutal.*
I think that's probably the way natural selection works on the 'Net. It does go through these periods of hyperspeciation with violent natural selection, settling down into a period of standardization and then there's another punctuated equilibrium. Nowadays, probably the best way to analyze what's happening on the Web is a biological/ecological metaphor.

*What do you think the future is of CGI and PERL? Do you think PERL will be around in 50 years or that it will be taken over by servlets and Java?*
I think for sure PERL will be around as long as I can foresee because of CGI, and I think CGI will be around at least another five to ten years. But more importantly than CGI is the

idea of server side logic, that's going to be around for good. Whether or not it's in PERL, it will always be a very useful language for server-side logic.

The technology of CGI, it was the first stab, so how likely is it that they were going to get it right on the first try? It's kind of unlikely. So I think CGI will be around for a while more because it has got lock in and a lot of people can do it now on the Web and they won't want to change. But in the long run, I don't think CGI will be here forever. And I don't see servlets necessarily being forever either. I'm not happy with any of the solutions yet. They're all cold. None of them seem to have the staying power that they might, like client/server databases. That's going to be around for a long time.

I'm not a standards designer or protocol maker, I just intuitively think that neither CGI nor servlets are going to be a long-term solution. I see them both as australopithecine against whatever it is that's going to come around.

*That's definitely a possibility. What we paid for and could do with computers 15 years ago does seem Cro-Magnon and what we're doing today, that's the scary part. If this seems Cro-Magnon, then in 15 years we'll be doing some pretty heady stuff. Where do you see the Internet heading in the future? What is one of your predictions?*
I see Asia being the next to really become Internet aware. I think Europe is going to be, . . . they're a little too nationalistic, so for instance you'll have pages where they want to see the English, Spanish, and French version and that just takes too much time on the 'Net. If the EC were really happening then I could see it happening here, but I think it's going to happen in Asia as soon as the economic crisis is over. It's going to happen in Asia in Mandarin and English.

## INFORMATIVE SITE!
**www.extropia.com**
**Selena Sol = digital soul**

## Summary

PERL is pretty much a public domain language. It doesn't get the front-page articles like HTML, DHTML, and Java, but it is certainly deserves a big hand for being the workhorse of the Web.

As you have seen, PERL is a tremendously powerful language. There is plenty more to PERL than you have seen here, but what you have seen can get you a long way. To learn more about PERL you can even download an online manual at no cost from reference.perl.com.

PERL scripts are abundantly available on the Web. PERL junkies seem to be willing to give away the easy ones. Some people actually make a living writing PERL! *The PERL Journal* (www.tpj.com) is the only commercial publication on PERL. You can also find useful information at the PERL Institute's Web site (www.perl.org).

# CHAPTER 10

# Internet Database Programming

Improved data storage and retrieval techniques are what drove the data processing explosion that started in the late 1950s and is still with us today. The Internet promises to make more data instantly accessible to the average person than anyone would have dreamed of even five years ago. Who would have thought the details of a high-level tryst would be available worldwide only hours after its delivery to Congress, allowing up-to-the-minute news on the American government? Terabytes of data are being put online every year and someday, probably within our lifetime, there will be very little left outside the reach of our capability for instant access.

This comes back to you, the programmer, whose job it is and will be to make this data available in a quick and efficient manner. What tools do you have available?

The world of Internet database programming can get very complex, with terms flying by you like bullets on a Normandy beach. In this chapter we are going to look at the simplicity of providing access to an online database.

In case you haven't suspected, the reason Chapter 9, "PERL and CGI," appears after Chapter 8, "Java," was so that we can use PERL again in this chapter to build a quick and simple online database. This will involve presenting the user with a search screen that sends a CGI query, reading through the database to find the query result, and delivering up the content in HTML dynamically generated by the PERL script!

These tasks can be done better by other languages and technologies, including Java, Active Server Pages, and sophisticated off-the-shelf database products. We will start here (with PERL), something we can use with no more than what we have learned so far.

## Internet Database Access

The first thing you have to realize is that an Internet database is no different from any other database. It is stored on a computer that may be just like the one you use at home or at work. The computer Internet database is stored on what happens to also be a network server. The difference in the task is how to receive a query from and transmit the data back to a remote user.

This is where the concept of client/server began. A database is stored in one or more data files, and in order to retrieve information from a data file, a program has to be run on the same computer on which the data file is located. It is important to be able to visualize the sequence of events in order to understand exactly what needs to occur. At the lowest level, the operating system contains a disk driver program that reads and writes the file tables on the disk drive. The file table translates filenames into physical disk sector locations where files are stored. The system driver program can then translate a request for a piece of data into a physical disk location and return that chunk of data to the program that requested it. This is automatic, so we thankfully don't have to do it ourselves. This driver program, at least today, cannot be called remotely, and if it ever will be you can be sure it will be under the tightest security. Imagine the havoc one could wreak on a computer by remotely invoking such a program!

In order to read the file, we have to run a program that is tied in to that same computer's system services and is run under that same computer's security restrictions. This is the server part of client/server.

The next challenge is to have the server program communicate with the remote user. In the past, this step has been bypassed by having users log in to the computer remotely and run database access programs over the phone line as if logged into the system locally. However, this requires additional security provisions, either giving out usernames and passwords or providing for anonymous logins with maximum restrictions.

The modern solution is to provide remote access using a client/server connection through a TCP/IP network connection using HTTP, as shown in Figure 10.1. Having an Internet or intranet already set up provides a basis for communications so we don't have to worry about the how of setting up a physical connection between our database and the user. Then any Web browser gives us the client part of client/server.

So what happens next? The user is looking at an HTML document. Two computers are just sitting there idling at several hundred million cycles per second. Somehow, the services of the server program must be made available to the remote user.

The starting point for our database service is the Web page. Through the Web page we invoke the server program, which gathers information and returns it to the client in the form of another HTTP delivered Web page.

## Creating a Database

There are two basic types of data file: *sequential* and *indexed*. These terms relate to how the data is stored, which in turn gives us certain options as to how it can be accessed.

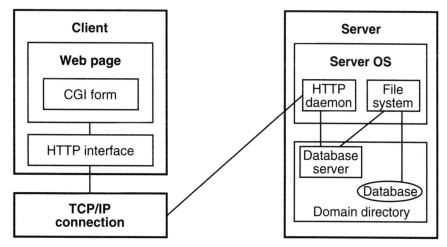

**Figure 10.1**   Two-way database radio.

## Sequential Files

Sequential data files are the easiest to handle. They are easy to maintain with the use of a plain text editor and especially easy for PERL to read through and search. The downside to this is that if the file is large it will slow down processing. You wouldn't want a 50,000 record data file being read every time somebody ran a search. At the most, several hundred records would be okay, maybe even a thousand or so, depending on how much processing each record actually had to undergo.

The simplest and most usual form of a sequential file is a text file, which can go by many names. They can be called *ASCII* files. ASCII (American Standard Code for Information Interchange) defines the binary representation of all possible characters, meaning the character set starting at hex 0 through hex 255. The term *ASCII file* is continually misused to mean a human-readable text file that does not contain unreadable characters. Since all characters, readable or not, can be represented in the ASCII set this is not only misused but redundant. Nevertheless, the term survives.

These files can also be called *flat files,* which simply means there is no index structure. I guess you could say each data record is a "flat" one-liner. And, of course, these files are called *sequential* because, since there is no index structure, they have to be read through from start to finish. You can't start in the middle or jump around.

In the examples later in this chapter we will be processing two types of sequential files: a small flat file with about a dozen fields in each record, and a series of text files stored in HTML format.

**NOTE**
**Sequential files are normally kept in some kind of order based on one of the fields, either alphabetical or numeric order, or possibly another order such as regional or categorical.**

## Indexed Files

Indexed databases come in many flavors. An easy one to set up for Internet access is, pun most likely intended, Microsoft Access, since this is supported by any Windows NT server. This kind of a database is very easy to set up. All you need to do is enter your data in a file on your local machine, save it, and upload it to your server. The first time you do this you will have to get your server administrator to make an entry in the server software recognizing your data file as an Access file, but after that all you have to do is upload a new version any time you want to change it. Of course this means your Web host has to have its server configured to support this kind of database, and that is something to be reckoned with for any type of indexed database support you want to implement, from Access to ColdFusion to whatever, and is actually the most formidable technical hurdle.

Any indexed data file is kept in a specific order based on one or more fields, and these fields combined are called the *key*. The key is used to access a specific record, or to at least set the position in the file to a specific location in the file order (such as at the start of the Ms) so that as few records as possible can be read while searching for the data.

Internally, indexed files use a multilevel *tree structure* as shown in Figure 10.2 to find data as quickly as possible. Each tree branch contains a list of keys and locations in the next lower level of the index where the first key in this range can be found. The bottom level contains a location for each individual record. In a data search, the file handler will start at the top branch and scan through each level until it finds the record being sought.

In this example let's say we're looking for a reference to Pearl Jam. The database file handler will scan the top-level index, finding P in the second top-level key reference. It will then jump to the second entry in the second-level index, finding P in the second key entry. It will then jump to the start of the third-level entry and scan through the key

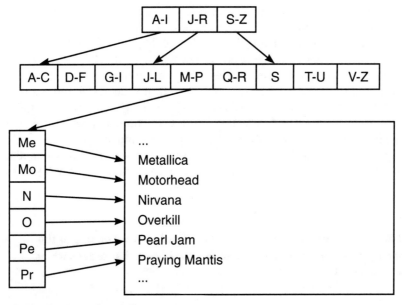

**Figure 10.2**   Indexed file tree structure.

values until it hits Pe, which in this case is the part of the key that is unique, the minimum needed to differentiate this key from all others. The bottom-level index contains a reference directly to the data.

Large indexed files can contain several levels of indices and several hundred thousand or even millions of records of data. The point is that an efficient index may allow direct access to any record in a database this size in as few as six or seven reads.

If access to the data based on different fields is needed, a database can be created using more than one key, but realize that this makes the database larger and more complex because each key needs a completely separate index. Additionally, when you access the database, you will have to specify which key to search by. In this case, the original or first key used to order the file is called the *primary key* and all other keys are called *alternate keys*. I have seen databases set up with seven or more keys. If the database handler is not very sophisticated yet allows this, the index becomes corrupted and the file is useless. The moral: If you're pushing the envelope here, always keep a very recent backup.

## NOTE

It is possible to create and maintain smaller databases in any database program and export the records to a sequential file in any of several formats, depending on the capabilities of the database program.

## Creating an Internet Database

The first thing we need to do is create a database. In this case, we're using an example from www.californiado.org that contains a list of osteopathic physicians in the state of California. Since there are less than a thousand of these, and the database can be searched on any of five different fields, the database is kept in a sequential file.

The sequential file holds 12 fields as broken out in Table 10.1, each field separated with a ":" character. I could have chosen anything here from "!" to "XXX" but the simple colon is not used in this kind of data so a ":" character serves well.

Here's one of the records:

```
Donna:D.:Alderman:Family Medicine, Prolotherapy::Shaw Health Center:5336
Fountain Avenue:Los Angeles:90029:213-467-5200::losangeles/dalderman/
dalderman.htm
```

The CGI form shown in Figure 10.3 will accept up to five different fields of data to search for, including *last name, specialty, city, zip code,* and *languages spoken*. It will then send the query string to the PERL script, which will search the respective fields for the data and return a Web page listing all doctors who match the search results. If we wanted, it would be very easy to add search fields to both the CGI form and the PERL script, but these five are all that are really necessary.

Figure 10.4 illustrates the core HTML written to produce the form shown in Figure 10.3. It uses the POST method to send the query data to a script called *cgi-bin/findadoc.pl*.

**Table 10.1**    Database Field Layout

| # | FIELD | SEARCH? |
|---|-------|---------|
| 1 | First name | |
| 2 | Middle name | |
| 3 | Last name | Yes |
| 4 | Specialty | Yes |
| 5 | Title | |
| 6 | Address1 | |
| 7 | Address2 | |
| 8 | City | Yes |
| 9 | Zip | Yes |
| 10 | Phone number | |
| 11 | Languages spoken | Yes |
| 12 | Web site address | |

**Figure 10.3**    CGI search form.

```
<FORM NAME="findadoc" METHOD="post" ACTION="cgi-bin/findadoc.pl">
Dr. last name: <INPUT TYPE="TEXT" NAME="lastname">
    Specialty: <INPUT TYPE="TEXT" NAME="specialty">
         City: <INPUT TYPE="TEXT" NAME="city">
     Zip code: <INPUT TYPE="TEXT" NAME="zipcode">
     Language: <INPUT TYPE="TEXT" NAME="language">
<INPUT TYPE="RESET" VALUE="Start over" NAME="Reset1">
<INPUT TYPE="SUBMIT" VALUE="Search!" NAME="Submit1">
```

**Figure 10.4** CGI search code.

Let's say someone accesses this page and enters "prolotherapy" under specialties. The CGI engine will send an HTTP header with the following information to the PERL script:

```
lastname=&specialty=prolotherapy&city=&zipcode=&language=&
Submit1=Search%23
```

Figure 10.5 contains the PERL script that powers this search engine. This is the entire script with several exceptional features, which we'll discuss in detail.

```
#!/usr/bin/PERL
#
# Main procedure:
# Read through database formatted with ":" separators as
#  first:middle:last:specialty:title:address1:address2:city:zip:phone:
#  languages:Website
# Then generate HTML doctor list based on CGI search criteria
#
read(STDIN, $buffer, $ENV{'CONTENT_LENGTH'});
chomp $buffer;
@pairs = split(/&/, $buffer);
foreach $pair (@pairs)
{
  ($name, $value) = split(/=/, $pair);
  $value =~ tr/+/ /;
  $value =~ s/%([a-fA-F0-9][a-fA-F0-9])/pack("C", hex($1))/eg;
  $name =~ tr/+/ /;
  $name =~ s/%([a-fA-F0-9][a-fA-F0-9])/pack("C", hex($1))/eg;
  $form{$name} = $value;
}
#change directory from cgi-bin and create HTML page banner
chdir("/www/htdocs/californiado");
&genheader;
                                                        Continues
```

**Figure 10.5** PERL database script.

```
$doccount = 0;
#read through database
open(DRS,"californiado.dat") || &safedie;
while (<DRS>) {
 chomp;
 @doc = split(/:/);
 $found = 0;
 if (defined($form{"lastname"}) && $form{"lastname"}) {
   $found = ($doc[2] =~ /$form{"lastname"}/i);
   }
 if (defined($form{"specialty"}) && $form{"specialty"}) {
   $found = ($doc[3] =~ /$form{"specialty"}/i);
   }
 if (defined($form{"city"}) && $form{"city"}) {
   $found = ($doc[7] =~ /$form{"city"}/i);
   }
 if (defined($form{"zip"}) && $form{"zip"}) {
   $found = ($doc[8] =~ /$form{"zip"}/i);
   }
 if (defined($form{"language"}) && $form{"language"}) {
   $found = ($doc[10] =~ /$form{"language"}/i);
   }
 if ($found) {
   $doccount++;
   &genhtml;
   }
 }
unless ($doccount) {
  print "<I>No doctors found matching your request, please try
again<I>";
   }
# end of doctor list
print "</UL></BODY>\n";
# end of main procedure
# subroutine to generate HTML banner page
sub genheader {
print "Content-type: text/html\n\n";
print <<'ENDPRINT';
<HTML><HEAD><TITLE>Find a DOctor</TITLE></HEAD>
<BODY BACKGROUND="http://www.californiado.org/images/dodocbg.gif">
<TABLE WIDTH="100%">
<TR>
<TD><IMG SRC="http://www.californiado.org/images/cadodrs.gif"
ALT="doctors" WIDTH="214" HEIGHT="138"></TD>
<TD>
<P><FONT SIZE="+3" COLOR="#C100B3">Find a DOctor</FONT></P>
</TD>
<TD><A HREF="http://www.californiado.org/aopsc.htm#home">
```

**Figure 10.5** *(Continued)*

```
<IMG SRC="http://www.californiado.org/images/home.gif" ALT="home"
WIDTH="115" HEIGHT="58" BORDER="0"></A>
</TD>
</TR>
<TR>
<TD></TD>
<TD><FONT SIZE="+1" COLOR="#FF0080">Search results!</FONT></TD>
<TD><FONT SIZE="+1"><A
HREF="http://www.californiado.org/findadoc.htm">
New Search</A></FONT></TD>
</TR>
</TABLE>
<UL>
ENDPRINT
}


#subroutine to generate doctor list
sub genhtml {
($first,$middle,$last,$spec,$title,$addr1,$addr2,$city,$zip,$phone,
 $lang,$site) = @doc;
    print "<LI>";
    if ($site) { print "<A HREF=\"",$site,"\">" } else { print "<B>"}
    print $first," ",$middle," ",$last;
    if ($site) { print "</A>" } else { print "</B>"}
    print "<BR>\n";
    if ($spec) { print $spec,"<BR>"}
    if ($title) { print $title,"<BR>"}
    print $addr1,"<BR>";
    if ($addr2) { print $addr2,"<BR>"}
    print $city,"  ",$zip,"<BR>";
    print "<I>",$phone,"</I><BR>";
    if ($lang) { print $lang,"<BR>"}
    print "<BR>\n";
}

#subroutine to die safely
sub safedie {
  print "<I>Sorry, could not open doctor list!<BR>($!)<BR></I>";
}
```

**Figure 10.5** *(Continued)*

## The Query

The script starts out with the standard handling for breaking down the POST method CGI query string. The contents of the query string are read using the *STDIN* file handle for a length given by the environment variable *CONTENT_LENGTH* into a variable declared on the fly called *$buffer*. We then *chomp* any newline characters off the end of *$buffer* and proceed to process the name/value pairs.

The pairs are loaded into the array *@pairs*, also declared on the fly, using the *split* function to chop up the string at each instance of the & sign. Then the *foreach* control loop iterates through the *@pairs* array, loading each element in turn into the *$pair* variable. Each instance of *$pair* is in turn split into *$name/$value* variables at the = sign. The *$name* and *$value* variables in turn have their + signs *transliterated* into a space and any instances of hex characters *substituted* with the actual ASCII character. Finally, a *hash array* is created using *$name* for the key and *$value* for the contents.

At this point we now have a hash array of name value pairs, and it's time to perform the search.

First the *chdir* statement sets our default directory to the location of the database file. This is server specific and depends on the exact structure of your Web site.

Then the *&genheader* subroutine call uses the print statement to write to *STDOUT*. This file handle is the default and does not have to be explicitly named. The *genheader* subroutine first writes a standard simple HTML header as shown next with two newlines following. This is because the end of an HTML header is recognized by all user agents as a blank line, so the two newlines are mandatory.

```
Content-type: text/html\n\n
```

Then the *print << 'endstring'* version of the print statement is used to output a long stream of HTML that will be ended by the string *ENDPRINT*. This HTML code creates a table containing all the markup up to but not including the search results.

**NOTE**
**This HTML code must include the full path to any image or link referenced, such as www.californiado.org/images/home.gif, because we are in the middle of a CGI script. If the full path to the file is not given starting with http://, it will most likely be somehow malformed by the browser when it tries to put 2 and 2 together.**

Now comes the fun part. The number of doctors found is set to 0 as *$doccount*, and the doctor data file is opened. The file handle *DRS* is assigned to the file *californiado.dat*, which is opened for input, the default open mode. The *OR* symbol causes the *&safedie* subroutine to be executed if the result of the *open* statement is false.

The *safedie* subroutine prints an explicit error message, "Sorry, could not open the doctor list!", followed by whatever error message the server reports, which is represented by the PERL string "$!" in parentheses. Figure 10.6 illustrates the result. The script does not actually die at this point, but having no file to read from terminates with the message, "No doctors found matching your request, please try again."

The next section is the heart of the search routine. This is enclosed in a *while* control loop that repeats as long as the *diamond operator* successfully retrieves the next line from DRS.

There is an element of PERL here at work that was not discussed in the previous chapter. PERL has two *default variables*, one for scalar values and one for array values. If no variable is specified for an operation, these are assumed. The scalar variable is $_, and the array variable is @_. These are at work in this loop when the *<DRS>* read loads the variable $_, and this variable is used in every statement that has no visible object for its actions, such as the following *chomp* and *split* functions.

**Figure 10.6** A CGI script's last words.

The *split* function loads the array *@doc* with the contents of the doctor database record retrieved by the most recent read. At this point, the array elements *$doc[0]* through *$doc[11]* are predictably loaded with the values of their corresponding columns in the database.

Now it's time to scan the database for a match.

## The Lookup

The variable *$found* is set to 0 before we check each of five search elements entered. This particular search is configured so that *all* search criteria must be satisfied to be included in the results.

Each search element is checked only if:

- A search criteria for that element was entered, *if (defined($form{"lastname"})*
- That search criteria is not empty, *if ($form{"lastname"})*

Each search element is checked by setting the value of $found to the result of using the =~ *match* operator to associate the array element, *$doc[n]*, with the contents of the search element, *$form"element"* with the *case insensitive flag* set. This could easily be changed to an OR-type search by prefixing each line with *if ($found = 0)*.

Finally, if *$found* is set, then *$doccount* is incremented to prevent the "No doctors . . ." message from being displayed, and the *&genhtml* subroutine is called.

## The Result

Notice that the last line of the *&genheader* print statement wrote the unordered list opening tag *<UL>*. The *&genhtml* subroutine now writes the contents of the ordered list. First it loads the contents of the *@doc* array into a list of scalar variables because now we're going to need them all to print all the doctors' information. If no doctors are found, *$doccount* will be 0 and the *unless* statement will cause the "No doctors found matching your request, please try again" message will be displayed.

For each doctor found, the doctor's *<LI>* list item contains the following HTML sequence:

1. If the doctor has a Web site, the "*<A HREF=$site>*" opening link tag is written using the site URL from the database record; otherwise, the *<B>* bold tag is written.

2. The doctor's full name is written, regardless, and if he or she has a Web site this will show up in link format.

3. If the doctor has a Web site, the *</A>* closing tag is written; otherwise, the closing bold tag *</B>*.

4. The doctor's specialty, title if not blank, address, and second address line if not blank, city, zip, phone number in italics, and languages if not blank, are written.

After the search loop has finished searching the file, the last thing the script does is write the closing tags *</UL>* and *</BODY>*.

Figure 10.7 shows the brilliant result of this superbly written search routine.

It would be very easy to write a CGI form combined with another PERL script to add, change, and delete records from this data file online, without having to do any uploading or downloading of the database. Of course it may be faster and easier to create the original database offline and upload it all at once, but once the data is online and as long as updates can be done in only a few minutes a day, it's much more efficient to skip the upload step and just enter the data directly into the Internet database.

In the next example we're going to do just that, in PERL. Why PERL again? PERL is everywhere. There should not be a single Web server that does not support PERL! Further, it's free, and you can do it yourself without needing anything from anyone else.

## Maintaining an Internet Database

As with any database update there are three tasks involved:

**Entering new data for the record** includes several possibilities. All new data is required for an addition, partly new data for a change, and specific enough key information to find the correct record for a change or delete and to make sure an addition is not a duplicate!

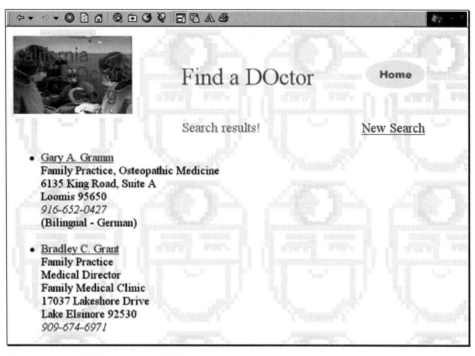

**Figure 10.7**  PERL-generated HTML.

**Making the requested update at the correct position in the file** requires reading through the file while writing a new version.

**Creating the new version of the file** requires locating the position in the file to update. This depends on how the file is sorted, and the location will have to be determined while reading through the file. When the position is found, the script will take action to make the add, change, or delete, or not do anything depending on what is found.

Figure 10.8 illustrates the update page. There is no link to this page because we don't want just anybody updating this. It's a simple page with one text box per field.

The first and last names are required because they are going to be used to sort the doctors. If we end up with two doctors with the same name we could always add the middle initial.

The user does not have to be trained and can just enter the data and select the add, change, or delete box, then press the button to execute the CGI script.

Figure 10.9 illustrates the PERL script. In case you hadn't noticed, these larger PERL scripts (PERL not being an object-oriented language, for a change) begin to take on the appearance of structured programming as was discussed in Chapter 3, "Programming, Scripting, and Applets." These scripts are much easier to read when you have a small main procedure that calls a set of subroutines in a specific order.

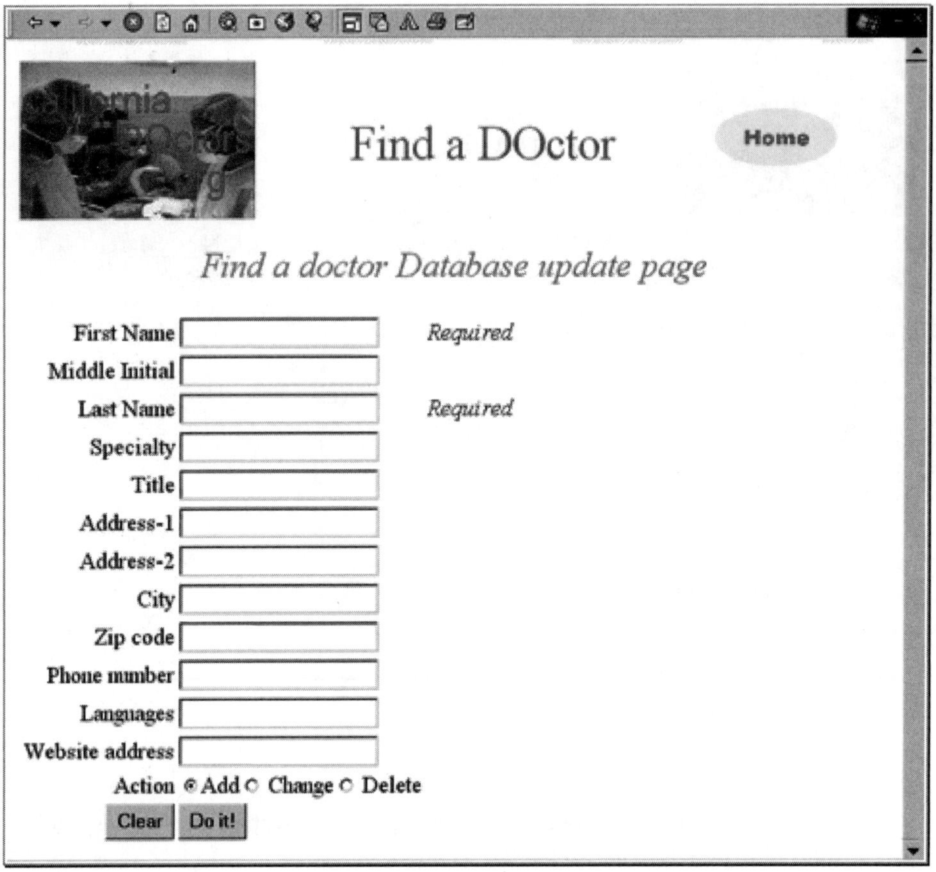

**Figure 10.8**   All-purpose CGI database tool.

```
#!/usr/bin/PERL
#
# Main procedure
# Read through database formatted with ":" separators as:
#
DRS=first,middle,last,spec,title,addr1,addr2,city,zip,phone,lang,site
# and update list with add, change or delete
#
&break_cgi;
&genheader;
$found = 0;
if ((defined($form{"lastname"}) && $lastname) &&
    (defined($form{"firstname"}) && $firstname)) {
```

**Figure 10.9**   PERL wrench behind all-purpose CGI database tool.

```
    chdir("/www/htdocs/californiado");
    &finddoc;
    if (!$found) {
      &genfounderr;
    } else {}
  } else {
  &genfielderr;
  }
# End of main procedure

# Subroutine to do CGI breakdown
sub break_cgi {
  read(STDIN, $buffer, $ENV{'CONTENT_LENGTH'});
  chomp $buffer;
  @pairs = split(/&/, $buffer);
  foreach $pair (@pairs)
  {
      ($name, $value) = split(/=/, $pair);
      $value =~ tr/+/ /;
      $value =~ s/%([a-fA-F0-9][a-fA-F0-9])/pack("C", hex($1))/eg;
      $name =~ tr/+/ /;
      $name =~ s/%([a-fA-F0-9][a-fA-F0-9])/pack("C", hex($1))/eg;
      $form{$name} = $value;
  }
  $lastname = $form{"lastname"};
  $firstname = $form{"firstname"};
  $middle = $form{"middle"};
  $title = $form{"title"};
  $specialty = $form{"specialty"};
  $address1 = $form{"address1"};
  $address2 = $form{"address2"};
  $city = $form{"city"};
  $zipcode = $form{"zipcode"};
  $phone = $form{"phone"};
  $languages = $form{"languages"};
  $Website = $form{"Website"};
  $action = $form{"action"};
}

# subroute to generate HTML header
sub genheader {
  print "Content-type: text/html\n\n";
  print <<'ENDPRINT';
  <HTML><HEAD><TITLE>Find a DOctor</TITLE></HEAD>
  <BODY BACKGROUND="http://www.californiado.org/images/dodocbg.gif">
  <TABLE WIDTH="100%">
  <TR>
```

*Continues*

**Figure 10.9**   *(Continued)*

```
      <TD>
        <IMG SRC="http://www.californiado.org/images/cadodrs.gif"
         ALT="doctors" WIDTH="214" HEIGHT="138"></TD>
      <TD>
        <P><FONT SIZE="+3" COLOR="#C100B3">Find a DOctor</FONT></P>
      </TD>
      <TD>
        <A HREF="http://www.californiado.org/aopsc.htm#home">
        <IMG SRC="http://www.californiado.org/images/home.gif"
         ALT="home" WIDTH="115" HEIGHT="58" BORDER="0"></A>
      </TD>
    </TR>
    <TR>
      <TD></TD>
      <TD>
        <FONT SIZE="+1" COLOR="#FF0080">Database update results</FONT>
      </TD>
      <TD>
        <A HREF="http://www.californiado.org/docdbmod.htm">
         Database update page</A>
      </TD>
    </TR>
    </TABLE>
    <UL>
ENDPRINT
}

# Subroutine to read through file and locate record to modify
sub finddoc {
  open (DRS,"californiado.dat") || &safedie1;
  open (NEWDRS,">newcaldo.dat") || &safedie2;
  while ($buffer = <DRS>) {
    chomp $buffer;
    if (!$found) {
      @doc = split(/:/,$buffer);
      $found = (($doc[2] eq $lastname) && ($doc[0] eq $firstname));
      if ($action eq "add") {
        &testdocadd;
        print NEWDRS "$buffer\n";
      } elsif ($action eq "change") {
        if ($found) {
          &testdocchange;
        } else {
          print NEWDRS "$buffer\n";
        }
      } elsif ($action eq "delete") {
        if ($found) {
          &testdocdel;
```

**Figure 10.9** *(Continued)*

```
          } else {
            print NEWDRS "$buffer\n";
          }
        }
      } else {
        print NEWDRS "$buffer\n";
      }
    }
    close DRS;
    close NEWDRS;
    rename ("newcaldo.dat","californiado.dat") || $safedie3;
}

# Subroutine to add doctor
sub testdocadd {
  if ($found) {
    &genduperr;
  } else {
    $found = (($doc[2] gt $lastname) ||
            (($doc[2] eq $lastname) && ($doc[0] gt $firstname)));
    if ($found) {
      $doctor = join (":",$firstname,$middle,$lastname,$title,

$specialty,$address1,$address2,$city,$zipcode,
                        $phone,$languages,$Website);
      print NEWDRS "$doctor\n";
      @doc = split(/:/,$doctor);
      &genresult;
    }
  }
}

# Subroutine to change doctor
sub testdocchange {
  if (defined($form{"firstname"}) && $firstname) {
    $doc[0] = $firstname;
  }
  if (defined($form{"middle"}) && $middle) {
    $doc[1] = $middle;
  }
  if (defined($form{"lastname"}) && $lastname) {
    $doc[2] = $lastname;
  }
  if (defined($form{"specialty"}) && $specialty) {
    $doc[3] = $specialty;
  }
  if (defined($form{"title"}) && $title) {
```

*Continues*

**Figure 10.9**  *(Continued)*

```
      $doc[4] = $title;
   }
   if (defined($form{"address1"}) && $address1) {
     $doc[5] = $address1;
   }
   if (defined($form{"address2"}) && $address2) {
     $doc[6] = $address2;
   }
   if (defined($form{"city"}) && $city) {
     $doc[7] = $city;
   }
   if (defined($form{"zipcode"}) && $zipcode) {
     $doc[8] = $zipcode;
   }
   if (defined($form{"phone"}) && $phone) {
     $doc[9] = $phone;
   }
   if (defined($form{"language"}) && $language) {
     $doc[10] = $language;
   }
   if (defined($form{"Website"}) && $Website) {
     $doc[11] = $Website;
   }
   $doctor = join(":",@doc);
   print NEWDRS "$doctor\n";
   @doc = split(/:/,$doctor);
   &genresult;
}

# Subroutine to delete doctor
sub testdocdel {
   print "DELETED!<BR>";
   &genresult;
}

# Subroutine to generate duplicate error
sub genduperr {
   print "<I>Add failed. Doctor already on file!<I>";
   print "</UL></BODY>\n";
}

# Subroutine to generate field error
sub genfielderr {
   print "<I>Can't update. Insufficient data!<I>";
   print "</UL></BODY>\n";
}

# Subroutine to generate found error
```

**Figure 10.9** *(Continued)*

```
sub genfounderr {
  print "<I>Could not perform database $action on $firstname $lastname
        </I><BR>";
  print "<I>No doctor found matching your request, please try
again<I>";
  print "</UL></BODY>\n";
}


# Subroutine to generate doctor list
sub genresult {
  ($first,$middle,$last,$spec,$title,$addr1,$addr2,$city,$zip,$phone,
   $lang,$site) = @doc;
  $basedir="http://www.californiado.org/";
  print "<LI>";
  if ($site) { print "<A HREF=",$basedir,$site,">" } else { print
"<B>"}
  print $first," ",$middle," ",$last;
  if ($site) { print "</A>" } else { print "</B>"}
  print "<BR>\n";
  if ($spec) { print $spec,"<BR>"}
  if ($title) { print $title,"<BR>"}
  print $addr1,"<BR>";
  if ($addr2) { print $addr2,"<BR>"}
  print $city,"   ",$zip,"<BR>";
  print "<I>",$phone,"</I><BR>";
  if ($lang) { print $lang,"<BR>"}
  print "<BR>\n";
}


# Subroutines to die safely
sub safedie1 {
  print "<I>Sorry, could not open doctor list for input!
        <BR>($!)<BR></I>";
}
sub safedie2 {
  print "<I>Sorry, could not open doctor list for output!
        <BR>($!)<BR></I>";
}
sub safedie3 {
  print "<I>Sorry, could not rename doctor list!<BR>($!)<BR></I>";
}
```

**Figure 10.9** *(Continued)*

Since we've already discussed CGI interpretation and basic HTML generation, we can skip the first two subroutines in the script that break down the CGI and generate the top of the document. Since the fields that are going to be updated are the same fields that were displayed in the original search, you would already be familiar with those.

## Entering Data

The code that drives this script is in the *&finddoc* subroutine. As long as the user has entered a first and last name, this is executed by the main procedure. Otherwise, the *&fielderr* subroutine displays an error message for the user's error, not the computer's. The main procedure will also generate an error message if *$found* still comes up 0 after *&finddoc* has run its course.

The first thing *&finddoc* does is to open the existing data file for input and a new data file with a different name for output. If the open for output used the same name, it would create a new file of 0 size and clobber the existing file. If either open statement fails, an informative error message will be displayed.

To follow the logic in the rest of the subroutine, sometimes it's easier to work from the outside in. Omitting the inner loop, the loop that reads the existing file in while writing the new file out is very brief. If the record to be updated has not yet been found, look for it; otherwise, just write the rest of the file out. This saves the server a lot of processing time and the user some waiting time.

```
while ($buffer = <DRS>) {
    chomp $buffer;
    if (!$found) {
      find a doctor
    } else {
      print NEWDRS "$buffer\n";
    }
  }
```

## Requesting Update

Finding the matching record is much the same as the original search-only script. The record is split into an array of fields so comparisons can be made, but that's as far as it goes.

To find the matching record there are different criteria for an add versus a change or delete. We only want to change or delete if we find a matching record; otherwise, we pass the current record to the new file unchanged. But add is different. We pass the current record to the new file unchanged regardless of whether we add or not, and we only add if we don't find a match. It will help to draw this out (they used to call it *flow-charting*) if you're unfamiliar with file maintenance programming.

### Subroutines

The simplest subroutine is the *&testdocdel*. In fact, there isn't any test at all. It simply omits writing the record to the new file, and displays a *DELETED!* message.

The *&testdocchange* routine is only slightly more complicated. It tests each CGI field for definition and content, and any field that is not blank replaces its corresponding field in the found record. The change routine creates a new record using the *join* function to reassemble the *@doc* array into a single string separated by the : symbol. Finally, *&testdocchange* prints the record to the new file, and splits it apart again. This last step is technically unnecessary but was included as a crutch to assure me that the data was correctly reassembled when the *&genresult* subroutine displays back the results of the database update.

Isn't this easy? *Split* and *join* are such a joy to use, they take any number of arguments and with one incredibly short line do what would otherwise take another language a half a page of code. They're so easy to use, they're going to make the last subroutine in this example, *&testdocadd*, really short.

The hardest thing about the add routine is finding where to add the record. How are we going to locate the one exact place to add a new person? Since our file is in alphabetical order, we read through it until the next last name in the file is less than the last name we want to add. We also need to check the first name, but we can't do this at the same time. What if the last name is smaller and the first name is bigger? We'll miss the location entirely. This might seem like a obvious point to bring up, but this error is made all the time by new programmers and programmers who are often in too much of a hurry (like me). So we only check the first name if the last name is the same.

This point is important not only for this routine, but has many implications for database indexing in general. Computers (actually computer languages) have written into them what is called a *sort order* or *collating sequence*. This is how one string value can be compared against another and a less than or greater than decision can be made.

This order is not, as one might assume, always identical to the binary value of the ASCII characters. This order is artificial and can be made into anything. If you look up the binary character sequence of the alphabet in ASCII, you will first find all the uppercase letters A–Z and then later on the lowercase letters a–z, giving a collation sequence of:

```
ABCDEFGHIJKLMNOPQRSTUVWXYZabcdefghijklmnopqrstuvwxyz
```

However, the writer of a programming language can specify any sort order; for example, it could be:

```
AaBbCcDdEeFfGgHhIiJjKkLlMmNnOoPpQqRrSsTtUuVvWwXxYyZz
```

You could even allow the programmer to declare a variable that replaces the default sequence. This is because when you get right down to string comparison at the assembly language level, where all languages eventually end up, it is done one character at a time. When you're working down at that level, it takes just about as much effort to compare a character to one thing as another.

Getting back to our add routine, we want to read through the file and find a record where the last name is smaller than the last name in the record to be added, or the last name is the same and the first name is smaller than the first name in the record to be added.

## Creating a New Version

Once this is found the rest is easy. The *join* function is again used to string the CGI variables together and the new record is written to the file. Finally, the old fail-safe is used again to reparse the assembled record before the result is displayed. The much labored over original record that was read from the existing file is passed to the new file when *&testdocadd* returns to *&finddoc*.

The update result looks very much like the original search page (since I'm using the same code to display it, there's no figure here).

# Text-Based Internet Databases

We'll now see an example of a search routine that can be used to search through a text-based database and return results to the user.

Text-based databases are completely different from record-based files. Of course you are familiar with these from the Internet, because the whole Internet is one huge text-based database! This example is going to be handled in PERL and is much different from the way it is handled by search engines. Search engines cannot do a real-time search through millions of pages to retrieve an up-to-the-second result. These use highly sophisticated relational databases to store word content against URL entries. These types of databases store not only the data, but define relations between the data and store the data with these links intact. This way they are able to associate results from hundreds of thousands of cataloged entries in a fraction of a second. A lot of this speed has to do with radically tuned hardware and huge memory caches that can rip through millions of cached records faster than you can say, "What?"

The PERL script will, however, search through several dozen HTML pages, returning a user-friendly list of what was found in just a few seconds. It's powered by the simplest of CGI pages, asking for only one text box and one radio button, as shown in Figure 10.10.

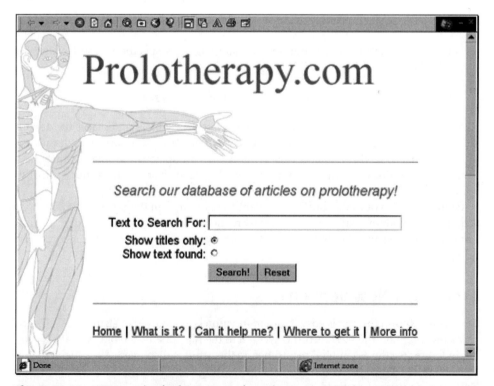

**Figure 10.10** CGI term intake for text search engine.

The radio button demands a tremendous addition of functionality to the search script. It's easy enough to search through a file for terms and return the text between the <TITLE></TITLE> tag pair; however, that's not a very informative response. When we want to show the exact portion of text that was found, then a decision has to be made as to what to show. How many words before or after? What if the search found the first or last word in the sentence?

I decided to aim for the entire sentence that the word or words are in. This means the script has to search backwards for the beginning, which will be either a previous period or HTML > bracket, and forwards for the end of the sentence, which will be either a period again or an HTML < bracket. I also decided to underline the search terms found.

Before going over the script, Figure 10.11 will give you an idea of how the result looks.

The article titles head up each list of sentences contained within and will link to the beginning of the respective HTML document. The sentences will not link, and I suppose you could put an HTML anchor at the start of each one and get some action there, but you have to agree this would really be overkill. Finally, each sentence starts on a new line. The script is shown in Figure 10.12.

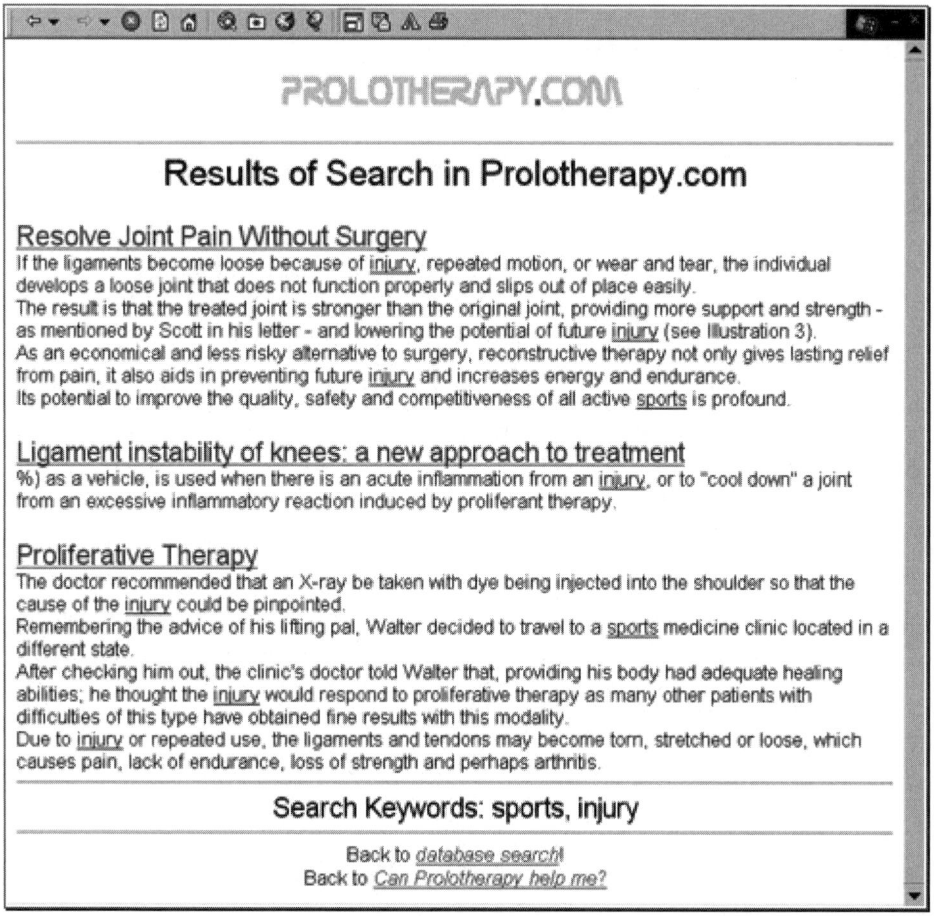

**Figure 10.11**   PERL text search engine output.

```perl
#!/usr/bin/PERL

# Define variables/constants
$basedir = '/www/htdocs/prolotherapy/articles/';
$baseurl = 'http://www.prolotherapy.com/';
$title = "Can Prolotherapy help me?";
$title_url = 'http://www.prolotherapy.com/prolohelp.htm';
$search_url = 'http://www.prolotherapy.com/prolohelp.htm#search';
@matches = ();
@types = ();

# Main Procedure

&parse_form;
&get_files;
foreach $file (@files) {
  &start_search;
  if ($found) {
    push (@matches,$file);
    push (@types,"FILE");
    push (@matches,$doctitle);
    push (@types,"TITLE");
    if ($show eq "text") {
      &search;
    }
  }
}
&gen_html;

# End of main procedure

# Subroutine to parse CGI data
sub parse_form {
    read(STDIN, $buffer, $ENV{'CONTENT_LENGTH'});
    @pairs = split(/&/, $buffer);
    foreach $pair (@pairs) {
        ($name, $value) = split(/=/, $pair);
        $value =~ tr/+/ /;
        $value =~ s/%([a-fA-F0-9][a-fA-F0-9])/pack("C", hex($1))/eg;
        $cgiarray{$name} = $value;
    }
    $show = $cgiarray{"show"};
    @terms = split(/\s+/, $cgiarray{'terms'});
}

# Subroutine to get list of .htm files and load array
sub get_files {
    chdir($basedir);
```

**Figure 10.12**  PERL text search and display engine.

```
      opendir (FILEDIR,$basedir);
      while ($file = readdir(FILEDIR)) {
        if ($file =~ /.*\.htm/) {
          push (@files,$file);
        }
      }
  }

  # Subroutine to read and scan document for terms and title
  sub start_search {
      open(FILE,"$file");
      @lines = <FILE>;
      close(FILE);
      $string = join(' ',@lines);
      $string =~ s/\n//g;
      $string =~ s/\s+/ /g;
      $found = 1;
      foreach $term (@terms) {
        if ($string !~ /$term/i) {
          $found = 0;
        }
      }
      if (($found) && ($string =~ /<title>(.*)<\/title>/i)) {
        $doctitle = "$1";
      }
  }

  # Subroutine to do text substring search
  sub search {
      $found = 1;
      $last = 0;
      while (($found > 0) && (@matches < 200)) {
        $found = 999999;
        foreach $term (@terms) {
          $test = index($string,$term,$last);
          if ($test > 0 && $test < $found && $test > $last) {
            $found = $test;
          }
        }
        if ($found == 999999) {
          $found = -1;
        }
        if ($found > $last) {
          $period = rindex($string,".",$found);
          $bracket = rindex($string,">",$found);
          $first = $period;
          if ($bracket > $first) {
```

*Continues*

**Figure 10.12**    *(Continued)*

```
            $first = $bracket;
        }
        $char = substr($string,$first,1);
        if ($char eq ">") {$first+=1}
        if ($char eq ".") {$first+=2}
        $period = index($string,".",$found);
        $bracket = index($string,"<",$found);
        $last = $period;
        if ($bracket < $last && $bracket > 0) {
          $last = $bracket;
        }
        if (substr($string,$last,1) eq ("<")) {
          $last--;
        }
        $sentence = substr($string,$first,($last-$first+1));
        if ($sentence ne $matches[$#matches]) {
          push (@matches,$sentence);
          push (@types,"DATA");
        }
      }
    }
  }
}

# Subroutine to return search results
sub gen_html {
   print "Content-type: text/html\n\n";
   print "<html><head><title>Results of Search</title></head>\n";
   print "<body><center><img src=\"/proloanim.gif\"
         alt=\"prolotherapy.com\"";
   print "width=320 height=67 border=0><hr>\n";
   print "<font size=+2 face=arial,helvetica,sans-serif>\n";
   print "Results of Search in
Prolotherapy.com</font></center><br>\n";
   if (@matches) {
     for ($i=0; $i < @matches; $i++) {
       if ($types[$i] eq "FILE") {
         print "<p><font face=Arial,Helvetica size=+1>";
         print "<a href=$baseurl$matches[$i++]>$matches[$i]</A>";
         print "<font face=Arial,Helvetica size=-1>";
       } elsif ($types[$i] eq "DATA") {
         $line = $matches[$i];
         foreach $term (@terms) {
           $line =~ s/$term/<U>$term<\/U>/g
           }
         print "<br>$line\n";
       }
     }
   } else {
```

**Figure 10.12**   *(Continued)*

```
      print "<font face=Arial,Helvetica size=-1><p><center>";
      print "Your search terms were not found or too general.<br>";
      print "Please try again!</p></font>";
  }
  if (@matches >= 200) {
      print "<font face=Arial,Helvetica size=+1><p><center>";
      print "<p><i>Too many matches! Please try again.</i></font>";
  }
  print "<center><hr><font size=+1 face=arial,helvetica>\n";
  print "Search Keywords: ";
  $i = 0;
  foreach $term (@terms) {
      print "$term";
      $i++;
      if (!($i == @terms)) {
         print ", ";
      }
  }
  print "<hr></font><font size=-1 face=arial,helvetica>Back to ";
  print "<a
href=http://www.prolotherapy.com/prolohelp.htm#search>\n";
  print "<i>database search</i></a>!<br>";
  print "Back to <a
href=http://www.prolotherapy.com/prolohelp.htm>\n";
  print "<i>Can Prolotherapy help me?</i></a>\n";
  print "</font></center></body></html>\n";
}
```

**Figure 10.12**   *(Continued)*

The part of this script that deals with sentence search and what could be called *framing* actually ends up being pretty complicated. The hard part is to only save each sentence that contains a search term once even though it may contain multiple search terms. I'll go through this when we get to it.

At the start of the script, several constants are set. These include the directory to be searched, which will be done using PERL directory access statements, and a few strings for HTML display.

Two arrays are declared as empty (another fail-safe). The *@matches* array will be filled with target file titles, filenames, and sentences found, and will have corresponding entries in the *@types* array to tell what kind of string is in each *@matches* element. Why not use a two-dimensional array, or a hash, or something else? This method is much easier to code, much easier to read, and I don't have to deal with complicated indexing.

The main procedure has only four steps:

1. *&parse_form* breaks down the CGI input.

2. *&get_files* creates a list of files to process (this step allows us to add content to be searched without changing the script).

3. A loop to process each file is created.

4. *&gen_html* feeds the HTML result back to the user.

## Title-Only Search

After *&parse_form* processes the search query, the *&get_files* subroutine uses the PERL *opendir* and *readdir* statements to create a list of files with the *.htm* string anywhere in the filename. This will get us all HTML files in the directory. Each one found is added to the *@files* array. There is nothing mysterious or difficult about reading through a directory in PERL, and these PERL statements work in any OS. *Readdir* returns the next file in the directory, whether it's text, graphic, another directory, or something else. It gives you the filename plain and simple, and it's your job to figure out what to do with it.

The *&start_search* subroutine and the code that calls it actually handles everything that is needed for a title-only search. Each file in the *@files* array is handled in turn, being read into the *@lines* array all at once before processing. The lines are then converted into one huge string using the *join* function, and two substitutions remove any line breaks (\n) and convert multiple spaces (\s+) to single spaces. At this point we have a one-line document, well formatted with markup.

Next, the *foreach* statement searches for all terms, and if any are not found, then *$found* is set to false. If found is true, the title is pulled out of the title bracket pair using the *$n* regular expression matching string. This was mentioned only in passing in Chapter 9. Specifying a regular expression, including any part of it in a pair of parentheses, will load the variables *$1, $2, $3* … and so forth, with each matched string in turn. Here the matched title string is returned in *$1*, which is then assigned to *$doctitle*. Upon returning to the main procedure, if *$found* is set then the document title is saved in the *@matches/@types* array pair.

## Text Search

A text search would follow this well thought-out algorithm:

1. Set a starting point in the document for the next scan.

2. Scan the document from the starting point to the end for the first occurrence of any search term.

3. When a term is found, scan backward from the found point to find the start of the sentence, then scan forward from the found point for the end of the sentence.

4. Save the found sentence.

5. Set the starting point for the next scan to after the sentence.

The value of each variable in this subroutine is vitally important to its success. Initial conditions are sometimes odd. In this case, the main loop is going to scan until *$found* is false, which causes us a problem for the first iteration. So in order to start off, $found is set to $true even though nothing has been searched yet. Since we know we're going to find at least one term, this is the simplest way to get around this initial condition problem. Then there is the *$last* variable, which is the starting point for the scan.

The reason it's called *$last* and not *$first* is that it represents the last position scanned through. If we were going to write a wordy program in COBOL we would find a better way to say this. However, PERL is short, fast, and mathematical in its methods. Hence, *$last* is initialized at 0.

The *while* loop scans as long as something is found and there are not too many matches. If we exceed some kind of memory limit the server will not return anything but an "Internal Server Error" to the user. So we have to keep from sending too many results back. The limit of 200 lines is really more than enough.

The *$found* variable is now confusingly set to a huge number. This is another initial condition problem and is done because we want to find the lowest index for the occurrence of the next search term. The first term found must successfully reduce the index to its location in the document, and setting the initial index to a number higher than any possible location will ensure success. If nothing is found the index won't change, so we'll artificially reduce it below 0.

I suppose it would be nice if a programming language had, in addition to 0 as an anchor for numeric tests, the number infinity. We could instead say *$found* = ∞, then *if* *$found* == ∞, etc., but we can't because there's no way to represent infinity in a computer, so we use an arbitrarily large number.

The *foreach* loop now searches for the next occurrence of a search term. The *index* function returns a number representing the location in *$string* of the first occurrence of *$term* starting at the location *$last*. This treats *$string* like an array of single characters string with 0. If nothing is found, then *$found* is set to less than 0 and the rest of the subroutine will be skipped. A few of the phrases in these statements are, again, fail-safe checks. The remainder of the loop only executes if *$found* > *$last*, but that has to be the case anyway if *$found* > 0. Perhaps I should embark on a formal study of algorithms, but experience tells me that writing code this way both makes my intentions clear and does its best to avoid bugs like the plague.

The *rindex* function is the same as *index* except searches in reverse gear. The *substr* function pulls one string out of another; in this case, *$char* is pulled out of *$string* starting at *$first* for a length of 1, giving us a single character. The sentence framing algorithm tries to format a nice-looking string by going from the exact beginning to the exact end based on earlier formatting that removed all multiple spaces. The following code shows the various possibilities where pointers, represented by ^ symbols, could end up based on search results for periods and HTML brackets. In this case, a picture is worth a thousand words because I'll leave it up to you to check the logic. This dummy content is called *greeked text*.

```
volutpat.  Lorem ipsum dolor sit amet. Ut wisi enim ad minim veniam.
         ^                 ^               ^

delit. <P>Lorem ipsum dolor sit amet<I>consectetuer adipiscing elit.</I>
     ^   ^              ^            ^                                ^
```

Another substitution could have been performed to remove all the HTML tags and avoid some of this complexity, but in some cases this could have added more complexity in other ways; for example, captions to illustrations that don't have periods. This script is not meant to be perfect but a close guess that works pretty well under the prevailing conditions. You can always get more sophisticated, but if you've studied the law of diminishing returns, or even if you haven't, it becomes obvious that at some point it's just not worth it.

Finally, the sentence is pulled out of the text and (another fail-safe) if the sentence does not match the last one saved it is added to the *@matches/@types* array.

You may find it interesting how the array pair is used to display the results (HTML generation). First, the *$baseurl* is not concatenated but simply strung together with the *@matches* file entry to create a usable filename in the returned HTML document. The *@matches* index is then autoincremented to display the document title in the same breath without having to use any intervening statements. Before printing the final result, each line is once again scanned for search terms and those found are substituted for themselves with surrounding underline tag pairs added.

With the tools shown here, your own study, and scripts available online, there is very little, perhaps nothing, you could not accomplish! Remember, there are only three things you need to provide online database access:

- A database that can be created in any computer as long as it's uploadable to the server.
- A script or program to reside on the server that can access the data.
- A CGI form or applet to send queries to the script or program on the server.

## INTERVIEW

*Jeremy Allaire, Allaire Corporation*

*How did you get into the ColdFusion business?*
It's a long story, of course! In all seriousness, Allaire got started early in 1995 with the mission to create tools that would enable developers to use the Web as an application platform. J.J. [my brother] and I, and some other close friends, had been doing a lot of experimental and commercial work with the Web throughout 1993 and 1994, and learned a lot about what was difficult (like interactive programming, CGI, etc.) and what its potential was. I saw the Web as potentially the foundation of a new computing platform, that treated the browser as a runtime for server-based applications. Global, distributed client/server, if you will.

J.J. built ColdFusion and launched the company and product because a lot of people wanted to use the Web this way, and he had great ideas about how to craft a product that could make it incredibly simple to program the Web, to enable live, dynamic, and interactive sites.

So, in many ways, the work with ColdFusion, the vision behind the products, and so on, were the natural evolution of work and thinking that we had been doing for years. The fact that a nascent market existed, and that the Web enabled us to sell, market, and service his product at almost no cost, had a huge impact on making this a true "business."

*That wasn't too long ago. Has growth really been that fast? What kind of experience has this been?*
The company has continued to grow at a very steady pace. Certainly nothing on the scale of Netscape, which went from a few hundred people to over two thousand in about a year, but definitely fast. But a slightly more paced growth has been good for the company.

For one, we never feel like we're out of control, and second, we didn't have to have an ultra-aggressive growth and investment strategy, which has the potential to defocus the company from building core infrastructure.

*I know there are a lot of people out there who need databases, but a lot of these are done in-house. How big is the database market really?*
Allaire is not in the database market. In fact, pretty much, we see that the database market has saturated with Microsoft Access, SQL Server, and Oracle, with a bunch of freeware and other commercial DBs comprising a small percentage of the rest of the market. Allaire sells a Web application server and visual tools for building Web sites and applications. This market is an enormous and growing market, what analysts think will be over $2 billion by 2002. We've got great market-share, over 20,000 corporations use our application server, and well over 60,000 developers are building with ColdFusion. In an early market, as a pre-public company, we think we've done pretty well.

*Sorry, didn't mean to pigeonhole Allaire Corp., but the Internet server market seems to me to be the most confusing, or maybe just the hardest to understand. It almost seems like server technology is where airplane technology was exactly 100 years ago. There are all kinds of ideas that are trying to take flight but who will stay in the air is anyone's guess. And visual application development is a real challenge in that kind of environment, like shooting ducks off the deck of a boat in a storm. Can you simplify any of this for us? Where do you think this market is headed? What will an Internet server be doing in five years?*
Well, as we look at the landscape we see this phenomenal growth in the number of servers and companies connecting themselves to the Web. Right now, the vast majority of that work is bringing static Web sites online, a smaller percentage are people actually building dynamic page applications with things like ColdFusion, CGI, ASP, etc. We expect over the next couple of years for that to turn in favor of the majority being true Web applications.

But this still doesn't fundamentally change the Web we have today. The Web of today is and was designed for end users, not for Web applications. What I mean by this is that when a company sets up a site—whether it's an application or just static content—they are essentially designing that with only the end user of the site in mind. The real opportunity, in my opinion, is starting to view the Web and its resources as a distributed network, where each node on the network provides value as data and services to every other node on the network. All of a sudden the value equations start exploding, and you have economic revolution, and so on. That's the exciting stuff, no doubt.

So, technically, this comes down to application servers that are focused on distributed data. Things like agents, event services, XML, etc., become significantly more important. That's the easy part, in many respects, and I expect the Web to simply evolve there just as it has evolved to where it is today. The tough problems are the business problems, the organizational challenges, and the ways in which this new infrastructure will radically redefine how society functions.

*Agents, event services, and XML? I know XML, but what are you thinking of when you say agents and event services?*
Agents simply refers to Web applications running on a Web server that automatically access and manipulate information on other servers on the network. For example, you

might have an agent that scanned data on several of your suppliers' networks, found a configuration you need, and ordered a product. The idea is that this happens automatically, over the HTTP network, without human intervention.

Event services are merely an extension of this model, but where the 'agents' respond to other events. For instance, let's say a supplier's product pricing changes on their server. An agent on their server would 'notify' your server—this would be an 'event'—and an agent on your server would respond. XML is what makes all of this possible, as for the first time there is a simple means for encoding messages and data for exchange over the Web. In this case, the agents would 'inform' each other of changes with a simple XML packet.

Our goal, of course, is to make this very simple and transparent for anyone who wants to do it. We want this kind of thing to fall out of your general Web application development, without forcing you to think about network programming, XML, and all that kind of stuff.

*I know the Web is important to some people, but how do you see it as an infrastructure of society?*
In many ways, most of the major social systems—the systems that run how the world works—are being radically transformed by the Internet. For instance, the primary means of communication—mail, FedEx, telephone, fax, and mass media—are all industries that are facing massive restructuring because of the Internet. Talk to the CEOs of any major telecommunications or media company, and ask them what they view as the biggest threat to their future, and what will transform their work the most, and I'd imagine that 99.9% of the time they'd answer the Internet.

But this extends into other places. For instance, models of learning and collaboration based on computing get opened up by the Web. It is now more cost-effective—and potentially a much richer experience—to build learning and information exchange systems on the Web, than in person. Asynchronous communities—where the community exists over time, in cyberspace, without being "there"—allows niche communities to thrive in a way that wasn't possible before.

All in all, these changes are redefining the face of industrial society, and I suspect that we are just at the early stages of this transformation.

*I'm really having a hard time getting my mind around the shifting base of server technologies. How do you envision this yourself? What do you see when you think of working with server software?*
Well, as we look at the landscape we see this phenomenal growth in the number of servers and companies connecting themselves to the Web.

What I mean is, [we think] in terms of what is on the servers, the software, the server engine, the protocol handlers, the server-side includes, PERL, ASP, etc. How do we get a grasp on this technology so we can make a choice of tools?

My sense is that over the next couple of years, you'll see two major trends on the server side. One is toward application development and deployment environments being more integrated into overall solution frameworks for solving problems like content management, personalization, and e-commerce. The tools, in many ways, will become part of a broader application framework provided by vendors like Allaire.

*You're killing me, Jeremy. Can you translate this?*
Basically, corporations are going to become less concerned about what programming languages and servers they are using, and more concerned with what kinds of solutions

they can develop based on these. With this, we think the landscape for 'packaged frameworks' for things like e-commerce, customer service, Web marketing, etc., becomes much more important.

The second major trend is toward application and content data exchange models that give Web applications a higher degree of interoperability. In other words, we see technology emerging, such as WDDX (www.wddx.org), based on XML, which provides a transparent way for developers building in one server environment (e.g., ColdFusion, PERL) to leverage data and services built with other server environments (e.g., ASP, Java). In this way, developers will be able to protect themselves from technology lock-in by leveraging interoperability standards such as WDDX.

*That sounds really cool, but what does WDDX stand for?*
Web Distributed Data Exchange (WDDX). WDDX is an open, Allaire-invented XML technology that enables the exchange of data between Web programming languages. More details can be found at www.wddx.org. I've also attached an FAQ.

What did you do before you started Allaire Corp, relating of course, to what attracted you to the Internet as a business enterprise?
As a correction, I did not start Allaire. J.J. Allaire, my brother, started the company. I was the key visionary behind the product, and was among the founders, but did not start the company.

Before Allaire Corp. I had been involved with the Internet for about five years, starting in 1990 while I was in college. I worked very closely with the Internet pretty much every day since then until now, and was simply fascinated by what this technology was going to do to the world—it became the center of all of my intellectual and professional work.

Specifically before Allaire, I was an Internet consultant and analyst. I worked with a variety of companies putting together their Internet technology strategy, doing consultative training, and writing for a variety of early newsletters focused on the online world.

I had a very clear vision of the Web as an application platform, as opposed to using it as a content or publishing medium, which is how people treated it—and still treat it—for years. I believe that the basic technologies of the Web—HTML, HTTP, TCP/IP—were sufficient to become essentially a new operating system for applications. With something like ColdFusion, you really do have a very rich platform for software applications. I wanted to see this built, and J.J. had the will, energy, and technical acumen to make that happen, with the close help of myself and a small group of friends close to this vision.

*How has the amount of success you've had changed your life?*
Very little, except for the fact that I travel way more than I used to or like to. It has certainly changed my perspective on the computer industry. I've learned a phenomenal amount in a very short time. Remember, neither J.J., nor myself, or any of the other founders had any real background in the industry, and in fact, few of us had formal technical education.

*Does Allaire need employees? What kind of people would you want working there?*
Allaire definitely is always growing and looking for great people. The company is really outstanding in terms of the people we've hired over the years. While we've got a huge range of people with different technical and professional backgrounds, there are some common themes to everyone we hire. Not surprisingly, we look for smart, highly motivated, high-integrity, professionals. Also, not surprisingly, it can be awfully hard to find these kinds of people.

*Is there a large demand out there for ColdFusion developers?*
Yeah, there appears to be enormous demand for ColdFusion developers. So many companies are moving their business to the Web, and ColdFusion is just such a cost-effective and productive way to make that happen. Our best developers report, universally, that there is far more work than they can even handle. We continue to see significant growth in our developer and solution partner base, which is a great sign. We estimate that there are over 80,000 developers using ColdFusion today.

*Regarding XML, I was at Microsoft last week talking about XML development. This is a wide open field, and a lot of developers are working on bright ideas. What does Allaire have in mind?*
We've been supporting XML for well over a year. First, in our visual tools, both HomeSite and Studio have been extensible to support any XML language that comes about. Second, in ColdFusion, we've had people using ColdFusion to dynamically generate XML content for IE4, which is currently the only browser with any XML support. With our latest product releases, we've significantly expanded our use of XML, both natively in our own internal engine, but for our customers through technologies like WDDX, noted earlier, or Visual Tools Markup Language (VTML), which is an XML technology for extending HomeSite and ColdFusion Studio.

*If you were just starting in the Internet business today (aside from ColdFusion!) what area would you head for and why?*
It seems like there are still huge opportunities for people in the applications business. With the Web platform only now stabilizing and standardizing around a few key technologies, there's a predictable and ubiquitous platform for application vendors to build on. So, there are huge opportunities still in creating vertical applications and selling these as 'hosted applications' on an ISP infrastructure. Rentable applications, which is something Oracle is already doing with its own applications business. In this model, you build an app and rent usage of it to corporations worldwide on a hosted ISP infrastructure.

*Do you have any advice for people who want to learn these new technologies?*
Like everything, learning to use these technologies and applying them in your work is an evolutionary problem. Get started simple, with HTML, move up into simple interactive sites by combining things like ColdFusion, and DHTML or JavaScript on the client. From there, you're already solving a huge range of problems, and extending into the world of advanced, distributed applications will come naturally—your customers will demand it, and your ideas will drive it.

*Thanks, Jeremy!*

# Summary

It is not as difficult to actually put a simple database online as it is to understand the jargon that goes with many of the more advanced database tools. PERL is by far the easiest and quickest way to get a database up and running, and is quite powerful in its capabilities, too.

By far the biggest obstacle to implementing any specific type of database tool is its availability on the Web server. PERL is universal and standard in its various implementations. Java is universal but will need to be tested on each specific platform. Other technologies may or may not be available depending on the server's OS and the ISP's choice to support it.

There is a database package available online for minimal or no cost called MySQL that implements PERL. You can check this out at www.tcx.se.

# Security and E-Commerce

The last Internet World show I attended left me with the strange experience of walking into a place where everyone suddenly decided to speak a different language. The booths were plastered with words and phrases undoubtedly churned out by writers in marketing departments across the world who were desperately trying to find buttons to push in a consumer audience no one really yet understood. I skillfully handled this by walking up to booth after booth and asking those present, "What the heck are you selling?"

The answer was everything from a way to accept money online to fully automatic database-driven electronic storefronts. The technology was all new and, in fact, was so new that nobody really knew what was going to sell, but they were all there to find out. We live in an interesting time for technology development. When a new technology is introduced, all manner of money is spent on developing applications for it, even though there may be little or no experience on which to make judgments as to what solution might be the most workable. As a result, every conceivable variety of online store service seemed to be available, and for just about any budget.

Although it has been less than a year since most of these off-the-shelf packages have been introduced, we are finding out several things:

- Combined shopping cart and electronic payment services are very popular.
- Security is a tremendous concern, especially regarding credit card and bank account numbers.

- An alternative for smaller businesses to avoid having to buy expensive store-front software is for Web hosting services to provide this for a monthly fee.

- There are two kinds of e-commerce: business to business (B2B) and business to consumer (B2C). I'm sure the Yellow Pages people are not at all surprised about this one.

Whereas it is possible to spend five figures on a high-end e-commerce package that does everything, leaving you only the installation and configuration to overcome, we are going to focus on the basics of e-commerce, getting to know what it's made of at the low end so there are no mysteries at either end.

# E-Commerce

E-commerce boils down to four basic actions:

**Building a list of products the consumer wants to buy.** You've seen this if you've bought something anywhere on the Internet that uses shopping carts, baskets, or lists. If a site has only a few products, all you may be required to do is check boxes and fill in quantities on a form.

**Transmitting the list of products to the seller.** This is done through e-mail, which is normally created by a CGI script, as illustrated in earlier chapters.

**Accepting payment information from the consumer.** This is a more complex arrangement that comes with several options. The bottom line is that the consumer has to enter a credit card number somewhere.

**Transmitting the payment information to the seller.** This data gets transmitted to the vendor, the vendor's bank, or both, depending on the setup.

These can all be done in a single HTML FORM as you've learned how to do, or they can be done using a fancy combination of all the tools shown in this book. The difference is in the scope of the number of products on the site, the security level of the transmissions, and the degree of sophistication of the funds processing. The last step not shown here, actually delivering the goods to the consumer, is not yet a part of e-commerce. Perhaps someday (probably very soon) someone will market a product that receives the e-mail, packages, addresses, and then ships the products. That would be true automation.

You already know how to create Web sites that illustrate products, and by this time you could most likely figure out how to write a shopping cart or how to use one downloaded from a PERL site. You can also write an HTML FORM and get an e-mail script to transmit it. In this chapter I am going to concentrate on two areas of e-commerce that are not quite so easy to figure out: security and payment processing.

# The Importance of Internet Security

Everybody knows that transmissions can be intercepted, and if they are in plain text their content is free for the taking. We've all seen these messages the browsers display when we're about to take that risk. But do you know what these messages really mean and what triggers them? How do you know if the site you're visiting encrypts the data you're sending or not, or how it's encrypted? How can you tell if you're buying from a real site or a spoof? More importantly, does the buying public really know what's going on, or do they just rely on their browser to tell them? If they were spoofed, would they even know it? Is this concern really merited or are most people just afraid of something they don't understand?

If someone asked you these questions today, could you answer them?

The primary definition of security is "freedom from danger." But the word *secure* is also defined as "confident." So I say we put these together to get the real purpose of Internet security in today's world: *confidence in a freedom from danger*. That leads to a different definition for each individual because now we involve the opinion of the individual as to what the danger is of transmitting information on the Internet.

For example, many people are frightened by news reports into believing that simply receiving an e-mail can land a virus on their system. But in order to really do this, a program has to be executed in order to transfer the virus from a received file to the memory and to start the virus running on its new host. Whether this program is a decompression utility, a setup wizard, or a file viewer, the program counter has to start running in the virus address space or it may as well just be another string of dead DNA. Or to put it another way, a virus in a text file is just another string of ASCII nonsense.

The point is that computer security involves winning the confidence of the browsing public by assuring them that their information is only going to be seen by those intended, and a large portion of the browsing public currently has one or both of these misconceptions:

- They are afraid that anything they send is susceptible to being intercepted and decoded.

- They don't have a clue as to how security works or as to their browser's security features.

I will not only clear up both of these misconceptions (which I am certain such a slayer as yourself does not have) but also give a thorough grounding in the area of Internet security so that you can explain the what, why, and how of the answers to these mysteries to others.

# How Does Internet Security Work?

There are three communication lines alone that secure documents travel, and each one has a different set of security options.

- Browser to server

- Server to server

- E-mail

There are also three issues involved in any of these security situations. Together, these ensure that a communication goes from sender to receiver without being intercepted, forged, or altered. Each of these steps is accomplished by a different security technology.

**Security issue #1:** The secure encryption and decryption of data.

**Security issue #2:** Verification that data was sent by the stated sender.

**Security issue #3:** Validation that data was received unaltered.

A few definitions are in order before diving into this topic.

# DEFINITION: CIPHER

This has several definitions, including (a) a method of encoding, (b) a message that has been encoded, and (c) the key to decoding the message. For our purposes, the first and last are the most relevant definitions since they define the specific method of encoding and decoding.

Cipher has a strange word origin. Cipher comes from the Arabic *sifr* meaning empty, or zero, and, in fact, the primary definition of cipher is zero. This implies that to cipher is to create a message that means nothing.

# DEFINITION: CRYPTOGRAPHY

This is the science of secret writing and symbols, specifically how to prepare encoded information.

# DEFINITION: CRYPTOANALYSIS

This is the reverse of cryptography, as the science of the analysis and deciphering of encrypted writing and symbols. Cracking the code. Breaking the cipher.

# DEFINITION: CRYPTOLOGY

This comes from the two Greek root words *kryptos*, meaning hidden, and *logos*, meaning word. Cryptology is the study of hidden words, and so the study of cryptography and cryptoanalysis.

# Encrypting and Decrypting Data on the Internet

There are many types of encryption/decryption algorithms in cryptology, ranging from the simple alphabetic offset used in secret decoder rings to supposedly unbreakable military grade ciphers.

Those responsible for Internet security have come to a combination of two technologies using both traditional secret keys and a newer technology called *public key cryptography*.

In simple ciphers of *secret key cryptography*, the same key is used to encode and decode information. This is called *symmetric encryption*. Public key cryptography uses two keys, one to encode and another to decode. This is called *asymmetric encryption* and is based on mathematical hocus-pocus involving prime numbers, and we will thankfully skip an explanation of this technique as it only has meaning to the truly serious cryptographer.

The key used to encode is called the *public key* because it is freely distributed. The key used to decode is called the *private key* because it is kept in a secure place by the owner. Someone wishing to send an encoded message uses the recipient's public key to encode the data. This ensures that no matter who intercepts the message, only the person who possesses the private key can decode it.

A simple example of symmetric key-based encryption is given in Figure 11.1.

This encryption uses a simple string as a key to encode a text message. This cipher uses the numerical position of each letter in the alphabet to add the value of the key and the value of the message to come up with the encrypted text. If the message were longer than the key, the key would simply be repeated. It would take more than a little work for this to be decoded without the key. The key can be any string, and the longer it is, the harder it will be for spies to decipher.

The primary problem in using symmetric ciphers is not that they are easily decoded, but that the keys are not secure. This technology alone is not up to the task of establishing secure Internet transactions because encoding-side keys need to be universally available. Let's take the example of dealing with encoded payment information for an online bookstore. If the store used symmetric keys it would have to give every buyer the same key to encode their transmission, and if everyone has the key, what's the point?

In public key cryptography the first thing that is needed is a program that will generate pairs of keys. Key pairs are not hard to generate. You can use one of these programs to crank out as many as you like. The task to be addressed is first to put the public key in a place where anyone can get to it, and second, to keep the private key secure. Public keys can be sent to those who specifically need them or can be generally published on *key servers*.

Figure 11.2 is an example of a public key linked to my e-mail address. This is a real key.

Secret key cryptography, on the other hand, depends entirely on the keys being kept absolutely secret as well as the messages. The secrecy of the key is weakened every time a message is intercepted, and if enough messages are intercepted the key will

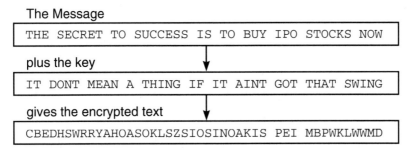

The Message

```
THE SECRET TO SUCCESS IS TO BUY IPO STOCKS NOW
```

plus the key

```
IT DONT MEAN A THING IF IT AINT GOT THAT SWING
```

gives the encrypted text

```
CBEDHSWRRYAHOASOKLSZSIOSINOAKIS PEI MBPWKLWWMD
```

**Figure 11.1**  Key-based encryption.

```
-----BEGIN PGP PUBLIC KEY BLOCK-----
Version: PGP for Business Security 5.5.2

mQENAzYMkRkAAAEIAMWkiDFRasti8qViO/6sY3a4j+A/gdWsPx18BzzPjRidvdV+
E6JyUGUCh/MR5aqYeiUzKAOdzKQHjkPIRks2V/OTmJwllrH7OMWb3L3gnKBFZcSg
QeX9JzkeK91Ejbv0ZmmJACgAnHazhOqatfWBXiRhfglnJsMBwRVR/ERImJ+GxTuU
PDphVCkC7P91yXkW050Dy3qhHFegDaVZjIjhHbfxUVCrmxzsygeyJIqB9h0gsNvH
CjEu+G+iRxFqPdhRWSXV1oUynJ25lWZvWZR3x5NznSUHrNLbI0j21g0+KGFEyhhN
ior2dQ8YSOorvdeVNT5Yf1CRQxHUSq8SDTEW76UABRG0JURhdmlkIEEgQ21udHJv
biA8c2Npb0Bjb21wdXNlcnZlLmNvbT6JARUDBRA2DJEZSq8SDTEW76UBAV4TB/9d
qHznx21FZcPnksGxcJ2W0Mj49E4esqiD99mrqDvgKDJkmk0UhAw78JI59maPCILa
nc63rlbrE8aqAs1CweWsywAb+spybXM2yGo/la4SV83ed+veod/qY+V6dwi7Rc8T
Ghnmu07Mb7aD8Y719YaSsdsYPVh+/SRzVDnG1K27WwdPQWmIK3fKAb8tWVoAg4Yn
hBXLvQPHPru6OGf1zATMqc4QosBaB14i54kutVjGXhnvBXeKTNBkUMWmEGZnRkGX
4ePRbbMzPVIiIdWIO2QO/1R6lRHIVC1R6qbXePl4fRUvQzfrZCnB3zMJQqFHA0ie
QibR4GVviPzIr9tgCaNL
=5Kjw
-----END PGP PUBLIC KEY BLOCK-----
```

**Figure 11.2**  Public side of key pair.

eventually be broken. Finally, the cipher becomes completely useless if the codebreaker has the ability to create a message and intercept the encoded version. Not so with asymmetric encryption.

**SECRET KEYS, SYMMETRY, AND SUCCESS**

The most successful secret key algorithm I know of is the Navajo code talkers of World War II. The United States Marines enlisted a group of Navajos to come up with a code using the Navajo language. Even though a Navajo captured by the enemy who did not know the code was able to translate the words, his captors were still completely unable to crack the code. The code was never broken in the three years it was used during the war in the Pacific, and played a major role in the success of many military campaigns.

# PGP

PGP (Pretty Good Privacy) is a specific implementation of public key cryptography. PGP was created in 1991 by a programmer named Phil Zimmerman as a way to encrypt e-mail. Phil did not invent the cipher technology; he simply made it available to the Internet public. PGP is also a company, but PGP, Inc. was not founded until 1996, well after PGP was first released on the Internet. PGP is also a product you can buy at any computer store, or download for free.

The PGP product has utilities that enable any user to create a key pair and publish the public key on a PGP key server. This solves the first security issue of ensuring that encrypted messages can only be decrypted by the recipient, but leaves the second security issue unaddressed, verification that data was sent by the stated sender.

The PGP technology alone is consumer-grade security that you can use to send and receive encoded messages. When you generate a key in PGP, it asks for your name and e-mail address, and, of course, you can type in anything you like. The hole in this security is that there is no verification of who you are. Just like you can enter any address in an e-mail program, you can claim to be anybody in your public key.

For example, it just now took me only 30 seconds to create a key pair in the name of the current president of the United States, as shown in Figure 11.3. If I combined this with a made-up e-mail account I could really fool somebody who didn't know any better.

Actually, the big damper on this little scheme is that very few people seem to know much of anything about PGP. My friend at Netscape is the only one I could find who has a public key registered on a PGP server. PGP seems to be used by a select few with a specific need for security, and these few are spread throughout the world. The PGP Web site claims this is used a lot in countries with a questionable or downright bad attitude toward human rights. That I can believe.

Figure 11.4 shows how PGP-encrypted e-mail works.

Actually, the e-mail program would not have to pull the public key off the Internet—it should be on your local *keyring*—but the idea is that public keys are universally available. The owner of a key can also create and upload a new key whenever he or she pleases, so your local keyring could be rendered obsolete at any time, without prior notice.

All the e-mail programs I know of currently support PGP messaging (more or less), although you still need PGP to create your own key. These include Microsoft Outlook, Netscape Messenger, and Eudora.

One trick in PGP is to encrypt any message you send with two public keys, the recipients and your own. That way, if the message gets returned for any reason, you'll be able to decipher what you wrote! This is an easy thing to do. When you tell PGP to encrypt the message you are given the option of assigning any number of public keys to the message. Mysteriously, adding keys does not increase the size of the message by very much.

This same PGP e-mail scheme is used in e-commerce transactions to transmit purchase information from the server to the seller, and payment information from the server to the bank. This is all right for a really small operation, but for high-volume, big-money sales it does not provide enough certainty that the buyer is being honest or that the payment request is bona fide. If we're a big retailer we don't want to be sending out thousands of

**Figure 11.3** My PGP keyring.

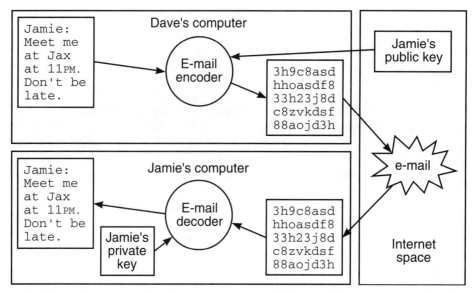

**Figure 11.4** The cycle of PGP e-mail communication.

dollars' worth of products that are not paid for or charging up credit cards willy-nilly. Not only will we lose money, but we'll upset a lot of people, too.

This security hole in PGP is why it's called PGP. It gives pretty good privacy, but it's not perfect. What needs to be added to PGP is verification of the identity of the sender, and that is where the subject of digital certificates comes in.

## INFORMATIVE SITES!

*www.pgp.com*

*www.nai.com*

**Network Associates is a merger of PGP, Inc.**

*www.nai.com/products/security/phil/phil.asp*
**The homepage of Phil Zimmerman, creator of PGP, offers a history of PGP.**

*www.pgpi.com*
**The PGP International homepage is different than www.pgp.com because it's run by the users!**

# Digital Certificates

Digital certificates are used by e-commerce vendors so you can be sure you're buying from a legitimate company that won't steal your money or misuse your payment information.

A digital certificate is two things:

- It's an electronic document issued by a Certificate Authority, or CA. A CA is a trusted source who has verified the identity of the person or organization applying for the certificate. This is not an electronic verification, it is done by a person who checks you out and approves the digital certificate to be issued.

- It's a piece of data that is transmitted to instantaneously validate your identity in electronic transactions. This is an electronic verification that is accepted without question on the basis of trust of the CA.

To see a list of recognized Certificate Authorities:

- In Explorer, select the *View* menu, *Internet options* item, *Content* tab, *Authorities* button.

- In Navigator, click the *Security* button, *Certificates* menu, *Signers* selection.

Two of the major CAs in e-commerce are Verisign *(www.verisign.com)* and Thawte *(www.thawte.com)*. They provide digital certificates, which are renewable each year for a yearly fee, to validate e-commerce transactions.

A digital certificate contains the following six pieces of information:

- The owner's public key
- The owner's identity
- The issuer's identity
- A serial number
- The issuing and expiration dates
- The issuer's digital signature

The bottom line on a digital certificate is that it is used to prove that a public key belongs to the owner and is genuine, so that a secure transmission can be initiated with the trust that the party on that end of the communication line is who they say they are.

Security is a two-way street, especially on the Internet. In a secure transaction, digital certificates go both ways. Both in browser-to-server and server-to-server transactions, each party validates the other's certificate before allowing the transaction to proceed. How this is done is explained later in this chapter, but that it is done at all may be a surprise to the user who never sees any of this going on.

You may be asking (or should be asking), "I see that the site I'm buying from should have a certificate, but what about me? I never asked for any stinking certificate!"

The answer is that your browser creates one on the fly because in order for you to receive an encrypted Web page, the server has to encode it to your browser's public key. Of course this certificate is not issued by any CA, but it does keep the pages the server is feeding to your browser from being intercepted and decoded by an unscrupulous third party. The browser can do this because there is more than one tier of Certificate Authority. In addition to the official CA, there can be a local server administrator CA. All you need is the right software to create a certificate.

The invisibility of server-side digital certificate validation leaves a wide gap in Internet security. You don't have to have your own certificate to validate e-commerce transactions unless you're going through a bank or payment processing service that specifically requires you to have one of your own. However, the user will never know this unless he or she specifically looks to see it (see the sections later in the chapter on Navigator and Explorer security).

So the submission of payment information to a small business e-commerce site will be validated by the browser against the Web host's certificate, which is the default certificate used for a site that doesn't have one of its own. If this were misused to gather credit card numbers and process fraudulent payments offline, the site would eventually be shut down and the Web host (and maybe the FBI) would go after the subscriber, but still it could be done without the user realizing anything was wrong.

## Digital Signature

Digital signatures are the solution to security issue #3, validation that the data was received unaltered. Remember from Chapter 9, "PERL and CGI," that a hash function is a programming technique. Originally it meant creating a unique index by mixing up the data in a way that would avoid duplication of results from different inputs. In PERL this is used differently, but in security it is used in the traditional sense.

Digital signature is nothing more than a hash function run on the message to be sent with the result, which is then encrypted. The digital signature is included with the message so that the decoding program can put it aside, run the same function on the same original message, and compare results as shown in Figure 11.5.

If they match, the data could not have been altered.

Here's the kicker: It is not only possible to encrypt with a public key and decrypt with a private key, it is also possible to encrypt with a private key and decrypt with a public key. After all, the only difference between these two keys is that one is secret and the other is not. The quality of each component of the key pair is the same.

Technically, the result of running the hash function on the message creates what is called the *message digest*, and an encrypted message digest is a *digital signature*. Digital

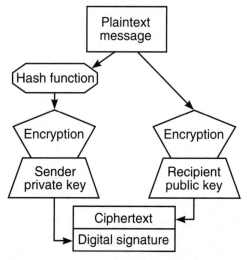

**Figure 11.5**   Digitally signing a document.

signatures are encoded to the sender's private key, because the signature is not a secret, and the signature really belongs to the sender, not the receiver. Anyone can decode the signature, but that's okay because it can't be used to decode the message, only to prove that the message received is the same one that was sent. The cycle of digital signature validation is shown in Figure 11.6.

Digital signatures combined with public/private key pairs and digital certificates round out the three-point security scheme used in Internet Public Key Cryptography, but there is more to this animal called *Internet Security*.

## SSL

SSL (Secure Socket Layer) is a client/server security scheme. SSL runs in a layer (recall your earlier lessons in Internet architecture) between HTTP and TCP/IP, so this means two things. First, HTTP data will continue to go back and forth but at some point it will become encrypted. Second, the SSL protocol will perform the encryption and decryption in a manner completely transparent to the user.

Figure 11.7 illustrates precisely how this is used in e-commerce. Documentation on the SSL protocol can be found in many places, specifically on the Netscape, Microsoft, and RSA sites.

The first thing that happens in the SSL layer when a document is requested from a secure server is that the client issues a CLIENT-HELLO message. This includes a list of ciphers supported by the client.

The server responds with a SERVER-HELLO message, sending back a list of ciphers compatible with the client and the server's digital certificate which, most importantly, contains the server's public key. At this time, the client may also take the steps of validating the server's certificate by checking the digital signature, the expiration date, and the Certificate Authority. Later on, the server may apply the same validation procedure to the client. This would be most applicable in server-to-server SSL data transfers.

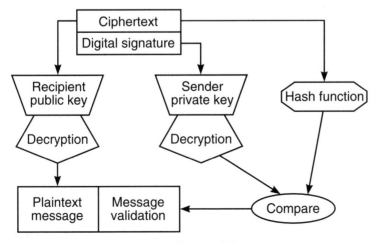

**Figure 11.6**   Validating a digitally signed document.

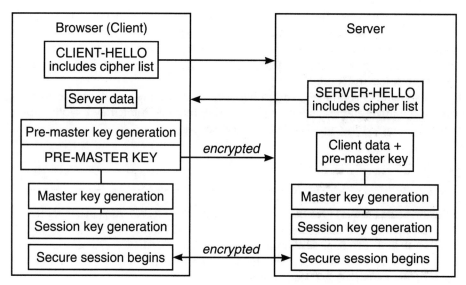

**Figure 11.7**    Secure Socket Layer security initiation.

As part of the SERVER-HELLO the client accepts the information from the server, which includes a piece of random data to be used in the process of creating a *pre-master key*. The piece of data used is in cryptographic terms called the *nonce* ("the number *n* used only *once*") and is typically the session ID number sent by the server, a random enough choice.

The client computes the pre-master key and sends this to the server encoded to the public key in the server's digital certificate as protection against a server spoof.

The server and client then separately go through a standard key generation process to create a pair of session keys. Because these keys are generated in secret and are valid only for the current session, and because symmetric ciphering is much faster than asymmetric ciphering, these are not public/private key pairs. These are symmetric keys.

Once this process is completed, the secure session can now get underway. If anything goes wrong such as intercepted, imitated, or corrupted key information, the client and server will simply go out of communication, since the encryption keys could not possibly match, and the session will end.

You may think this is a bit much for a lesson on e-commerce, but to truly understand the process you have to go just a little bit farther, and here's why: When you get involved with configuring security for an e-commerce site you are going to have to choose the level of security you are after, and in order to do that you're going to have to understand the choices available in the cipher list mentioned earlier.

# Encryption Options

The first thing you have to do is to separate the subject of key generation from the subject of encryption technique to realize that there are two types of algorithms at work here: those for key generation and those for encryption.

Key generation algorithms work differently for Public Key and Secret Key Cryptography. The two preferred algorithms implemented by PGP in Public/Private key pair generation are called RSA and Diffie-Hellman, with only Diffie-Hellman being supported in newer versions. In Secret Key generation, there are several algorithms in use, including RC2, RC4, DES, and Triple-DES.

Encryption algorithms implemented by PGP are different than for key pair generation and include CAST, IDEA, and Triple-DES, with the preferred method being CAST. Secret key encryption algorithms are combined with their key generation methods so they have the same names. As you can see, the only algorithm that Public and Secret Key Cryptography currently have in common, as implemented on the Internet, is Triple-DES.

Now it's time to put all this in perspective.

Public Key Cryptography algorithms are used for e-mail, digital signatures, and digital certificate authentication. As such, they are not really used for e-commerce security, only for introducing one party of the transaction to the other party through a reliable source. The quality and specifics of the methods used are not particularly relevant to a discussion of e-commerce security options, and besides, there's really not much to say unless you plan to be a cryptographer.

Secret Key Cryptography algorithms, on the other hand, have very specific parameters that are totally relevant to e-commerce, and I'll be digging into these right now.

But first, a little background. Many of the encryption technologies in use today were invented in the 1970s when computer security first became involved with national security.

RSA is a "public key cryptosystem" that defines both key pair generation and message encryption. RSA was invented by three guys whose initials are, what else?, R, S, and A. These are Ron Rivest, Adi Shamir, and Leonard Adleman. RSA is a patented and licensed technology. The RSA patent expires in the year 2000. RC2, RC4, and the newest version, RC5, were designed to be faster, more secure, and an exportable (as in selling overseas) replacement for DES. Ron Rivest went on to devise further security tools in the form of the RC secret key methods. RC means either Rivest's Cipher or Ron's Code, depending on how Ron feels on any given day.

DES stands for Data Encryption Standard and came out of IBM. A really big deal has been made out of DES in the last 20 years because it was originally such a superior method that it became a U.S. Department of Defense standard. As such, export of the technology was severely restricted. That era in history is now over. DES is scheduled to be replaced by a more sophisticated algorithm under the name AES.

One of the interim solutions to the weakened status of DES has been Triple-DES, an enhanced version of DES that makes it much harder to break. (You can't use the word *impossible* in cryptography). DES is patented by IBM but IBM has placed it in the public domain.

Diffie-Hellman was also invented in the 1970s by two guys named, no surprise here, Diffie and Hellman, and is not an encryption method but a *key agreement protocol*. It only defines how users can exchange secret keys over a public medium.

Finally, IDEA (International Data Encryption Algorithm), SAFER (Secure and Fast Encryption Routines), CAST (Carlisle Adams and Stafford Tavares), and Blowfish, along with many more clever methods, are all newer encryption algorithms of the 1990s.

# INFORMATIVE SITES!

*www.rsa.com*
**RSA Laboratories, Inc. offers a course in cryptography.**

*www.uni-mannheim.de/studorg/gahg/PGP/cryptolog1.html*
**Crypto-Log: Internet Guide to Cryptography includes everything you wanted to know about cryptography!**

*www.lasalle.edu/~danylir1/privacy/crypto/crypto.htm*
**Roman's Haven: Cryptography is another site filled with cryptography knowledge!**

*www.ssh.fi/tech/crypto*
**Cryptography A-2-Z offers tons of cryptography information if you know where to look!**

# Message Authentication Options

In addition to reliable and secure encryption and decryption, we have the task of verifying that the message has not been altered. This is called *message authentication* and uses a hash algorithm, as discussed earlier, to produce a digital signature, which in SSL is called a *message digest*.

There are only two of these algorithms in use in the SSL protocol. These are MD5, or Message Digest 5, also developed by Ron Rivest, and SHA, or Secure Hash Algorithm, developed by NIST, or the National Institute of Standards and Technology, a division of the U.S. Department of Commerce. Both of these are, like the newer encryption algorithms, products of the 1990s.

# Security Options in SSL

When we look at security options we are looking at defining how hard it will be to crack a certain code. The longer the key is, the harder the code will be to crack. This is a central theme in Internet security for two reasons:

**Reason #1.** Keys used in Public Key Cryptography must be longer than those used in Secret Key Cryptography because the public key is broadly published and so must be more difficult to crack. Because longer keys increase processing time, Public Key and Secret Key Cryptography prefer different ciphers.

**Reason #2.** Being the connected Net surfer that you are, I'm sure you've heard about restrictions that U.S. Government export laws put on cryptographic software. This forces servers processing secure transactions for international clients to support a dual standard of high and low versions of the same security ciphers.

There are currently two versions of SSL in use, the most recent version being SSL 3.0. The difference between SSL 2.0 ciphers and SSL 3.0 ciphers is really only in the message authentication techniques. SSL 3.0 uses an improved version of MD5, and SSL 3.0 DES ciphers have replaced MD5 authentication with SHA.

Table 11.1 shows how the key length for SSL ciphers varies from the legally U.S. exportable 40-bit maximum for the RC2 and RC4 ciphers to the Triple strength DES 168-bit whammy. Remember, these key sizes are for Secret Key ciphers.

# Cracking a Cipher

The argument as to which cipher to use hinges on statistics, experience, and periodic attempts by cryptoanalysts to break certain codes.

Statistically, a 40-bit key gives $2^{40}$, or a little more than 1 trillion possible combinations. A 56-bit key gives 72 quadrillion. A 128-bit key gives $3 \times 10^{38}$ possible keys, and it goes up from there. A 128-bit key is considered adequate for commercial security. A key the size of Triple DES is now considered military grade.

To put this in perspective, in early 1997 RSA Labs offered a challenge: Anyone who could break the 56-bit DES code would receive a $10,000 prize. A group of Internet users responded to the challenge and for the first time ever, broke a DES code, and it only took them about three months. They did this by writing a client program that participants could download. The program would retrieve a range of keys to test from an Internet server, then run through the keys and report the result.

During the project, over 78,000 computers participated in the task. On the peak day of their code-breaking work, over 14,000 computers were working on the job processing about 6 billion keys per second and a total of over $10^{12}$, or 600 trillion, keys were tested. That's in a single day. In the three months of testing, a total of less than half of all the possible 72 quadrillion key combinations were tested before someone came up with the winning number.

This type of attempt, trying all possible combinations, is called an *exhaustive key search* or *brute-force attack*. Using improved techniques, the most recent 56-bit DES code-breaking success undertaken by the Electronic Frontier Foundation took only 56 hours using a computer built for $250,000. It is estimated that a $1 million computer built specifically for the task using today's technology could bang out a solution in about $3\frac{1}{2}$ hours.

So it can be concluded that at least for important data, 40-bit keys are worthless and it's time to move up to something that will not also be rendered worthless in a few more years. Not only is computing power increasing pretty fast these days, but the Internet shows the awesome increase in power you can get with distributed processing!

**Table 11.1**  SSL Cipher Options

| KEY LENGTH<br>MA ALGORITHM | RC2 | RC2 | RC4 | RC4 | DES | TRIPLE<br>DES |
|---|---|---|---|---|---|---|
| SSL 2.0 | 40-bit<br>MD5 | 128-bit<br>MD5 | 40-bit<br>MD5 | 128-bit<br>MD5 | 56-bit<br>MD5 | 168-bit<br>MD5 |
| SSL 3.0 | 40-bit<br>MD5+ | 128-bit<br>MD5+ | 40-bit<br>MD5+ | 128-bit<br>MD5+ | 56-bit<br>SHA | 168-bit<br>SHA |

To put the rest of the key sizes into perspective, if we use the $3\frac{1}{2}$ hour estimate as a starting point it would take just over a month to break a 64-bit key. To break an 80-bit key would take 7,000 years, and a 128-bit key would put us off effectively forever. Even with a dramatic 100,000-fold increase in computing power, the 80-bit key may fall in as little time as the 56-bit key, but the 128-bit key would still take over a trillion years to crack, at least if you're using the brute force method. So, barring an unforeseen leap forward in cryptoanalysis, this size key is felt to be secure enough for some time to come.

Public key ciphers are a great deal longer than secret key ciphers. As a rough comparison, a 40-bit secret key is considered equal to a 512-bit public key; a 56-bit secret key to a 768-bit public key; an 80-bit secret key to a 1024-bit public key; and a 168-bit secret key to a 2048-bit public key. This is the main reason public key processing takes a good deal longer.

The export restrictions on cryptographic software that can process keys greater than 40 bits is very controversial. The reality is that such software can be downloaded from anywhere, to anywhere. Of course, such a download would be illegal. This would certainly not bother a foreign government, but a commercial business may not want the trouble. For these entities, an alternate solution has been found that is perfectly legal. The source code is published in books, and books do not have export restrictions. Remember the First Amendment? So anyone can buy these books, which are printed in OCR fonts, then scan in the source and have the code.

## INFORMATIVE SITES!

**www.frii.com/~rcv/deschall.htm**
**The $10,000 DES Challenge page includes the full story on how the code was cracked!**

**www.eff.org**
**The Electronic Frontier Foundation is run by the guys who continue to explore the crypto frontier.**

# SET

SET (Secure Electronic Transaction) was developed by Visa and MasterCard as a method to increase security specifically for e-commerce purposes. SSL is a general security protocol not specifically directed towards e-commerce. SET uses all the tools SSL does: public and secret key encryption, digital signatures, and digital certificates. Some see SET as being a great thing, some feel it's no better than SSL. It's too early to tell just what effect SET will have on the world.

The SET 1.0 specification was released in 1997, and the 2.0 spec is due out in 1999. SET currently uses 40- and 56-bit DES for secret key encryption and RSA for public key encryption. Now, from your newly educated viewpoint, you can see that the DES part may need to be revised at some point. Of course, not everyone has a DES-cracking machine, at least not yet, and remember that 56-bit DES is still export restricted.

Some of the new things that the SET spec provides for is a new Certificate Authority and a testing service to ensure both server and client SET software comply with SET specifications. This means that someone will have authority over who can and who cannot use SET, something certainly not true with SSL. But the question is, is all this really necessary?

## INFORMATIVE SITE!
*www.setco.org*
**SET Secure Electronic Transaction Web site offers the scoop on the SET standard.**

## Navigator Security

When submitting a form (using a simple search engine or posting credit card numbers to an online store) to a secure server or not, and no matter to whom it is submitted, Navigator displays the warning show in Figure 11.8, but only if certain security features are turned on. As the checkbox states, you can easily turn off this notice and never see another warning again.

The question is, would the user even remember having turned off this warning and think twice before slinging another set of credit card numbers through thousands of miles of fiber optic cable? I know that when I'm shopping on the Web I figure that, right or wrong, it's all set up for me and if someone did steal my numbers I'd just dispute the purchases anyway. But what I'd like to know is, how much electronic commerce do these messages deter, and is it really worth it?

On one of my Web sales sites I have an alternative form for faxing or mailing, and every now and then I receive one of these. So somebody who was already on the Internet decided to print and fax or mail the form instead. How do they know somebody's not tapping their fax line, or steaming open their letters? The answer is, trust and confidence. The phone company and U.S. Mail have earned their trust. The Internet has not.

In my opinion this warning is not really a true statement of the facts but is provided for legal, public relations, or politically correct reasons. Browsers do have security features and even though a secure message can be broken, it would take the perpetrator a

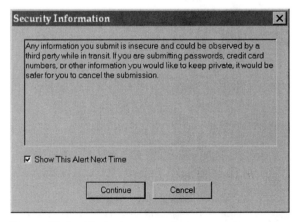

**Figure 11.8**     Navigator transmission security warning.

great deal more work than it's worth. Of course it would be safer to cancel the submission, but it would also be safer if I never left the house, wore a bullet-proof vest all the time, and ate five helpings of vegetables a day.

Another version of this warning shown in Figure 11.9 will occur when you get transferred to a new URL. I'm not sure what the intention is here, because there's another set of messages that can display when you're entering or leaving secure server space. Maybe they're afraid secure information will be echoed back to the user?

An even more remote piece of data the average user will never see is the certificate information for the secure server he or she has accessed. In order to get to this screen you have to select the *View* menu, *Page Info* item.

Figure 11.10 tells us that this site uses 40-bit encryption at a security level suitable for U.S. Export and was issued a digital certificate certified by RSA Data Security, Inc. on May 18, 1998. Sounds good to me. Could you explain why this is good or bad to a potential buyer?

Finally, Figure 11.11 gives a shot of the Netscape security settings screen. To get to this screen, select the *Communicator* menu, *Security Info* item, *Navigator* tab. Or just click on the *Security* icon on the toolbar. The *Security Info* tab will also display a button to *View Page Info* that gives the same security settings screen as shown in Figure 11.11.

Friendly browser security is apparently the last frontier. And a big frontier it is.

I think this screen illustrated in Figure 11.11 would intimidate most users who would probably be afraid to change these settings, much less figure out what half this stuff means. If I were an average user I'd be thinking to myself, "What is an encrypted site? And what does it have to do with credit cards? Who cares if the site is encrypted, all I care about is my information. The last checkbox is the only one that seems to make much sense. And what the heck is all this stuff about certificates? Nobody seems to have one listed!"

This screen also acts a bit strange, at least in Version 4 of Navigator. Half the window controls don't work and the screen format seems to be a refugee from Windows 3.1, almost as if Netscape never expected anyone to actually visit this section, or forgot it was there. Clicking on the Help button gives a more sophisticated screen with basic explanations of cryptography.

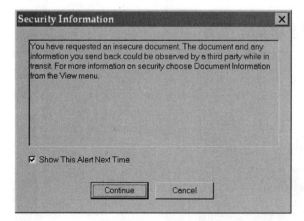

**Figure 11.9**  Navigator secure document warning.

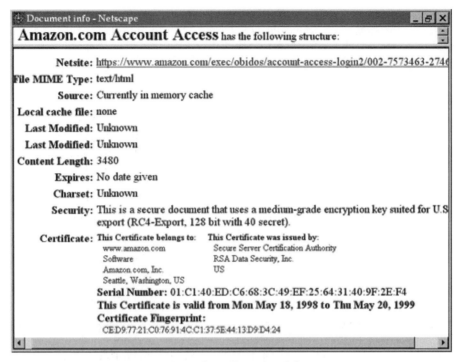

**Figure 11.10**   Navigator security and certificate breakdown.

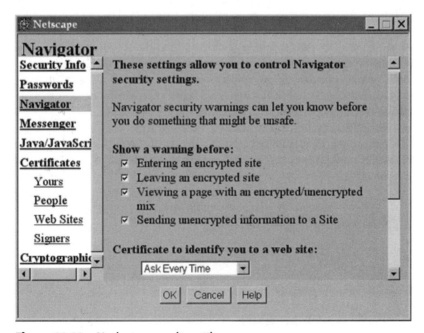

**Figure 11.11**   Navigator security settings.

Navigator Version 4 supports a standard cryptography package called PKCS #11. PKCS stands for *Public Key Cryptography Standard.* These standards are published by RSA Laboratories, which can be found at www.rsa.com. PKCS #11 is a specification for an API for cryptography and is also called *Cryptoki,* which is pronounced "crypto-key," not "crypt-oki." Crypto-key in turn is short for *cryptographic token interface.*

This is all very new stuff and very secret. The truth is, you can download documentation on this, if you're interested, from the RSA Web site at www.rsa.com. In fact, RSA's site is a whole course in cryptography.

Cryptoki, and so Navigator, supports all the current cryptographic standards, which are explained in this chapter.

# Explorer Security

Explorer displays a message similar to Navigator but not quite as scary, and gives you the option of checking the box to prevent the message in the future, as shown in Figure 11.12.

Explorer also has the redirect message, shown in Figure 11.13, which occurs when the browser is rerouted to a new URL. This happens in search engines using the GET method to transmit the query string in the URL.

Unlike Navigator, Explorer offers the option of applying different security settings to different zones including Internet, intranet, trusted sites, and not trusted (restricted) sites. The Internet zone, however, is the default zone as it is the only one that does not have to have its exact sites listed.

The information on this message is a bit more informative than Navigator as it gives the specific reason for the security precaution, that a URL could contain a cookie in the form of query string information that is then handed off to the new URL. Despite the accuracy of this message, I'm still very skeptical that the average user has any idea what this means, and I suspect that it is more of a nuisance than a help. Again, and this time just like in Navigator, these messages only show up if you set the security options to make it happen, and allow you to turn them off permanently simply by checking the box.

Is this kind of security really helpful? There's a job out there just waiting for someone to figure this out, and it could be you.

Explorer also has a window in which to view security information for the Web page currently loaded, as shown in Figure 11.14. In the *File* menu, *Properties* item you can access a window that gives a pretty worthless breakdown of the page, except for the *Certificates* button.

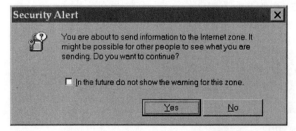

**Figure 11.12**  Explorer transmission security warning.

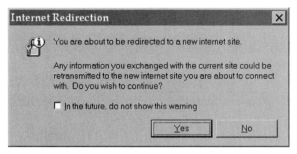

**Figure 11.13**   Explorer secure document warning.

Pressing the Certificates button will give you a security menu more friendly than Navigator but still meaningless to the average Web user. It shows to whom the certificate belongs, and has an Issuer tab as well, as shown in Figure 11.15.

The educated computer security student will see that the Explorer Certificate page gives you a little more data than the Navigator Document Info page, but it takes a little more work to get to it. Clicking each of the tabs tells us what kind of security standards *amazon.com* uses, how it encrypts pages being sent from the secure server, what kind of message authentication is used, and what size of key exchange is supported. These topics were discussed earlier in this chapter.

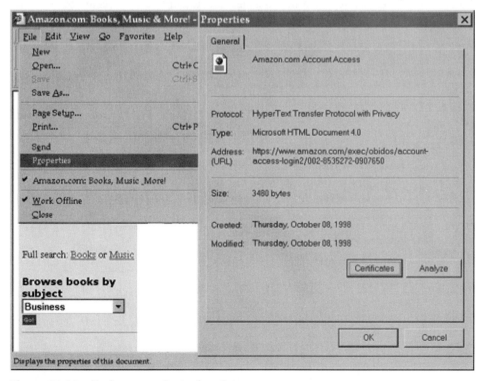

**Figure 11.14**   Explorer security explanation.

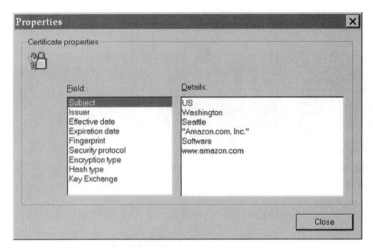

**Figure 11.15**   Explorer certificate breakdown.

The advanced security settings for Explorer (see Figure 11.16) show that it supports SSL 2.0 and 3.0, which covers all the same security options present in Netscape. A document in the Microsoft library states that Explorer and Navigator both support PKCS #7, which, according to RSA, is a general syntax for cryptographic enhancements.

Microsoft also offers PCT security, its own version of SSL called Private Communications Technology. How much this is in use outside of Microsoft is anyone's guess.

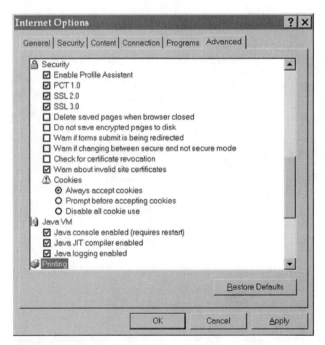

**Figure 11.16**   Explorer advanced security settings.

If you are interested, you can read the PCT spec online in the support library at www.microsoft.com.

Additionally, Explorer offers to check the validity of certificates checking for revoked or invalid certificates.

# Accepting Electronic Payments

Once trust and understanding in credit cards, electronic checks, and digital cash builds amongst the general public, look out. There's tons of work to be done in this area, but first, let's start simple. Accepting credit cards over the Internet can be as easy as having a form the customer has filled out e-mailed to you.

But whatever scheme you use, the first thing you need is a merchant account with a bank that has approved your company to accept credit card payments. This is not always easy, but it can always be done. Even if you can't get that kind of action yourself, there are companies that will provide this service to you for the purpose of Internet payment processing. They're approved to accept credit card payments so you just set up your site to have the payments routed to them, and they pay you.

Figure 11.17 illustrates a simple four-step Internet ordering scheme for those with their own bank account.

Beyond this is where things start to get interesting, because now you're talking about having the customer's payment information sent somewhere else and this means it's going to be processed electronically. There are a lot of options for making this happen, but when it does happen there's really only one way to go about it, at least as far as credit cards are concerned.

A site like this is not practical for too small of a business because the cost of processing electronic payments in real time online begins to grow at this stage. One answer for this in the future is to have a lower-cost service that will process payment requests all at once at the end of the day. We seasoned Internet veterans are not used to this in the instant-gratification world of online buying, but it's really no big deal for a mail order business to wait a few hours to process its orders.

The full-service e-commerce Web site, more commonly called a *storefront*, will have a sequence of several Web pages to process the customer's order: One or more pages for building the list of goods to buy, a different page to process each different type of possible

---

1. The customer submits the CGI form to the merchant's Web server, secure or not.

2. The CGI script generates an e-mail to the merchant, with or without PGP encryption.

3. The CGI script transfers the customer to an acknowledgment page.

4. The merchant processes the credit cards offline, using a separate computer program, card reader with numeric keypad, or (gasp) by filling out paper slips!

---

**Figure 11.17**   No frills e-commerce.

payment, and a thank you or acknowledgment page as usual. Or, if you're selling something that can be downloaded immediately, then the customer is routed to what is called the *fulfillment area*, where they get the stuff like, right now.

Figure 11.18 illustrates a sophisticated storefront work flow in eight easy steps. Some of these steps can be broken down into more steps and it's possible to add other steps, like e-mailing the customer to verify the order before processing the payment, but these show the required order of the essential steps to fully automated electronic payment processing.

1. The customer submits the completed order form to the merchant server, which then prompts for and accepts the payment information. The pages that accept payment information contain and/or call scripts that are written by the payment processing service.

2. The merchant server encrypts the payment information and sends it to a server run by an electronic payment processing company with which the merchant has an account.

3. The payment processing server relays the encrypted payment information to a server that can verify the customer's payment information, most likely run by the customer's bank or credit card company.

4. The customer's bank server accepts or declines the transaction.

5. If accepted, the payment processing server routes the payment information to a server that can deposit the electronic payment into the merchant's bank account.

6. The payment processing server also relays the results of the payment request to the merchant's Web server so the order can be processed or declined.

7. The merchant's Web server e-mails the results of a successful transaction to the merchant.

8. The merchant's Web server generates a page that tells the customer if his or her payment was accepted or declined. If declined, the customer may try again.

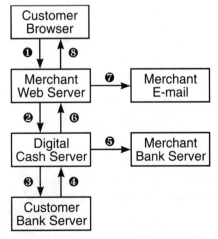

**Figure 11.18** E-commerce with the works.

# Cybercash

Cybercash is a digital payment processing service. It's been around since the beginnings of the World Wide Web and offers an electronic payment processing service to merchants. Cybercash also recently acquired ICVerify, which is the offline credit card processing program mentioned earlier. To use Cybercash, just as with any credit card payment service, you need a merchant account. Then you can establish an account with Cybercash and decide how you are going to implement the software.

The challenge here, as in any such system, is if you decide to install it yourself. You can download what's called the Merchant Development Kit for any server OS and go to work. Version 2 of the Cybercash MDK was much more difficult and time consuming to install than Version 3. With the new version, Cybercash has taken the burden of all the processing that it possibly could off of the merchant server and put it on its own servers, so installing Version 3 is relatively easy. It comes with about 300 pages of good documentation. In its simplest form it consists of a few templates for Web pages that will be accepting payment information, a few CGI scripts to relay that to the Cybercash servers, and three executables: one for Triple DES encryption, another for Triple DES decryption, and another for MD5 hash computation.

If you're working on your own server it's easy enough to install, but if you have a remote Web host, you'll need to get a shell account and use a telnet login to install the Cybercash software. Then it will be time to sharpen your PERL skills and integrate the CGI scripts and HTML templates with your Web site. There is also a testing script so you can be sure you're connected!

Cybercash is now offering a new service called Insta-Buy. The future of payment processing may actually lie in Java applets! Rather than having a series of payment processing screens, the applet shown in Figure 11.19 can pop up and take the payment data and relay it directly to the payment processing center, completely bypassing the need for any HTML forms or CGI scripting. Plus, the applet will become a familiar format to the consumer, thus inspiring trust and confidence in this form of payment. And what's more, the applet may be able to recognize the buyers and access the buyers' payment information already on file so they don't have to enter their credit card numbers every time, as is currently done using the traditional HTML forms and CGI script methods at www.amazon.com.

# Wallets

A wallet (Figure 11.20) is an application that keeps track of the buyer's payment information. Explorer contains the Microsoft Wallet, which can be accessed through the *View* menu, *Internet Options* item, *Content* tab, *Payments* button. This wallet happens to be on the buyer's computer, though it could be anywhere as long as it's secure.

The idea of a wallet is that you enter all your credit card information in the wallet, which can be automatically launched when it's time to pay for something. You may not ever recall having seen this happen, but Cybercash tells me that Microsoft Wallet is the same wallet it uses, so this must tie in somehow!

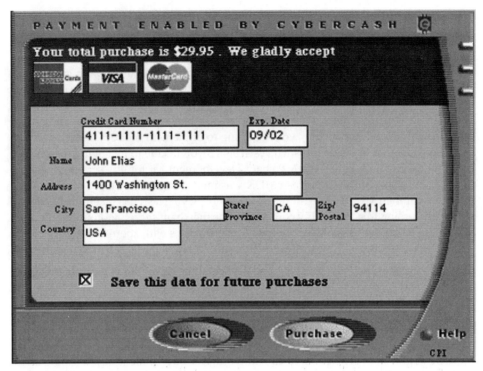

**Figure 11.19** Insta-Buy applet sports cool design.

## Digital Cash

The first and most familiar form of digital cash is credit cards. But that's where familiarity ends.

There is a lot of talk about *digital cash*, which literally means what it says. The question is, how do you give out digital cash without having it forged (another issue where the public trust is really all that is keeping this from coming to life)?

Digital cash is cash given out in the form of files, and we all know how easy it is to copy files. So what's the catch? The bank has to have a server that keeps track of valid digital cash certificates, with the term *valid* meaning they haven't been spent yet. So when the digital cash is spent, it can't be used again. The cash file is encrypted to the bank's public key so that the certificate number is protected.

There are a lot of interesting issues that come up when you think of exactly how this will work.

First, to buy digital cash, you'd have to download it from the bank.

Second, like paper money, it would have to come in unalterable denominations.

Third, you'd have to have a way to make change. This brings us to the potential scene where any company can issue digital cash. All it really is in this case is an I.O.U.! Think about how money works. Paper money was originally issued as a substitute for gold kept at the Federal Reserve Bank, and was supposedly exchangeable for that gold. Every country in the world has a different form of money and its relative worth is based on how

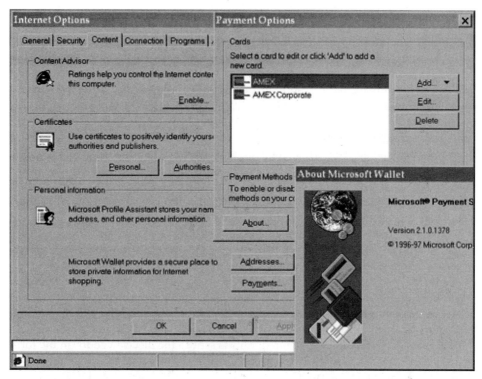

**Figure 11.20**   Your hidden wallet.

well that country can back it up. It's illegal for just anyone to print money because of the obvious potential for fraud. But it's not illegal to issue what's called *scrip*, which is just a form of money that can only be exchanged with one business.

Perhaps someone will start an electronic clearing house for digital cash where you can exchange privately issued certificates for more publicly useful ones. Currently, the government is not involved in issuing digital cash, so it would have to be bought from and redeemed by a bank or other issuing institution. This limits the usefulness of digital cash, but with the integration of this type of exchange, its use could easily become as universal as that of credit and debit cards.

And fourth, you'd have to either delete spent digital cash from your computer or have a way to keep track of spent and unspent digital cash files.

I'm sure there are other issues. As you can see, this field is pretty wide open right now.

# INFORMATIVE SITES!

***www.cybercash.com***
**Cybercash**

***www.verisign.com***
**Verisign**

***www.thawte.com***
**Thawte**

# EDI

EDI (Electronic Data Interchange) has been around since its start in the late 1980s and is a B2B e-commerce technology. Consumers will never use EDI. In its current form, EDI is a very complex, hard to support method of computerized business. XML and the Internet promise to change all that.

Traditionally, *EDI transactions* are processed over private networks for security reasons. SSL technology has plenty of security for EDI, but this is an industry that has been resisting change. The private networks, called VANs for *Value-Added Networks*, provide a secure mailbox system of EDI communications between buyers and vendors and charge a hefty price for sending and receiving EDI information. Internet mail servers could do the same job using PGP encryption at no cost and with no security risk. There is a certain amount of support and verification the VANs supply, but somehow this is going to have to shift to the Internet sector.

An EDI transaction can be just about a piece of data you can imagine that would go from one business to another, from a hazardous materials list to a college transcript. In business, the most basic form of EDI normally consists of a *purchase order* sent from a buyer to a vendor, followed by an *invoice* sent back from vendor to buyer.

An example of retail EDI in use would be this. Let's say you order a bicycle from a JC Penney catalog. This transaction would be entered in the JC Penney computer and an EDI transaction would be generated. This is sent to the bicycle vendor in the form of an EDI purchase order with your shipping address. The vendor ships you the bicycle and sends an EDI invoice to JC Penney. In EDI terms, the vendor and JC Penney are called *trading partners*, though the term is more frequently applied to the buyer, who is usually the larger of the two companies.

EDI transactions are based on text files sent in exact formats that are outlined in 1000-page books. Further, every year these *EDI standards* are slightly revised, forcing everyone to buy another book and reprogram to add the new version. For experienced programmers this may start to sound like the IRS, and it is. If you can't keep up with EDI business requirements you could lose thousands or millions of dollars of revenue from trading partners who dictate which standard they will send in and what data will be sent in which field.

Figure 11.21 is an example of an EDI purchase order transaction. Each line is called a *segment* and has a three-character segment identifier that shows what kind of information it contains so it can be correctly translated. These identifiers are supposed to be somewhat mnemonic but are not always easy to figure out. The segments must follow an order defined in the EDI standards. Each individual field within each segment also has a specific minimum and maximum size, data type and list, range, or some definition of what values are allowed.

Table 11.2 is an attempt to loosely translate these segments (in the last six years I have been completely unable to find a written reference as to what the abbreviations really mean).

Another challenge for businesses using EDI is to take this information from the EDI software (which has received this data in EDI format) and export it to a format that can be imported into whatever accounting software they are using. The alternative is to manually enter dozens, hundreds, or even thousands of EDI transmitted purchase

```
ST*239423
BEG*00*SA*0070817**980701
REF*DP*20-07
DTM*010*980720
N1*ST*Hillary Clinton
N3*1600 Pennsylvania Avenue
N4*Washington*DC*20008
PO1*001*1*EA*239.88**CB*3334290
PID*F****BRACELET 6  STY/PPK/PP
CTT*1.
SE*239423
```

**Figure 11.21**  EDI gibberish.

orders every day. And then on the flip side there's another challenge, to export invoices from the accounting package back to the EDI software. Not to mention that these are not by any means the only types of transactions sent and received through EDI!

XMLEDI is the Internet solution to all this complexity. As you have seen, XML could provide position-independent data in the form of a structure using an agreed-upon DTD tag set. It's going to be a big job to get people to change the way EDI is done. There has been a vast amount of effort put in to making it work the way it does, and "migrating" to XML is more like going to a new planet entirely rather than flying south for the winter.

**Table 11.2**  EDI Decoded

| SEGMENT | CONTENTS |
| --- | --- |
| Start Transaction | Transaction ID # |
| BEGinning | 00=Original PO, SA=Standalone, PO #, PO date |
| REFerence | DP=Department, Dept # |
| Date/TiMe | 010=Requested ship date, 7/20/98 |
| Name 1 | ST=Ship to, Name |
| Name 3 | Address |
| Name 4 | City, state, zip |
| Purchase Order 1 | Line item #1, Quantity 1, Each, Price 239.88, CB=buyer's catalog #, the # |
| Product Identification | F=free format, (skip 3 fields), description |
| Current Transaction Total | 1 line item |
| Start-End | Transaction ID# (same as ST) |

There is a much work to be done in this industry, but it is not for the impatient.

# INFORMATIVE SITE!

*www.disa.org*

**Data Interchange Standards Association is the only existing EDI standards Web site.**

## Summary

I hope you've enjoyed this tour of security and e-commerce. If you've gotten this far, congratulations, it's a hard road to get this stuff figured out. If you haven't, you wouldn't be reading this anyway. But even if you are, this is one area in which you have be sure you understand one concept before moving on to the next. *Applied Cryptography* by Bruce Schneier (John Wiley & Sons, 1995) is a book that deals with the subject of security in more detail.

# CHAPTER 12

# Multimedia and the Future

When the Web was first getting popular back in 1993 and 1994, those of us who are members of the Internet old timer's club were using 9600-baud modems *at best*. Even with the improved streaming media software available today, these would not be adequate to carry even the lowest quality of Internet audio.

With our 56K modems today, there is no comparison to the motionless online world we left behind. We can listen to Internet radio whenever we want, and some of us even have access to full or partial T1 connections, cable modems, or ADSL lines that can deliver streaming video at full speed.

Every year that goes by brings higher modem speeds and better software to deliver content. Where will this take us? In this chapter we're going to look at how media is created for the Web, the state of the art in Web media delivery, and the future of multimedia on the Web in view of the up and coming technologies of digital and high-definition television and ongoing research in the area of a new ultra-high-speed Internet.

Finally, we'll wind down with a few observations on the future of content delivery in terms of new markup languages and the integration of XML into the existing Web paradigm.

You're going to learn a lot about how digital audio and video are put together in the next section, so get ready for a Vulcan mind meld, of sorts!

**371**

# Streaming Media

When audio and video files first became available on the Web, they had to be downloaded in their entirety before they could be played. Streaming media changed all that by providing a player program that would play back content as it was received. There is a price to pay for this, however, which is that the quality of the sound or video file that you are playing is limited by the speed of your modem. Streaming audio and video can be delivered at any speed, but it wasn't until 28.8 modems became available that music-quality audio could be delivered—video is still struggling to get out of the gate even at 56K.

## DEFINITION: BANDWIDTH

*Bandwidth* **is the technical term for the amount of data you can put through your modem.**

Bandwidth is not a new concept. It is a term born out of the need to squeeze more wireless broadcasting (read that as radio and television) stations into a limited range of frequencies. Radio more than TV has used the term *band* in the past with reference to long-, medium-, and short-wave bands, and AM and FM bands. Each of these bands covers a different range of frequencies, which are represented by their physical *width* on the tuning dial. Hence the term *bandwidth*.

Cable, satellite, and digital transmissions change the traditional concept of bandwidth by providing new ways to deliver increasing amounts of content through higher-capacity transmission media, such as coaxial cables and digital multiplexing. Multiplexing simply means combining many channels into one, and is a technology used in anything digital, including cellular phones, fiber optic communications, and satellite uplinks. Digital multiplexing allows a number of lower-bandwidth channels to be funneled through a single larger bandwidth channel.

We'll discuss how the quality of audio and video relates to bandwidth later in this chapter.

# Audio

The first thing that one must realize about audio on computers (whether on the Internet or not) is that it has been found that people become much more annoyed when the audio is interrupted than the video. In case you hadn't noticed, audio always takes precedence over video, and audio does not skip like video does. This is not because audio takes less bandwidth than video (which it does), it's because audio becomes incomprehensible when it skips, and that is not necessarily true with video. In fact, the way computer audio/video delivery has been configured to work is that the video is actually slaved to the audio to the point where video frames will always be dropped as necessary to maintain audio continuity and synchronization.

Computer audio has been assigned three quality settings: telephone quality at the low end, radio quality in the middle, and CD quality at the high end. These all have an assigned *sampling rate*.

Sampling solves the problem of converting what is normally a continuous sound wave (analog) into a series of numbers (digital). The explanation for how this works forces us to cross over into the technology of sound recording, because if you're going to put audio on the Internet you can't get by without knowing what you're dealing with!

## Analog versus Digital

Traditional sound recording equipment is *analog*. Analog comes from the Greek root words meaning "*proportionate gathering*," and so an analog signal is shown as a continuous unbroken curve on a graph or oscilloscope that represents a voltage proportionate to the loudness of the signal as recorded at any given instant. The reason voltage is used is because the ultimate destination for this wave is always a loudspeaker, which is powered by electricity.

Figure 12.1 shows the relationship between an analog wave, voltage as amplitude, and time as wavelength.

Digital audio is based on the technology of *sampling*. It takes this analog signal and measures it at specific intervals. The frequency of measurement determines the quality of reproduction, meaning how faithfully the original sound will be recreated on the other end, and is called the *sampling rate*. This quality also depends on the perception of the listener.

Human hearing ranges from about 20Hz (Hertz, or cycles per second) on the low end to 20,000Hz on the high end. 20KHz is really a very, very, high-pitched signal. Consider that the highest key on a piano is only around 8KHz. Many people cannot hear anything above 15KHz, but even if you can't pick them out in a hearing test, it's those highs that give that crisp and clear sound to your favorite music.

There's a rule to this: In order to reproduce a signal at a specific frequency, the sampling rate must be at least double that frequency. Consider for a moment why that is. If you took a ruler to Figure 12.1 and measured the signal at every inch mark, and then connected the dots, you'd come out with a pretty poor representation of it.

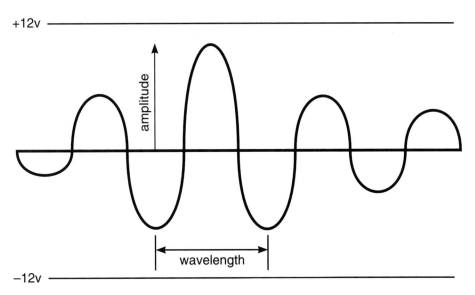

**Figure 12.1** Analog signal breakdown.

But if you instead marked it off at every eighth of an inch, you'd get a much better representation.

So it is with digital audio. Each sampling point is translated into a number that represents the signal amplitude at that point. This is stored as an 8-bit or 16-bit number depending on the recording format. Digital recording formats are called *codecs*. Just as modem stands for *modulation-demodulation*, codec stands for *compression-decompression*. It seems this term is applied to any digital media encoding algorithm even if the digital format is not compressed.

## Audio Quality

Digital audio on computers has been categorized into three standards of quality based on the sampling rate, which translates to bandwidth and file size. A higher sampling rate will require a higher bandwidth and a larger file size. These formats are only applicable to a static audio file. Streaming audio is encoded at a single sampling rate (which would be one of these standards) but can be downloaded at any of a couple of dozen different rates depending on the bandwidth of the connection. But remember, the streaming rate is an instantaneous rendering and is only transitory, disappearing after the packet is delivered to the listener.

- CD quality audio is sampled at a 44.1KHz sampling rate, just over twice the limit of human hearing. This is the rate at which all CDs are recorded.

- Radio quality is sampled at half the CD rate, or 22,050Hz, which will still carry an 11KHz tone, high enough for decent quality music but without as much brilliance as CD quality.

- Telephone quality is sampled at half the radio rate, or 11,025Hz. This really doesn't sound too hot. Don't confuse the term *telephone quality* with the fact that your telephone modem can carry CD quality sound. If you have any doubt that music sounds really bad over the telephone, just call somebody and try it. Modems use a very special technology to squeeze 56KHz of bandwidth into a telephone signal.

The bit rate of digital audio sampling is important because this now relates to the ability of the human ear to discern different levels of sound, and it is surprising to see how sharp the average ear really is.

Anyone familiar with samplers used in music studios will tell you that 12 bits is a bare minimum for decent quality, even though it may seem that the 4,096 levels of sound amplitude this provides are more than enough. The truth is that 8 bits, which gives you 256 levels, is just not worth listening to! On the other hand, 16 bits gives you 65,536 possible levels and produces excellent quality sound. In fact, more resolution is beyond our ability to perceive. The human ear really is a very finely tuned instrument!

### Quality Factors

There are three factors that are balanced in the continuing battle of quality versus bandwidth for the delivery of digital audio content. These are compression, noise reduction, and the need for stereo sound.

**Compression.** Compression allows us to squeeze more content through the same bandwidth and is discussed later in this chapter in the section on how digital video works. The purpose of compression is to reduce the size of the file without losing its content. The most common example of compression is the universal use of the "zip" program to compress text files for download on the Internet. The number of people and businesses who depend on this technology to accurately recreate the compressed contents of files never ceases to amaze me, and it seems to faithfully perform its duties millions of times daily around the globe.

**Noise suppression.** Noise, being a low-level, nonzero signal, will be picked up and encoded with an amplitude of 1 or 2. In an 8-bit sample this will play back as a very audible hiss, whereas in a 16-bit sample it will hardly be noticed at all.

**Mono versus stereo.** Another consideration in calculating the bandwidth required for digital audio is the fact that you can have mono (1 channel) or stereo (2 channel) sound. Speech is normally recorded in mono, while music is normally delivered in stereo. Stereo takes twice as much bandwidth as mono, but if bandwidth is limited, the two stereo channels can be mixed together into a single mono channel.

Figure 12.2 illustrates the Creative Labs WaveStudio display of a sample CD quality stereo audio file. WaveStudio is a simple digital audio editing program that comes with the SoundBlaster product. You can see that the high sampling rate causes the dots to blur into a very high-quality signal. In reality, sound waves are not nearly as simple as the sine wave shown in Figure 12.1.

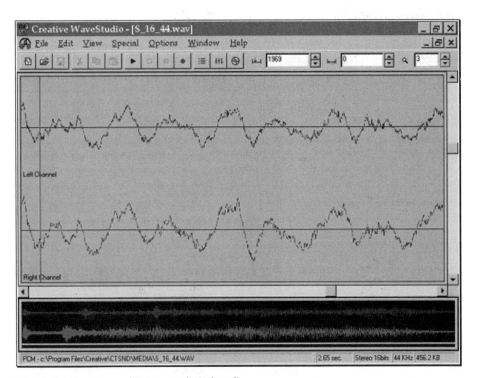

**Figure 12.2**   CD quality stereo digital audio.

**Bandwidth.** As far as raw modem speed, a 28.8 modem can deliver 28,800 bits divided by 8 bits per byte of data per second, or 3.6KB/second. This isn't very much. A 56K modem (if running at full speed) will deliver about 7KB/second. One channel of CD quality audio at 16 bits/sample will take 88.2K of bandwidth. We're running a little bit behind here. Even a single channel of telephone quality audio at an 8-bit rate will take 11K of bandwidth to deliver in real time, still beyond the speed of a 56K modem! Table 12.1 shows the demand for the various formats for streaming audio.

## NeXT/Sun Audio Format

There is one more digital audio standard I didn't mention earlier because it stands aside in its own category. This is based on an 8KHz sampling rate that got its start at Sun Microsystems and is supported by a Java API. This format is called *u-law* where the letter u is really μ and so is pronounced mu-law. This was intended to allow programmers to manipulate audio content with a built-in set of routines and without having to worry about codec encoding and decoding.

As you might have guessed, this sounds pretty bad. This quality of sound will do okay with speech, but that's about it because voice quality audio is not as demanding as music and can at least be understood at a sampling rate as low as 8KHz at 8 bits. Unfortunately, this seems to be the only format slow enough for today's modems.

## Streaming Audio

In practice, streaming audio may not even live up to a standard as low as this 8KHz level of expectation. Even though a modem may run at 56K, some of the bandwidth has to be set aside for protocol transmission. After all, we can't receive the data without some TCP/IP activity! In response to this, RealNetworks (www.real.com) suggests that the encoding rate be 25 percent below the data rate, and the RealNetworks encoder, RealPublisher, supports sampling rates for streaming audio that take as little as 5Kbps (5K bits/second) of bandwidth, mostly used to squeeze as much video in as possible.

Although the standards by which digital audio is measured have been constant for some years, the technology of digital audio encoding is constantly being improved, and as with all Internet technologies, better ways of streaming audio content are always under development.

**Table 12.1**  Audio Bandwidth Demands

|  | 8-BIT MONO | 8-BIT STEREO | 16-BIT MONO | 16-BIT STEREO |
|---|---|---|---|---|
| 8K | 8KB | 16KB | 16KB | 32KB |
| Telephone | 11KB | 22KB | 22KB | 44KB |
| Radio | 22KB | 44KB | 44KB | 88KB |
| CD | 44KB | 88KB | 88KB | 168KB |

Both Microsoft and Sun are coming out with brand new Internet-friendly digital audio technologies as of early 1999. Microsoft has ASF (Advanced Streaming Format). Sun has Java Sound. ASF was developed by a consortium of digital audio companies and promises to carry all the major digital audio formats. Java Sound also supports many digital audio formats, but is primarily a new feature of the Java language, released with Sun's Java 2 platform in the JDK (Java Development Kit).

## Putting Audio on the Web

The key to putting audio on the Web is having a way to encode (record) and decode (play) the audio files.

Players are downloadable for free, and if you want to put audio on the Web, you must choose a format that has a wide availability of players. RealNetworks has been the dominant player in this arena, and has recently released a new technology in the form of its RealPlayer G2. The difference in this player from previous versions of this and other players is that it supports what is called *scalable content delivery*. This means that a single file, encoded for streaming, can be delivered at any bandwidth.

Before scalable delivery, a separate streaming file had to be created for each separate bandwidth of delivery. Say, one for a 14.4 modem, another for a 28.8 modem, another for a 56K modem, and yet another for something higher. This led to "high bandwidth" and "low bandwidth" versions of sites. This is no longer the case, although just as with any technology, it will be a while before most existing Internet audio files are converted to scalable streaming format.

There are five steps needed to put audio on the Web. The entire cycle from recording to playing is shown in Figure 12.3 and is detailed next.

1. **Recording.** There are many ways to do this, from recording audio through a computer microphone (which I have not found very rewarding) to recording

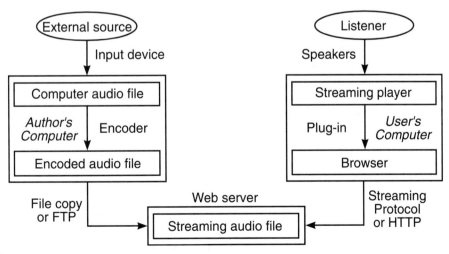

**Figure 12.3**  Internet audio from source to speaker.

direct from CD. My favorite recording medium for speech is first through a video camera with a high-quality external microphone attached, and transferring the audio from the camera into the computer.

2. **Encoding.** In order to prepare audio files for streaming you need an encoder. Personally, I use RealPublisher from RealNetworks, which is now a scalable encoder. There is also the True Speech converter from the DSP Group (at www.truespeech.com), which encodes to the 8KHz 8-bit codec.

3. **Publishing.** The streaming audio file can now be copied or uploaded to the Web server. Of course you also have to write a Web page to cause the player to load, and there are always special instructions to be followed to create the HTML for the streaming file, depending on the format. These instructions come with the encoder documentation.

4. **Streaming.** The streaming file is now ready to be played. When a user jumps to the Web page there will be a button or URL to click on to play the audio file. In case the user doesn't have the player, there should also be a button to download the player.

5. **Playing.** If the user does have the player, the browser calls it as a plug-in. The rest is up to the player, and the user can continue browsing other sites if he or she chooses.

The HTML code to deliver the RealAudio files on the Web page in Figure 12.4 is shown in Figure 12.5.

RealPublisher throws in a few comment lines, but all that is really needed is the <A HREF=> link that causes the RealPlayer to pop up. These lines are shown in bold type.

All that the *.ram* files contain is the full URL address of the encoded audio files, which in this case would be "http://www.prolotherapy.com/success1.rm", and likewise for success2.rm and success3.rm.

There are a few things to consider when choosing a method of streaming delivery. First, if the Web server does not have special streaming software running (for example, the RealNetworks RealServer, which delivers streaming media using a streaming media protocol), the server will use HTTP to deliver the file. This works just fine but slows down the transfer a bit. The real point here is that since the full-blown versions of these servers are not free, many Web hosts do not support them. You can download a free smaller version of your own, but it will require a shell account and permission from your Web host.

Further, a streaming media server application takes up a lot of memory and puts a load on the physical server. Also, if you're paying your Web host provider for user access by the megabyte, there's nothing like huge media files to run up the bill, so be aware!

# MIDI

MIDI (Musical Instrument Digital Interface) is a computer music standard that dates back to the late 1980s and was developed to hook synthesizers together in a way that one could be used to control another. It is also used in music sequencers, which are dedicated

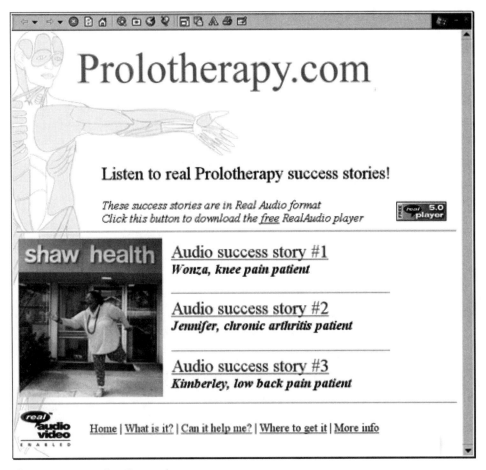

**Figure 12.4** RealAudio Ready.

sequencing machines or sequencing programs running on personal computers that are used to record from and play back to multiple synthesizers and drum machines.

MIDI is also on the Web in streaming format in the form of the Crescendo player from LiveUpdate (www.liveupdate.com), and of course in nonstreaming format as well. These files are small enough that streaming is not always necessary and because of this, many Web sites have MIDI files that automatically play when the page loads.

MIDI files contain no audio, they instead contain commands that are sent to a sound card that has a built-in music synthesizer. For this reason, MIDI files are limited to music, are extremely slim, and download quickly. MIDI files, however, depend heavily on the quality of the sound card's synthesizer for the quality of the sound, since the music is not actually contained in the file but is reproduced from the commands in the file.

A few years ago a standard called *General MIDI* was introduced that states exactly which instruments are to be assigned to the first 128 synthesizer voices on sound cards.

```
<HTML>
  <HEAD>
    <TITLE>Prolotherapy Real Audio</TITLE>
  </HEAD>
  <BODY BACKGROUND="images/Musclesb.GIF">
    <TABLE WIDTH="100%">
      <TR>
        <TD WIDTH="139" ROWSPAN="2"></TD>
        <TD WIDTH="599" COLSPAN="2"><FONT SIZE="+2">
        Listen to real Prolotherapy success stories!</FONT></TD>
      </TR>
      <TR>
        <TD WIDTH="499">
         <I>These success stories are in Real Audio format <BR>
         Click this button to download the <U>free</U>
         RealAudio player</I></TD>
        <TD WIDTH="100">
        <A HREF="http://www.real.com/products/player">
        <IMG SRC="images/realaudio.gif" ALT="RealAudio"></A></TD>
      </TR>
    </TABLE>
    <HR>
    <TABLE>
      <TR>
        <TD ROWSPAN="3"><IMG SRC="images/Wonza.JPG"></TD>
        <TD WIDTH="380" ALIGN="LEFT">
<!-- RVEncoder
-- pagelayout="pop-up"
-- serverpath="http://www.prolotherapy.com"
-- mediafile="success3.rm"
-- metafile="success3.ram"
/!-->
        <FONT SIZE="+2" COLOR="#FF0080">
        <A HREF="success3.ram">Audio success story #1</A></FONT><BR>
        <FONT SIZE="+1">
        <B><I>Wonza, knee pain patient</I></B></FONT></TD>
      </TR>
      <TR>
        <TD WIDTH="380" ALIGN="LEFT"><HR>
<!-- RVEncoder
-- pagelayout="pop-up"
-- serverpath="http://www.prolotherapy.com"
-- mediafile="success1.rm"
-- metafile="success1.ram"
/!-->
        <FONT SIZE="+2" COLOR="#FF0080">
        <A HREF="success1.ram">Audio success story #2</A></FONT><BR>
        <FONT SIZE="+1">
```

**Figure 12.5** RealAudio HTML.

```
            <B><I>Jennifer, chronic arthritis patient</I></B></FONT></TD>
        </TR>
        <TR>
          <TD WIDTH="380" ALIGN="LEFT"><HR>
<!-- RVEncoder
-- pagelayout="pop-up"
-- serverpath="http://www.prolotherapy.com"
-- mediafile="success2.rm"
-- metafile="success2.ram"
/!-->
          <FONT SIZE="+2" COLOR="#FF0080">
          <A HREF="success2.ram">Audio success story #3</A></FONT> <BR>
          <FONT SIZE="+1">
          <B><I>Kimberley, low back pain
patient</I></B></FONT><BR></TD>
        </TR>
      </TABLE>
      <HR>
      <TABLE WIDTH="100%">
        <TR>
          <TD WIDTH="99"><B><IMG SRC="images/ravenab.gif"></B></TD>
          <TD WIDTH="535"><A HREF="proloindex.htm">Home</A> |
           <A HREF="prolodefine.htm">What is it?</A> |
           <A HREF="prolohelp.htm">Can it help me?</A> |
           <A HREF="proloshaw.htm">Where to get it</A> |
           <A HREF="proloinfo.htm">More info</A> </TD>
        </TR>
      </TABLE>
    </BODY>
</HTML>
```

**Figure 12.5**    *(Continued)*

Before this standard was set, it was anyone's guess as to what instruments would actually be used to play an MIDI file, because MIDI assigns notes to channels, not specific instruments, and there is no voice information in the MIDI file. Imagine what a song would sound like if the guitar track were played by the drum kit, the drum track by an oboe, and so forth. General MIDI allows MIDI authors to predict which instrument will be used on playback, even if the quality isn't what they had in mind.

MIDI files consist mainly of *note on* and *note off* commands, which include what note at what exact time and at what velocity. Velocity translates to volume and refers to the force with which the key is struck, since this was intended to record live performances from a synthesizer keyboard, although MIDI is now used with other instruments. There are also *system exclusive* commands that carry information on pitch bending, modulation, foot pedals and other controls, voice channel assignments, and program changes.

MIDI files can be placed on the Web just as audio files can. No special encoding is required, but as always, the player should be downloadable from anywhere a streaming file is offered.

There is a new trend in Internet MIDI. RealNetworks and LiveUpdate have combined forces to create a synthesis (pardon the pun) of the RealPlayer G2 and Crescendo Forte. These will download a single stream consisting of combined MIDI and digital audio, giving a higher quality of instrumental reproduction with a much lower bandwidth. The digital audio portion is reserved for vocals and instruments that would be hard to reproduce with MIDI, such as virtuoso-quality solo work and sound effects. This is not new to the computer music world as MIDI sequencing programs have combined digital audio with MIDI for years, but it is totally new to the Internet. Done right, MIDI sounds great.

The reason this has not hit the Internet sooner is that the primary technological difficulty to overcome is synchronizing the two audio streams, especially because they each use completely different sound technologies. This is achieved by using a brand new Internet technology called SMIL (Synchronized Multimedia Integration Language).

# SMIL

SMIL (pronounced just the way it sounds, *"smile"*) is a tag-based XML type language complete with its own DTD. SMIL is supported by the RealNetworks G2 player, which is what makes G2 a true multimedia player. Unlike previous versions of RealPlayer, G2 is not only for audio and video but it is something that can be programmed using SMIL to deliver entire presentations including digital audio, MIDI, text, images, and video!

Figure 12.6 is a short example of SMIL that does a lot.

This SMIL file is meant to be processed by the RealPlayer, not the Web browser, so it exists in a separate file with an *.smi* extension that is passed to the RealPlayer.

The structure of an SMIL file is very HTML-like. The entire file is enclosed in a set of <smil></smil> tags and has *head* and *body* sections. All SMIL tags are lowercase and, as in XML, unpaired tags end with a "/".

The *head* section *meta* tags should be familiar and include information that will appear in the RealPlayer "Clip info" box and the Help menu "About this presentation" window.

The *body* section is shockingly simple. There is of course much more to SMIL than is shown here, but this simple example accomplishes a great deal of multimedia work in itself.

The <par> and <seq> tags simply mean play in parallel, meaning at the same time, and play in serial, meaning one after the other. These tags can actually be nested as they are in this case, with a sequence of songs playing in parallel with either a picture or video presentation, which in turn is linked to the user's bandwidth.

The <switch> tag set denotes that only one of the enclosed files should be played depending on the attributes of the tag. In this case, depending on the "system bit-rate," you will either see a still .jpg image or a streaming video. If you get the still image, then the *fill* attribute specifies that after the image is displayed it will *freeze* on the screen for the duration of the presentation. Without this attribute set the image would be cleared after it had fully downloaded, as is the default action for all streaming media.

```
<smil>
<head>
  <meta name="author" content="Dave Cintron"/>
  <meta name="title" content="Rockin out"/>
  <meta name="copyright" content="(c)1999 Cintronics"/>
</head>
<body>
  <par>
    <switch>
      <video src="electricwarrior.rm" system-bitrate="56000"/>
      <img src="ewarrior.jpg" fill="freeze" system-bitrate="14000"/>
    </switch>
    <seq>
      <audio src="neversaydie.ra"/>
      <audio src="firstcontact.ra"/>
      <audio src="rockforthedevil.ra"/>
      <audio src="warpdriverockandroll.ra"/>
    </seq>
  </par>
</body>
</smil>
```

**Figure 12.6**   SMILing Dave in multimedia.

SMIL also has instructions to leave images on the screen for specific time periods, to start and stop an audio or video file at a specific point in its timeline, and much more. In fact, the entire SMIL specification is not yet supported by the RealPlayer G2, but they're working on it.

You might guess that SMIL has a big future. That would be my guess, too. The W3C specification and more information on SMIL is available at the W3C multimedia Web page (www.w3.org/AudioVideo).

# Live Audio Webcasts

Live Internet streaming audio broadcasts are specialized applications of streaming audio. In order for live Webcasts to work, the listener must be able to join the audio stream at any point from start to finish, so there's a little more to it than just download-ing a file. Also, anyone doing a live broadcast would expect that there would be many people listening at the same time; otherwise, why bother to take the trouble to do it live?

Live Webcasts can take a huge amount of bandwidth on the server end so there are two ways this can work. First, it can be done in traditional format where each listener has his or her own audio stream. This method is called *unicasting*. You can immediately see how only a thousand listeners would put a huge strain on any server. A 28.8KB/sec live link to 1000 listeners gives you a 28.8MB/sec demand!

A *multicast*, on the other hand, relays a single Webcast stream through a network of servers called *splitter sites*, which in turn relay individual streams to those hooked in to the domain to which the streaming multicast server belongs. This spreads the bandwidth burden to a much more tolerable level. The only way to do this today, aside from creating your own private multicast network, is through a specialized server network such as RealNetworks Real Broadcasting Network multicasting service.

In Figure 12.7, the RBN broadcasts to a network of splitter sites, which in turn deliver unicast content.

# Video

Much of the technique of streaming video is the same as streaming audio, but formatting video is another story. Video is different because first, it takes up a lot more bandwidth than audio; and second, video can be played back at varying rates and still be recognizable.

**NOTE**
There is a terminology stumbling block when we talk about computer video, and that is the term *digital video*. Of course, all video on a computer is digital video. There is a new Digital Video technology, however, where video is not just stored digitally, but is recorded digitally. I will capitalize as shown to distinguish between the two.

There are three unique parameters to be considered when dealing with video: *frame rate, window size,* and *compression.* These all add up to *frame size,* which translates to bandwidth.

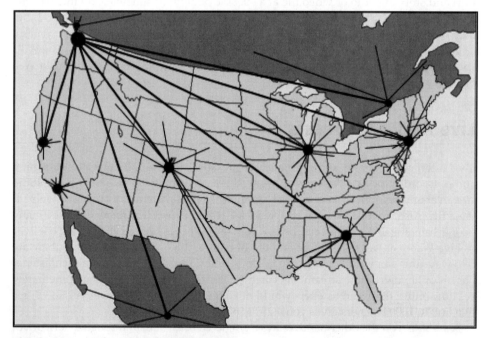

**Figure 12.7** Web multicast method map.

# Frame Rate

Video as seen on television or any full-motion medium is 30 frames per second, or 30fps. Not to even mention the Internet yet, consumer-grade personal computer video adapter cards were not capable of displaying full-screen/full-motion video until a couple of years ago. Even now, most computer video runs at only 15fps for several reasons:

- There is downward compatibility with older systems.

- Running full-speed video puts a huge demand on the hard drive to deliver content, and most hard drives just can't keep up unless they're dedicated to video only or otherwise specially optimized.

- Full-motion/full-screen video takes up a lot of space, which is becoming less of an issue as time goes by, but it's still an issue.

Internet video is not restricted to these limitations because it doesn't even get that far. The bandwidth issue is huge, so video on the Net ends up running as low as 1fps, not much better than a slide show! In order to speed this up we can sacrifice size, which means we end up with a smaller video window but more frames per second.

# Window Size

A full-size television signal has 525 lines of vertical resolution, and because of its 4:3 aspect ratio (the ratio of the width of the image to its height), this would work out to 700 lines of horizontal resolution. Because of the way television is transmitted, this is not quite as high as the quality of a low-resolution $640 \times 480$ computer screen.

Most computer video is recorded at quarter-screen size, or $320 \times 240$. Internet video is most often recorded at a quarter of that, which is 1/16th screen size, or $160 \times 120$. Anything below that is what I call postage-stamp video. Of course, the smaller the frame is, the more frames per second we can see, but at some point you have to follow the law of diminishing returns.

# Compression

Compression is a very important subject because it is the one thing that tries to improve bandwidth without sacrificing frame rate or size. What does get sacrificed is quality, or sharpness of image. There are several different compression algorithms: some are *lossy*, meaning more image quality is lost with increased compression, and others won't compress below a certain standard of quality.

Digital Video compression is standardized at 5:1. This was settled on for one reason and one reason only. Uncompressed video is really not recognizably better than this, because all video has some redundancy. It's not like audio where the signal is constantly changing. Any video image is full of areas where the color and shading do not change for several pixels in a row and can be compressed without loss of image quality. So 5:1 is an acceptably high standard for video compression. Anything less than this is really unnecessary, and anything more than this starts to lose quality, at least with today's technology. The Digital Video compression rate is fixed and cannot be changed because it is written right into the file format.

Before Digital Video came along there was digital video. You can plug a non-Digital Video capture card into your computer, such as one of the MiroVideo series (www.pinna-clesys.com), and digitize video at any compression rate from almost no compression all the way up to 40:1. Figure 12.8 shows the difference in quality between the two extremes.

The video on the left was compressed at 40:1. Notice the jagged lines on the window blinds in the lower left corner and the pixelating of the face, especially in the forehead area. The video compression algorithm decided that these large blocks of pixels were close enough to assign the same color. After all, something had to go.

The video on the right was compressed only at 10:1 and comes out much smoother. The fuzzy borders are artifacts caused by saving a moving video frame as a bitmap, where the interlacing is showing up as slightly offset lines.

## Interlacing

Television frames are recorded in two parts. If you take your fingers and interlock them, you'll get the idea. The reason this was decided upon (sometime around 1937) was to prevent motion across the screen from causing a lagging effect between the time the signal started to be displayed at the upper left and was finished at the lower right. The scan time was cut in half by displaying only half of the lines, then scanning a second time for the other half of the lines. Each half is called a *field*. Today's solid-state (no tubes) technology makes interlacing unnecessary, but there it still is.

I go into such depth only because there is a conflict in standards being sorted out right now. Computer monitors are not interlaced. TV screens are interlaced. Soon the two will converge. To interlace or not to interlace, that is the question. Whether 'tis better on the screen to suffer the slings and arrows of noninterlaced video, or to take arms against a sea of standards and by merging, view them. Interlacing is discussed in more detail in the digital television section later in this chapter.

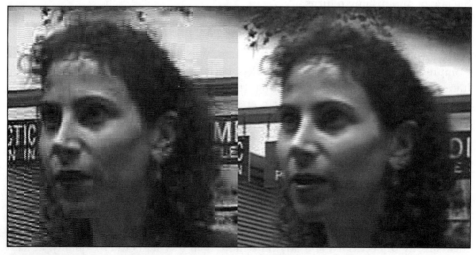

**Figure 12.8**    High versus low compression.

### *Algorithms*

The two main compression algorithms in use are motion JPEG and MPEG. Motion JPEG is simply JPEG applied to video, whereas MPEG is a video-specific algorithm. JPEG stands for Joint Photographic Experts Group, and MPEG stands for Motion Picture Experts Group, and as far as I know, these groups are completely separate.

JPEG is a *lossy* algorithm, and each frame in the video is compressed separately as an individual picture. MPEG, on the other hand, works by compressing one full frame called a *key frame* or an *I-frame*, and sending a series of frames that contain only the differences between the key frame and that frame, called *delta frames*, continuing with another key frame, and so on. Because of this, MPEG video is a lot harder to work with and more expensive to encode.

Originally, MPEG encoding required so much processing that it could only be done by a dedicated encoding board, but computing power has increased to the point where software encoding is now practical. MPEG can give a compression ratio of up to 200:1 and is constantly being improved. MPEG is the current standard for consumer digital video including most, if not all, CD ROM and DVD products.

## Frame Size

Frame size is the bottom line as far as bandwidth goes and we can measure this in KB/frame. Recall the discussion about modem bandwidth. A single frame of $640 \times 480$ full-screen video at 5:1 compression takes 108KB. Think of it as a still picture and you'll get the idea. This means that only five minutes of full-motion, full-screen video will take 1GB to store or download. At 10:1 compression this goes down to only 60KB per frame, at 20:1 it is 30KB/frame, and at 30:1 it's 20KB/frame (now down to about 200MB for the five-minute video).

If we compromise and cut to a quarter screen with 10:1 compression, we now get 15KB per frame, and if we then cut the frame rate to 15fps, the five minutes take only 25MB. Even this low-quality image is still way over the top for today's modems. The only way video is going to be viable on the Internet is to get everybody using the high-speed cable and ADSL modems currently being implemented by cable TV and telephone companies.

## Digital Video

As noted earlier, Digital Video is video that is recorded digitally. Before the introduction of digital editing systems for television, video was recorded on one tape, transferred to another tape for editing (because you always want to keep your master tape in pristine condition), then edited onto a third tape, which was then used to make copies. This means that you are now three or four *generations* down from the master, and you experience what is called *generation loss*. This is the main reason professional video recording equipment is so expensive. The quality of the original image has to be high enough to suffer this amount of loss in quality and still be good enough for broadcast.

Digital Video recording blows all that away. Because the original signal is digital, now your final copy can be just as good as your master tape, so you don't need a $30,000 camera to make broadcast-quality video. In fact, ENG (Electronic News Gathering) is now being done with cameras like the new Sony VX1000 that you can buy for a paltry $4,000.

The compression standard for Digital Video is 5:1, which is built right in to the file formats, so you're not going to see much of this on the Internet until the bandwidth comes up remarkably. The funny thing about Digital Video is that when you transfer the digitized video from the camera to the computer, you're actually just doing a file copy, and it does not have to be done in real time, meaning the speed at which the video was recorded. It could be faster or slower and it wouldn't matter because it's just data. Timing only counts for video playback.

## Putting Video on the Web

The real question here is, what kind of video is the Web ready for? Only those who have ADSL or cable modems can view Web video with any quality, and these are becoming more readily available. Testing the G2 player running on a 384MB/second line, which equates to either a partial T1 (a high-speed connection option offered by the phone company) or bidirectional ADSL line (which sacrifices some of the high download speed of ADSL for a higher upload speed), I find that it can almost display a 160 × 120 video with CD quality audio in real time, meaning you don't have to wait for it to download.

Figure 12.9 shows how encoding video with RealPublisher is just as easy as point and click.

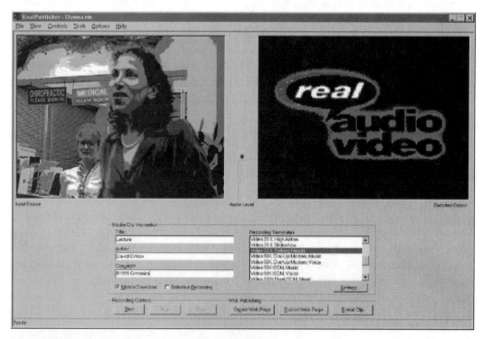

**Figure 12.9**    RealPublisher video encoding screen.

In just a few years there may be enough high-speed new technology modems installed to make Web video practical. Just as there are now RealAudio splitting servers all over the world, there will have to be some kind of channel for video as well. This idea has at least started with a project called the MBONE, or *Multicast Backbone*, which provides multicasting services for audio and video with the goal of integrating its multicasting protocol into the set of standard Internet protocols.

This leads to the concept of a specialized video server, something that would be the video counterpart of the multicast audio server, that would do nothing but deliver video across the Web over dedicated channels. Video servers are not a thing of the future. They exist today, but only on private networks within television stations and video production houses where they can run at full-bore Ethernet speed. To find out more about these you can get involved in the digital video world through trade publications such as *Digital Video* magazine (www.dv.com).

## INFORMATIVE SITES!

*www.real.com*
**RealNetworks provides information on G2, streaming audio and video authoring, SMIL, and more.**

*www.liveupdate.com*
**This site is home of the Crescendo player and includes information on streaming MIDI and integrating G2 with Forte.**

*www.w3.org/AudioVideo/*
**The W3C Audio, Video, and Synchronized Multimedia site offers information about multimedia on the Web, including links to a great tutorial on SMIL.**

*www.truespeech.com*
**DSP Group Inc.'s True Speech Digital Speech Technology features low-bandwidth streaming speech delivery.**

*www.vdolive.com*
**Club VDO offers Videophone, Videoconferencing, Videomail, and more streaming video.**

*www.vivo.com*
**Vivo Software Inc.'s homepage offers VideoNow, another product that creates streaming media for the PC and the Mac.**

*www.vosaic.com*
**Vosaic Corp.'s homepage offers information on streaming media with an accent towards business and multicasting.**

*www.xingtech.com*
**Xing Technology Corporation offers streaming MPEG and is oriented toward high-bandwidth delivery technology.**

*www.microsoft.com/ntserver/nts/mediaserv*
**Microsoft Media Services provides streaming media for NT servers.**

# Digital Television and HDTV

Digital television and HDTV are two different things. Digital television is simply television transmitted digitally. HDTV (High Definition Television) is one specific standard within the digital television realm. HDTV transmits a signal with as many as 1,100 lines of vertical resolution at a 16:9 aspect ratio, which is the same you see on the big screen, 16 units wide by 9 units high. This means the signal contains about four or five times as much information as our analog TV signals. It is comparable to revving up the resolution on your monitor to a whopping 1920 × 1080, which is as high as it will go. If it weren't bad enough trying to download video at 160 × 120, now what are we doing to do?

There are in fact many accepted standards for digital television, as shown in Table 12.2. Most standards are not interlaced but are *progressive,* meaning one continuous scan from top to bottom. Only 1080i is interlaced because at 60fps there is not enough bandwidth in the FCC assigned channels for transmitting progressive scans. Depending on whom you ask, HDTV is either the highest-quality 1080 alone or either of the higher-quality 720 or 1080 standards. The 480 standard is what some people would like to see replace current broadcasts with a digital format, that's also compatible with computer monitors, without going to increased resolutions. Based on the fact that 480 digital is still better than 525 analog, this would leave bandwidth for more digital channels.

There is a huge debate now among those in the broadcasting industry because the federal government has issued a mandate that digital television broadcasts were to begin in 1998. The argument centers around the question: "Why should we spend all our TV bandwidth on a single HDTV channel when we could broadcast several channels at normal resolution?" The answer is not available yet; however, HDTV is still a novelty in the United States. Japan has had an analog version of 1080 HDTV for years.

The Federal government has set a goal that within five years, all TV broadcasts be switched to digital. This means that everyone is going to have to either buy a new TV or get a converter. Either way, the new TVs and the new converters will be programmed to accept a variety of digital TV formats and standards until the standards issue is resolved. Maybe we'll just have to deal with all the options for some time to come.

This is all important because, as I mentioned earlier, it is inevitable that the television and computer monitor will converge into a single instrument. The questions are, how will this happen, how will it affect Internet video as far as bandwidth goes, and how will the Internet feed back to digital television? Right now, it's hard to say.

**Table 12.2**    Digital Television Standards

| NAME | VERTICAL RESOLUTION | HORIZONTAL RESOLUTION | INTERLACED? | FRAME RATE |
|---|---|---|---|---|
| 480p | 480 pixels | 640 pixels | Progressive | 24, 30, 60 |
| 720p | 720 pixels | 1024 pixels | Progressive | 24, 30, 60 |
| 1080p | 1080 pixels | 1920 pixels | Progressive | 24, 30 |
| 1080i | 1080 pixels | 1920 pixels | Interlaced | 60 |

# VRML

VRML (Virtual Reality Modeling Language), or "vermal," is meant to create 3D worlds that we can explore through the Internet. Actually, VRML is not considered a true modeling language but a 3D exchange format. In order for VRML to do its job, a 3D world has to be created, saved in VRML format, and downloaded and interpreted by a VRML player.

There are two primary reasons why we haven't seen more of VRML: First, it's an incredibly complex language. VRML is filled with huge tables of numbers that lend description to virtual objects. Although there are more VRML authoring tools coming out every month, these aren't as easy to use as a drag-and-drop HTML editor.

If you've ever done any 3D modeling you know that for every 3D object you have to specify a huge number of parameters. Once you have the basic shape down (a task of its own that takes quite a bit of practice), you have to assign it a position, orientation, size, surface, texture, transparency, color, and brightness. If you want it to move, that's another story. In short, objects aren't really that hard to create, but it takes a lot of patience and understanding to make things look the way you want.

Second, VRML files are rather large. Aside from the new VRML banner ads, a small VRML world may only take 250K; a large one can take several megabytes. Displaying VRML worlds also puts a heavy load on the processor, so between file size and number crunching, this does not yet lend itself to quick viewing.

Yet VRML holds incredible promise for the future of the Internet in many areas. For example:

- Online shopping can be conducted with actual 3D models of products.

- Educational sites offer 3D representations of the actual subject, including things that cannot be seen, such as molecular construction and abstract 3D data representation.

- Entertainment sites offer 3D games and animation.

- Animated VRML ad banners offer animated Internet commercials.

Currently, the Cosmo player is the dominant player for what there is of VRML on the Web. Figure 12.10 shows a VR world that can be found at www.blitcom.net. Blitcom is one of the companies developing technology for streaming VRML, which promises to overcome the problem of waiting to download large VRML world files.

If you look along the bottom of the screen, you'll see the Cosmo player controls that allow you to do such things as zoom, tilt, pan, float, and anything that involves moving through the virtual world.

More applications, tools, and implementations of VRML are certain to come our way in the next few years. This is one technology that has hardly scratched the surface of its Internet potential.

We're going to take a look at where the Internet is heading today in two parts: hardware in the form of architecture and protocols, and software in the form of markup languages.

**Figure 12.10** "Bliss.com", VRML Cyber-grrrl.

## INFORMATIVE SITES!

*www.vrml.org*
The VRML Consortium provides links to anything and everything about VRML!

*vrml.sdsu.edu*
San Diego State University VRML Repository is another site with links to anything and everything about VRML!

*www.cosmosoftware.com*
Cosmo Software is the maker of the Cosmo VRML player/viewer, and this site provides tons of data on VRML.

*www.verbal-imagery.com*
The Verbal Imagery site belongs to Andrea Ames, a VRML guru I met at Web98.

*www.blitcom.net*
Streaming VRML may be available online by our publication time!

# The Future

Where is Internet technology heading today? That's a wide-open question, especially considering that in the few months between completing this book and its publication that an Internet year will pass in which whole trends could be started, new technologies released, and announcements made about some new company's Big Plans.

## Architecture and Protocols

Speaking of Big Plans, there are several in progress right now to bring into being an Internet with speeds 100 to 1000 times faster than what is today's Internet. These networks are being developed, and in fact by early 1999 are going to be up and running (at least in their early phases).

These include:

- NGI (Next Generation Internet)
- Internet2 and the Abilene Project
- vBNS (very high-performance Backbone Network Service)

### *Next Generation Internet*

NGI is a U.S. government enterprise. It evolved from a need to recover the connectivity advantage the key federal agencies involved in the original Internet had when the Internet was primarily a service facility for government and academic research. Not only is the NGI a U.S. government agency concern, it is being funded to the tune of $500 million over a five-year period that started in 1998.

The plan is not to build a new fiber optic network from scratch, but to utilize existing networks already in place to build a network in parallel with the existing Internet backbone. The important difference from the way the Internet is currently configured is that the Next Generation Internet does not have its ultra-high-speed connections limited by low-bandwidth routing bottlenecks. The connections are to be ultra-high-speed from start to finish.

The first goal is to build a network of 100 selected sites that will deliver 100Mbps connectivity between all nodes in the entire network. The second goal is to take 10 selected sites and deliver 1Gbps connectivity. Finally, the third goal is to achieve the technological capability to deliver a 1 Terabyte/second connection. At the same time, new and innovative applications are to be developed to take advantage of this incredible bandwidth.

The government agencies involved in planning and development include:

- DARPA (Defense Advanced Research Project Agency), a founding agency of the original Internet
- DOE (Department of Energy)
- NASA (National Aeronautics and Space Administration)

- NSF (National Science Foundation), another current generation Internet founder

- NIST (National Institute of Standards and Technology)

The NGI Implementation Plan, as of February 1998, is available online at www.ccic.gov/implementation, and it states the following:
"The NGI initiative has three goals:

1. To advance research, development, and experimentation in the next generation of networking technologies to add functionality and improve performance.

2. To develop a Next Generation Internet testbed, emphasizing end-to-end performance, to support networking research and demonstrate new networking technologies. This testbed will connect at least 100 NGI sites—universities, federal research institutions, and other research partners—at speeds 100 times faster than today's Internet, and will connect on the order of 10 sites at speeds 1,000 times faster than the current Internet.

3. To develop and demonstrate revolutionary applications that meet important national goals and missions and that rely on the advances made in goals 1 and 2. These applications are not possible on today's Internet."

Table 12.3 shows the five-year timetable for the NGI from their implementation plan.

**Table 12.3** NGI Time Line Summary

| DELIVERABLES | FIRST ACHIEVED |
| --- | --- |
| 100+ site high-performance testbed providing OC-3 (155Mbps) connections over OC-12 (644Mbps) infrastructure | 1999 |
| Federal, academic, and industry partnerships conducting applications/networking research on the 100x testbed | 1999 |
| 10+ site ultra-high-performance testbed providing OC-48 connections (2.5Gbps) | 2000 |
| Networking/applications research conducted on the 1,000x testbed | 2001 |
| Tested models for NGI protocols, management tools, QoS (Quality of Service) provisions, security, and advanced services | 2000 |
| 100+ high-value applications being tested over the high-performance testbed (for example, remote, real time, collaborative NGI network control of select laboratories) | 2000 |
| Integrate QoS over a variety of technologies and carriers | 2001 |
| Terabit-per-second packet switching demonstrated | 2002 |
| 10+ advanced applications being tested over the ultra-high-performance testbed | 2002 |

# INFORMATIVE SITES!

*www.ngi.gov*
**Next Generation Internet (NGI) Initiative is the NGI homepage.**

*www.ccic.gov/implementation*
**The NGI Implementation Plan is available through the National Coordination Office for Computing, Information, and Communications).**

*smithsonian.yahoo.com/nextgeneration.html*
**Yahoo! Next Generation Internet site is Yahoo!'s tribute to cutting-edge developments in Internet connectivity.**

## Internet2 and the Abilene Project

I2 is very similar to NGI. The difference is that it was originated by the academic community and is a project that involves over 150 universities and private corporations under the banner of the UCAID (University Corporation for Advanced Internet Development).

I2 does not have access to the government funding that the NGI does, but it's not far behind, receiving nearly as much funding from its corporate members. Nevertheless, I2 will also be working with NGI, and many I2 sites will also be test sites on the NGI network, so NGI's federal funding will also end up helping the I2 project as well. The real difference is that I2 is run by the academic and business sectors for their own interests, which are different from the interests of the U.S. government.

The I2 project evolved through the need to improve Internet connectivity over that which the original Internet delivered. The Internet that used to belong to the academic and research world has now become a worldwide enterprise that has left the original members at the same place they were five years ago. Since that time, data communications technology has evolved to the point where it is now possible to improve the speed of Internet connections from the sub-100Mbps bandwidth average of the past to super-Gbps multimedia capability and beyond.

I2 will not be building a new network, but like NGI will be buying into existing high-speed networks, and this will be easier for I2 because the speed goals are not quite as high as those of NGI. In fact, I2 was expected to be online by the end of 1998. These bandwidth goals were outlined as:

- Desktop access: 10Mbps
- Campus LAN backbone: 500Mbps
- I2 network connectivity: 155Mbps

I2 calls the points of access to the high-speed networks *GigaPoPs* (Gigabit capacity Points of Presence), and it looks like this term is going to be around for a while.

Just as the original NSF backbone provided Internet connectivity through NAPs, as discussed in Chapter 1, "What Has the Internet Become?," the I2 GigaPoPs will actually be implemented as NAPs to vBNS. Whereas I2 is involved with vBNS as a backbone provider, the Abilene Project is a completely separate network intended to provide I2 with superior connectivity.

Abilene is a special project also run by the UCAID, and their goal is to go beyond the bandwidth goals of I2 and set up a network that will deliver bandwidth to GigaPoP connections as high as possible, meaning OC-192 at 9.6Gbps and beyond! And like NGI, Abilene expects to go online in early 1999 and that their Research and Development timetable will run about five years.

Internet2 is not by any means a final goal. There is talk of Internet3, Internet4, and . . .

## INFORMATIVE SITES!
**www.Internet2.edu**
**Find out all about I2 at the UCAID I2 homepage.**

**www.ucaid.edu/abilene**
**Find out all about Abilene at the UCAID Abilene homepage.**

## vBNS

In 1995, the National Science Foundation and MCI began a five-year venture together to accomplish the same goals as NGI and I2, only they were first. Like I2, vBNS is primarily in the interests of its originators. It was intended to return the NSF to the superior connectivity of their early Internet days, only in today's optical fiber terms. As a result, the NSF now has a private OC-12 622Mbps backbone for its supercomputing network, as shown in Figure 12.11.

As mentioned earlier, vBNS is the main network provider for the first phase of I2, assuming that Abilene will take over at some point. Not to be outdone by Abilene, vBNS expects to upgrade to OC-48 2.4Gbps bandwidth in 1999. And one can certainly expect that the future of an alliance between a supercomputing organization and a major communications company will not stop at anything short of the fastest connections imaginable.

The three networks discussed here, NGI, Abilene, and vBNS, are all designed to take advantage of the latest in Internet technologies, including IPv6 (discussed in Chapter 2, "How Does the Internet Work?"), streaming media, and multicasting. The incredible investment of time and money spent on this project is very exciting since, between the U.S. government and corporate interests, it looks like a good billion dollars is going to go into these broadband Internet R&D projects. Keep in mind that access to the highest-bandwidth connections is going to be reserved for those at the top of the Internet food chain, meaning high-priority government communications traffic and big money research networks. But the public will certainly get a much improved Internet in many ways.

## INFORMATIVE SITE!
**www.vbns.net**
**Find out all about MCI's and NSF's very high-speed Backbone Network Service from the MCI vBNS Web site.**

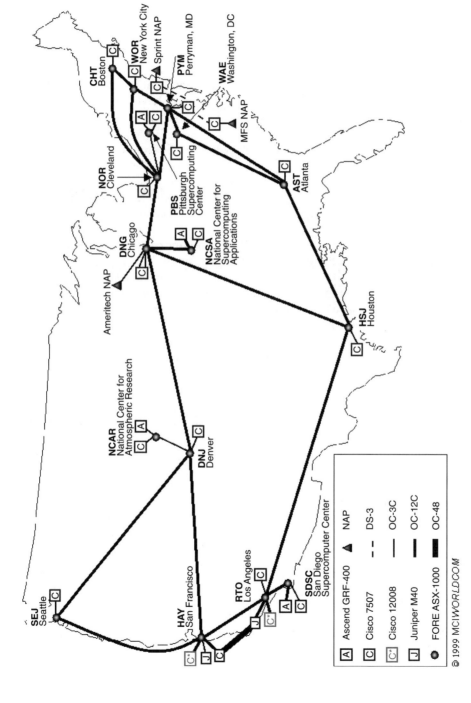

**Figure 12.11** Twenty-first century backbone.

# Markup Languages

The markup world is currently undergoing a transformation with XML, challenging HTML's dominance and offering new and better solutions to at least some of the difficulties involved in an HTML-only world. This metamorphosis is affecting two areas: the display of Internet content and the storage of Internet data.

## HTML and XML

XML is getting a lot of attention these days. Some think that it will replace HTML, others think it's overrated. Our interviews with Microsoft have shown that XML has found its place in data storage and communication, but the jury is still out on its role in the markup world.

It is at this point anyone's guess as to what the future holds for HTML and XML. Not only are developers busy at work thinking up new ways to use these languages, but the standards for parts of the XML world haven't even been finalized yet. At present, XML engines are built into both Explorer and Navigator and are capable of applying style sheets to XML code through the XSL language to generate displayable HTML documents.

Scripting capability is even built into XML by including the scripting statements in the HTML code generated by XSL. XSL (eXtensible Stylesheet Language) is the XML counterpart of CSS, but XSL goes beyond CSS in that XSL does not just define styles, but assigns HTML tags, attributes, and styles to XML content based on rules defined in the XSL style sheet. These rules can be extremely sophisticated and are designed specifically for the XML document.

Once the HTML is generated, the DHTML is no different than what we're already used to, but fitting the script into the XSL code turns out to be more difficult than sticking to conventional DHTML. Then if you want to add a server-side script, we're back where we started, having to embedding XML as a data format within a script within a conventional Web page.

The main feature that seems to be missing from XML is a better solution to create a "Dynamic XML." I believe the process of implementing better interactivity within XML will most likely be guided by the model that is currently followed in generating Web pages, shown in Figure 12.12 and detailed next.

As a Web page is transferred from server to client it goes through several stages of interpretation and translation, starting with server-side scripting all the way through the interactive content replacement of Dynamic HTML. This can be broken down into the following steps, useful toward understanding a more universal content delivery model.

1. The interpretation and translation begins with a Web page and its associated files residing on a server.

2. When the page is accessed, the server reads the file and executes any server-side script.

3. The server then creates a modified version of the Web page that is transmitted to the client.

4. When the client receives the page, it interprets the page executing any client-side script.

5. The client then passes this modified Web page to its display engine, which displays the Web page including any Dynamic HTML scripting that will be executed interactively by the user.

Between HTML and XML, there are currently two different models for adding server, client, and dynamic scripting into a Web page. The HTML model is illustrated in Figure 12.13 and shows all of the scripting options built into the HTML along with the style sheet. True, we can separate the style sheet and DHTML scripting out into their own files, but these files are still read in and interpreted according to this same model.

In the XML model shown in Figure 12.14 (as interpreted by myself according to the facts at hand at this moment and subject to change at the whim of any authoritative Internet body), we have quite a different story.

First of all, the style sheet is separated into its own XSL language file. The way XSL works is that it contains a set of rules that are applied to a particular XML tag to create the appropriate HTML markup. This means all the HTML ends up in the XSL style sheet, including any scripting that is to be interpreted by the browser on the client side. If that is as far as we wanted to go, all that would be needed is the XML file and the XSL file.

If we do want to go further and perform scripting on the server side, we have to again invert the process and use a scripting language to generate the XML and its style sheet. This could be JavaScript embedded in HTML, XML embedded in PERL, or something else like ASP.

This server-side scripting process should be pretty common since the whole point of XML is to support interactive data structures without display attributes. So right away this puts a whole new twist on XML, at least in its current form.

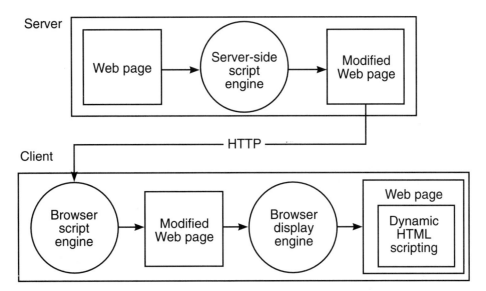

**Figure 12.12**   Web language processing path.

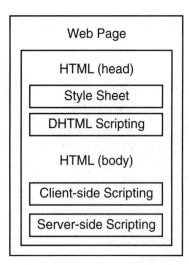

**Figure 12.13** HTML model for dynamic scripting.

In the area of data storage, one area that has avoided examination is search engine indexing. XML has the potential of bringing a revolution to search engine discovery and cataloging, including the potential for a new way to tell search engines how content should be cataloged instead of leaving it to the search engine itself to figure out.

But whatever happens with markup languages, there are several areas of emerging technology that will be integrated in new ways in the near future, including all the technologies we have reviewed in the last 12 chapters.

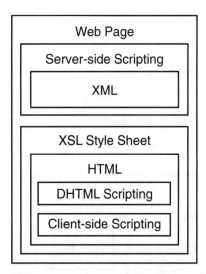

**Figure 12.14** XML model for dynamic scripting.

*Kevin Epstein, Real Networks*

RealNetworks is located in downtown Seattle. These guys, like all Internet companies, only started a few years ago, yet they now take up several floors in a large office building. In case you didn't know, RealNetworks makes software that plays audio and video files over the Internet, like RealPlayer, and server software for multimedia streaming.

The entrance is way up on the 31st floor and the windows face out to Puget Sound, one of the largest inland waterways in the United States. You have to admit, this would be a pretty nice place to work.

*What exactly do you do at RealNetworks?*
I'm the Server Product Manager. It basically involves coordinating the entire product management and launch cycle. Some places product management focuses more on the engineering side, other places it focuses more on outbound marketing. I'd say that the job I'm doing right now has a good quotient of outbound marketing, spending time training the sales people, tracking sales, doing pricing, product placement promotion, all of that good standard marketing stuff.

But also, in my case, product management certainly has a large element of inbound side. Talking to customers, getting feedback on the product, thinking about the impact and the shape of new features and new products, and then working directly with the engineering teams to see those things spec'd out and built and tested.

*That sounds like a huge job. I've been studying the RealNetworks products line and it's interesting in that the high profile product that people see is the player, but that seems to be backed up by this humongous server technology. I've looked at the different products that you have on the server line and I'm trying to understand them a little better. Can you help me out?*
Sure, I can go into the multiple details. Much like any product, you want to have flavors, or versions, for a wide range of audiences. There will be folks who are just starting out with audio and video who want to do something very simple. You've got a small Web site and all you want to do is put up some A/V like home movies converted to video, or conversations, what have you. And for folks like that we want to have a nice straightforward, easy-to-use, guides-you-through-the-steps type of product.

On the high end, if you're CNN or someone like that, obviously you probably would be willing to sacrifice some of the ease of use for power and additional functionality. If you think about video cameras, for instance, there's a significant difference between the little portable home video cam and the standard TV news industrial video cam.

What we're trying to do is do the same thing on the software side. So on the low end we've got something we call the basic server. There's a free version, which is truly the Basic Server, and then a paid-for version, the Basic Server Plus that has a few additional features and functionality. And that's for the basic person starting out. And then on the higher end we have our Internet solution and our Commerce solution. When you say solution instead of server it correctly implies that it comes with more than just the software. The software itself is more fully featured, and then it comes with a set of tools, and a set of additional services and support. At the core of it, it comes down to this great server software that delivers audio, video, text, and other multimedia data types. Just like the flavors of handy cam versus video cam, we have different levels.

*I was looking at the free version, which was something you can just download and install under your own personal Web account. How many streams does that support?*
The free one these days is the basic server and at this point I think it supports somewhere between 25 and 60 streams. It varies. We basically try and design the free server to have enough stream capacity to fill a T1 line.

*Now we have HTTP streaming, and then you have something else?*
There are actually two protocol issues. There's HTTP streaming, as you pointed out, if you create a RealAudio or RealVideo file and just put it on your Web site it will stream via HTTP just the way a Web page will. The concern there is that there's no control protocol. HTTP was designed for packet data delivery. Great for Web pages, but for consistent even data flow, it's not originally what it was designed for, so you end up with a situation where if you want to do pause, play, fast forward, if you encounter data loss while you're transmitting it will break up significantly. HTTP was never really designed to do a nice smooth, even data flow.

So instead we use something else. The old version was "pnm," but the new version, RealSystem G2, is the first player to use the open RTSP, or Real Time Streaming Protocol which is an IETF open, published, anybody can build a server that uses it. We happen to be the first because this is our primary business. We keep an eye on these things and aggressively participate in these standards bodies to contribute our knowledge and expertise. So our RealSystem G2 server uses RTSP versus HTTP. The advantage that gives you is that this is a protocol that was designed to compensate for the fact that those dropped packets is not a consistent flow of information.

*Plus HTTP has a pretty high overhead, doesn't it?*
Yes, exactly. HTTP uses, underneath it, TCP and that was designed to make sure you got every bit of data, which is great if you're looking for a Web page or a document and don't want to be missing some words. But it's not so great if you're trying to get video or audio for a smooth experience because the fact is, if you're watching a movie and you snipped out a few frames of that movie, you'd hardly notice it. You'd see a flicker, perhaps. But the overall experience would be great as opposed to watching the movie, and you're watching and watching and oops! You're missing those frames so the movie stops and waits for someone to replace those frames and then keeps going. It's a much more disconcerting experience.

The advantage is RTSP, which uses UDP (User Datagram Protocol) as the underlying protocol, versus HTTP using TCP. HTTP using TCP is the situation where you stop the movie and you wait for every frame and UDP just keeps on blasting along.

*UDP doesn't wait for the acknowledgments, it just keeps going. [UDP is a parallel to TCP and is called a connectionless protocol because once the communication line is established it does not depend on receiving data back from the other end confirming receipt of transmissions. During these brief periods of UDP transmission you're actually using UDP/IP instead of TCP/IP.]*
Exactly, no acknowledgment, no resend; if you miss a packet you just keep going.

*I was looking at what makes G2 special, is the streaming combined with SMIL.*
If I was to pick three things that made RealSystem G2, and there are a lot more than three, but if I was to pick the top three that really made it something unique, I'd say it's the use of SMIL, it's the extensibility of the system to do streaming of native data types,

and its use of some neat technologies like SureStream to compensate for the variability of the Internet. And in that order: SMIL, data types, and SureStream.

SMIL looks like HTML. It is XML, which is a tag language. It lets you do what HTML did for Web pages, for synchronized multimedia in a time sense, a choreographed time sense. It lets you take different elements that would have appeared in a static sense like a picture, a title, an audio clip, and in a very simple language, say, in the window put the video on top with the title underneath, put the audio behind it, and at 50 seconds into the presentation bring in this picture on the side.

*Yeah, I saw a demo on the Web and I was very impressed.*
The fact is that most multimedia, you don't pause to think about this when you're watching TV these days, but multimedia isn't just audio or video. If you watch a standard news broadcast, the audio and video will be the main focus but then you'll have a stock ticker along the bottom, you'll have the CNN logo in the corner, you'll have a little icon when they talk about the latest news story that appears next to the talking head. And those are all multiple elements that aren't just audio and video. Audio, video, images, text, different types of audio like the CNN blurb audio versus the actual voice talking over versus the background music and the commercial.

So the ability to synchronize all these elements is extremely important, and logically. And SMIL is an open standard that allows folks to do that and again, being an open standard is great, because it means we don't have to build all the pieces. No one can go out and create a world by themselves, so we can rely on or ask others or provide the opportunity to others to build tools, to build other SMIL-compliant players and SMIL compliant content and expand the universe that way.

*It's an interesting concept, having an entire news broadcast controlled by some computer language.*
It's a script. SMIL reduced to its most elemental terms is a script. It's choreography for a multimedia presentation. So SMIL was item one. Item two was this concept of extensibility. In RealSystem G2 we took this very straightforward audio video streaming and said, well, why should we focus on streaming certain types of audio and video? Let's design a system that's an engine underneath that talks this RTSP and UDP protocol and then you can plug in chunks of code on top of that to stream different data types. So, in other words, once the computer understands the data type, all packets are just 1s and 0s.

*The idea of streaming text struck me. What is that, a piece of text that just keeps going, that's not static, like a time-based text?*
Imagine the difference between reading a page of text in the browser versus a page of text streamed to the browser. If you're downloading it, you connect, you wait x number of seconds while in the background the text comes to your browser and then the whole page is sitting there and you can scroll up and down the page. The question is, since you're only reading one line at a time anyway why shouldn't the first few lines start appearing as the data comes to your computer? Then by the time you get to the bottom, the rest of it will have appeared.

*People think in text in such a static way because text is everywhere, but the idea of time-based text is different.*
It's more than just time-based. If you're to generalize one more step, the primary difference between streaming and downloading is, downloading sends you a big few blobs and then

once the data is at your computer, renders it. Versus streaming, which starts sending the data in a thin long stream and starts rendering it as soon as it gets to your computer, so again the end result is the same, you end up with data on your computer but it uses the bandwidth differently. If you have thin bandwidth, particularly or you have a long presentation, you'll notice the difference. If everybody had fiber optics to their house you could in theory take a full-length movie, spend five minutes downloading it, and watch it.

So concept one is SMIL, concept two is the idea that we built this architecture that you can plug any data type into and stream it. It's fairly novel because players have existed for a long time that will play things when they're sitting on your hard drive. How many things can you think of that will read text documents off your hard drive? Tons of them. Or things that will play .WAV files? There are literally hundreds of tools out there that you can download to your computer that will play it. But the concept of streaming these things is very new and we're in fact the only folks right now who stream data as opposed to playing it locally. There are a lot of companies out there that will say we play anything. The answer is yes, but playing doesn't matter; it's streaming it that's the hard part, across the Internet with a smooth flow.

*That's why I was impressed with the integration with MIDI because, especially if you have a good sound card, you get such a much higher quality, because you don't have to stream the high bandwidth. Howard Stern used to do this commercial, which one is the CD and which one is the tape, and I could always tell because the crisp highs come off the CD but they're missing from the tape.*

Item three that's neat about G2 is this concept called SureStream. The idea is that we do have different bandwidths, everybody has different bandwidths, and you want the appropriate data type and bandwidth stream delivered to you.

*Is this scalability what the SureStream is all about?*

Yes, SureStream is scalable. SureStream is this concept of, when you initially create a streamed file why should you have to pick your audience ahead of time, why should you have to say, I'm going to create audio and it's going to be voice audio for 28.8? Oh wait, now my audience is listening in the office, I'm going to create voice and music, there's a good bandwidth for it at 100 kilobits per second. Instead, this concept of SureStream says, use our encoding technology to compress and encode all the bandwidths you want into one file. And then, and this is the subtlety, not just two or three bandwidths but as many as you want, 6, 8, 10, 12, and then, while the person is listening, adjust the bandwidth appropriately! This is new. The concept that when you're listening to something across the Internet, just as in your car you can listen to the radio and you get bad reception in some areas and good reception in others. Well, the Internet, if you're logged on early morning on a Sunday I expect that there are fewer people on the 'Net, there's less traffic, data flows better versus a high traffic time.

*So it adapts to the bandwidth dynamically?*

Exactly, just because I have a 28.8 modem doesn't mean I'm always going to get 28.8 throughput. In fact, literally, I can connect at 28.8 and then while I'm online have things slow down. That's happened to the best of us; you can't control it. And yes, this dynamically adjusts in real time, dropping or raising the stream being sent to you, so it's kind of neat. Because it's the principle of, if you're listening to music you'd rather have the music get fuzzier than have it stop, rebuffer, and restart.

*It's interesting that how if the audio input is broken up something becomes incomprehensible, but if the video is broken up they kind of fill it in, in their head.* And if the audio input becomes fuzzy, like if I put my face further away from the phone, like this, you can still understand what I'm saying. Versus if I stop . . . and restart . . . like this. So SureStream says you'd rather listen to an ongoing fuzzy stream than a perfect clarity, broken up stream, and adjusts accordingly.

*But with the video it's better to have it broken up than fuzzy, so it's the opposite.* So what happens is it literally adjusts accordingly. With video it will drop frames so the video will be crisp, but will start slowing down, as it were.

*Multimedia seems to be the culmination of everything because you get all these Web technologies and you put them together and now you've got to do something with it, and the future of the Web is going to be in interactive and motion and high bandwidth.* What I've sort of come to at the end as a conclusion is the Web, when you come right down to it, it's a communications medium. And anything that can be done, or was done before for different types of communications media, may or may not be appropriate for the Web. But certainly multimedia is a very efficient form of communication, so it's not illogical to see it head in that direction.

*What about Next Generation Internet and all this high-bandwidth stuff they're going after? Along with the flexibility of the new streaming technologies, do you guys have any outlook on that?* SureStream is a kind of early indicator on that. One of the things that we've always followed is, go with the best technology that's out there. RealAudio wanted to work with audio only, 14.4 modem, very, very sort of elemental, but of course that's where everyone was at that point. As we've moved forward we've continued to improve at the low end, so if you listen, for instance we still support 14.4 audio. We can stream audio at levels that might even work over a 9600 baud modem. So if you go listen to our low end audio, compare the RealAudio one with RealSystem G2, apples and apples at that low bandwidth, it's much better. We've significantly improved it. At the same time, we have SureStream, we have higher bandwidth technologies.

At this point we've shown off what is essentially full-motion 30 frames per second video at 100 kilobits to 1 to 2 megabits. We can stream MPEG 1, not a problem, so we're certainly prepared for the high end and we're obviously aggressively looking into where does this thing go? We've got satellite, multicast, fiber optics, and ADSL. It all points to interesting, new, different forms of bandwidth.

The answer is, who knows where it will go, but we've followed the market to date and innovated by pushing the market in certain areas. The modularity of RealSystem G2 combined with the new technologies like SureStream really put us in the position where, if people stick with the existing data types great, we've got improvements on those. If bandwidth comes up, great, SureStream will take care of that. You can encode megabit SureStream right now and that content will still then be useful when you've got megabit transmission. At the same time, the extensibility of the system says if someone comes up with new data types we just plug them in.

*What do you think it will take to get full-motion, full-screen video in the home?* Computer processing power has gone up, bandwidth has gone up, and at the same time requirements due to compression have gone down. We can do it on lower end machines at much lower data rates right now, so there's still a slight disconnect because you still have the majority of people on really low bandwidth modems on 28.8 and the majority of video requiring say, 100 to 200 kilobits minimum. So we're still a little ways apart, but not that far. People are certainly upgrading, getting cable modems and so forth, and bandwidth needs are still falling. Even a year ago you pretty much wanted 300 kilobits and now we're down to more like 100, so somewhere they're going to meet.

*Thanks, Kevin!*

## Thank You!

I sincerely expect that you have learned a great deal from what you have studied here. Now that you have reached the end, it is time for you to choose an area to get involved in and explore more deeply. Whatever area this may be, good luck in your new Internet career.

# Internet Standards Index

0013    Domain Name System. P. Mockapetris. November 1987. (Also RFC1034, RFC1035)

0014    Mail Routing and the Domain System. C. Partridge. January 1986. (Also RFC0974)

0015    Simple Network Management Protocol. J. Case, M. Fedor, M. Schoffstall, J. Davin. May 1990. (Also RFC1157)

0016    Structure of Management Information. M. Rose, K. McCloghrie. May 1990. (Also RFC1155, RFC1212)

0017    Management Information Base. K. McCloghrie, M. Rose. March 1991. (Also RFC1213)

0018    Exterior Gateway Protocol. D. Mills. April 1984. (Also RFC0904)

0019    NetBIOS Service Protocols. NetBIOS Working Group. March 1987. (Also RFC1001, RFC1002)

0020    Echo Protocol. J. Postel. May 1983. (Also RFC0862)

0021    Discard Protocol. J. Postel. May 1983. (Also RFC0863)

0022    Character Generator Protocol. J. Postel. May 1983. (Also RFC0864)

0023    Quote of the Day Protocol. J. Postel. May 1983. (Also RFC0865)

0024    Active Users Protocol. J. Postel. May 1983. (Also RFC0866)

0025    Daytime Protocol. J. Postel. May 1983. (Also RFC0867)

0026    Time Server Protocol. J. Postel. May 1983. (Also RFC0868)

0027    Binary Transmission Telnet Option. J. Postel, J. Reynolds. May 1983. (Also RFC0856)

0028    Echo Telnet Option. J. Postel, J. Reynolds. May 1983. (Also RFC0857)

0029    Suppress Go Ahead Telnet Option. J. Postel, J. Reynolds. May 1983. (Also RFC0858)

0030    Status Telnet Option. J. Postel, J. Reynolds. May 1983. (Also RFC0859)

0031    Timing Mark Telnet Option. J. Postel, J. Reynolds. May 1983. (Also RFC0860)

0032    Extended Options List Telnet Option. J. Postel, J. Reynolds. May 1983. (Also RFC0861)

0033    Trivial File Transfer Protocol. K. Sollins. July 1992. (Also RFC1350)

0034    Routing Information Protocol. C. Hedrick. June 1988. (Also RFC1058)

0035    ISO Transport Service on top of the TCP (Version: 3). M. Rose, D. Cass. May 1978. (Also RFC1006)

0036    Transmission of IP and ARP over FDDI Networks. D. Katz. January 1993. (Also RFC1390)

0037    An Ethernet Address Resolution Protocol. David C. Plummer. November 1982. (Also RFC0826)

0038    A Reverse Address Resolution Protocol. Ross Finlayson, Timothy Mann, Jeffrey Mogul, Marvin Theimer. June 1984. (Also RFC0903)

0039    Interface Message Processor: Specifications for the Interconnection of a Host and an IMP (Revised). BBN. December 1981.

0040    Host Access Protocol specification. Bolt, Beranek, and Newman. August 1993. (Obsoletes RFC0907) (Also RFC1221)

0041    Standard for the transmission of IP datagrams over Ethernet networks. C. Hornig. April 1984. (Also RFC0894)

0042    Standard for the transmission of IP datagrams over experimental Ethernet networks. J. Postel. April 1984. (Also RFC0895)

0043    Standard for the transmission of IP datagrams over IEEE 802 networks. J. Postel, J. K. Reynolds. August 1993. (Obsoletes RFC0948) (Also RFC1042)

0044    DCN Local-Network Protocols. D. L. Mills. August 1993. (Also RFC0891)

0045    Internet Protocol on Network System's HYPERchannel: Protocol Specification. K. Hardwick, J. Lekashman. August 1993. (Also RFC1044)

0046    Transmitting IP traffic over ARCNET networks. D. Provan. August 1993. (Obsoletes RFC1051) (Also RFC1201)

0047    Nonstandard for transmission of IP datagrams over serial lines: SLIP. J. L. Romkey. August 1993. (Also RFC1055)

0048    Standard for the transmission of IP datagrams over NetBIOS networks. L.J. McLaughlin. August 1993. (Also RFC1088)

0049    Standard for the transmission of 802.2 packets over IPX networks. L. J. McLaughlin. August 1993. (Also RFC1132)

0050    Definitions of Managed Objects for the Ethernet-like Interface Types. F. Kastenholz. July 1994. (Obsoletes RFC1623, RFC1398) (Also RFC1643)

0051    The Point-to-Point Protocol (PPP). W. Simpson, Editor. July 1994. (Obsoletes RFC1549) (Also RFC1661, RFC1662)

0052    The Transmission of IP Datagrams over the SMDS Service. D. Piscitello, J. Lawrence. March 1991. (Also RFC1209)

0053    Post Office Protocol—Version 3. J. Myers and M. Rose. May 1996. (Obsoletes RFC1725) (Also RFC1939)

B

# Escaped Characters

| NAME | SYMBOL | DECIMAL | DESCRIPTION |
|------|--------|---------|-------------|
| quot | " | &#34; | Quotation mark |
| amp | & | &#38; | Ampersand |
| lt | < | &#60; | Less than |
| gt | > | &#62; | Greater than |
| nbsp | |   | Nonbreaking space |
| iexcl | ¡ | &#161; | Inverted exclamation mark |
| cent | ¢ | &#162; | Cent sign |
| pound | £ | &#163; | Pound sign |
| curren | ¤ | &#164; | Currency sign |
| yen | ¥ | &#165; | Yen sign = yuan sign |
| brvbar | ¦ | &#166; | Broken bar = broken vertical bar |
| sect | § | &#167; | Section sign |
| uml | ¨ | &#168; | Diaeresis = spacing diaeresis |

*Continues*

| NAME | SYMBOL | DECIMAL | DESCRIPTION |
|---|---|---|---|
| copy | © | &#169; | Copyright sign |
| ordf | ª | &#170; | Feminine ordinal indicator |
| laquo | « | &#171; | Left-pointing double angle quotation mark |
| not | ¬ | &#172; | Not sign |
| shy | - | &#173; | Soft hyphen = discretionary hyphen |
| reg | ® | &#174; | Registered sign = registered trade mark sign |
| macr | ¯ | &#175; | Macron = spacing macron = overline |
| deg | ° | &#176; | Degree sign |
| plusmn | ± | &#177; | Plus-minus sign = plus-or-minus sign |
| sup2 | $^2$ | &#178; | Superscript two = superscript digit two |
| sup3 | $^3$ | &#179; | Superscript three = superscript digit three |
| acute | ´ | &#180; | Acute accent = spacing acute |
| micro | µ | &#181; | Micro sign |
| para | ¶ | &#182; | Pilcrow sign = paragraph sign |
| middot | · | &#183; | Middle dot = Georgian comma |
| cedil | ¸ | &#184; | Cedilla = spacing cedilla |
| sup1 | $^1$ | &#185; | Superscript one = superscript digit one |
| ordm | º | &#186; | Masculine ordinal indicator |
| raquo | » | &#187; | Right-pointing double angle quotation mark |
| frac14 | ¼ | &#188; | Fraction one quarter |
| frac12 | ½ | &#189; | Fraction one half |
| frac34 | ¾ | &#190; | Fraction three quarters |
| iquest | ¿ | &#191; | Inverted question mark |
| Agrave | À | &#192; | Latin capital letter A with grave |
| Aacute | Á | &#193; | Latin capital letter A with acute |
| Acirc | Â | &#194; | Latin capital letter A with circumflex |
| Atilde | Ã | &#195; | Latin capital letter A with tilde |
| Auml | Ä | &#196; | Latin capital letter A with diaeresis |
| Aring | Å | &#197; | Latin capital letter A with ring above |
| AElig | Æ | &#198; | Latin capital letter AE |

| NAME | SYMBOL | DECIMAL | DESCRIPTION |
| --- | --- | --- | --- |
| Ccedil | Ç | &#199; | Latin capital letter C with cedilla |
| Egrave | È | &#200; | Latin capital letter E with grave |
| Eacute | É | &#201; | Latin capital letter E with acute |
| Ecirc | Ê | &#202; | Latin capital letter E with circumflex |
| Euml | Ë | &#203; | Latin capital letter E with diaeresis |
| Igrave | Ì | &#204; | Latin capital letter I with grave |
| Iacute | Í | &#205; | Latin capital letter I with acute |
| Icirc | Î | &#206; | Latin capital letter I with circumflex |
| Iuml | Ï | &#207; | Latin capital letter I with diaeresis |
| ETH | Ð | &#208; | Latin capital letter ETH |
| Ntilde | Ñ | &#209; | Latin capital letter N with tilde |
| Ograve | Ò | &#210; | Latin capital letter O with grave |
| Oacute | Ó | &#211; | Latin capital letter O with acute |
| Ocirc | Ô | &#212; | Latin capital letter O with circumflex |
| Otilde | Õ | &#213; | Latin capital letter O with tilde |
| Ouml | Ö | &#214; | Latin capital letter O with diaeresis |
| times | x | &#215; | Multiplication sign |
| Oslash | Ø | &#216; | Latin capital letter O with stroke |
| Ugrave | Ù | &#217; | Latin capital letter U with grave |
| Uacute | Ú | &#218; | Latin capital letter U with acute |
| Ucirc | Û | &#219; | Latin capital letter U with circumflex |
| Uuml | Ü | &#220; | Latin capital letter U with diaeresis |
| Yacute | Ý | &#221; | Latin capital letter Y with acute |
| THORN | Þ | &#222; | Latin capital letter THORN |
| szlig | ß | &#223; | Latin small letter sharp s = ess-zed |
| agrave | à | &#224; | Latin small letter a with grave |
| aacute | á | &#225; | Latin small letter a with acute |
| acirc | â | &#226; | Latin small letter a with circumflex |
| atilde | ã | &#227; | Latin small letter a with tilde |
| auml | ä | &#228; | Latin small letter a with diaeresis |

*Continues*

| NAME | SYMBOL | DECIMAL | DESCRIPTION |
|---|---|---|---|
| aring | å | &#229; | Latin small letter a with ring above |
| aelig | æ | &#230; | Latin small letter ae |
| ccedil | ç | &#231; | Latin small letter c with cedilla |
| egrave | è | &#232; | Latin small letter e with grave |
| eacute | é | &#233; | Latin small letter e with acute |
| ecirc | ê | &#234; | Latin small letter e with circumflex |
| euml | ë | &#235; | Latin small letter e with diaeresis |
| igrave | ì | &#236; | Latin small letter i with grave |
| iacute | í | &#237; | Latin small letter i with acute |
| icirc | î | &#238; | Latin small letter i with circumflex |
| iuml | ï | &#239; | Latin small letter i with diaeresis |
| eth | ð | &#240; | Latin small letter eth |
| ntilde | ñ | &#241; | Latin small letter n with tilde |
| ograve | ò | &#242; | Latin small letter o with grave |
| oacute | ó | &#243; | Latin small letter o with acute |
| ocirc | ô | &#244; | Latin small letter o with circumflex |
| otilde | õ | &#245; | Latin small letter o with tilde |
| ouml | ö | &#246; | Latin small letter o with diaeresis |
| divide | ÷ | &#247; | Division sign |
| oslash | ø | &#248; | Latin small letter o with stroke |
| ugrave | ù | &#249; | Latin small letter u with grave |
| uacute | ú | &#250; | Latin small letter u with acute |
| ucirc | û | &#251; | Latin small letter u with circumflex |
| uuml | ü | &#252; | Latin small letter u with diaeresis |
| yacute | ý | &#253; | Latin small letter y with acute |
| thorn | þ | &#254; | Latin small letter thorn |
| yuml | ÿ | &#255; | Latin small letter y with diaeresis |

# What's on the Web Site

The companion Web site can be found at www.wiley.com/compbooks/cintron. This site offers links to everything in the book that you might want to download, all the sites you can view, and all of the code for you to copy.

## Downloads

First of all, the site has links to downloads for all the software used in the book, be it freeware, shareware, or limited use demo packages, whatever, it's all there whether you need it or not.

- Microsoft Internet Explorer 4
- Netscape Navigator 4.5
- Prudens Inc. Spy Suite
- Telix shareware
- Internet RFCs
- Alchemy Mindworks Graphic Workshop
- SoftQuad HoTMetaL PRO
- Visual Basic Control Creation Edition

- Sun Java Development Kit (JDK)
- PERL Development Kits

# Links

Second, each and every Interesting and Informative site listed in the book has a link on the companion site. This will save you some time searching through the book and typing, and you can use it as a jump page to visit all the sites more easily.

# Code Examples

And last but not least, links to running and source code examples from the book are included to save you even more typing. And remember:

*Every code example in this book has been written and tested for real.*

# Index